Communication and Organizational Knowledge

Communication and Organizational Knowledge provides an overview of communication-centered theory and research regarding organizational knowledge and learning. It brings together scholarly work from multiple disciplines to address emerging knowledge issues facing today's organizations. Chapters provide important insights regarding the communication of organizational knowledge, characteristics of knowledge processes, and resources for effectiveness. Taking an intensively communication-centered perspective, contributors to this volume question assumptions about organizational knowledge that often go unexamined when adopting information-centered or technology-centered perspectives. Each chapter offers implications for practice to bridge the gap between theory and practice.

This volume will serve as an important resource for scholars and practitioners studying or working in organizational knowledge management, concepts of knowledge as interactive or social, and organizational learning. It also provides a unique forum in which scholars may consider new directions for future research and theorizing.

Heather E. Canary is Assistant Professor in the Department of Communication at the University of Utah. Her research interests include family and organizational communication processes, particularly involving issues such as disability and public policy where organizational and family processes intersect.

Robert D. McPhee is Professor in the Hugh Downs School of Communication at Arizona State University. His research interests include structuration theory, organizational constitution, and communication theory.

COMMUNICATION SERIES
Jennings Bryant/Dolf Zillmann, General Editors

Selected titles in Organizational Communication (Linda Putnam, advisory editor) include:

Cooren/Taylor/Van Every – *Communication as Organization: Empirical and Theoretical Explorations in the Dynamic of Text and Conversations*

Cooren – *Interacting and Organizing: Analyses of a Management Meeting*

Kramer – *Managing Uncertainty in Organizational Communication*

Nicotera/Clinkscales with Walker – *Understanding Organizations Through Culture and Structure: Relational and Other Lessons From the African–American Organization*

Parker – *Race, Gender, and Leadership: Re-Envisioning Organizational Leadership from the Perspectives of African American Women Executives*

Putnam/Nicotera – *Building Theories of Organization: The Constitutive Role of Communication*

Taylor/Van Every – *The Emergent Organization: Communication as Its Site and Surface*

Communication and Organizational Knowledge

Contemporary Issues for Theory and Practice

Edited by Heather E. Canary
and Robert D. McPhee

Routledge
Taylor & Francis Group

NEW YORK AND LONDON

First published 2011
by Routledge
270 Madison Avenue, New York, NY 10016

Simultaneously published in the UK
by Routledge
2 Park Square, Milton Park, Abingdon, Oxon OX14 4RN

Routledge is an imprint of the Taylor & Francis Group, an informa business

© 2011 Taylor & Francis

Typeset in Sabon by Wearset Ltd, Boldon, Tyne and Wear
Printed and bound in the United States of America on acid-free
paper by Sheridan Books, Inc.

Library of Congress Cataloging-in-Publication Data
Communication and organizational knowledge : contemporary
issues for theory and practice / edited by Heather E. Canary and
Robert D. McPhee.
p. cm.
1. Knowledge management. 2. Communication in organizations.
3. Organizational learning. I. Canary, Heather E. II. McPhee,
Robert.
HD30.2.C635 2010
658.4'038–dc22

2010004935

ISBN13: 978-0-415-80403-5 (hbk)
ISBN13: 978-0-415-80404-2 (pbk)
ISBN13: 978-0-203-87450-9 (ebk)

This book is dedicated to Dan and Dale.
Your love and support sustain us.

Contents

Foreword

Representation, Signification, Improvisation – A Three-Dimensional View of Organizational Knowledge

Haridimos Tsoukas

"An empire is partly a fiction," writes Thomas Richards (1993, p. 1) in his brilliant *The Imperial Archive*. "No nation can close its hand around the world; the reach of any nation's empire always exceeds its final grasp." What is true of empires is true of organizations too. After all, empires are organizations.

An organization is partly a fiction. It is the assumption of belonging to a single whole, created out of the ordering of disparate and often geographically distant units. "Most people during the nineteenth century," notes Richards (1993, p. 3), "were aware that their empire was something of a collective improvisation," an ongoing struggle to create order out of multiplicity and heterogeneity. Running an empire is an enormous administrative challenge – something Victorians were soon to find out. Maps, surveys, statistics, censuses, etc., were the new types of knowledge to be enlisted in the service of the British Empire; they brought closer – *re-presented* – far away places to those in charge (Cooper & Law, 1995). The knowledge generated was classified and organized into ever more comprehensive archives. Controlling knowledge was co-extensive with controlling the Empire. Just as the Empire was partly fictive, so too was its knowledge base – the imperial archive: the latter's comprehensiveness, namely the singular, complete, and global character of knowledge included in it, was more assumed than real. "The imperial archive was a fantasy of knowledge collected and united in the service of state and Empire," writes Richards (1993, p. 1).

The information explosion we are experiencing in late modernity is not really new (although it has taken a qualitatively new turn). It started with the British Empire in the second half of the 19th century, when, for the first time, knowledge-producing and knowledge-conserving institutions such as the British Museum and the Royal Geographical Society were created. The idea of comprehensive knowledge being indispensable for running an organization (be it an empire, a state, or a corporation) goes hand in hand with the rise of bureaucracy. What is the latter if not a vast knowledge system, which, through its emphasis on written standardized procedures and merit-based rise through the hierarchy, codifies knowledge, makes it available to organizational members, and assumes that a hier-archy of office broadly correlates with a hierarchy of knowledge?

True, today we are beginning to question the possibility of comprehensive-cum-centralized knowledge, mainly due to the emergence of post-bureaucratic organizations (Sennett, 2006), the realization that a self-generating pattern may be created through open-ended processes of organizing (Weick, 1979, 1995), and our late modern incredulity towards universal narratives (Bauman, 1993). Nonetheless, purposefully organized systems, be they bureaucratic or spontaneously collaborative, in so far as they consist of rela-tively bounded socio-technical activities, within which cooperative human action is to be secured under some kind of authority relations, rely for their effective functioning on stocks of knowledge, on which they regularly draw. This is so because for organized action to be effective over time, some form of institutional memory is required. That memory may be codified in formal rules and routines, be immanent in informal understandings and norms, or be widely distributed (see Chapters 7 and 8 in this volume, on transactive memory, by Palazzolo, and by Hollingshead, Brandon, Yoon, and Gupta, respectively). More likely, it is a combination of all three.

However, what distinguishes *modern* purposeful organization is the relentless process of disembedding (de-contextualizing): the lifting of social relations out of their spontaneously occurring local contexts of interaction and their re-combination in abstract space and time (Giddens, 1990, p. 21; 1991, p. 18). Through the process of disembedding, social systems extend their reach beyond the here and now of interaction in conditions of co-presence. Purposeful organization is a process of abstraction. Social rela-tions are lifted out from their local contexts and recombined across time and space. It is the ability to systematically coordinate absent others (i.e., beyond conditions of face-to-face interactions) and therefore undertake action at a distance, which is the most distinct feature of modern organized systems. The dialectic of presence and absence becomes the central prin-ciple of modern organization – human interaction is no longer limited by the context of co-presence (Tsoukas, 2001, 2005).

For example, a service technician repairing a photocopier at a custom-er's site (Orr, 1996) acts within the boundaries of an abstract role and follows, *inter alia*, an abstract body of knowledge about how broken pho-tocopiers may be repaired. Moreover, the technician–customer interaction is an abstract one insofar as both the technician and the customer embody abstract roles and their relationship is quasi-independent from the particu-larities of local context. Action becomes organized insofar as it can be instantiated across different contexts. Overcoming the contingencies of local contexts is an achievement that modern organization makes possible. The abstraction of social relations and their subsumption under generic rules enables coordination over indefinite spans of time-space.

Insofar as purposefully organized systems entail abstraction, they con-stitute what Giddens calls "expert systems" – namely, impersonal systems of knowledge and expertise whose validity is independent of those drawing on them. An expert system, notes Giddens (1990, p. 28), provides "'guarantees' of expectations across distanciated time-space." As customers, we expect the photocopier we bought will work as it is supposed to, and trust the coffee we drink at Starbucks is, indeed, "fair trade" coffee. Expert systems draw on techno-scientific knowledge, professional norms, and idiosyncratic organizational know-how.

Expert systems provide *synoptic knowledge.* The latter consists of abstract representations of a particular domain, patterns of association between representations, and propositional statements (i.e., "if ... then" statements) that function as rules for action. Abstract representations create generic categories for attention (e.g., classes of objects, behaviors, roles, etc.), which are connected in particular ways to achieve particular results. To organize is to create, explicitly or tacitly, an ensemble of distinct categories, logically related to one another.

For example, repair manuals issued to photocopier service technicians contain canonical images of what a broken machine is and how it may be repaired (Orr, 1996). For the designers of such manuals, photocopiers are abstractions whose reliable operation can be statistically described. Designers investigate patterns in machine breakdowns, codify them, relate types of breakdown to types of repair action, and incorporate the relevant information in the manual. Without turning the photocopiers into abstract representations, organized action by the repair technicians cannot be undertaken (Tsoukas, 2005, p. 78). This applies even in cases in which there is a tacit body of knowledge concerning how work is to be carried out – as, for example, is the case of the flute-making companies described by Cook and Yanow (1996). Although there is a paucity of explicit representations to guide the work of flute makers, nonetheless, in the course of time, generic notions of what a good or a "clunky" flute is have emerged that guide flute-making work. Singling out, labeling, categorizing, and connecting are necessary components of the collective effort to carry out work in both cases.

However, representations can be used insofar as organizational members know *how* to use them. That knowledge is obtained through individuals' immersion in socio-material practices, in which they have learnt how to make competent use of relevant categories and their associations (see Chapter 15, by Murphy and Eisenberg, and Chapter 16, by Myers, in this volume). For example, abstract terms such as "faulty photocopier" (Orr, 1996), "pathological change" (Polanyi, 1962, p. 101), or "clunky flute" (Cook & Yanow, 1996), derive their meaning from the way they have been *used* within the respective practices. One learns to recognize, say, a faulty photocopier, a pathological lung, or a clunky flute because one has been taught to *use* the respective category ("faulty photocopier," etc.) in practice, within a practice. The activities carried out within a practice are teleologically structured in so far as they are oriented toward attaining certain ends that determine it as the activity it is (e.g., teaching, nursing, flute making, photocopier repairing).

Organizations, therefore, as well as being carriers of synoptic knowledge, are the sites of *cultural knowledge*: collective meanings that provide an organized system with a distinct identity and enable its members to act in coordinated ways. Through their immersion in a practice, actors (such as, for example, service technicians or flute makers) gradually learn to relate to their surroundings "spontaneously" (Wittgenstein, 1980, §699) – that is to say, without explicitly thinking about them. It is when unreflective immersion in a practice has not taken place – as, for example, in the case of a trainee physician described by Gawande (2002) – that the practitioner is explicitly aware of what he or she does. When, however, the practitioner is absorbed in the task at hand, the tools she uses, her body, and the surroundings are not explicit objects of thought, but form an interrelated network that recedes from explicit awareness. Absorption in the task at hand provides practitioners with "subsidiary particulars" (Polanyi & Prosch, 1975, pp. 37–38) – taken-for-granted aspects of the normal setting – on which the practitioner draws in order to attend to the task at hand. For representations, patterns of their association and propositional statements to be competently used, practitioners must form a *sensus communis* – they must share a common sense of what they mean (see Chapter 16, by Myers, in this volume). Expert systems cannot be self-sustained if they are to be usable, but must be grounded on collective self-understandings.

The synoptic knowledge included in an expert system, no matter how abstract it is, needs to be related to the world – to encounter experience, with all the latter's messiness and complexity. That encounter is mediated by *personal* knowing. As Polanyi and Prosch (1975, p. 31) remark, "even the most exact sciences must [...] rely on our personal confidence that we possess some degree of personal skill and personal judgment for establishing valid correspondence with – or a real deviation from – the facts of experience." Whereas cultural knowledge provides practitioners with the ability to competently *use* synoptic knowledge, it is how they relate to *particular* instances of the world they confront that is actually important. A service technician may have developed the generic skill of repairing photocopiers, but his skill is tested and further developed any time he encounters particular photocopiers in customers' settings.

A practitioner needs to fill in the "phronetic gap" (Taylor, 1993, p. 57) that inescapably crops up between a representation and the world encountered. The circumstances confronting a practitioner always have an element of *situational uniqueness* that cannot be expressed through an abstract representation or cultural know-how. The "interaction order" (Goffman, 1983/1997) in which representations are enacted is infinitely richer than the synoptic order in which representations are formulated. Since, like all categories, abstract representations have a radial structure, they consist of a stable part made up of prototypical (central) members, and an unstable

part made up of non-prototypical (peripheral, marginal) members radiat-
ing out at various conceptual distances from the central members (Johnson,
1993; Lakoff, 1987). Patterns of action stemming from acting on prototypical cases (what several authors in this volume call "determinate situations") tend to be "by the rule book" (e.g., repairing a typical fault in a
photocopier). But the world also throws at practitioners peripheral cases
(again what several authors, especially Kuhn and Porter, Chapter 2 in this
volume, call "indeterminate situations"), which they are, in varying
degrees, puzzled by as to how to respond. The customer, for example, may
have been using the machine in idiosyncratic ways, leading to a somewhat
unusual pattern of faults (Orr, 1996). As a result of the radial structure of
categories, there is an intrinsic *indeterminacy* when organizational
members interact with the world – hence the need for them to fill in the
phronetic gap by imaginatively extending a category beyond prototypical
cases to peripheral ones (Johnson, 1993; Lakoff, 1987; Tsoukas & Chia,
2002). The effort to close the phronetic gap leads inescapably to improvisation and, thus, the development of *improvisational knowledge*. For
example, Orr (1996) has reported how service technicians improvise as
they go about their work. Similarly, Orlikowski (1996) has shown how
specialists enact ongoing situated accommodations, adaptations, and alter-
ations in response to previous variations, while anticipating future ones.

To sum up, organizational knowledge consists of three distinct types of
knowledge: synoptic, cultural, and improvisational (see Canary, Chapter
14 in this volume, for similar types of knowledge: "encoded," "encultured," and "embedded" knowledge). Synoptic knowledge includes abstract representations and their patterns of association, either formally
articulated or informally picked up. Through synoptic knowledge the par-
ticularities of context are sought to be overcome and economy of effort to
be achieved. Information and Communication Technologies (ICTs) provide
the technical means through which synoptic knowledge may be stored,
retrieved, and communicated. But synoptic knowledge cannot be effectively used in practice unless organizational members share the meanings of
synoptic-knowledge categories. While through representation human
action is sought to be decontextualized, insofar as representations are sig-
nifications, they are necessarily rooted in the practice of a particular community, through which they acquire collectively shared meanings. Insofar
as meanings are coached in language, they enter signification, hence they
are open-ended (Castoriadis, 1997). Representations (syntax) and meanings (semantics) are applied by concrete people in a concrete world, which
is infinitely more complex than any representations. There is always a
phronetic gap between representations and the world, which is filled in
through actors improvising in situ. Representations and meanings are
instantiated through the pragmatics of human action.

To put the above in process language, organizational knowledge consists of, or is accomplished through, three processes: a process of *represen-*

tation, a process of *signification* (meaning-making), and a process of *improvisation*. Moreover, in so far as organizational knowledge is put into action, it is irreducibly *personal*. Since practitioners necessarily act in the real (i.e., complex) world, they inevitably rely on their judgment for aligning representations and cultural meanings with "the facts of experience" (Polanyi, 1962, p. 31). Synoptic and cultural knowledges are drawn upon in situated circumstances, which cannot be fully described *ex ante*, and this is what makes organizational knowledge *in toto* ultimately unsurveyable and non-codifiable at any point in time. Insofar as practitioners need to improvise to reduce the phronetic gap, their knowledge, rooted in the experience of partly unpredictable situated interactions as it is, retains an irreducibly *emergent* character that is unavailable to anyone in its entirety; there is no higher ground from which a synopsis may be provided (Tsoukas, 2005, p. 290).

The partly emergent character of organizational knowledge makes the latter more complex, since emergent knowledge cannot be reduced to a reproducible synoptic pattern – that is to say, it is not algorithmically compressible (Tsoukas & Hatch, 2001). The reason the "imperial archive" is incomplete is that, seen in process terms, it is always instantiated *in concreto* – its key categories are applied in specific, unpredictable, circumstances, thus generating open-ended (emergent) outcomes. Moreover, any system of synoptic knowledge is inherently unstable: insofar as cultural meanings change over time, key categories and representations change too. Synoptic, cultural, and improvisational knowledges form a dynamic triangle.

In light of the above, let me suggest a way to understand the chapters included in this splendid book edited so competently by Heather E. Canary and Robert D. McPhee. A communication perspective is strongly processual (Cooren, Taylor, & Van Every, 2006; Fairhurst & Putnam, 2004; McPhee & Zaug, 2009; Taylor & Van Every, 2000). It brings to light the processes of communication through which organization is constituted. Communication involves both redundancy and surprise, standardization and novelty (Eco, 1989; Hayles, 1990; Tsoukas, 2005). Representation processes involve standardization: the representation of the world in abstract categories (see Corman and Dooley, Chapter 9 in this volume, for how explicit knowledge may be represented and systematized in a research university). But representation is inherently incomplete, due to the improvisation processes instantiated when representations encounter the complexity of the world. Representation is also dynamic due to the self-interpreting character of the collective meanings generated in social practices. In other words, signification is inherently open-ended and changes over time. Incompleteness and open-endedness bring about the possibility of novelty. A communication perspective sensitizes us to these dynamic processes: representation, signification, improvisation. Most chapters in this book deal with one or more of those processes. Indeed, an important feature of most chapters is the extent to which they adopt a practice-cum-process perspective on organizational knowledge. The latter is seen as both an outcome and a process, and several chapters explicate how the two (outcomes and processes) are mutually constituted. Let me provide a few illustrations.

Kuhn and Porter's focus on "knowledge-accomplishing activities" approaches "knowledgeable action" as dependent on judgments of situational appropriateness tied to identity and legitimacy. In other words, questions of collective meaning (i.e., cultural knowledge) that make certain knowledge claims "appropriate" are tied to "sensitivity to situational affordances" (i.e., improvisational knowledge). Shifting emphasis from knowledge to knowing, Kuhn and Porter invite us to explore how continuous problem-solving in more or less "determinate situations" is accomplished through situational resources in the context of shared meanings generated in social practices.

A strong emphasis on the epistemic importance of "community" (i.e., cultural knowledge) is evident in Chapter 3, by Iverson. Focusing on "communities of practice," Iverson captures how communities are enacted when knowledge is enacted, and vice versa. Knowing, being enacted through relating to others, is co-extensive with belonging, since the latter enables practitioners to spontaneously relate to their surroundings through the competent use of the key categories of their practice. Others are a condition for one's knowledgeable action.

Jackson and Williamson (Chapter 4) capture the interplay between the drive to represent and systematize knowledge in databases (and therefore make it more accessible, searchable, retrievable and replicable) and the inherently open-ended emergence of knowledge in experiential processes of improvisational action. Organizational knowledge becomes more complex and thus less imitable insofar as "indeterminate solutions are responded to, usually through highly localized practices" (p. 62). "Leverage the power of emergence, the moments of serendipity that occur in communication that underpins indeterminate knowledge seeking practices" (p. 66) creates a unique context that is less likely to be copied by others. In other words, the effort to close the phronetic gap generates improvisational knowledge that is strongly personal and contextual, thus making organizational knowledge at large more idiosyncratic and, therefore, more valuable, more rare, more inimitable and more non-substitutable. Knowledge becomes a strategic asset not only when it becomes efficiently systematized but, crucially, when it becomes idiosyncratic – when emergence is embraced.

Focusing on how knowledge is represented, how shared meanings are constructed and how improvisation takes place enables us to look at the politics of knowledge. In Chapter 5 in this volume, Lyon and Chesebro raise several interesting questions: "whose version of organizational reality becomes normalized? Whose values guide our decisions? Whose priorities do organizational members pursue? In whose voice or interests are members speaking?" (p. 71). Knowledge involves *ac-knowledgment*: that others acknowledge our knowledge and we acknowledge theirs. This is an inherently political issue, involving the use of power and rhetoric (see also Murphy and Eisenberg, Chapter 15 in this volume).

As well as political, knowledge is deeply cultural. Leonardi (Chapter 6 in this volume) explores how different conceptions of key organizational categories among engineers in a global firm stifled sharing and impeded learning. Here was not a question of inadequate systematization and poor retrievability (i.e., low representation), but a culturally shaped problem of where knowledge lies. ICTs cannot solve such problems; better cultural awareness and informal socialization might (see also Myers, Chapter 16 in this volume).

The dynamic interplay between knowledge management systems, enabled by the use of ICTs, and flows of knowledge is explored by several chapters (see Chapters 10, 11, and 12 in this volume, by Flanagin and Bator, Shumate, and Deng and Poole, respectively). While the role of ICTs is important, it should not be overestimated; it is rather important to acknowledge the enabling role of technology without equating technological connectivity with the practice of actors' relating to one another in the context of socio-material practices. ICTs and web applications are useful for providing "content" (representation) and connectivity, thus supporting situated practice. But ICTs' representational and connectivity capabilities should not be seen as equivalent to knowledge creation, learning, and transfer. The latter are primarily socio-material practices, not merely technological constructions.

In conclusion, the illuminating studies in this volume show the tension between *entitative* and *enactive* approaches to organizational knowledge. The tension cannot be eliminated because organizations ontologically are systems of institutionalized interactions designed to generate patterns and regularities that are representable; *and* sites of socialization and meaning-making; *and* interaction orders calling for personal situated judgments. As a result, organizational knowledge involves processes of creating stable entities in the form of representations *and* using them in open-ended contexts. While entitative approaches highlight the representational aspects of organizational knowledge and the systems that are created for their effective management, enactive (or process or relational) approaches emphasize the use of representations in practice, and the consequent communicative constitution of such knowing. From the perspective of using knowledge, the "personal coefficient" (Polanyi, 1962, p. 17) is visible as well as ineliminable in all knowing. Seeking to construct an ever more comprehensive archive is inherent in organized contexts, and failing to do so is as inevitable as persistent is the effort. The reach of any organization's knowledge always exceeds its final grasp. Victorians had the chance to find out, although it did not stop them creating an Empire.

References

Bauman, Z. (1993). *Postmodern ethics*. Oxford, UK: Blackwell.

Castoriadis, C. (1997). The logic of magmas and the question of autonomy. In D. Ames Curtis (Trans. and Ed.), *The Castoriadis reader*. Oxford, UK: Blackwell.

Cook, S. D., & Yanow, D. (1996). Culture and organizational learning. In M. D. Cohen & L. S. Sproull (Eds.), *Organizational learning* (pp. 430–459). Thousand Oaks, CA: Sage.

Cooper, R., & Law, J. (1995). Organization: Distal and proximal views. *Research in the Sociology of Organizations, 13*, 237–274.

Cooren, F., Taylor, J. R, & Van Every, E. J. (2006). *Communication as organizing*. Mahwah, NJ: Lawrence Erlbaum.

Eco, U. (1989). *The open work* (A. Cancogni, Trans.). Cambridge, MA: Harvard University Press.

Fairhurst, G. T., & Putnam, L. (2004). Organizations as discursive constructions. *Communication Theory, 14*, 5–26.

Gawande, A. (2002). *Complications*. New York, NY: Metropolitan Books.

Giddens, A. (1990). *The consequences of modernity*. Cambridge, UK: Polity.

Giddens, A. (1991). *Modernity and self-identity*. Cambridge, UK: Polity.

Goffman, E. (1983/1997). The interaction order. In C. Lemert & A. Branaman (Eds.), *The Goffman reader* (pp. 233–261). Malden, MA: Blackwell.

Hayles, N. K. (1990). *Chaos bound*. Ithaca, NY: Cornell University Press.

Johnson, M. (1993). *Moral imagination*. Chicago, IL: University of Chicago Press.

Lakoff, G. (1987). *Women, fire, and dangerous things*. Chicago, IL: University of Chicago Press.

McPhee, R. D., & Zaug, P. (2009). The communicative constitutions of organizations. In L. L. Putnam & A. M. Nicotera (Eds.), *Building theories of organization* (pp. 21–48). New York, NY: Routledge.

Orlikowski, W. J. (1996). Improvising organizational transformation over time: A situated change perspective. *Information Systems Research, 7*, 63–92.

Orr, J. (1996). *Talking about machines*. Ithaca, NY: ILR Press.

Polanyi, M. (1962). *Personal knowledge*. Chicago, IL: University of Chicago Press.

Polanyi, M., & Prosch, H. (1975). *Meaning*. Chicago, IL: University of Chicago Press.

Richards, T. (1993). *The imperial archive*. London, UK: Verso.

Sennett, R. (2006). *The culture of new capitalism*. New Haven, CT: Yale University Press.

Taylor, C. (1993). "To follow a rule…" in C. Calhoun, E. LiPuma, & M. Postone (Eds.), *Bourdieu: Critical perspectives* (pp. 45–59). Cambridge, UK: Polity Press.

Taylor, J. R., & Van Every, E. J. (2000). *The emergent organization*. Mahwah, NJ: Lawrence Erlbaum.

Tsoukas, H. (2001). Re-viewing organization. *Human Relations, 54*, 7–12.

Tsoukas, H. (2005). *Complex knowledge*. Oxford, UK: Oxford University Press.

Tsoukas, H., & Chia, R. (2002). On organizational becoming: Rethinking organizational change. *Organization Science, 13*, 567–582.

Tsoukas, H., & Hatch, M. J. (2001). Complex thinking, complex practice: The case for a narrative approach to organizational complexity. *Human Relations, 54*, 979–1013.

Weick, K. E. (1979). *The social psychology of organizing* (2nd Ed.). Reading, MA: Addison-Wesley.

Weick, K. E. (1995). *Sensemaking in organizations*. Thousand Oaks, CA: Sage.

Wittgenstein, L. (1980). *Remarks on the philosophy of psychology*. Vol. II (G. H. von Wright & H. Nyman, Eds.; C. G. Luckhardt & M. A. E. Aue, Trans.). Chicago, IL: University of Chicago Press.

Acknowledgments

We would like to take this opportunity to acknowledge the assistance of several key people in moving this project from a kernel of an idea to a finished book. First, we appreciate that Dan Canary encouraged us to pursue this idea in the first place. Second, we thank our editor at Routledge, Linda Bathgate, for being open to this book idea, for giving us easy-to-follow explanations of each step in the process, and for her patience as we muddled through this experience. We also appreciate the comments of Linda Putnam and anonymous reviewers at Routledge whose suggestions consistently created even further muddle.

We also appreciate the willingness of each of our contributing authors to work with us through the stages of the book. We made some mistakes along the way, and our authors were gracious not to point them out to us but rather to move along with the project as it developed. In addition, we are grateful to Hari Tsoukas for consenting to read and react in limited time to our whole manuscript.

Of course, the behind-the-scenes team at Routledge also deserves our acknowledgment. We are especially grateful to Kate Ghezzi for handling our many questions with ease. Dale Kalika did a wonderful job developing the index in a timely manner, and we thank her for that contribution to the book. We don't know the names of the production team, but we want also to acknowledge their dedication and care with our work.

Contributors

Contributors represent senior and emerging scholars of organizational communication and related disciplines. Contributors are listed in alphabetical order:

Melissa Bator is a doctoral student, Department of Communication, University of California Santa Barbara.

David P. Brandon is General Administrator, Theoretical and Computational Biophysics Group, University of Illinois at Urbana-Champaign.

Heather E. Canary is Assistant Professor in the Department of Communication at the University of Utah.

Joseph L. Chesebro is Associate Professor, Department of Communication, SUNY College at Brockport.

Steven R. Corman is Professor, Hugh Downs School of Human Communication, Arizona State University.

Liqiong Deng is Assistant Professor, Department of Management, Richards College of Business, University of West Georgia.

Kevin J. Dooley is Professor, Department of Supply Chain Management, W. P. Carey School of Business, Arizona State University.

Eric M. Eisenberg is Dean, College of Arts and Sciences, and Professor of Communication, University of South Florida.

Andrew J. Flanagin is Professor, Department of Communication, University of California, Santa Barbara.

Naina Gupta is Assistant Professor of Strategy, Management, and Organization, Nanyang Business School, Nanyang Technological University.

Andrea B. Hollingshead is Professor, Annenberg School of Communication, University of Southern California.

Joel O. Iverson is Assistant Professor, Department of Communication Studies, University of Montana.

Michele H. Jackson is Associate Professor, Department of Communication, University of Colorado at Boulder.

Katherine M. Kelley is a doctoral student in the Department of Communication, University of Oklahoma.

Timothy Kuhn is Associate Professor, Department of Communication, University of Colorado at Boulder.

Paul M. Leonardi is Assistant Professor and Breed Junior Chair of Design, Department of Communication Studies and Department of Industrial Engineering and Management Sciences, Northwestern University.

Alexander Lyon is Assistant Professor, Department of Communication, SUNY College at Brockport.

Robert D. McPhee is Professor, Hugh Downs School of Human Communication, Arizona State University.

Alexandra G. Murphy is Associate Professor, Department of Communication, DePaul University.

Karen K. Myers is Assistant Professor, Department of Communication, University of California, Santa Barbara.

H. Dan O'Hair is Dean, College of Communications and Information Studies, University of Kentucky.

Edward T. Palazzolo is Assistant Professor, Hugh Downs School of Human Communication, Arizona State University.

Amanda J. Porter is a graduate student in the Department of Communication, University of Colorado at Boulder.

Marshall Scott Poole is Professor, Department of Speech Communication, University of Illinois at Urbana-Champaign.

Michelle Shumate is Assistant Professor, Department of Speech Communication, University of Illinois at Urbana-Champaign.

Haridimos Tsoukas is the George D. Mavros Research Professor of Organization and Management at the Athens Laboratory of Business Administration (ALBA) Graduate Business School, Greece, and a Professor of Organization Studies at Warwick Business School, University of Warwick, UK.

Kathy L. Williams is Principal of Tulsa Met Lombard High School, Tulsa, Oklahoma.

Julie Williamson is a doctoral candidate in the Department of Communication, University of Colorado at Boulder.

Kay Yoon is Assistant Professor, College of Communication, DePaul University.

Chapter I

Introduction

Toward a Communicative Perspective on Organizational Knowledge

Heather E. Canary and Robert D. McPhee

A primary reason people choose to organize is to achieve a common purpose with knowledge and abilities of multiple people. Accordingly, interests in who knows what, how they know it, and what they do with it are as old as the phenomenon of organizing. This volume attests to the complexities involved in understanding organizational knowledge, and to the many ways *organizational knowledge* is conceptualized. The book brings together several approaches to organizational knowledge, and many important issues scholars and practitioners grapple with as organizational members adapt to contemporary exigencies. The unifying element throughout this book is a focus on the communicative nature of organizational knowledge. That is, contributors to this volume address in varying manners how organizational knowledge is developed, manifested, managed, and/or utilized through communication. Organizational knowledge researchers and theorists have not consistently considered the interactive elements of knowledge, although much empirical research in the area "points to" communication (Bartel & Garud, 2003; Hayes & Walsham, 2003).

Accordingly, this volume is devoted to explicating communicative perspectives of organizational knowledge. In this introduction, we discuss theoretical foundations of organizational knowledge research and articulate connections among the chapters included in the book. We start by reviewing major scholarly movements in the emergence of organizational knowledge as background for theory and research. This historical review is followed by a discussion of current perspectives on the topic as a vehicle for introducing the work that this volume comprises. Third, we discuss a general theoretical template that is used throughout the book for delineating knowledge processes. Finally, we discuss the four sections of this volume as they represent four problem fields emergent in the organizational knowledge literature.

Emergence of a Focus on Organizational Knowledge

Because scholarly attention to organizational knowledge is a fairly recent phenomenon, we use this section to briefly summarize major movements in organizational theory and practice which have led to the current focus on organizational knowledge. Importantly, although the term *organizational knowledge* has only been commonly used within the past couple of decades, interest in the phenomenon of organizational knowledge has been emerging since the early days of organizational theorizing.

Bureaucracy and Scientific Management

Collection of information about production is one of the oldest practices in human history, a contributor to development of such phenomena as writing, agrarian society, empires and cities, and pre-modern as well as modern patterns of commerce (Giddens, 1981). However, real recognition of knowledge use in organizing appeared early in the 20th century. One of the fundamental principles of bureaucratic organizing is division of labor based on expertise (Perrow, 1986). However, early efforts at bureaucratization were much less focused on member knowledge than on such concepts as standardization and efficiency (Perrow, 1986). Early Weberian bureaucratic emphases included setting up systems for file processing, determining qualifications for job assignments, and prioritizing rationality in organizations. All of these endeavors revolve around the notion of organizational knowledge, although that term was not referenced or highlighted in early bureaucratic movements of organizational studies. As Perrow noted, the bureaucratic movement encouraged organizational leaders to abandon nepotism and other forms of particularism for the more rational concepts of systematization, specialization, and expertise. In the contemporary lexicon, developing divisions of labor and hierarchies based on expertise and specialization was the first movement for harnessing and prioritizing organizational knowledge. Before the bureaucratic movement, knowledge and ability counted much less than did reputation and loyalty (Perrow, 1986).

An alternate path toward knowledge manipulation to serve organizational control was the scientific management movement, which emphasized the division of tasks so specialized knowledge was not needed and so production could be performed by multiple employees who had little knowledge of the overall product. Accordingly, overall *knowledge* of the process and product was seen as extracted by studying workers executing tasks, then developed and administered by a staff of "scientific managers" (e.g., a factory works best when industrial engineers conceive and design it). Taylorism valorized internal study of organizations to optimize productivity. Of course, hindsight provides a clear view of the downside of this deskilling of production – lack of worker motivation and commitment, underutilization of worker creative abilities, and the dehumanization of work organizations. Hence, scientific management, as a way of viewing organizational processes, played a significant role in the emergence of a focus on *organizational* knowledge as opposed to *individual* knowledge and one-way knowledge processes.

Human Resources

The dehumanization of work organizations inevitably led to a backlash which has become known, using the term broadly, as the human resources movement. As Wheatley (2000) recently noted, knowledge is *human* knowledge, so employees are best treated as having useful knowledge. With a more educated workforce, and greater emphasis on service industries and white-collar jobs, theorists and managers began to place more emphasis on flatter structures, participative decision-making, group norms, job redesign, intrinsic motivation, and open communication. Structural contingency theory articulated a difference between routine jobs and a class of jobs or departments that confronted high uncertainty, using expertise and information collection. The interpretive notion of organizational culture did include informal practices and norms, but it also recognized stocks of knowledge, employee creativity, the tacit dimension of knowledge, and organizational memory. Although many human resource management ideas were more relevant to motivation, the varied notions of organizational learning, increased employee responsibility, and cultural knowledge naturally led to more reliance on looser management, socialization, expertise, and group cooperation to make room for employee contributions. And all of these are early concepts whose interrelatedness is part of the concept of organizational knowledge.

The Recent Sources of Knowledge Studies

Taking an historical look at the development of organizational knowledge as a focus of theory and research brings into sharp relief how different conceptualizations of knowledge drive the diverse streams of literature on the topic. Scholars of organizational knowledge have, for one thing, studied a variety of *processes* of development and storage of knowledge. For instance, cognitive psychologists, but arguably also the whole range of disciplines, have studied:

> (a) schema theory and related conceptions of mental representations (especially the notion of mental models), (b) behavioral decision theory (especially work on heuristics and biases), (c) attribution theory, (d) social identity theory and related conceptions, and (e) enactment and the related notion of sensemaking [These can be more broadly grouped as] computational and interpretive perspectives on cognition in organizations.
>
> (Hodgkinson & Healey, 2008, p. 391)

Obviously, some of these individual-level foci inherently depend on social/communicative groups engaged in processes of "making available and amplifying knowledge created by individuals as well as crystallizing and connecting it to an organization's knowledge system" (Nonaka & Von Krogh, 2009, p. 635). Here, an increasingly focal concept is that of "practice." Theorists of practice emphasize the grounding of explicitly stated, and/or technologically manifested or stored and distributed, knowledge on a background of tacit and socially grounded knowledge, which is always in complicated relation to the first type. A broad range of theorists and researchers have been exploring the question of how such arrays of knowledge can be organizational (Tsoukas, 2005). Throughout this volume, we explore the ways such organizational knowledge is also, in essence, communicative.

A sense of the importance of groups and social interaction implies a related conception of knowledge as emergent and maintained in nets of *connections*. Social/communicative studies of knowledge processes contextualized in networks have ranged from information flow in webs of relations among specific persons, to studies of network patterns that generate social and intellectual capital, to studies that describe the nets of work-related knowledge in global commodities markets as flows so unstable that they constantly recreate transient networks (Carlile, 2004; Knorr-Cetina & Prada, 2007; Monge & Contractor, 2003; Stewart, 2003).

Connections, though, are partly but increasingly dependent on communication technologies. Emphasis on innovation and constant change, on the especially dynamic domain of communication technology, and on communication networks and inter-organizational coordination led to a focus on technology-grounded knowledge sharing and "informating" even in factory jobs (Zuboff, 1985). The notions of quality control, particularly in Japanese corporations, and of high reliability organizations involved increasing employees' control and knowledge of the whole organization. Organizational knowledge research has examined the technology-dependent capacity to gather or receive knowledge, to store it, to translate or transform it, and to use it, in organizational situations imposing a variety of constraints and opportunities (Baskerville & Myers, 2002; Bhatt, 2001; Carlile, 2004). Of course, technological effects are two-way, with technology and its effects transfigured by social processes. And of course, "gathering" usually includes reflexive surveillance that is technologically grounded, and there is a constant temptation to see knowledge as reified, as *being* the technology (Trethewey & Corman, 2001).

Finally, organizational knowledge process research has increasingly recognized the importance of context. Organizations in different industries, in different markets, in different national or ethnic cultures, with different levels of capital, have different technological resources, and appropriate them differently. The sheer number of academic journals devoted to knowledge management and knowledge processes is evidence of the importance placed on knowledge processes across contexts and disciplines. A recent issue of the *Journal of Knowledge Management* ranked the top 20 knowledge management journals, many of which are devoted to specific organizational contexts (Serenko & Bontis, 2009, p. 11). Additionally, several typologies of organizational knowledge have been proposed in recent scholarly literature, with scholars recognizing that different types of knowledge are used and valued in different contexts (Lam, 2000). We will not elaborate here on these typologies, because Heather Canary addresses knowledge typologies in Chapter 14. It is clear from the volume of research generated in recent years across disciplines and contexts that organizational knowledge remains an important phenomenon to understand, and that increasing that understanding requires recognition of a complex interplay of processes.

A Theoretical Template

Evident in the literature is a sense of the variety of ways communication is part of the complex web of organizational knowledge processes. Due to the broad range of approaches and issues represented in organizational knowledge research, we thought it productive to use a theoretical template to describe issues in this book. We found a useful beginning in Glaser's (1978) model of the "six Cs," which included context, condition, cause, covariance, contingent, and consequence as they relate to some object, "A." Glaser presented the six Cs as a way of conceptualizing coding families and variables/constructs, which can be used to develop grounded theory. However, it is also valuable in clarifying the relations among variables or constructs in many types of theories. Such relations sometimes are unclear or have a mixed identity in theoretical writing and research application. Also, the model is a stimulus to innovative questions and new developments, as scholars consider the types of additional concepts they could add to their own theoretical structures.

We modified Glaser's original figure to account for the complexity of knowledge processes and the different ways in which knowledge is addressed by our contributors. Figure 1.1 presents our adaptation, which includes an extra "C." As shown in Figure 1.1, we added *constitutive subprocesses* and retained context, conditions, causes, covariances, contingencies, and consequences in our model. Each chapter addresses one or more of these constructs as they relate to organizational knowledge.

As shown in Figure 1.1, the 7C model concerns a central phenomenon under investigation that is being explained, such as knowledge construction or knowledge utilization within organizations. Glaser (1978) used the generic label "A" for this central phenomenon, but we label this central part of the figure *events* or *processes*. In this book, these are typically processes of knowledge development or use.

Importantly, social processes occur within particular contexts. This is represented in the figure by arrows, connected to the *context* box, which encompass the rest of the figure. For instance, several contributors discuss transactive memory theory, which proposes that knowledge needed to

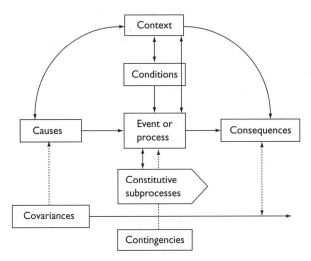

Figure 1.1 The 7C theoretical template.

accomplish organizational tasks resides within a group of connected people rather than in one particular isolated individual. Although the focus is on the group as unit of analysis, this approach to organizational knowledge recognizes the influence of the larger organizational context within which a group exists.

The second "C" in Figure 1.1 is *conditions*, which we consider to be circumstances necessary and constraining (but also enabling) for the knowledge communication process to occur in a standard way. Among these are complexities and mixed motives characteristic of systems of community health risk communication, as described in Chapter 13 by O'Hair, Kelley, and Williams. As Deng and Poole argue in Chapter 12, a condition underlying knowledge communication processes in an electronic network is the level of centralization of the array of information system-based knowledge repositories.

Conditions are not to be confused with the third C, *causes*, which are seen as direct sources or reasons for the knowledge process or event rather than grounding/limiting/enabling conditions. For example, hospitals, fire stations, and police stations are considered high-reliability organizations that require intense newcomer training. The cause of a particular knowledge process in this context would be new members entering the organization, who cause or cue organization members to teach specific procedures for safely performing tasks. In Chapter 8, Hollingshead, Brandon, Yoon, and Gupta mention reward structure as a prerequisite causing movement toward cognitive interdependence and a further cycle of knowledge communication processes.

The fourth C is *constitutive subprocesses*, which we added to the model in order to cope with the arguments and findings of our authors. In many cases, they analyzed a knowledge practice and found typical subprocesses vital for carrying out the practice in a routine or successful way. For instance, among the subprocesses in transactive memory system-based knowledge communication is the ongoing development of "meta-knowledge" about the system, as Shumate points out in Chapter 11. Meta-knowledge could be thought of as a consequence, but impressions of others' knowledge are developed, tested, and used in an ongoing support-ive cycle in knowledge communication. Or knowledge communication importantly involves the emergence and enactment of knowledge heteroge-neity, which can be foreshadowed, expressed, and reacted to in a variety of ways, as Kuhn and Porter elucidate in Chapter 2.

The fifth C is *covariances*, which are simultaneous but not intrinsically or typically related to the focal process. For instance, "ceremonies honor-ing firefighters" might be a regular event, rarely impactful on firefighter knowledge but shaping and shaped by firefighter actions and culture (e.g., "So *that's* how to get a citation in my file").

The sixth C is *contingencies*. These are atypical events or situations that affect focal knowledge communication practices. For example, "number of other fires also going on in the city" might be a contingency for a specific localized firefighting event in Myers' study of knowledge in firefighter organizations in Chapter 16. If there are multiple fires, firefighters might have to know how to adapt to situations where they have little back-up, but that isn't a typical or marked sphere of knowledge.

The seventh and final C is *consequences*, the meaning of which is pretty obvious. One type of relevant consequence is the range of outcomes for various stakeholders of the organization. But another central consequence in this book is the maintenance or transformation of organizational know-ledge and knowledge communication practices. For instance, Flanagin and Bator mention in Chapter 10 the development of electronic procurement systems in corporations, which replace manual purchasing routines. These electronic systems (themselves parts of informated knowledge processes) are the consequence of demanding reflexive knowledge work by purchasers as well as collection of information from and about suppliers.

Communicative Perspectives on Organizational Knowledge

It is clear from our discussion thus far that interest in organizational know-ledge phenomena both includes and extends beyond the subfield of organ-izational communication. Undeniably, a majority of research and theorizing about organizational knowledge has been conducted by those aligning themselves more with disciplines of management, organization science, and information technologies than with the discipline of commu-nication studies (Easterby-Smith & Lyles, 2003). However, recent work outside of the communication discipline certainly points to the importance of communication in organizational knowledge (Boer, 2005; Hayes & Walsham, 2003), and there now exists a critical mass of communication researchers who have made important contributions to the area. Indeed, one reason for this book is to bring together in one place the several focal areas of communication-centered research regarding organizational knowledge. Past and recent literature presents four overlapping problem fields that indicate the communicative nature of organizational knowledge processes. The sections of this volume reflect these problem fields: (1) the communicative *practices* of organizational knowledge, (2) the communicative *connections* of organizational knowledge, (3) the communicative *technologies* of organizational knowledge, and (4) the communicative *contexts* of organizational knowledge.

Communicative Practices of Organizational Knowledge

Practice-based approaches have been adopted by many organizational communication scholars due to the emphasis on the social and interactive nature of knowledge. If knowledge is conceived as existing in practices, several challenges are present for communication scholars: to explain the difference between knowledgeable practice and mere communication behavior, to explain how a "single" or unified web of practice can accommodate different and even inconsistent performances, to reconcile practice with complex organization, and to elucidate the connection between practice and deeper human relations. All the authors address the first challenge, Kuhn and Porter especially address the second, Jackson and Williamson and also Lyon and Alexander focus on the third, and Iverson focuses on the fourth and, to some extent, the second.

Several chapters in this book use practice approaches to examine organizational knowledge and communication. For example, Tim Kuhn and Amanda Porter take a practice-based approach to that topic in Chapter 2 by focusing on knowledge accomplishment and the role of heterogeneity in organizational knowledge processes. Kuhn and Porter compare their practice approach to cognitive-representational views of knowledge, highlighting that a communication-centered view of organizational knowledge prioritizes the process of knowing over the possession of knowledge, and over communication behavior considered as a mere conduit among psychological knowers.

Chapter 4 presents an approach to organizational knowledge that combines practice theory with systems theory. Michele Jackson and Julie Williamson present challenges practitioners face when organizational structure and practice collides. This chapter also calls into question the view that knowledge is simply an asset to be managed. Rather, Jackson and Williamson point out the paradox that traditional knowledge management procedures seek to transform knowledge into a centralized organizationally managed text, and thus typically threaten the strategic and innovative quality of organizational knowledge processes they are intended to protect. They offer as an alternative a view of knowledge processes that combines practice and systems views to both create and protect strategic organizational assets.

An emphasis on practice in knowledge processes became well-recognized after Lave and Wenger (1991) introduced the concept of communities of practice. In Chapter 3, Joel Iverson uses communities of practice (CoP) theory to discuss the role of belonging in organizational knowledge. He addresses several critiques that have been raised regarding CoP, and elaborates on the usefulness of this approach for communication-centered investigations of organizational knowledge. As Iverson points out, CoP theory maintains unique benefits for understanding the development of organizational knowledge that withstand critiques of over-simplification. Iverson primarily focuses on the role of belonging in organizational knowledge development/communication, noting that the CoP lens is uniquely suited to providing insight into how belonging (or not belonging) influences organizational knowledge processes – far more fundamentally than communication behavior, considered as a mere conduit among psychological knowers.

Importantly, knowledge practices are not value-neutral. The construction, use, and management of knowledge are inherently related to power and organizational politics. Alexander Lyon and Joseph Chesebro examine this political side of communication practices in Chapter 5, adopting a critical approach to organizational knowledge that critiques functionalist and managerialist assumptions. Although not as prevalent in the organizational knowledge literature bases, the critical approach is valuable for investigating ways in which communication practices serve varying interests as organizational knowledge is constructed, used, and managed. They argue that knowledge in organizations is inherently politically biased and rhetorical, heterogeneous and inconsistent, control- and identity-laden. Thus, a unified web of practice must conceal or neutralize, at the level of practice, these jolts. Lyon and Chesebro use a case study to demonstrate the political side of knowledge development practices.

Communicative Connections of Organizational Knowledge

Another focal area that continues to attract interest by both researchers and practitioners is the importance of connections in organizational knowledge processes. Organizational communication researchers, as well as those within technological disciplines, focus on how connections among knowers are implicated in, and both influence and are influenced by, various knowledge processes. Work on this problem field among communication researchers aims to add to our knowledge of ways that communicative limitations are involved in and, especially, constrain knowledge practices.

For example, transactive memory (TM) is a network-based approach to explain how second-order "knowledge about knowers" affects knowledge use and diffusion within particular groups. Several chapters in this book draw on transactive memory as a theoretical approach to understanding organizational knowledge processes. For example, Ed Palazzolo discusses transactive memory theory in organizational communication terms in Chapter 7, presenting measurement developments and future directions for applying the theory across organizational contexts for the benefit of practitioners. He notes how innovative methods, especially computational modeling, can develop our specific understanding of complex reflexive impacts of member impressions of knowledge resources and networks of knowledge possession/sharing practices.

Hollingshead, Brandon, Yoon, and Gupta provide a theoretical look at knowledge-sharing errors in Chapter 8. Their chapter presents a dynamic model of TM growth in situations characterized by task ambiguity and change, the need to find or create matches of knowledge distribution to task structure, and the need to develop trust in relationships. They describe several dimensions of resulting transactive memory errors that impede effective knowledge sharing within working groups.

The other two chapters in this section analyze other aspects of the communicative connections that constrain organizational knowledge practices. Paul Leonardi presents an interesting case, in Chapter 6, of how task-required and attempted connections in a multinational corporation did little to facilitate the development and use of knowledge across global workgroups. Leonardi points out the importance of cultural assumptions in organizational knowledge processes, such that simply establishing connections with technology and procedures is ineffective if those who are connected are unaware of fundamental knowledge assumptions of others with whom they are connected.

Likewise, Corman and Dooley present, in Chapter 9, the difficulties involved in getting organizational members connected who share common stocks of knowledge and who could use their shared knowledge bases to develop valuable projects. As Corman and Dooley point out, there are significant operational divides between (unknowingly) sharing mutually relevant knowledge resources, identifying such potentially valuable connections, and actually developing those connections in useful ways. Together, the four chapters in this section of the volume present ideas that are both stimulating and challenging for scholars and practitioners alike who are interested in the communication of mutually relevant knowledge within and across organizations.

Communicative Technologies of Organizational Knowledge

A third problem field that has emerged in the literature is that of technologies associated with organizational knowledge processes. Scholars have noted that many organizational practitioners have lionized technology as the panacea for all problems related to knowledge management, use, and sharing, without taking into account social processes that work concomitantly with technology in organizations (Bhatt, 2001; Hayes & Walsham, 2003). A rival viewpoint has claimed that knowledge practices are fundamentally social-interactional, and that focusing on technology as more than an extra tool clouds our knowledge. Our chapters aim to contribute, in varied ways, to realistic resolution of this conflict.

Flanagin and Bator present a communicative view of organizational knowledge in Chapter 10 that refigures the technological and relational views of knowledge management. They note that organizational practitioners charged with knowledge management functions should neither underestimate nor exaggerate the role of information communication technologies (ICTs) in the knowledge management process. While some organizational technology arrangements (especially hierarchical control in varied guises) can thwart knowledge development and use, others can facilitate emergence of knowledge grounded in social practice, and even organize such practices, as in the case of open-source software.

The technological features of knowledge management systems are also discussed by Michelle Shumate in Chapter 11 through her presentation of a network model of knowledge flow. Shumate draws on public goods and exchange theory to develop a model of network, technology, and social knowledge sharing. She notes that her network model is well-suited to address knowledge management challenges as workgroup boundaries blur across organizational boundaries, people increasingly use Web 2.0 technologies, and individuals become more aware of the enabling and constraining role of technology in social processes.

Deng and Poole take a different approach to technology in Chapter 12 through their discussion of electronic networks of practice. Deng and Poole combine a practice approach to organizational knowledge with transactive memory theory to develop the concept of electronic networks of practice. This chapter offers several insights into characteristics of ICTs, both social and structural, that contribute to effectively facilitating knowledge sharing and development through interpersonal practice network development, supplemented and stimulated by electronic resources in ways that merge network technology and socially distributed practice.

Communicative Contexts of Organizational Knowledge

An important issue evident in the former three sections of this book is that context matters. Indeed, Figure 1.1 presents context as an over-arching construct for consideration when explicating knowledge processes. The final section of this volume includes four examples of contexts that present unique nuances to organizational knowledge processes. Each chapter in the section also addresses one or more of the first three problem fields through discussion of knowledge processes situated in specific communicative contexts. For example, O'Hair, Kelley, and Williams recognize blurred boundaries in organizational knowledge processes in their Chapter 13 discussion of a community-communication infrastructure approach to managing community risk. The authors recognize the importance of knowledge networks and technology in risk management, but provide an integrated approach for developing community resilience through more collaborative knowledge development processes.

Chapter 14 also addresses a context that crosses organizational boundaries as Heather Canary discusses knowledge development regarding public education policy. This chapter addresses the texture of the concept of communicative practices, but does so within the specific context of public policy and multiple stakeholders. The chapter presents structurating activity theory as an integrative framework for examining cross-system knowledge processes and different types of knowledge that emerge when policy implementers interact with each other, with administrators, and with policy beneficiaries to construct policy knowledge.

Murphy and Eisenberg examine the health care context in Chapter 15, delineating three frames of knowledge in that context: knowledge as routinized, knowledge as emergent, and knowledge as political. These frames are connected to each other through three dimensions of knowledge: instrumental, performative, and relational. The authors present a case study of how the three frames and dimensions of knowledge are useful for understanding and improving knowledge processes in hospitals and other health care contexts.

Myers builds upon Chapter 15 with her discussion, in Chapter 16, of another high reliability organizational context: firefighting organizations. This chapter addresses the role of informal socialization in organizational knowledge processes for the unique context of high reliability organizations. Myers emphasizes the importance of tacit knowledge in organizational socialization, and provides useful insights regarding both knowledge and socialization processes in this very important context.

Concluding Remarks

We are confident readers will find that each of the following chapters presents compelling issues, relevant examples, and useful insights for moving toward a communicative perspective on organizational knowledge. We have attempted in this chapter to lay out historical and theoretical foundations for the work presented in this volume, and to display a few of the interrelations among the chapters – those that led to our organization of the volume. But we hope our categories and summaries do not deter readers from exploring all of the chapters, since they illuminate varied facets of a focus on knowledge as communicative.

References

Bartel, C. A., & Garud, R. (2003). Narrative knowledge in action: Adaptive abduction as a mechanism for knowledge creation and exchange in organizations. In M. Easterby-Smith & M. A. Lyles (Eds.), *The Blackwell handbook of organizational learning and knowledge management* (pp. 324–342). Oxford, UK: Blackwell.

Baskerville, R. L., & Myers, M. D. (2002). Information systems as a reference discipline. *MIS Quarterly, 26*, 1–14.

Bhatt, G. (2001). Knowledge management in organizations: Examining the interaction between technologies, techniques, and people. *Journal of Knowledge Management, 5*, 68–75.

Boer, N. I. (2005). *Knowledge sharing within organizations: A situated and relational perspective.* Rotterdam: Erasmus Research Institute of Management.

Carlile, P. R. (2004). Transferring, translating, and transforming: An integrative framework for managing knowledge across boundaries. *Organization Science, 15*, 555–568.

Easterby-Smith, M., & Lyles, M. A. (2003). Introduction: Watersheds of organizational learning and knowledge management. In M. Easterby-Smith & M. A. Lyles (Eds.), *The Blackwell handbook of organizational learning and knowledge management* (pp. 1–15). Oxford, UK: Blackwell.

Giddens, A. (1981). *A contemporary critique of historical materialism*, Vol. 1: *Power, property, and the state.* Berkeley, CA: University of California Press.

Glaser, B. G. (1978). *Theoretical sensitivity.* Mill Valley, CA: Sociology Press.

Hayes, N., & Walsham, G. (2003). Knowledge sharing and ICTs: A relational perspective. In M. Easterby-Smith & M. A. Lyles (Eds.), *The Blackwell handbook of organizational learning and knowledge management* (pp. 54–77). Oxford, UK: Blackwell.

Hodgkinson, G. P., & Healey, M. P. (2008). Cognition in organizations. *Annual Review of Psychology, 59*, 387–417.

Knorr Cetina, K., & Preda, A. (2007). The temporalization of financial markets: From network to flow. *Theory, Culture & Society, 24*, 116–138.

Lam, A. (2000). Tacit knowledge, organizational learning, and societal institutions: An integrated framework. *Organization Studies, 21*, 487–513.

Lave, J., & Wenger, E. (1991). *Situated learning: Legitimate peripheral participation.* Cambridge, UK: Cambridge University Press.

Monge, P. R., & Contractor, N. S. (2003). *Theories of communication networks.* New York, NY: Oxford University Press.

Nonaka, I., & Von Krogh, G. (2009). Tacit knowledge and knowledge conversion: Controversy and advancement in organizational knowledge creation theory. *Organization Science, 20*, 635–652.

Perrow, C. (1986). *Complex organizations: A critical essay* (3rd Edn). New York, NY: McGraw-Hill.

Serenko, A., & Bontis, N. (2009). Global ranking of knowledge management and intellectual capital academic journals. *Journal of Knowledge Management, 13*, 4–15.

Stewart, T. A. (2003). *The wealth of knowledge: Intellectual capital and the twenty-first century organization.* New York, NY: Currency.

Trethewey, A., & Corman, S. (2001). Anticipating k-commerce: E-commerce, knowledge management, and organizational communication. *Management Communication Quarterly, 14,* 619–628.

Tsoukas, H. (2005). *Complex knowledge: Studies in organizational epistemology.* Oxford: Oxford University Press.

Wheatley, M. (2000). Can knowledge management succeed where other efforts have failed? In D. Morey, M. Maybury, & B. Thuraisingham (Eds.), *Knowledge management: Classic and contemporary works* (pp. 3–8). Cambridge, MA: MIT Press.

Zuboff, S. (1985). Automate/informate: The two faces of intelligent technology. *Organizational Dynamics, 14,* 5–18.

Part I

The Communicative *Practices* of Organizational Knowledge

Chapter 2

Heterogeneity in Knowledge and Knowing

A Social Practice Perspective

Timothy Kuhn and Amanda J. Porter

Research on organizational knowledge is dominated by a set of assumptions that should give communication scholars pause. Research frequently claims that knowledge is the center point of organizational existence, and the lion's share of theorizing emanating from such a view asserts that when organizations seek competitive advantage they must nurture "knowledge work," extract knowledge from its locations, build "collaborative" technologies, possess more and better information, protect knowledge from getting into the wrong hands, and understand "who knows what" in a given site (see, for example, Grant, 1996; Schultze & Leidner, 2002). In both empirical and theoretical literatures, analyses tend to portray knowledge as a *cognitive entity*, possessed by actors in either tacit (procedural) or explicit (declarative) form, but rarely both (Maier, Prange, & von Rosenstiel, 2001). It is a stance reflecting a *representational* orientation, where social settings are discrete and unitary entities can be modeled with precision, and knowledge is seen to consist of technical expertise, technical skill, and abstract principles (Chia & Holt, 2008). This conception portrays knowledge as a transferable commodity located in the individual or the collective mind; its guiding concern is to show how the accumulation, management, and protection of this commodity produces organizational effectiveness (Walsh & Ungson, 1991).

For organizational communication scholars, the cognitivist-representational perspective runs the risk of violating some core beliefs about organizing. If we view communication as a process in which contextualized actors use symbols and make interpretations to coordinate and control activity and knowledge (Kuhn, 2008), and if we increasingly desire to see how communication constitutes organization (see, for example, McPhee & Zaug, 2000; Taylor, 2000), the cognitive-representational perspective is unhelpful. Four harmful consequences of taking this view stand out. First, it sees knowledge as an entity ontologically separate from action (and context), reinforcing a dualism against which many in communication studies argue (Conrad & Haynes, 2001). Second, in the cognitivist-representational literature, "knowledge" is seen to serve primarily technical and instrumental concerns, where its functional benefits can be realized only if it is quantified, captured, and transferred to others; communication scholars at least since the interpretive turn express concern about the domination of managerialist ideologies of this ilk. Third, the orientation leads to the valorization of efficiency and accuracy in knowledge transfer, reducing the role of communication to that which transmits the object of interest. Communication, then, is rendered *epiphenomenal*: it becomes the mere surface, rather than the substance, of organizing. And fourth, the cognitive-representational view depends on a conception of organizational settings as functioning on a relative stability of rules and situations, which "simply avoids the empirical experience of managers acting in situations where any such 'rule' is constantly negotiated through an entire weave of habits, norms, and emotional dispositions" (Chia & Holt, 2008, p. 474). The underlying problem is that the cognitivist-representational view fails to provide explanations of how knowledge is constituted, appropriated, and altered in complex organizing practices, while it also pays little attention to how knowledge is shaped by a wide array of other dynamic social and organizational phenomena. Such issues are generally considered central for organizational communication scholarship, and the aim of this chapter is to show that there exists a better alternative.

Drawing on theories that place social practice at the conceptual core, we employ a framework for investigating knowledge that examines communicative activities, and their situational shaping, in episodes of problem-oriented action. We present this perspective in the next section, showing the connections along the way with the "7C model" modified by McPhee (2008). We follow that by engaging with what we think is a unique account of heterogeneity in knowing, portraying it as generative of several interesting consequences for organization studies scholarship. We hold that if this perspective is to be of benefit for understanding organizing, it must produce novel insights on practice; we address these in the chapter's final section.

Knowledge-accomplishing Activity as an Alternative Explanatory Focus

The alternative conception of knowledge we take up here, a *practice-based* view, is advocated by a growing interdisciplinary group of organizational scholars. Influenced by several related streams of theorizing, a practice-based view provides a vision of social life based on connections between culture, activity, minds, objects, and interactions (Reckwitz, 2002). Knowledge becomes not an identifiable and commodifiable entity, but rather an active presence in, or attribution made about, practice. Analytical concern thus turns away from identifying the existence or uniqueness of knowledge, and instead turns to *processes of knowing*, seeing these processes as always embodied, embedded in particular socio-historical settings and communities, and intimately connected to the material factors through which they emerge.

Foregrounding knowing implies that knowledge is a *capacity to act within a situation*, where this capacity should always be seen as intersubjectively negotiated and continually in flux (Ewenstein & White, 2007; Styhre, 2003). Knowing, as a social practice, suggests that our explanatory focus should not be knowledge (seen as a commodity), but rather the complex interactive processes that apply and invent (that which we take to be) knowledge in situated problem-solving.[1] Scholars working from this view suggest that action involves significantly more "wayfinding" (Hutchins, 1995), and significantly less rational calculation, than the dominant cognitive-representational perspective would allow. The point is not, however, that organizing, as practice, is devoid of "knowledge" – indeed, it is infused with knowledge in ways outside the scope of the cognitive-representational view – but instead that knowledge is always a provisional *accomplishment* that responds to the myriad contingencies of organizational situations, as well as to an understanding of the distinctions marking particular discursive moves as locally relevant or irrelevant. Examining what we shall call "knowledge-accomplishing activities" encourages insight into *how* situated actors create and reclaim capacities to act while also acknowledging the effects of language, reflexivity, and struggles over meaning.

Despite the potential attractiveness of a practice-oriented view, two concerns animate our argument. First is a lack of specificity among proponents of these practice perspectives regarding concepts and their relationships to scholarship and intervention. Although practice-based writing can provide a novel vocabulary and a set of heuristic devices (Nicolini, Gherardi, & Yanow, 2003), the view generally lacks clear guidelines for research (Kuhn & Jackson, 2008). Given the challenges in studying mundane, tacit, and embedded action, the absence of directives is a concern. In response, we base this chapter on a practice-based methodological framework that distinguishes between performances and practices. *Performances* are interactive moves, expressive and collaborative communication acts that "emerge in a productive tension between participants' expectations for good form and content in particular situations and the unpredictable human powers of creativity and improvisation" (Lindlof & Taylor, 2002, p. 6). Practices are "embodied, materially-mediated arrays of human activity centrally organized around shared practical understanding" (Schatzki, 2001, p. 2). We hold that performances and practices exist as a duality in that individuals author performances, while these performances' status as exemplars of (and contributions to) practice simultaneously make them properties of collectives. Our explanatory focus, then, is not actors, communities of practice, or knowledge as an entity, but is instead the form and content of the communication process generating the performance–practice duality. Understanding the factors shaping performances, the array of potential performances characterizing a practice, and the ways performances can challenge practices can provide necessary methodological guidance.

A second concern involves the heterogeneity of knowledge in organizational life. Those who advocate a practice-based view tend to argue for its superiority over a cognitive-representational perspective because it honors the complexity of organizing processes, acknowledges the myriad contextual and communal influences on knowledge, and refuses to engage in reification. They argue for the importance of communities in shaping what "counts" as knowledge, and thus argue for the importance of old-timers involving novices in experiences and narratives that bring them into the pre-existing community as full members (Orr, 1996; Wenger, 1998). But many critics note that such moves often generate simplistic assumptions about intra-community consensus and shared knowledge, while ignoring important organizational and identity-based divisions – divisions common to organizing (Kuhn & Corman, 2003). These assumptions about sharing, in turn, prevent examinations of difference, and the forms of power that create and maintain it (e.g., Contu & Willmott, 2003; Østerlund & Carlile, 2005). Our two concerns require careful consideration. We argue that a framework informed by communication theory is up to the task.

The Conditions and Contexts of Knowledge-accomplishing Activity

As Kuhn and Jackson (2008) argue, the development of such a framework starts with recognizing the centrality of *problematic situations* – as the *context* of knowing-in-practice – for explaining social action. A problematic situation is the state of affairs formed by a stream of past and projected future practices in which actors perceive the need to take action to address a (current or potential) opportunity in, or threat to, ongoing action. In problematic situations, actors sense the deficiencies in their abilities to meet claims of appropriateness and engage in the performance of pragmatic action that can either reclaim a capacity to act or create a new capacity (Cronen & Chetro-Svizos, 2001; Dewey, 1938; Fisher, 1982). This takes the concept of immanence (Chia, 1999) seriously, yet situates knowing in the constant present. The principle of immanence suggests that the past is always immanent in the present; each situation necessarily incorporates and absorbs the events of its past. Each "event" represents the realization of one of the many possibilities presented by the past configuration of events (Chia, 1999, p. 220). This creates potentialities for the future while simultaneously constraining those potentials; in this sense, problematic situations should be seen not as obstacles encountered in organizing, but rather as a configuration of elements that require knowledgeable action in response. Thus, problematic situations emerge and are transformed in interaction; they are constructed by persons and are shaped by the "culturally constituted relations of persons, settings, and activity" (Suchman, 1996, p. 56). Variations across problematic situations imply that some situations will appear to participants as open and unstructured, while others will seem straightforward and closed.

Our conception of the problematic situation recognizes at its core a relational epistemology, which recognizes the source of knowing as an intersubjective function of relating to others within situations, where similarities and differences between participants emerge in responsiveness to one another. This projects a view of knowing-in-practice as different from knowledge of facts or skills; "it is a moment-by-moment changing *felt* kind of practical knowing to do with how to *organize* or *manage* our own behaviour *from within* our lives together with the others around us" (Shotter, 2008, p. 507, emphasis in original). In this sense, relations as constructed in situated activity portray our anticipation of, interpretation of, and responsiveness to, others' moves as crucial to realizing individual and collective capacities to act. More to the point, our engagement with others in problematic situations constructs the normative claim of appropriateness on actions. Such a normative claim can be understood as forming the contours of the situations which both mediate and are the outcome of problem-oriented action.

Such claims about situations are evocative, yet – to echo a point made above – provide little guidance for research or practice. Linking action that defines situations to knowledge claims, Kuhn and Jackson's interpretation of Lazega's (1992) situational features recognizes that claims regarding the appropriateness of particular discursive moves are a function of the factors shaping actors' identifications, the legitimacy of their actions, and sources of their accountability. In other words, a person's claim to knowledgeability in a given setting takes the form of appropriateness, as judged by the community, regarding the content and form of his or her problem-solving moves. Thus, judgments of appropriateness are tied to identities, as actors assess their own and one another's identifications as they frame situations. Identifications are, at least in part, allegiances that index an organization's or community's control over individuals. The discursive production of identities is an ongoing activity, as actors attempt to predict others' likely actions and project valued identities. This is tied to the second situational feature, legitimacy of action, which refers to motivation to act, spurred by an actor's perception of the organization's expectations of him or her. Finally, sources of accountability acknowledge that individuals look to particular members of the audience for direction and validation. In our continual responsiveness to others, we perform for a constituency.

Identification, legitimacy, and accountability can best be understood as resources in knowledge-accomplishing activity. The process of framing of a situation is the negotiation of these three resources and the resulting judgments regarding the appropriateness and outcomes of discursive moves. Kuhn and Jackson's framework shows how knowledge-accomplishing activity responds to and, in turn, participates in the construction of, situation-defining resources. The model also displays that situations vary in the types of discursive activity considered appropriate. Specifically, many problem-solving situations appear straightforward and routine (i.e., determinate), but others are more indeterminate; they are considered ambiguous and "irrational," and neither the grounds of action nor the consequences of decision are well understood (Alvesson, 1993). Such ambiguous cases exist when participants evince little common understanding of the bases for identification, accountability, and/or legitimacy; when there is ambiguity regarding these, the resources to validate action (and actors) are uncertain.

Episodes and Knowledge-accomplishing Activities as Constituent Subprocesses

Discursive moves, then, can be *knowledge-accomplishing activities* that apply and/or generate knowledge in an attempt to realize a capacity to act (incidentally, we assume no particular objective toward which a capacity to act is directed). These moves are the interactional strategies by which knowledge accomplishing is carried out, but they always occur within *episodes* of organizing. Although isolating episodes of interaction could be accused of the same sort of reduction we lodged against the cognitive-representational view, episodes should be seen within the stream of ongoing practice, and therefore as a participant in continuous system structuration (Harrè & Secord, 1972; Knorr-Cetina, 1981; Pentland, 1992). More importantly, because they are characterized by beginnings and (at least a semblance of) endings, they have a structure that lends itself well to analysis. The moves we call *knowledge-accomplishing activities* are those that frame the situations, make bids for action within them, and bring them to a close. The form and content of the moves that respond to determinate or indeterminate situations – the variations of which Kuhn and Jackson (2008) describe as information transmission, information request, instruction, and improvisation – can become "textual" and can later be taken to be knowledge in a manner fitting with the cognitive-representational view. These activities, then, can become what members employ in subsequent problem-solving, and their appropriateness becomes a matter of that future emergent – and continually interactionally reconstituted – situation.

Heterogeneity in Knowing

Diversity in knowledge is a key concern for many students of organization. Research frequently considers how experts and novices interact (Lave & Wenger, 1991), how boundary objects enable coordinated action across knowledge divisions (Carlile, 2002; Flanagin, 2002; Tenkasi & Boland, 1996), how diversity and conflict can engender group-level creativity (Hargadon & Bechky, 2006), and how to locate people with unique knowledge profiles (Child & Shumate, 2007; Contractor & Monge, 2002). In much of this work, that which is heterogeneous is the knowledge *possessed* either by a person or by a group of ostensibly-homogeneous persons (e.g., those within a particular workgroup). The problem is that such a view overlooks *knowing* – the communicative accomplishment of problem-oriented action – in its desire to shed light on the ways differences in knowledge present obstacles to, and opportunities for, the production of "desirable" organizational outcomes or the exercise of power.

Recovering a focus on knowing is possible with the practice-based view, but it runs into its own problems. As suggested above, some in the practice camp examine communities' influence on practices, but oversimplify and sterilize practice while rendering elements homogeneous (Chia, 1999). The difficulty appears to be locating how difference matters in practice-based, situated perspectives on knowing. Despite these difficulties of attending to and conceptualizing heterogeneity, there is continued recognition that heterogeneity matters in knowing (Bruni, Gherardi, & Parolin, 2007; Lave, 1996). Knowledge-accomplishing activity offers conceptual tools to display how difference is constitutive of knowing in practice. The necessary move is to examine the ways in which heterogeneity *generates* knowing.

Consequences: Heterogeneity as Generative

Heterogeneity as generative of knowing points to the varied nature of materials, social positions, and trajectories of activity upon which actors draw in knowing. Heterogeneity, in other words, is a source from which knowledge accomplishment proceeds. Thus, the theoretical conception of the social world is one in which actors base interpretations on differing contextual social positions (Lave, 1996) and construct meaning from relations made up of heterogeneous materials (Bruni et al., 2007; Cooren, 2004). To understand heterogeneity as generative is to acknowledge the ways in which difference is used as a resource to call forth and construct judgments of situational appropriateness and, as such, to compel or enable actors to engage in knowledge-accomplishing activity. From such a perspective, heterogeneity is portrayed as a resource that is performed into existence in a situation, and the interactive responses to that construction have implications for organizational structuring. In Kuhn and Jackson's framework, then, there exists no *a priori* assumption about heterogeneity; rather, heterogeneity can only be understood situationally, as produced through performances that index contrasting practices and resources for identification, accountability, and legitimacy. In what follows, we consider three implications of understanding heterogeneity in this way.

A first consequence touches upon potential sources of change in practice. As actors frame problematic situations – drawing upon the resources of identification, legitimation, and accountability – differences in loyalties, preferred procedures, and responsibilities frequently surface (Schön, 1983),

and these differences can produce ambiguity by contributing to the indeterminacy of situations. Additionally, heterogeneity may generate conflict
via exertions of expertise to validate personal knowledge, or personal
preferences for activity trajectories, against others' preferences (Alvesson,
1993). Importantly, ambiguity and conflict can also signal the possibility
for a reframing of the larger practice in which a set of problem-solvers is
engaged. When a discursive move occurring within a practice is perceived
by members as ambiguous, or when it produces disagreement, practice-
based theories assume that members refer to their encompassing practice
to make sense of the act; their shared meanings for the practice suggest
that they will be able either to fold the ambiguity into the practice or to
attribute it to some idiosyncrasy of the person. When those shared meanings are not in place, are not fully shared, or are unstable, however – cases
that are likely to be more common than shared meanings – ambiguous
performances can point up gaps or ruptures in the practice. A *non
sequitur* offered in a routine meeting can become an occasion for metacommunication – reflection on the multiple meanings embedded in
ongoing communication practices – seeking to understand the source of
the difference and, potentially, as an opportunity to introduce a new conception of knowing into the ongoing practice. When a new member joins
a workgroup, for instance, he or she may base performances on the policies and procedures of a previous group while simultaneously seeking to
understand the new one, and a case in which a contribution produces
ambiguity or conflict can serve as an opportunity to step outside the
assumptions of practice to interrogate (and perhaps reinscribe) the local
configuration of resources for identification, accountability, and
legitimacy.

A second consequence of taking a knowledge-accomplishing perspective
is that it provides the possibility for understanding how heterogeneity (re)
inscribes power differences. Because one consequence of knowledge-
accomplishing activity can be the routinization of performances, another
potential response to ambiguity and conflict is to codify or strengthen the
distinctions and classifications marking practice, establishing or solidifying
the value of some forms of knowing over others. Such a possibility is well
known to critical theorists who examine how a given group's claims over
texts and practices become taken for granted within a given setting (as well
as across settings). Examining how performances such as stories, moves
toward discursive closure, linguistic distinctions, images, and the like shape
– and are shaped by – both local and broader-scale resources for identification, legitimation, and accountability can produce insight into how practices of knowing are bound up in struggles over meaning where power is a
central concern.

A third implication considers the organization-constituting properties of
situated knowing. Drawing on both the notion of knowing as situated
problem-solving practice and the generation of "texts" that signify the

knowledge accomplished through activity, the nascent *communicative theory of the firm* holds the potential to connect scholarship on knowledge with scholarship explaining the constitution of complex commercial organizations. Although a thorough explication of this theory is beyond the scope of this chapter, we draw upon two themes in Kuhn's (2005, 2008; Kuhn & Ashcraft, 2003) articulation of such a theory, which in turn builds on theorizing about the ways communication constitutes organizations associated with the "Montréal School" (Cooren & Taylor, 1997; Taylor, Cooren, Giroux, & Robichaud, 1996). In this theory, the coordination and control seen in knowing are depicted as an organizing "game" – one which lacks a designated end and where rules are provisionally and internally negotiated (Carse, 1986; see also Chapter 5 in this volume). The ongoing, infinite, nature of such game – as opposed to economists' version of games, which are based on fixed interests and a drive for limited iterations – is key to understanding constitution, because it implies both continued player involvement and the likelihood that its lessons extend beyond any given site as players, artifacts, and texts circulate. Further, games are important conceptual tools because they provide players with goals, strategies, roles, audiences, definitions of success and failure, and visions of meaningfulness (Koppl & Langlois, 2001; Long, 1958). Knowledge, in turn, is both medium and outcome of the game-playing we have called problem-oriented knowing.

The second theme in this communicative view of the firm centers on texts. Specifically, the theory describes the emergence of an abstract text produced as communicative practices employ similar resources across space and time. This "authoritative" text comes to represent the relations of legitimacy and power in firm-specific practice, depicting the firm's structure in a way that specifies the valuing of knowledge (and thus capital) and activities, as well as the roles and authority, in the firm. It is authoritative in a dual sense: in that its content and form are the product of active (and potentially conflict-laden) authorship, and also in that its use in situated episodes of interaction provides its users authority. Accordingly, a given firm will be characterized by only one authoritative text, but the degree of abstraction or dispersion of its elements depends on the differences among those who vie to author it.

The authoritative text, then, becomes the representation of the "official" organization, but is neither immutable nor monolithic. Rather, it can be modified through "saturation" by other texts, particularly through encounters with groups beyond organizational boundaries. The authoritative text could, for instance, become extended through textual supplement through an inter-organizational collaborative enterprise, or it could converge on a reduced set of tenets through interactions with stakeholders. This has implications for investigations of how the text is employed intra-organizationally as a guide in engaging with problematic situations occasioned by knowledge heterogeneity. In this way, a communicative theory of the firm encourages a conceptual connection between knowing-in-practice and the constitution of the organization – two bodies of work that are infrequently of benefit to one another.

This is of potential interest to practitioners, too, because it suggests that those issues typically chalked up to "communication problems" (Gilsdorf, 1998) may instead involve divergent social practices, or trajectories of those practices (Schatzki, 1996). Addressing those issues, therefore, is not served by merely "managing" diversity or repeating messages to ensure understanding. Instead, managers and other members require a sensitivity to situational affordances (i.e., textual and material resources for legitimacy, accountability, and identification) as they design practices that respond to difference. For example, Kuhn and Corman (2003) studied processes of collaborative change in a city's real-estate planning department, finding that the recognition of divergent knowing practices across subgroups was interpreted not as a threat, but as a resource for generating a regime of accountability to the whole. In that case, members' arguments about change drew on both authoritative texts (both of the department and the larger city government) and the "brute facts" of local land use. The point, then, is that scholars who pursue communicative explanations regarding practices of knowing in firms will be guided by a research question that asks how the intersections of the material and the ideational (i.e., textual) manifest in the resources for – and the forms of capital implied in – organizing practice.

These three consequences of a knowledge-accomplishing perspective on heterogeneity highlight issues of interest primarily to scholars, and to organizational communication scholars in particular. For this to be a compelling perspective on knowledge, however, the implications for understanding and influencing knowing practice must be appealing to practitioners as well, and we address these in the next section.

Heterogeneity and Implications for Practice

By this point, it should be clear that seeing knowing as knowledge-accomplishing activity provides a starting point that differs markedly from the cognitive-representational view. Here, knowledge is understood as a relational, communicative accomplishment that cannot be simply broken into explicit and tacit forms. The practice-based view redirects attention from "knowledge" to the activity of knowing in problematic situations. In doing so, it encourages a focus on knowing as continuous problem-solving accomplished through the use of situational resources. Understanding the locus of social activity as the problematic situation can help organizational practitioners resist objectifying knowledge and rendering it static. From this perspective, heterogeneity in knowledge and forms of practice are not encumbrances to organizing, but instead are descriptions of normal states of affairs that can generate either stability or change in ongoing problem-solving. With this in mind, we advance two contributions to organizing practice based on the framework outlined above.

Rethinking Knowledge Management

The rise of attention to knowledge in organization studies was accompanied by a number of knowledge management (KM) initiatives in both scholarship and practice. Although KM, as a managerial strategy, may have been displaced as the buzzword of choice for consultants several years ago, its central tenets – involving locating, extracting, sorting, codifying, and, in particular, transferring knowledge to serve organizational goals – continue to shape organizational action. From the knowledge-accomplishing perspective, however, the concern for transferring knowledge is fundamentally misguided.

The problem, put bluntly, is that knowledge simply *cannot* be transferred. Although information (rather than knowledge) is amenable to transfer through typical media of exchange, the concern here is less terminological than epistemological, and communication scholars who rail against linear transmission models of communication should recognize this claim. Communication scholars hold that meaning – as that around which communication revolves – is too precarious, too tied to context, and too embedded within layers of discourse to make transfer a possibility. Knowledge, as a capacity to act and a *"tool at the service of knowing"* (Cook & Brown, 1999, p. 388, emphasis in original), evinces the same qualities. That which is deemed appropriate to contribute to problem-oriented action (i.e., knowledge) is inherently formed by the local configuration of situational resources and, *contra* the cognitive-representational camp, cannot be divorced from the stylistic characteristics of the actor(s) performing it. And, as suggested above, our notion of knowledge "deployment" depends on situational factors being aligned in ways that enable performances such as information transfer to "come off" as adequate knowledge-accomplishing activity. Accordingly, to assume that knowledge can be transferred is to ignore or erase the contingencies of context, condition, and performance, and doing so runs the risk of rendering organizing (and communicating) as simple and straightforward.

Most members of organizations would reject such a narrow vision of organizing, recognizing that tasks that become simple and straightforward tend to be the result of deliberate structuring, just as the practice-based view does. If this is the case, is there a perspective on KM that moves beyond simplified versions of knowledge transfer? Some in the practice-based view argue that KM should be reformed with an eye toward managing the context within which knowing occurs (rather than the content of knowledge), which would include establishing the conditions by which communities of practice might productively work together. Although such claims are not radically different from those coming from a cognitive-representational view influenced by complex adaptive systems thinking (see, for example, Anderson, 1999), we agree with the point about managing context, at least for some types of organizations and situations. But we additionally argue that practitioners can benefit from re-framing the notion of "management" in KM to signify not merely control and authority over persons, activity, and knowledge, but also as both a practice and a performance. Thus, management is not a separate function that organizes, directs, or controls knowledge. It is implicated in knowing as a practice and performance. Yet making explicit to members the ways in which the *telos* of managerial work provides affordances to, or exists in tension with, the aims of a particular practice implies that managers must find ways to reduce (or, depending on the situation, enlarge) community-based differences in knowing (Iverson & McPhee, 2002; Kuhn, 2002). The particular performances constituting management can demonstrate the coherence or incoherence of practices, and reflect how those practices can be socially monitored and enforced. In other words, a basic task of management from a practice-based conception of KM is to foster understanding of, reflection upon, the situational resources making particular forms of knowledge and knowing appropriate and desirable.

From our perspective on heterogeneity in knowing, then, KM requires collaborative metacommunication across communities. This is because groups' boundaries in actual organizations are rarely completely clear, and because work often bleeds across the boundaries taken for granted in organizational charts. Metacommunication about the practice(s) that connect individuals and groups can aid in generating awareness, and perhaps reformation, of the resources for identification, accountability, and legitimacy. Ideally, this would involve managerial efforts to (1) aid members to understand as legitimate the interests and situation-framing techniques of the "others" implicated in knowing, even if those others are not co-present; (2) confront participants in a practice with values that encourage ongoing reflection on the processes and products of practice; and (3) encourage productive conflict and the interrogation of difference as a means to both surface assumptions and clarify the standards upon which "knowledgeable" performances rest (Bauman, 1998; Kuhn & Deetz, 2008). These endeavors would do little to create stocks of information (as in traditional versions of KM), but would aid in developing a sensitivity to affordances of situations.

Unintended Consequences of Arrays of Activity

The types of knowledge-accomplishing activities used by actors in determinate situations differ from those employed in indeterminate ones. As a consequence, there are various ways by which an organizational practitioner may seek to support and foster knowledge-accomplishing activity. In indeterminate situations, for instance, practitioners should be wary of simple information transfer as problem-solving, for it is unlikely to foster performances complex enough to navigate the heterogeneity characterizing the situation. In a study of customer service supervisors in a large airline, Kuhn (2006) found that techniques for managing subordinates were developed for – and were often rather effective in – dealing with determinate situations: i.e., where resources for identification, accountability, and legitimacy were not called into question. The firm and the supervisors generated several types of knowledge-accomplishing activities to quell routine problems with passengers, baggage handling, and employees, but each activity responded to relatively straightforward problems – generally, those either with a "correct" answer or where the supervisor's authority made contestation unlikely. Not surprisingly, they trained employees to deal with the routine and to be able to interpret exceptions within a set of routinized procedures. In other words, they constructed a system in which their repertoire of knowledge-accomplishing activities was well-suited to most situations, but when they encountered indeterminate situations that could not easily be rendered determinate (such as cancellations without obvious causes, and employees who accidentally or deliberately offended passengers), employees and supervisors struggled to develop a capacity to act.

An unintended consequence of designing a system around the knowledge required by determinate situations is that it may be less capable of supporting knowing under indeterminacy. Moreover, this airline's approach ironically resulted in supervisors creating more work for themselves in these indeterminate situations. Given their position of authority in the system and a belief in their superior knowledge, supervisors were the only ones deemed capable of dealing with irate customers, system malfunctions, or flight/baggage connection problems. In other words, the local resources for accountability and legitimacy placed additional pressure on supervisors' knowledge-accomplishing activity under indeterminacy. On the one hand, this heterogeneous knowledge presented a supervisor as indispensable to the firm's practice; on the other hand, it held overwhelmed supervisors in crises.

For practitioners, this implies that an ongoing interrogation of the typified approaches to knowledge-accomplishing activity is desirable. Such an interrogation can not only protect against inflexibility; it can also aid in generating adaptation. Accordingly, what is required is a vantage point from which one can examine *sets* of knowledge-accomplishing activity across practices and can introduce performances that expand the repertoire (Wenger, 1998).

The potential value of these implications for practitioners becomes more salient with an example of knowing in practice. A recent popular press article on the 2008 crisis in the financial industry caught our eye, for it illustrates well our claims. Nocera (2009) recounts how a common measure employed in financial services, Value at Risk (VaR) – a calculation of a firm's probability of incurring losses in its portfolio of investments, based on complex statistical models and expressed as a dollar value – was associated with what turned out to be tremendously poor decisions in many firms. It was alluring to managers because it is quickly calculated and makes investors accountable for more than just large profits; moreover, financial executives were typically aware of their daily VaR within minutes of the market close (Nocera, 2009). Over time, VaR became a form of taken-for-granted knowledge within the financial system.

Whereas most firms did little to interrogate the meaning of VaR, managers at the investment bank Goldman Sachs engaged in knowing practices that questioned the assumptions and standards that constituted the "knowledge" of risk represented by VaR. In a series of meetings beginning in 2007, about 15 managers from a variety of specializations encouraged reflection and interrogation of use of VaR, giving primacy to the context of risk by attempting to make sense of this number in relationship to other practices. The heterogeneity in problem-solving practices across the meeting's participants surfaced assumptions and clarified the standards upon which VaR, as "knowledge," was located, particularly as they discussed how the market "felt." Based on these knowing practices, Goldman Sachs decided to reduce investments in mortgage-backed securities and, in turn, avoided much of the pain suffered by the rest of Wall Street (Nocera, 2009). Although there are good reasons to suspect that much of Goldman Sachs's success is borne of its cozy relations with governments (Bernstein, 2009; Taibbi, 2009), in arriving at this decision its managers acknowledged the contingencies of context, fostered reflection on situational resources, and encouraged ongoing reflection. Nocera notes that "a handful of human beings at Goldman Sachs acted wisely by putting their models aside," making decisions on "subjective degrees of belief about an uncertain future" (p. 27). For our purposes, the case points out that heterogeneity of perspectives, ongoing cross-unit interrogation and metacommunication, and a desire to avoid rigidity of practice are forms of knowing associated with organizationally-desirable outcomes.

Conclusion

Our aim in this chapter has been to show that organizational communication theory would benefit from a turn to theorizing practice, but that practice theory presently provides little in the way of methodological guidance. Consequently, we turned to Kuhn and Jackson's (2008) articulation of a framework on "knowledge-accomplishing activity," which foregrounds the contextualized performances constituting practices. In this sense, the framework encourages analyses of the "how" of knowing, focusing attention on the form and content of discursive moves that frame problematic situations (mediated by, and productive of, resources for identification, accountability, and legitimacy) and bring them to some semblance of resolution. When considering knowledge heterogeneity in organizing, our perspective promises to aid scholars in understanding how processes of problem-oriented knowing generate (and respond to) ambiguity and change, power differences, and the organization itself. We also addressed two implications of our perspective designed for practitioners: a reframing of knowledge management, and insight into the unintended consequences of arrays of knowledge-accomplishing activity, both of which suggest the need for an ongoing interrogation of, and metacommunication about, routinized approaches to knowing in organizations. Our hope, in the end, is that the knowledge-accomplishing perspective will provide a resource for those who wish to examine and re-shape conceptions of the situational and communicative constitution of knowledge.

Note

1. Of course, not all knowledge is oriented toward problems in an instrumental fashion. But if we seek to employ a perspective on knowing to explain the constitution of organization, the knowledge that becomes incorporated in formal structure and becomes part of the "authoritative text" that shapes the trajectory of the organization (Kuhn, 2008; McPhee, 1985), the moves that allow a practice to "go on" become essential. In other words, problem-oriented action is a logical condition on our explanatory focus.

References

Alvesson, M. (1993). Organizations as rhetoric: Knowledge-intensive firms and the struggle with ambiguity. *Journal of Management Studies, 30,* 997–1015.

Anderson, P. (1999). Complexity theory and organization science. *Organization Science, 10,* 216–232.

Bauman, Z. (1998). What prospects of morality in times of uncertainty? *Theory, Culture, and Society, 15,* 11–22.

Bernstein, R. (2009, Oct. 22). Imperialism, Goldman Sachs style. *New York Times.* www.nytimes.com/2009/2010/2022/us/2022iht-letter.html.

Bruni, A., Gherardi, S., & Parolin, L. L. (2007). Knowing in a system of fragmented knowledge. *Mind, Culture, and Activity, 14,* 83–102.

Carlile, P. (2002). A pragmatic view of knowledge and boundaries: Boundary objects in new product development. *Organization Science, 13,* 442–455.

Carse, J. P. (1986). *Finite and infinite games.* New York, NY: The Free Press.

Chia, R. (1999). A "rhizomatic" model of organizational change and transformation: Perspectives from a metaphysics of change. *British Journal of Management, 10,* 209–227.

Chia, R., & Holt, R. (2008). The nature of knowledge in business schools. *Academy of Management Learning & Education, 7,* 471–486.

Child, J. T., & Shumate, M. (2007). The impact of communal knowledge repositories and people-based knowledge management on perceptions of team effectiveness. *Management Communication Quarterly, 21,* 29–54.

Conrad, C., & Haynes, J. (2001). Development of key constructs. In F. M. Jablin & L. L. Putnam (Eds.), *The new handbook of organizational communication:*

Advances in theory, research, and methods (pp. 47–77). Thousand Oaks, CA: Sage.

Contractor, N. S., & Monge, P. R. (2002). Managing knowledge networks. *Management Communication Quarterly*, *16*, 249–258.

Contu, A., & Willmott, H. (2003). Re-embedding situatedness: The importance of power relations in learning theory. *Organization Science*, *14*, 283–296.

Cook, S. D. N., & Brown, J. S. (1999). Bridging epistemologies: The generative dance between organizational knowledge and organizational knowing. *Organization Science*, *10*, 381–400.

Cooren, F. (2004). Textual agency: How texts do things in organizational settings. *Organization*, *11*, 373–393.

Cooren, F., & Taylor, J. R. (1997). Organization as an effect of mediation: Redefining the link between organization and communication. *Communication Theory*, *7(3)*, 219–260.

Cronen, V. E., & Chetro-Szivos, J. (2001). Pragmatism as a way of inquiring with special reference to a theory of communication and the general form of pragmatic social theory. In D. K. Perry (Ed.), *American pragmatism and communication research* (pp. 27–65). Mahwah, NJ: Erlbaum.

Dewey, J. (1938). *Logic: The theory of inquiry*. New York, NY: Holt, Rinehart, and Winston.

Ewenstein, B., & Whyte, J. (2007). Beyond words: Aesthetic knowledge and knowing in organizations. *Organization Studies*, *28*, 689–708.

Fisher, B. A. (1982). Communication pragmatism: Another legacy of Gregory Bateson. *Journal of Applied Communication Research*, *10*, 38–49.

Flanagin, A. J. (2002). The elusive benefits of the technological support of knowledge management. *Management Communication Quarterly*, *16*, 242–248.

Gilsdorf, J. W. (1998). Organizational rules on communicating: How employees are – and are not – learning the ropes. *Journal of Business Communication*, *35*, 173–201.

Grant, R. M. (1996). Toward a knowledge-based theory of the firm. *Strategic Management Journal*, *17*, 109–122.

Hargadon, A., & Bechky, B. A. (2006). When collections of creatives become creative collectives: A field study of problem solving at work. *Organization Science*, *17*, 484–500.

Harrè, R., & Secord, P. (1972). *The explanation of social behaviour*. Oxford, UK: Basil Blackwell.

Hutchins, E. (1995). *Cognition in the wild*. Cambridge, MA: MIT Press.

Iverson, J. O., & McPhee, R. D. (2002). Knowledge management in communities of practice: Being true to the communicative character of knowledge. *Management Communication Quarterly*, *16*, 259–266.

Knorr-Cetina, K. D. (1981). The micro-sociological challenge of macro-sociology: Toward a reconstruction of social theory and methodology. In K. Knorr-Centia & A. V. Cicourel (Eds.), *Advances in social theory and methodology* (pp. 1–48). Boston, MA: Routledge and Kegan Paul.

Koppl, R., & Langlois, R. N. (2001). Organizations and language games. *Journal of Management & Governance*, *5*, 287–305.

Kuhn, T. (2002). Negotiating boundaries between scholars and practitioners: Knowledge, networks, and communities of practice. *Management Communication Quarterly*, *16*, 106–112.

Kuhn, T. (2005). Engaging networks of practice through a communicative theory of the firm. In J. L. Simpson & P. Shockley-Zalabak (Eds.), *Engaging communication, transforming organizations: Scholarship of engagement in action* (pp. 45–66). Cresskill, NJ: Hampton.

Kuhn, T. (2006, November). *Supervising customer service: Accomplishing knowledge in airline work*. Paper presented at the annual meeting of NCA, San Antonio, Texas.

Kuhn, T. (2008). A communicative theory of the firm: Developing an alternative perspective on intra-organizational power and stakeholder relationships. *Organization Studies, 29*, 1227–1254.

Kuhn, T., & Ashcraft, K. L. (2003). Corporate scandal and the theory of the firm: Formulating the contributions of organizational communication studies. *Management Communication Quarterly, 17*, 20–57.

Kuhn, T., & Corman, S. R. (2003). The emergence of homogeneity and heterogeneity in knowledge structures during a planned organizational change. *Communication Monographs, 70*, 198–229.

Kuhn, T., & Deetz, S. A. (2008). Critical theory and corporate social responsibility: Can/should we get beyond cynical reasoning? In A. Crane, A. McWilliams, D. Matten, J. Moon, & D. Siegel (Eds.), *The Oxford handbook of corporate social responsibility* (pp. 173–196). Oxford, UK: Oxford University Press.

Kuhn, T., & Jackson, M. (2008). Accomplishing knowledge: A framework for investigating knowing in organizations. *Management Communication Quarterly, 21*, 454–485.

Lave, J. (1996). The practice of learning. In S. Chaiklin & J. Lave (Eds.), *Understanding Practice: Perspectives on Activity and Context* (pp. 3–32). New York, NY: Cambridge University Press.

Lave, J., & Wenger, E. (1991). *Situated learning: Legitimate peripheral participation*. New York, NY: Cambridge University Press.

Lazega, E. (1992). *The micropolitics of knowledge: Communication and indirect control in workgroups*. New York, NY: De Gruyter.

Lindlof, T. R., & Taylor, B. C. (2002). *Qualitative communication research methods* (2nd Ed.). Thousand Oaks, CA: Sage.

Long, N. E. (1958). The local community as an ecology of games. *American Journal of Sociology, 64*, 251–261.

Maier, G. W., Prange, C., & von Rosenstiel, L. (2001). Psychological perspectives of organizational learning. In M. Dierkes, A. Berthoin-Antal, J. Child, & I. Nonaka (Eds.), *Handbook of organizational learning and knowledge* (pp. 14–34). Oxford, UK: Oxford University Press.

McPhee, R. D. (1985). Formal structure and organizational communication. In R. D. McPhee & P. K. Tompkins (Eds.), *Organizational communication: Traditional themes and new directions* (pp. 149–178). Beverly Hills, CA: Sage.

McPhee, R. D. (2008). *Revision of Glaser's 6C model*. Unpublished paper.

McPhee, R. D., & Zaug, P. (2000). The communicative constitution of organizations: A framework for explanation. *The Electronic Journal of Communication/ La Revue Electronique de Communication, 10*.

Nicolini, D., Gherardi, S., & Yanow, D. (2003). Introduction: Toward a practice-based view of knowing and learning in organizations. In D. Nicolini, S. Gherardi, & D. Yanow (Eds.), *Knowing in organizations: A practice-based approach* (pp. 3–31). Armonk, NY: M. E. Sharpe.

Nocera, J. (2009). Risk mismanagement: Were the measures used to evaluate Wall Street trades flawed? *New York Times Magazine*, Jan. 4, pp. 24–33.

Orr, J. E. (1996). *Talking about machines: An ethnography of a modern job.* Ithaca, NY: ILR Press.

Østerlund, C., & Carlile, P. (2005). Relations in practice: Sorting through practice theories on knowledge sharing in complex organizations. *The Information Society, 21*, 91–107.

Pentland, B. T. (1992). Organizing moves in software support hot lines. *Administrative Science Quarterly, 37*, 527–548.

Reckwitz, A. (2002). Toward a theory of social practices: A development in culturalist theorizing. *European Journal of Social Theory, 5*, 243–263.

Schatzki, T. R. (1996). *Social practices: A Wittgensteinian approach to human activity and the social.* Cambridge, UK: Cambridge University Press.

Schatzki, T. R. (2001). Introduction: Practice theory. In T. Schatzki, K. Knorr-Cetina, & E. von Savigny (Eds.), *The practice turn in contemporary theory* (pp. 1–14). London, UK: Routledge.

Schön, D. (1983). *The reflective practitioner: How professionals think in action.* New York, NY: Basic Books.

Schultze, U., & Leidner, D. E. (2002). Studying knowledge management in information systems research: Discourses and theoretical assumptions. *Management Information Systems Quarterly, 26*, 213–242.

Shotter, J. (2008). Dialogism and polyphony in organizing theorizing in organization studies: Action guiding anticipations and the continuous creation of novelty. *Organization Studies, 29*, 501–524.

Styhre, A. (2003). Knowledge as a virtual asset: Bergson's notion of virtuality and organizational knowledge. *Culture and Organization, 9*, 15–26.

Suchman, L. (1996). Constituting shared workspaces. In Y. Engestrom & D. Middleton (Eds.), *Cognition and communication at work* (pp. 35–60). Cambridge, UK: Cambridge University Press.

Taibbi, M. (2009, July 13). The great American bubble machine. *Rolling Stone* (issue 1082–1083). Available: www.rollingstone.com/politics/story/29127316/the_great_american_bubble_machine.

Taylor, J. R. (2000). Thinking about organization in a new way: An inquiry into the ontological foundations of organization. *Electronic Journal of Communication, 10*(1), available: www.cios.org/www/ejc/v10n1200.htm.

Taylor, J. R., Cooren, F., Giroux, N., & Robichaud, D. (1996). The communicational basis of organization: Between the conversation and the text. *Communication Theory, 6*, 1–39.

Tenkasi, R. V., & Boland, R. J. (1996). Exploring knowledge diversity in knowledge intensive firms: A new role for information systems. *Journal of Organizational Change Management, 9*, 79–91.

Walsh, J. P., & Ungson, G. R. (1991). Organizational memory. *Academy of Management Review, 16*, 57–91.

Wenger, E. (1998). *Communities of practice: Learning, meaning, and identity.* Cambridge, UK: Cambridge University Press.

Chapter 3

Knowledge, Belonging, and Communities of Practice

Joel O. Iverson

The recent history of community of practice (CoP) research begins with Lave and Wenger (1991) exploring CoPs as an exemplar of the social aspects of learning. CoPs were intended to be a social psychology alternative to cognitive theories of learning. A CoP is a set of people who "share a concern, a set of problems, or a passion about a topic, who deepen their knowledge and expertise in this area by interacting on an ongoing basis" (Wenger, McDermott, & Snyder, 2002, p. 4). A CoP can be seen as a group that shares similar skills, such as a profession (communication professors, medical technicians, truckers, etc.), connected through similar skills and a common profession or vocation (groups of people who tie flies, cross-stitch, etc.). Also, CoP can refer to groups of people with divergent skills and possibly different departments within an organization that are formed to deal with a complex problem or to generate new knowledge. In both cases, a sense of community is focused on a practice.

CoPs are unique, interesting, and popular in organizations attempting to capitalize on organizational knowledge, because CoPs can be viewed as a social mechanism for understanding or even creating knowledge without the limitations of pure technological and cognitive solutions. After all, CoPs directly demonstrate the social way people learn (Lave & Wenger, 1991). However, attempts to institute CoPs are difficult because they are complex social phenomena that develop in situ as interactive, communicative groups. As Zorn and Taylor (2004, p. 110) contend,

> the notion of communities of practice captures the complexities of how knowledge is created and shared by those who work and talk together regarding shared objects and in shared situations, and simultaneously it captures the difficulties of attempting to transfer that knowledge to others.

CoPs can be evaluated at the macro level as a community, but can be simultaneously understood as sets of individuals who are enacting knowledge. Although proponents advocate CoPs as the key to solving organizational knowledge (read managerial) problems, significant critiques of CoPs emerge contending they are vague and useless concepts. I argue that both of these claims have merit when viewing CoPs as entities. However, when the communicative processes of the enactment of CoPs is explored processually, organizational knowledge scholars and practitioners can better understand the interconnections and tensions of knowing in organizing, as well as connect organizational knowledge processes to larger organizational processes such as identification and belonging. CoP theory offers a way to move beyond seeing CoPs as entities, along with the accompanying definitional questions of what is and is not a CoP. Instead, the communicative processes enacted in knowledge practices demonstrate how knowledge is accomplished (Kuhn & Jackson, 2008), as well as provide a framework to connect the concepts of organizational knowledge to other organizational processes.

In this chapter, I focus on demonstrating the usefulness of CoP theory for understanding and explaining organizational knowledge processes as well as for demonstrating the centrality of communication to the process of organizational knowledge. Specifically, I contend that the elements of CoP theory as demonstrated by Iverson and McPhee (2002, 2008) provide a means based in communication for examining the enactment of knowledge communities. Additionally, I analyze the connection of the community facet of CoPs to organizing in general through an analysis of belonging. I conclude with theoretical and practical contributions of CoP theory.

Reviewing CoPs and Critiques

Though CoPs were introduced as a social view of learning (Lave & Wenger, 1991), they focused primarily on guilds and apprenticeships. Wenger (1998) examined CoPs as a part of everyday organizational work life through an ethnography of insurance claims processors. In this work, Wenger expanded the constructs of a CoP and establishes a basis for CoP theory. Others have extended the use of CoPs as a knowledge management tool. Wenger and Snyder (2000) focus on "cultivating CoPs as entities for creating and sharing knowledge in organizations." This strand of research has been extended in substantial business research. Brown and Duguid (2000) contend that CoPs represent interactive processes. CoP theorists have emphasized the context, embeddedness, and situational nature of knowledge, rather than treating knowledge as a commodity or an overly reified thing that can be traded, stored, exported, and mined.

In the field of communication, scholars have explored the complexities of CoPs as well as the communicative nature of CoPs (Iverson & McPhee, 2002, 2008; Kuhn, 2002; Vaast, 2004; Zorn & Taylor, 2004). Kuhn explored how students can act as boundary spanners into organizations, since they share the academic training and thus are members of our CoPs. Zorn and Taylor explain that knowledge management can have up to four independent meanings, including comprehensive programs to manage knowledge as capital and a resource; software applications that store, sort and allow for the retrieval of information to enacted; small-scale projects to use databases; and, finally, communicative definitions of managing knowledge through socially embedded groups such as CoPs. In this case, Zorn and Taylor indicated that the former three do not have a complex understanding of the communicative nature of knowledge and knowledge management and are thus "doomed to failure" (Zorn & Taylor, 2004, p. 110). Instead, CoPs demonstrate the difficulties of communicating and enacting knowledge, as well as the lack of direct control management has over some important knowledge processes.

Iverson and McPhee (2002) advocate using the elements of a CoP based on Wenger (1998) as theoretical constructs for understanding the communicative nature of knowledge and knowledge management as well as for examining knowledge in action. " 'Management' of knowledge processes works best from within the community, by members aware of its norms and resources. Knowledge managers must achieve dual loyalty, to the community and to their organization" (Iverson & McPhee, 2002, p. 264). Vaast (2004) also utilizes Iverson & McPhee's adaptation of Wenger through a differentiation of CoPs and networks of practice (NoPs) as different constructs, contending that NoPs are distanciated and rely on intranet systems, whereas CoPs require more social interaction (see Chapter 12, this volume, for further discussion of NoPs). Iverson & McPhee (2008) extend the use of CoP theory by comparing two very different groups as CoPs. As a result, they see CoP theory as a mechanism for examining the "CoP-ness" of groups through the three elements based on Wenger's analysis: mutual engagement, shared repertoire, and negotiation of a joint enterprise. At a very basic level, CoP theory allows for the clear comparison between different groups. Recall the different uses of CoPs as professionally similar people versus a team assembled within an organization to tackle a specific problem or advance knowledge in general. Each of these two groups can be considered a CoP. More importantly, CoP theory allows the exploration of differences between them. The first, a profession, has a high level of shared repertoire and perhaps limited mutual engagement (mostly at conferences, within some larger departments, with students) and the joint enterprise that is negotiated is the field of knowledge, governing organizations, standards for educating students, for limited groups, running a department. For the organizational team, negotiation of a joint enterprise is strong as well as mutual engagement, but repertoires are not always shared. In fact, one of the strengths of those internal problem-solving CoPs is that they bring different repertoires together to interact in order to come to new understandings and potentially "new knowledge" (even though that term is rife with problems, but also may serve as an emergent repertoire).

Critiques of CoPs certainly exist in the literature. While most of them focus on Lave and Wenger's earlier conceptions, Wenger's later works are also included in these critiques and deserve mention here. Fuller (2007) summarizes six themes of these critiques. First, critics have claimed that defining learning as participation is inadequate. Further, Wenger does not explain the origins of new learning very well, according to Fuller. However, the view of practice from a structurational perspective (Cohen, 1989; Iverson & McPhee, 2002, 2008) does allow for new knowledge to be enacted through reflective agency as well as other forms of learning. Additionally, practice and participation does not simply mean mindless repetition of techniques learned from others. Rather, creative, innovative, and new forms of learning can occur through participation.

The second critique is the lack of precision for the definition of a community of practice. The boundaries of communities of practice are imprecise, and virtually any group can be examined as a CoP. The validity of this critique is precisely why Iverson and McPhee (2008) critique the notion of treating all CoPs as similar. In my opinion, a precise and rigid definition of CoPs has the danger of eliminating many communicative processes from analysis as well as providing a means for understanding the need for development of a group that desires to become a CoP. Also, Iverson and McPhee go beyond determining which groups truly are or are not CoPs to emphasize the emergently bounded communicative processes of a CoP. In this way, CoP theory is a useful tool for examining the level and nature of the social and situated knowledge in practice for a group.

Third, Fuller (2007, p. 24) points out that Lave and Wenger do not adequately deal with "the ability of communities of practice to transform." According to Fuller, the presence of change makes a static entity like a CoP unhelpful for understanding how new learning takes place. However, CoP theory does deal with new learning, as well as with organizational and situational change. Negotiating the joint enterprise is analyzed as being within a larger situation or the organization and environment. Wenger (2000) specifically addresses how participating in social learning systems, especially those that cross organizational boundaries, is essential to change and thus success of organizations.

The fourth critique decries the lack of stability of the novice and expert. Originally, when examining apprenticeships, Lave and Wenger examine the process of going from the periphery of knowledge to expertise and thus CoP membership. However, Wenger (1998, 2000) and others deal with this issue through the negotiation of a joint enterprise, sharing repertoires, and the complexity of participation. Participation within the CoP requires shared repertoires, not just experts teaching outsiders to move them into the circle. Iverson and McPhee (2008) recognize the different way the Docents of the Sonoran Garden learn from each other, shadow each other, bring in a variety of experiences, and rely on one another for those participating (not just "learning") in the CoP. None of these elements requires a set expert and a paired novice. Those situations can exist in the dynamic flow of action, but are not the exclusive nature of a learning relationship.

The last two critiques deal with the different types of participation and boundary crossing for learning. First, critics recognize that learning is not the only type of participation. Wenger (1998) recognized this limitation and increased the types of participation. Different individuals can relate to the CoP in different ways. The last critique focuses on the ability to participate across CoPs. Wenger (2000) contends that boundary crossing between CoPs is not only typical but also important for learning. Again, CoP theory is adequately flexible to deal with each of these situations. Since CoP theory focuses on the practices, not the community as the foregrounded construct, the CoP does not act as a container. Rather, CoPs are constituted in the process of communicating. Several CoPs may be enacted simultaneously. Being a scholar and teacher, for example, can both be enacted in the same actions. CoPs are not guilds. Rather, the communicative enactment of knowing is social and present in multiple situations that are not simply contained in a CoP.

These critiques take a very static image of CoPs that is not present in the communicative view of CoP theory. However, they do point to a degree of situatedness and dynamism that has emerged in CoP theory from the early work of Lave and Wenger. Current CoP theory avoids treating all CoPs as similar entities, and provides a means of rudimentary analysis of groups enacting knowledge. However, such analysis does not tell us much about the nature of communication or knowledge. Indeed, such a brief analysis treats the elements of a CoP as mere consequences of a community of practice. They are treated as signs of knowledge activity that can be pointed to as proof of the existence or absence of a CoP. McPhee and Iverson (2008) work to go beyond that type of analysis, which I elaborate below.

CoP Theory Elements

According to CoP theory (Iverson & McPhee 2002, 2008), each of the three facets of the communicative enactment of knowledge in CoPs – mutual engagement, shared repertoire, and negotiation of a joint enterprise – binds these practices to the connectivity of the community. Additionally, the interactive enactment is centered around the practices, thus centering knowledge in activities. Mutual engagement focuses on the interaction for the CoP. Obviously, without any sort of interaction no sense of community can exist, let alone a CoP. Members must engage one another, and engagement can be used to define insiders from outsiders. However, all types of interaction do not count for mutual engagement, or CoPs would be no different from other groups or communities. Rather, the communicative interaction must be about or through the practice(s) they share in common. Again, the assumption for CoP theory is that the mutual engagement is one of the central processes for sharing knowledge. Mutual engagement is also essential for creating knowledge, such as Orr's (1996) example of the photocopier technicians engaging in the creative, improvisational interaction to fix a copier. Additionally, mutual engagement is the way that some CoPs provide a means to coordinate complex responses. "This mutual engagement allows activity coordination and overall understanding of the larger task at hand. Thus, the team members mutually engage around a shared practice" (Iverson & McPhee, 2008, p. 185). Iverson and McPhee point out that mutual engagement can be enacted differently by different CoPs. Since each CoP is unique, mutual engagement can vary in frequency as well as in the nature of the engagement. Groups can share best practices overtly, work together side by side, or even observe actions of each other. Iverson and McPhee state that

> the level and nature of mutual engagement are not inherent in a practice, but varying them is a flexible option for increasing or decreasing the level of interaction for the CoP, with likely growth in the quality of knowledge shared.
>
> (p. 187)

Thus, mutual engagement can be encouraged, facilitated, and directed in an attempt to "manage" the way knowledge is communicatively enacted as well as impact the nature of the CoP.

The second element of a CoP is a shared repertoire. Members of a CoP do not simply mutually engage over anything; the central focus for a CoP is the sharing of a common repertoire that comprises the common practice(s) of the CoP. "Because the repertoire of a community is a resource for the negotiation of meaning, it is shared in a dynamic and interactive sense" (Wenger, 1998, p. 84). I contend that communication provides the means for sharing meaning (and repertoires, for that matter) and dynamic interaction. Iverson and McPhee (2008) report that, when comparing two communities, the repertoires shared some similar elements but also differed in significant ways. Both included terminology and desired sets of skills, but also negotiated and invented skills were shared within the groups. "The repertoires add to the sense of community through the sharing of specialized knowledge, and this shared repertoire is critical in socializing new members into the CoP" (Iverson & McPhee, 2008, p. 188). The two groups compared differed in the way they enacted sharing of repertoires. Both had initial training, but beyond the initial training, differences emerged. One CoP had more formal, continual sharing, as well as structured times that sharing could occur – such as lunch time together – whereas the other simply shared techniques when happening to be on call. Thus, for Iverson and McPhee, CoP theory allows the ability to differentiate between groups on the basis of not only the different repertoires, but also the manner in which they are shared, structured, and enacted. These elements are critical for understanding how a CoP functions and enacts knowledge through communicative activity.

The final element of CoP theory is negotiation of a joint enterprise. Members of a CoP exist in a larger environmental context and they must negotiate, not in a bargaining sense but more in a navigational sense, the larger environment as well as the internal processes of being a CoP. As Iverson and McPhee (2008, p. 190) state:

> Negotiation of a joint enterprise constitutes a collective response to external forces, such as staff or situational characteristics, that defines the nature and enactment of the enterprise. In addition, we must remember the orientation of a CoP toward knowledge, learning, and mastery of the practice: negotiation constitutes mastery and makes members knowers, and thus creators, of the enterprise.

Negotiation of the enterprise includes negotiation of what counts as knowledge, such as what is defined as mainstream or fringe or not knowledge in medical practices. Members of a CoP adapt to unique circumstances, innovate, and share best practices. Also, at a group level, individual CoPs must choose how to relate to larger fields of knowledge, where to be rebellious, where to adopt standards, and how to enact the enterprise of knowing. This negotiation is obviously communicative action. Negotiation of the joint enterprise is the communicative enactment of the community through practices.

CoP Theory and Communication

CoP theory and its elements of a CoP provide a means for understanding and analyzing the central processes of communicating knowledge within a group or organization. By examining how groups mutually engage, share repertoires, and negotiate their joint enterprise, the central process of enacting, developing, sharing, and altering practices is evident. Along with those practices, the knowledge enactment occurs as well. Each of the three – engaging, sharing, negotiating – are essentially communicative processes. Iverson and McPhee (2008, p. 193) articulate that CoP theory

> not only allows researchers to identify important processes of communicative enactment of CoPs and articulate important differences between CoPs, but also provides a basis for evaluating the pragmatic effect of different communicative enactments of knowledge in CoPs.

Iverson and McPhee (2002, 2008) conclude that CoP theory identifies important communicative processes of enacting knowledge, provides a mechanism for articulating differences between different CoPs, and is useful for understanding how ways in which knowledge is communicatively enacted change organizational knowledge contexts. The theory recognizes that organizations cannot simply use intranet systems or other technological systems to list and explain knowledge practices (also recognized by Vaast, 2004), but must also have the ability to mutually engage in order to share ideas and live out the knowledge experience. Additionally, CoP theory recognizes that knowledge is enacted in the process of negotiating the joint enterprise. Knowledge is not simply the accumulation of ideas, but is communicatively enacted in the enterprise. Orr's (1996) copier technicians, as well as the two CoPs examined by Heaton and Taylor (2002), demonstrate that joint activity and negotiation of that activity generate knowledge in the process of communicating. Thus, first, CoP theory centers communication and practice while it does not look at CoPs as mere entities, but as a way to evaluate the processes of a range of groups. One can imagine examining a workgroup using CoP theory to understand their level and type of mutual engagement, sharing (or lack of sharing) a repertoire, and the way they do or do not negotiate a joint enterprise.

Second, and related to the first, CoP theory does not treat all CoPs as alike or *blackbox* what happens in a CoP. Gherardi's (2006) critique of CoPs is that theorists treat the group as a priori before the knowledge, ignoring how the CoPs developed through knowledge and how knowledge led to the existence of the CoP. CoP theory bypasses that problem by not having to assume a fully formed group before analyzing. Instead, the three elements can provide insight into the formation or the lack of formation of a CoP because it focuses on the communicative processes instead of an outcome. This provides a flexible, practice-based examination of knowledge that can both recognize the communicative and emergent nature of knowledge in practice and also demonstrate some of the routinization of practices that comes with the development of repertoires and enacted enterprise over time. The enacted routinization of practices can lead, over time, to sedimented, structured ways of enacting practice. CoP theory moves beyond classifying groups in organizations as CoPs or not to explaining the nature of enacting knowledge in organizations. That is, CoP theory explores *how* groups are mutually engaging, sharing repertoires, and negotiating a joint enterprise. Thus, CoP theory serves as an understanding of knowledge that communication theorists such as Zorn and Taylor (2004) call for by understanding how knowledge is enacted through talking and working together. It is through the communicative processes of developing practice and communicatively enacting knowledge that the *community* facet of the CoP is constituted.

Figure 3.1 summarizes how current conceptualizations of CoP theory can be viewed in terms of connections among the 7C theoretical constructs identified in Chapter 1, borrowed from Glaser (1978). From the perspective of this 7C model, the early emphasis for many examining CoPs as entities creates a false sense of a clear "A" as an event that is actually a process. Gherardi's concerns that CoPs are treated as a priori to knowledge, making knowledge a consequence of the CoP, or that the CoP causes knowledge, are resolved with CoP theory. The entity of a CoP does not precede the knowledge. Rather, the CoP is constituted in the process of communicating knowing and interacting as co-knowers/learners engaged

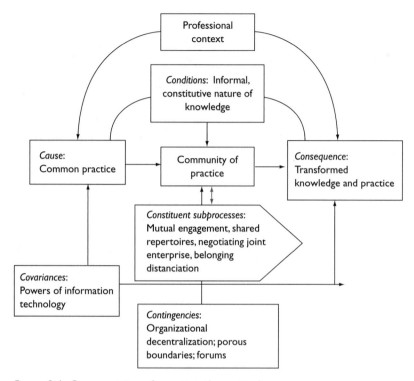

Figure 3.1 Communities of practice theoretical constructs.

in practice. CoP theory focuses on the subprocesses, how those subprocesses are communicatively enacted as knowing is enacted in this process. CoP theory also connects to larger organizing issues, such as belonging and organizational identification.

Community and Belonging in CoPs

The collective enactment of CoPs also produces a community. Individuals simultaneously belong to the CoP and are enacting the CoP. This section begins the exploration of the community aspect of CoPs, the communicative nature of enacting community through belonging, along with the implications for organizational knowledge. It is important to note that belonging is enacted *through* the mutual engagement, sharing or repertoires, and negotiation of the joint enterprise(s). Also, belonging is not a discrete set of actions separate from enacting knowledge. Rather, while engaging, sharing, and negotiating, CoP members are also enacting the community, which has meaning that is not simply tied to knowledge; it is an inextricable part of the process. The formation of a CoP as a community is not simply an entity, but also a source of identity that is enacted in the process of knowing. As Hara (2009, p. 119) indicates:

> Communities of practice provide milieus for professionals to learn from each other and become better at their profession. A professional practice provides the framework for a community of practice because a community of practice, by definition, emerges around a particular field of practice. I found the development of professional identity to be one of the most important components of face-to-face communities of practice. A group's sense of professional identity makes or breaks a community of practice.

However, this source of identity is not simply enacted on an individual level with an accompanying individual identification. Rather, this is enacted in a group and is a group-level phenomenon. Wenger (1998) examines modes of belonging as integral to identity as part of the social element of learning. I contend that Wenger uses belonging and identity interchangeably, but that these are connected processes that require articulation. To explore this difference, consider the following example from World War II (Dugan & Stewart, 2002, p. 114):

> Ben Kuroki had volunteered for the service on the night of Pearl Harbor and was turned away because of his [Japanese] ancestry. He besieged the Army and was accepted for a "nonsensitive" clerk's job in the infant Circus bomb group, whose members shunned him. His name was not on the shipping list when the group was sent to England. He pleaded with Ted Timberlake, who was at first confused, then touched and honored by the tears of Private Kuroki. Timberlake put his name on the list and Ben went to Britain on the Queen Elizabeth, scrubbing pots and sleeping on coiled decklines. In England, Ben slipped into air-gunnery classes and graduated with top qualifications, but no air crew would have him. Exactly one year after Pearl Harbor, Jake Epting needed a last-minute replacement gunner, and rather than ground his plane, took Kuroki on a mission.

The individual actions of Kuroki are quite exemplary and he turned out to be an amazing air gunner, but, despite his best efforts, the community did not include him. Based on individual analysis, Kuroki is a competent, knowledgeable member of a CoP of air gunners who is highly identified with the group and the mission. However, Kuroki belongs to the CoP in substantially different, marginalized, and contested ways than the other Americans belong. Here, what "counts" as knowledge is not independent from other processes such as power, politics, prejudice, etc. The community and belonging are collectively enacted in the process of practice in the CoP. The belonging of Kuroki and others also impacts the enactment of the organization. CoPs are not neutral sites where knowledge is the only criteria of inclusion. However, the examination of belonging for CoPs points to how knowledge is tied to those larger processes and to how CoPs can enact a collective level of inclusion beyond our current conceptualization of organizational identification. Kuroki highly identifies with the organization and is willing to endure much to gain clandestine mastery of the repertoire, but that does not explain how belonging is enacted at a collective level of analysis.

The general notion of belonging has multiple definitions, including a synonym for membership, being combined with "sense of" to articulate a perception of belonging, and as an enacted process in a group. Each meaning of belonging illuminates a facet of belonging as it is enacted in CoPs, and they require further exploration. First, belonging focuses on formal membership in an organization or group, such as an employee (Masterson & Stamper, 2003), a member of a church (Davie, 1994), a student of a university (Kember, Lee, & Li, 2001), or someone who embodies a group's traits such as race or sex (Fortier, 1999). Research focusing on membership also extends to perceived organizational membership (Masterson & Stamper), influences leading to membership choice (Kember et al., 2001), and membership requirements (Graham, 1991). Membership connects to larger organizational processes, such as membership negotiation (McPhee & Iverson, 2009; McPhee & Zaug, 2000), as a part of constituting the organization. The connection for membership to CoPs is also enacted, but meaning beyond inclusion is important. Kuroki was a member of the military, a trained member of the gunners, but this view of belonging has at least two central problems. First, belonging as membership is contested. From a current, external point of view, Kuroki *was* a gunner, but that answer was not enacted when he was officially left behind. Only after he was taken on a mission did he become a *belonging member* in the fullest sense of the term. Second, attempting to examine belonging as membership does not account for the actions of the rest of the group. Formal membership is only part of the belonging equation. Belonging is about knowledge and repertoire, but also about the actions of others who are members of the group. When knowledge is enacted collectively (through communication, of course), attempting to separate the repertoires from those enacting the knowledge is counterproductive.

Perhaps the most common use of belonging is in the phrase "sense of belonging" that is "closely equated to integration" (Kember et al., 2001, p. 327). In this use, belonging is "feeling comfortable," and is contrasted with otherness and alienation (Reed, Archer, & Leathwood, 2003). A sense of belonging can refer to the organization overall, or to various groups within the organization (Kember et al., 2001). One of Wenger's modes of belonging in his communities of practice, imagination, is "the creative process of producing new 'images' and of generating new relations through time and space that become constitutive of the self" (Wenger,

1998, p. 177). Imagination is based on past (reflection), future (exploration), and current (orientation) perceived relationships relative to others. Apker and Eggly (2004) demonstrate that medical students learn to think and identify with the ways of knowing through interaction with physicians in a process of morning report (see Chapter 15, this volume, for further discussion of ways of knowing in health care contexts). The connection of CoPs to perception is an important facet of belonging. However, it is important not to disconnect the sense of belonging from the activities that enact belonging and identification. The communicative enactment of CoPs demonstrates that the connection is not simply to knowledge and learning, but that identity and belonging are enacted through learning and enacting knowledge.

A promising conceptualization of belonging articulates a participative process as a part of an organization or a group, such as a work team, CoP, gang, or group of volunteers. Although this definition is not expressed specifically and precisely in the literature, seeds of its conceptualization can be found in Nishida's (1987) Japanese philosophy through *ba* and *basho*, along with Wenger's (1998) examination of identity in communities of practice. First, the Japanese concept of *basho* (*ba* is also used synonymously) that is derived from Nishida's philosophical works from the early 1900s (Nishida, 1987) roughly translates into *place* (Haugh, 2005; Nonaka & Konno, 1998; Nonaka & Nishigushi, 2001). However, the meaning of place with *basho* is not about a static point, such as geographic or hierarchical place; instead, place creates a way of understanding a dynamic and relating sense of belonging requiring further explanation (because different authors use place, *ba*, or *basho*, I treat them as interchangeable terms).

Basho *and Belonging*

As an explanation of Japanese connectedness and identity, Nishida's (1987) concept of *basho* (*ba*) evaluates the place of individuals and the identity derived from place (Haugh, 2005; Nonaka & Konno, 1998; Nonaka & Nishigushi, 2001). In fact, Haugh (2005) contends that Japanese politeness is better explained by place than face theory (Jensen & Meckling, 1976). Nonaka and colleagues have used the concept of place (the term *ba* instead of *basho* is used) in relation to knowledge itself and organizational teams, where the collective enacts the individuals' place and identity. "Ba is a shared time and space for emerging relationships – either physical, virtual, or mental – shared by two or more individuals or organizations" (Nonaka & Nishigushi, p. 4). Though Nonaka and colleagues address knowledge as having its own *ba*, I contend that the concept of place is better used to understand the organizing processes involved in *basho* by digging deeper into the details of *basho*. Further, place is not static, it is enacted in relationships. The analogy of a constellation of stars works well for *basho*. Each star has its own individual place and is meaningful only in relation to the other stars. The interaction and place relative to the other stars enacts meaning for the stars as well as the constellation. However, place is not the same as space. "Unlike abstract space, *basho* is loaded, it is the locus of tension, where the contradictory self-identities are acted out" (Raud, 2004, p. 46). Place is a fluid, impermanent, enacted construct of selves collectively enacting identity through "communicative construction of identity as individuals interact with one another" (Larson & Pepper, 2003, p. 531). I contend that place extends the enacted view of identity and offers exploration of its concertively constituted nature as well as the tensions of identities and meaning of place.

The most detailed analysis that translates place into its subcomponents is done by Haugh (2005). Haugh engages in a comprehensive analysis of Japanese language usage of place, and how the components of place work together for a complex understanding of place. Haugh summarizes, "The two most important senses of 'place' are *tokoro* (location) and *ichi* (one's position relative to others)" (p. 46). *Tokoro* focuses on insideness (*uchi*), or the place one belongs. *Ichi* emphasizes the place where one stands. Based on an analysis of the related terms to *tokoro* and *ichi*, Haugh (2005, p. 47) concludes:

> From this analysis it appears that the senses of "place" important for an understanding of Japanese interaction include the "place one belongs" (*uchi*) and the "place one stands" (tachiba). The "place one stands" refers not only to one's rank or circumstances, but also one's social standing and public persona … The notion of place in Japanese thus encompasses what could be glossed as "inclusion" (the place one belongs) and "distinction" (the place one stands). Inclusion is generally defined as being a part of something else (such as a particular set or group), while distinction is defined as being different or distinguishable from others. Place in Japanese, then, refers to acknowledgement of someone's rank/position or circumstances that distinguish them from others.

For CoPs, inclusion is important for belonging and connecting to identity formation. Being part of a particular CoP, or even socialization (see Chapter 16 for discussions of socialization) into the CoP, means learning and enacting knowledge and simultaneously enacting belonging. Beyond that, examining distinctions within CoPs and between various communities also provides an opportunity to explore the connections of knowledge for interactions in the organization. The connective power of knowledge is especially salient when we operate from the view that knowing is communicatively enacted. CoP theory allows us to understand not only the elements of mutual engagement, sharing repertoire, and negotiating a joint enterprise, but also the connections of enacting knowing to organizing, identifying, belonging, and the meaning that is enacted. For example, Iverson (2003) found that members of a disaster response CoP enacted belonging through actions such as collectively agreeing to break rules in order to better help clients. Examples such as Kuroki demonstrate that CoPs are enacted within the larger organizational and societal contexts (see Figure 3.1).

Inclusion or exclusion is thus one facet that is enacted by the group. Distinction is not the opposite of inclusion, but allows for a unique place within a group, just as a particular star in a constellation has a unique and important role relative to the others. Although Nonaka and others currently focus on knowledge having *ba* in organizations, and Haugh examines the centrality to politeness in interpersonal interactions, both recognize that *ba* is a collectively enacted, group construct. Haugh focuses on the communicatively enacted process that requires others to establish place. *Ba* provides the beginning of a group-based understanding that connects to identity as well as organizing processes.

Belonging and Identification

I contend that this view of belonging is consistent with and extends Scott, Corman, and Cheney's view as they demonstrate the need for an interactive and enacted notion of identification. Additionally, they position identity and identification in an interactive, structurational view of identity. Belonging and community as facets of the CoP also fit their interactive, structurational view, but go beyond the individualistic focus of identification. Belonging also contextualizes knowledge as communicatively enacted co-processes (Iverson, 2008) that instanciate more than one organizing process in the same set of communicative acts. This demonstrates both the difficulty and the beauty of communication. When knowledge is enacted, shared, and developed in organizations, communities are developed, and communities are enacted through processes of belonging and identification, knowledge is also shared and developed (enacted). CoP theory attempts to capture both of these processes, as well as the interaction between them.

Overall, CoP theory and belonging connect knowledge processes to identification and enactment of the organization. Bringing together processes of organizing, knowing, and belonging is one of the most meaningful connections CoP theory affords. CoP theory also provides advantages for recognizing how enacting organizational knowledge connects with and extends other organizational co-processes, such as the development of professional identity.

Practical Applications

CoP theory offers several useful insights into the nature of knowledge in organizations. First, the focus on process rather than structure avoids the problems of foregrounding the CoP as an entity (Gherardi, 2006). Organizational decision-makers as well as scholars should focus less on the entity and more on the dynamic processes of enacting a CoP in order to avoid trying to determine whether or not a group is or is not a CoP, but instead examine the processes of knowing that are or could be occurring. Second, focusing on the processes of engaging, sharing, and negotiating also avoids the dangers of overly reifying knowledge (Iverson & Burkart, 2007) while allowing researchers and organizational members to explore each element of a CoP. Understanding where mutual engagement and sharing of repertoires is and is not occurring can lead to a better understanding of how knowledge is enacted in the organization. Further, recognizing opportunities for the CoP members to negotiate their joint enterprise is beneficial (Iverson & McPhee, 2008). By recognizing that knowledge is enacted communicatively, CoP theory foregrounds the practices while recognizing that communities do develop from sharing those practices.

Belonging extends the understanding of meaning that emerges from being in a community. Again, CoP theory and the complexity of belonging, with its contested and situated nature, allows for the dynamics of community to be further explored. Belonging, conceptualized not only as membership and the sense of belonging, but also as place (*ba, basho*), affords the opportunity to extend our understanding of multiple organizational concepts, including organizational identification. Belonging extends the generally individualistic focus of organizational identification to a more collective level. Future research should extend and explore the connections of identification and belonging. For organizational practitioners, belonging is important to understand as it relates to work teams and concertive control (Barker, 1993). Belonging can also offer understandings of the contested nature of belonging to an organization at one level in contrast to or in concert with how members enact belonging to the CoP. Finally, CoP theory allows for extending our understanding of organizational knowledge in relation to these and other organizational processes.

Conclusions

From a communication perspective, the central focus for CoPs is not whether or not a particular group is a CoP or not. Nor is it the focus to determine whether CoPs create knowledge or knowledge creates CoPs. Rather, by viewing the enactment of knowledge as occurring through communicative engagement in the knowledge practices every day, the CoP is constituted at the same time as knowledge is accomplished (Kuhn & Jackson, 2008). Given the enacted perspective shared by many organizational knowledge scholars in communication, the focus of this chapter has been to explore CoP theory (Iverson & McPhee, 2002, 2008), the usefulness of CoP theory in understanding organizational knowledge, and the connection of knowledge process to belonging processes and thus to other organizational processes. These connections demonstrate the usefulness of understanding and exploring the mutual engagement, sharing of repertoires, and negotiation of a joint enterprise as a means of understanding organizational enactment of knowledge. Additionally, the constructs of belonging provide an insight into the communicative enactment of belonging in CoPs through the enactment of knowledge.

References

Apker, J., & Eggly, S. (2004). Communicating professional identity in medical socialization: Considering the ideological discourse of morning report. *Qualitative Health Research*, *14*, 411–429.

Barker, J. R. (1993). Tightening the iron cage: Concertive control in self-managing teams. *Administrative Science Quarterly*, *38*, 408–437.

Brown, J. S., & Duguid, P. (2000). *The social life of information*. Boston, MA: Harvard Business School Press.

Cohen, I. J. (1989). *Structuration theory: Anthony Giddens and the constitution of social life*. New York, NY: St Martin's Press.

Davie, G. (1994). *Religion in Britain since 1945: Believing without belonging*. Cambridge, MA: Blackwell.

Dugan, J., & Stewart, C. (2002). *Ploesti: The Great Ground–Air Battle of 1 August 1943, Revised Edition*. New York, NY: Random House.

Edwards, A. (2005). Let's get beyond community and practice: the many meanings of learning by participating. *Curriculum Journal*, *16*, 49–65.

Fortier, A. M. (1999). Re-membering places and the performance of belonging(s). *Theory, Culture & Society*, *16*, 41–64.

Fuller, A. (2007). Critiquing theories of learning and communities of practice. In J. Hughes, N. Jewson, & L. Unwin (Eds.), *Communities of practice: Critical perspectives* (pp. 17–29). New York, NY: Routledge.

Gherardi, S. (2006). *Organizational knowledge: The texture of workplace learning*. Oxford, UK: Blackwell.

Glaser, B. (1978). *Theoretical sensitivity*. Mill Valley, CA: Sociology Press.

Graham, J. W. (1991). An essay on organizational citizenship behavior. *Employee Responsibilities and Rights Journal*, *4*, 249–270.

Hara, N. (2009). *Communities of practice: Fostering peer-to-peer learning and informal knowledge sharing in the work place*. Berlin, Germany: Springer.

Haugh, M. (2005). The importance of "place" in Japanese politeness: Implications for cross-cultural and intercultural analyses. *Intercultural Pragmatics*, *2*, 41–68.

Heaton, L., & Taylor, J. R. (2002). Knowledge management and professional work: A communication perspective on the knowledge-based organization. *Management Communication Quarterly*, *16*, 210–236.

Iverson, J. (2003). *Knowing volunteers through communities of practice*. Unpublished doctoral dissertation, Department of Communication, Arizona State University, Tempe.

Iverson, J. O. (2008). *Examining the organizational communication landscape through cotheories*. Paper presented at the Alta Revisited Conference, Alta, Utah.

Iverson, J. O., & Burkart, P. (2007). Managing electronic documents and work flows: Enterprise Content Management at work in nonprofit organizations. *Nonprofit Management and Leadership, 17(4)*, 403–419.

Iverson, J. O., & McPhee, R. D. (2002). Knowledge management in communities of practice: Being true to the communicative character of knowledge. *Management Communication Quarterly, 16*, 259–266.

Iverson, J. O., & McPhee, R. D. (2008). Communicating knowing through communities of practice: Exploring internal communicative processes and differences among CoPs. *Journal of Applied Communication Research, 36(2)*, 176–199.

Jensen, M. C., & Meckling, W. H. (1976). Theory of the firm: managerial behavior, agency costs and ownership structure. *Journal of Financial Economics, 3*, 305–360.

Kember, D., Lee, K., & Li, N. (2001). Cultivating a sense of belonging in part-time students. *International Journal of Lifelong Education, 20*, 326–341.

Kuhn, T. (2002). Negotiating boundaries between scholars and practitioners: Knowledge, networks, and communities of practice. *Management Communication Quarterly, 16*, 106–112.

Kuhn, T., & Jackson, M. (2008). Accomplishing knowledge: A framework for investigating knowing in organizations. *Management Communication Quarterly, 21*, 454–485.

Larson, G. S., & Pepper, G. L. (2003). Strategies for managing multiple organizational identifications: a case of competing identities. *Management Communication Quarterly, 16*, 528–557.

Lave, J., & Wenger, E. (1991). *Situated learning: Legitimate peripheral participation*. New York, NY: Cambridge University Press.

Masterson, S. S., & Stamper, C. L. (2003). Perceived organizational membership: an aggregate framework representing the employee–organization relationship. *Journal of Organizational Behavior, 24*, 473–490.

McPhee, R. D. & Iverson, J. O. (2009). Agents of constitution in Communicad: Constitutive processes of communication in organizations. In L. Putnam & A. Nicotera (Eds.), *Communicative constitution of organization* (pp. 49–88). Mahwah, MJ: Laurence Erlbaum.

McPhee, R. D., & Zaug, P. (2000). The communicative constitution of organizations: A framework for explanation. *The Electronic Journal of Communication/ La Revue Electronique de Communication, 10*.

Nishida, K. (1987). *An inquiry into the good* (M. Abe & C. Ives, Trans.). London, UK: New Haven.

Nonaka, I., & Konno, N. (1998). The concept of "Ba": Building a foundation for knowledge creation. *California Management Review, 40*, 1–15.

Nonaka, I., & Nishigushi, T. (Eds.) (2001). *Knowledge emergence: Social, technical, and evolutionary dimensions of knowledge creation*. New York, NY: Oxford University Press.

Orr, J. E. (1996). *Talking about machines: An ethnography of a modern job*. Ithaca, NY: ILP Press/Cornell University Press.

Raud, R. (2004). "Place" and "being-time": Spatiotemporal concepts in the thought of Nishida Kitaro and Dogen Kigen. *Philosophy East & West, 54*, 29–51.

Reed, B., Archer, L., & Loathwood, C. (2003). Challenging cultures? Student conceptions of "belonging" and "isolation" at a post-1992 university. *Studies in Higher Education, 28*, 261–277.

Vaast, E. (2004). O brother, where are thou?: From communities to networks of practice through intranet use. *Management Communication Quarterly, 18,* 5–44.

Wenger, E. (1998). *Communities of practice: Learning, meaning, and identity.* Cambridge, UK: Cambridge University Press.

Wenger, E. (2000). Communities of practice and social learning systems. *Organization, 7,* 225–246.

Wenger, E., & Snyder, W. E. (2000). Communities of practice: The organizational frontier. *Harvard Business Review, 78,* 139–145.

Wenger, E., McDermott, R. A., & Snyder, W. M. (2002). *Cultivating communities of practice: A guide to managing knowledge.* Boston, MA: Harvard Business School Press.

Zorn, T. E., & Taylor, J. R. (2004). Knowledge management and/as organizational communication. In D. Tourish & Owen Hargie (Eds.), *Key issues in organizational communication* (pp. 96–112). London, UK: Routledge.

Chapter 4

Challenges of Implementing Systems for Knowledge Management

Static Systems and Dynamic Practices

Michele H. Jackson and Julie Williamson

Consider the following scenario. An employee needs to find something for a client. As per her company standard, she starts by looking in the company's "knowledge repository." Coming up short, she searches her hard drive, and looks on the Internet for some good information on the topic. This is the prescribed order of events according to the company's knowledge management process, and should result in a successful discovery of how to best serve the client. Consider a second practice which might more accurately represent what really happens. She starts by looking on her hard drive. She might call a friend or two for advice or suggestions. After about an hour of searching, she hasn't found quite what she's looking for, so she sends out a global e-mail to her colleagues, asking for help. Within about 10 minutes, she has a dozen replies, two of which have exactly what she thinks she needs. In addition, three people reply and indicate that they too would like to know what she is looking for, and would she please forward along anything she finds. She does so, and also calls one of the individuals who had what she needed, and has a short conversation about the information, which helps her to contextualize it in a way that would be critical for her client. Furthermore, she learns that her colleague has a particular affinity for the problem she's working on, and that he is willing to be a resource to her going forward. She also gives him some feedback on what he provided based on her own experiences in the area. Next time, she'll probably just call him directly.

The second process described here may be systematically discouraged and technically deemed inappropriate within the organizational policies. Management wants to make sure the knowledge repository is seen as the ultimate resource, and believes that discouraging the global e-mail or local network approach will encourage people to make sure knowledge assets are appropriately uploaded and stored in a searchable format. They provide monthly reports on how many assets are stored in the repository, how many searches were executed, and other various bits of data about its use, and present awards to people who add to the repository. They also keep track of who sends global e-mails to find information, and count it against individuals in their performance evaluations. There is no discernible effort to track the quality of the assets in the repository, the value of the information shared between individuals outside of the repository, or the new ideas generated when people connect directly. They believe they have a full commitment at an executive level to supporting managing knowledge as a strategic and competitive asset. This belief is supported by both the dollars invested in the knowledge management system (KMS) and the enforcement policies that have been developed and implemented. There is a view within senior management that the knowledge base itself is both a strategic asset and a competitive advantage.

This scenario is a composite of several experiences across organizations working to implement systematized knowledge management. It isn't limited to any particular industry or company; it is played out in many different kinds of business environments every day. The drive to systematize and manage knowledge, to create a database of knowledge assets, and to document and codify processes for using knowledge is pervasive, but it is also difficult to deliver. Furthermore, when attempted in the absence of formal approaches to and investment in network development and knowledge-sharing practices, knowledge management cannot deliver a complete asset.

Knowledge management (KM) has been researched in many disciplines, particularly in the past 15–20 years. Management science, information systems, human resource management, and other areas have all taken up the challenge, examining the idea of knowledge management from a variety of angles, and offering innumerable instruments for measuring, evaluating, and promoting KM tools and processes. In practice, while some companies like British Petroleum (BP) have experimented with and implemented ways to nurture knowledge development within coordinated KM efforts (Collison & Parcell, 2004), many more are stuck in the rut of tactical IT systems implementations or HR training program development. They are in what Maier and Remus (2003) refer to as the "knowledge management starter" phase, with a small group of KM enthusiasts working to build a repository of KM assets, but lacking a full KM strategy to build processes, practices, and assets together.

These tactical efforts are often defended by positioning the KM repository as a strategic asset. This position is typically supported by numbers – the number of artifacts, the number of users, the number of queries, the number of terabytes in the database, and the number of members of a community or network, all of which provide management with reassurance that they have knowledge within the organization and that it is under control. While this is useful in some ways, we maintain that the systems and tools-based approach, applied in isolation, actually results in knowledge being a less strategic asset. In their business analysis of knowledge management at work in BP and other organizations, Collison and Parcell (2004) draw an apt analogy for knowledge repositories. They point out that spring water is marketed as "bottled directly at the source" rather than "drawn from the lake." In the same sense, knowledge drawn from a repository may be valid, but it lacks the freshness of knowledge taken from "the source" – the originator of the documentation, or a current practitioner of a particular skill. It lacks context, currency, and, at times, applicability. But it can be measured, managed, and controlled, it can be useful, and its breadth and depth can be visualized by the average executive, shareholder, employee, or other interested stakeholder. The managerial need to account for tangible assets must be complimented by recognition of the inherent value of less tangible knowledge practices, built on the enduring connection between communication and knowledge. Without this balance, organizational knowledge cannot be counted as a strategic asset.

Despite extensive work done within the disciplines of management, organization, communication, human resources, and others, interdisciplinary examinations of knowledge management are less common. In this chapter, we focus on the intersection of managerial/systems theory and communication theory relative to knowledge management and knowledge as a strategic asset. Specifically, we leverage a resource-based view (RBV) of the firm with a practice perspective that sees knowledge as inherently communicative. In this, we look for ways to integrate the theories, suggest enhancements to organizational activities, and extend the view of communication practices that impact the positioning of knowledge as a strategic asset. We recognize that the managerial view of knowledge management is typically conceived as asset based, and exploring the integration of communication practices and managerial assets provides a dimension of interest.

Through this examination, we challenge the assumptions around what has traditionally been required for knowledge to be a strategic asset, the ways in which knowledge is understood as a strategic asset, and how support for both systems and practices is important for knowledge to be positioned as strategic.

We start with a review of knowledge management as a business area and the conceptual development of knowledge as a strategic asset. We build on existing case studies available in the business press to understand ways in which knowledge is managed and tracked. We explore ways in which managerial instincts to reduce knowledge to text and to reduce knowledge-seeking to defined processes through systemization need to co-exist with dynamic, ambiguous, and difficult to measure individual and group knowledge practices. We argue that businesses need to value and invest in both sides of the equation to support the placement of knowledge as a strategic asset. We conclude with a proposed combined model of a framework for understanding knowledge practices together with the application of explicit knowledge assets. In taking a practice-based view in coordination with a systems view, we believe a more robust model of knowledge as a strategic asset can be understood, based both on the tangible, explicit assets created and gathered and the communicative practices that lead to a "capacity to act," driving new knowledge creation (Kuhn & Jackson, 2008). In summarizing, we discuss ways in which joint research efforts that attend to both the systems and practice measures can contribute to theory development and organizational application.

Knowledge Management Review

In today's work environment, we see a situation where knowledge and knowledge workers are an assumed part of many organizations. According to Jonathan Spira (2005), who has built a business (Basex) around serving the knowledge economy, "at the beginning of the 20th century, unskilled labor accounted for about 90% of the workforce, today that figure is closer to 20%." Spira further estimates that "Knowledge workers spend at least 20% of their time each day searching.... That costs companies thousands of dollars per worker, and more significantly, delays completion of work." He estimates that this lag-time costs businesses approximately $25B in 2004 – a number that would only increase, going forward. He quotes IBM's Vice President of Strategy, Mike Wing, saying "We should be long past congratulating ourselves for the simple epiphany that intellectual capital is better than physical capital" – a comment that is indicative of why knowledge management is no longer an emerging concept that businesses should consider, but rather an imperative that has come into its own for any competitive business. These kinds of statistics demonstrate the significant role knowledge plays in defining both organizations and workers.

Despite its 40-plus year history, the idea of an economy fueled by knowledge seems to have had its coming-out party in the 1990s, as evidenced by both investment in and research on knowledge management as a field – enough of a spike in interest to consider it as a management fad, but with characteristics to make it a fundamental part of a business (Swan, Newell, Scarbrough, & Hislop, 1999). Throughout this decade and beyond, companies began to act, through significant investment, on the corporate view of knowledge as an asset to be captured, valued, and marketed. This has been spurred by tremendous improvements in communication, storage, and search/retrieval technologies, improvements in business processes for sharing information, and the ongoing risk of attrition of old and new workers from Baby Boomer retirements to Gen Y's habit of churning employment. The goal of these KM efforts has typically been that of making visible, systematizing, and cataloging organizational knowledge in a tangible, explicit form, generally through IT systems, or learning and development tools.

To understand the scope of the investment, consider that the market size for basic content management systems alone is estimated to reach approximately $4B in the United States in 2010 (Rockley, 2006). The addition of newer forms of knowledge management systems, including blogs, wikis, intranet and extranet sites, ERP systems, customer information systems, and the tracking and indexing of e-mails and text messages, will only accelerate this growth. Today, there is little argument in the business world that organizational knowledge exists, that it is valuable, and that it should be collected, monitored, and managed, and many organizations view organizational knowledge as a strategic asset, resulting in resources (people and dollars) being committed to systematize KM.

The industry that has built up around KM has been a combination of IT systems developed to create large, searchable repositories and the development, usually in human resources (HR) departments, of extensive training materials and approaches to push information about documented processes to employees. Even in process-oriented KM environments, the primary measures of success often come from explicit documentation of process models, procedure steps, or other forms of tangible assets that can be catalogued and searched. As a result, KM has become heavily supported by IT departments or HR departments, sometimes simultaneously and/or competitively, and often with little coordination. This divide is sometimes referenced in association with the split between systematized and process-oriented approaches to knowledge management. In both cases, thinking back to the analogy from Collison and Purcell (2004), the goal seems to be to "fill a lake" rather than to "bottle the source." IT departments build repositories, search engines, and other technology-centric tools to capture and catalogue knowledge, while HR departments write process and training documents to provide individuals with a pre-determined set of steps by which they can navigate the organizational knowledge base. In both cases, efficient and effective KM is often presented as a strategic asset to a knowledge-based organization.

Knowledge as a Strategic Asset

The IT and HR approaches are similar in their zeal to reduce knowledge to an accessible, searchable, retrievable, and replicable asset. This reductionist approach actually presents a challenge to the idea of knowledge as a strategic asset. Using the resource-based view of the firm (RBV), a strategic asset meets the criteria defined as valuable, rare, inimitable, and non-substitutable, often referred to as the VRIN criteria. Within the RBV, the VRIN strategic attributes are often considered as a bundle, meaning that having an individual attribute does not normally constitute a strategic asset. However, understanding each individual attribute is helpful as we work to connect systems and practices into the bundle that represents knowledge as a strategic asset. Bowman (2006, pp. 415–416) provides a useful set of definitions for each individual attribute, highlighting *valuable* as being something that supports revenue flowing into the company. *Rare* is a resource that is not found in competing firms, and that generates superior revenue off the same cost basis. Bowman (2006) points out that these two measures represent a point in time, and may change quickly depending on market conditions. An *inimitable* resource is something competitors have a difficult time replicating, either because the conditions whereby it is created are ambiguous, or because of inherent dependencies that exist to create the resource. A *non-substitutable* resource is one that cannot be produced outside of the unique conditions of the organization that holds the resource. Resources that are inimitable and non-substitutable represent more enduring value to the organization over time. These definitions will be important as we unpack the differences between systematized knowledge assets and indeterminate knowledge practices, and how they both contribute to knowledge being a strategic asset.

Strategic assets provide a means of differentiating from competition, and a way to assign tangible value to the resources of the organization. In combining RBV with knowledge theory, Bollinger & Smith (2001, pp. 10–11) suggest that "collective and cumulative organizational knowledge" meets the VRIN characteristics, adding that "organizations that wish to remain competitive should develop mechanisms for capturing relevant knowledge, and disseminating it accurately, consistently, concisely and in a timely manner…." They encourage combining this with a focus on the processes of knowledge development and transfer, acknowledging the value of process in addition to systems. We build on this idea, knowing that in application, many organizations focus primarily on the systems and tools required to support capture and dissemination. The challenge we see with the systems and process-based knowledge management approach is that it still drives to documentation and storage, and these two activities may result in organizational knowledge becoming less able to fulfill the VRIN requirements.

Knowledge as a Strategic Asset: The Systems Approach

The managerial approach tends to rely on familiar measures to determine success – for example, Jones (2003) provides a case study of a global financial institution that developed a balanced scorecard approach to measuring their knowledge management implementation, based on four dimensions: (1) designing and building … an intranet site; (2) replacing filing systems with a unified records management procedure; (3) storing "know-how" in a single knowledge base; and (4) providing a single point of contact for IT support. Measures were then taken regarding the use of the various dimensions – for example, how many times the Sharepoint site was accessed, and the amount of time spent searching. As Jones notes in the case study, adoption and use remained low throughout the study period, although levers of forced behavior changes, executive encouragement, and advertising benefits did create measurable changes in contributions. This type of benefits assessment based on contribution numbers, usage statistics, and customer satisfaction surveys is not uncommon in companies attempting to implement a KM strategy. Other case studies provide process-based and practice-based examples of KM; however, the connection back to how these different approaches support KM as a strategic asset is more limited. As a result, business cases are evaluated based on quantitative metrics that are used to validate continued investment in systems and tools for KM.

This systems perspective is consistent with the managerial approach to strategic assets that requires explicit, tangible assignment of value and return, measured against the VRIN attributes. Similar to the limitations noted in the strategic contingencies theory of power (Hickson, Hinings, Lee, Schneck, & Pennings, 1971), when only one dimension of a phenomenon is examined, the results fail to fully conceptualize the theory. The systems perspective serves its purpose of providing organizations with a business rationale for investment, attention, and experimentation relative to systems and processes to grow a repository of organizational knowledge. However, its embedded assumptions of knowledge reductionism and centralization leave this approach with a limited vision of knowledge as a dynamic, somewhat messy, and often amorphous thing, and focuses investment on systems implementations. It is this ambiguity that creates the possibility for knowledge to fully meet the requirements of the VRIN attributes to be seen as a strategic asset, but a purely systems-based view neglects or attempts to remove ambiguity from the system. Combining the systems view with a communication perspective grounded in practice allows for a full articulation of the VRIN characteristics relative to knowledge and knowledge management.

Knowledge as a Strategic Asset: Practice Theory

An expanded perspective to include the generative aspects of knowledge-seeking practices provides a way of challenging the limitations of systems and tools-based approaches to valuing knowledge management. Practice-based communication theory is action oriented. It places the emphasis on the activities and communicative aspects of knowledge development and distribution. Through a practice lens, the role of knowledge can be seen as both a static response to an inquiry and a generative stimulus to solving for unanticipated needs. This assumes organizational movement and change, where dynamic organizational knowledge supports an ability to respond to unpredictable situations.

Allowing for a perspective that assumes action, change, and unpredictability opens the door to realizing the promise of KM as a way of improving a firm's position relative to its competition through the placement of organizational knowledge as a strategic asset. For example, when a knowledge seeker in an organization has a need, he or she has several choices. If the organization has invested in knowledge management tools (as most have), there may be systematized procedures to follow to access a knowledge repository, talk with a knowledge manager, or access a defined network of knowledge owners. The degree to which people follow these procedures is measured and reported, and individuals are often encouraged (positively or negatively) to follow them. The knowledge seeker also has less obvious choices – he or she can follow an indeterminate path of discovery which might involve talking with friends or colleagues, referencing outside information, or calling on subject experts outside of the official procedure. These choices are more difficult to measure quantitatively and assign value to because they are often hidden in the organization and personal in nature. The selected course of action may be driven by the level of determinacy in the need, the knowledge seeker's preferences and experiences, or the degree to which the systematized tools have accurately predicted the contexts and conditions under which knowledge is sought. In some cases, the knowledge seeker may experience a moment of emergence based on the coming together of information, experiences, and community engagement, and non-standard practices and realize a new solution, create a new idea, or otherwise address his or her knowledge needs in a way previously undocumented.

Many knowledge seekers employ a combination of all three activities, regardless of organizational policy, rules, or other guidelines attempting to enforce systematized processes. Through these activities, there is the ongoing opportunity for the coming together of what is discovered and what is known to create something new and to support developing a "capacity to act" (Kuhn & Jackson, 2008) based on the tools used and practices engaged. This may be responding to a client request, providing "real time" assistance (as in the case of a call center), preparing a sales presentation, creating a new product, understanding a competitive threat, or myriad other business-related problems that present themselves to knowledge workers. The level of determinacy associated with the need impacts the suitability of different knowledge-seeking practices. The less determinate the need, the more important practices become, while systems and tools become less useful. Figure 4.1 provides a perspective on

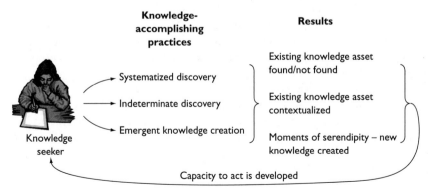

Figure 4.1 Knowledge-accomplishing practices.

knowledge-accomplishing practices. The three practices form a triad of knowledge assets that support knowledge being strategic to an organization, according to the VRIN attributes.

By means of review, assets are *valuable* when they support revenue generation, *rare* when they are unique to the organization and support margin competition, *inimitable* when they cannot be replicated by the competition, and *non-substitutable* when they can only exist within the organizational context. We suggest that bringing together dimensions of determinacy and centralization can drive the way in which knowledge assets, both systematized and practice-based, as a body represent a strategic asset. Choosing to evaluate organizational knowledge based only on assets in a repository or only on practices observed will limit its strategic value across the VRIN attributes, because determinate situations may be served by systematized assets that are often *valuable* and *rare*, meaning that they can be tangible assets to be sold or traded at a point in time. In less determinate situations, where the knowledge seeker is in need of ambiguous, non-specific, or yet undiscovered knowledge, the localized practices employed to gain the capacity to act become the knowledge asset. These practices are often *inimitable* by the competition because they are highly localized, and they become *non-substitutable* because the local context is what enables them to support a capacity to act. Kuhn and Jackson (2008) point out that ambiguity offers a rich environment for improvisation and emergence of new ideas. Likewise, taking an RBV perspective, ambiguity is a factor in maintaining an asset as inimitable for the competition (Bowman, 2006); that is, as the way in which an asset is produced becomes clear, it also becomes more subject to imitation and possibly substitution.

Knowledge as a Strategic Asset: Bringing it Together

A fully systematized approach to knowledge management cannot materialize knowledge as a strategic asset for an organization because it fails to satisfy the unanticipated, indeterminate needs that can only be met through communicative practices. An integrated approach is imperative to elevate knowledge to a strategic asset within a firm. In an integrated approach, the dimensions of determinacy and centralization become evaluative factors in understanding organizational knowledge and knowledge practices as a strategic asset. This encapsulates both the repository/documented processes supported by traditional IT and HR approaches, and the practice-based view supported by a communicative perspective of knowledge. Table 4.1 summarizes an integrated view of knowledge as a strategic asset, based on the determinacy of the needs being addressed.

A centralized repository of information and documented processes is *valuable* and may be *rare* compared to the competition in situations where knowledge needs are highly anticipated or determinate. These types of needs might include product specifications, contract information, pricing,

Table 4.1 An integrated view of knowledge as a strategic asset

Type of need	Centralized	Localized
Anticipated/determinate	Systematized resources that are valuable and rare	
Unanticipated/indeterminate		Communicative practices that are inimitable and non-substitutable

locations, previous experience with a particular client or product, answering common customer questions, or documented results from a previous situation. In these situations, a well-filled and searchable knowledge management system has the potential to provide faster response times, the perception of better customer service, faster quote to cash, and other measurable benefits relative to the competition. Many organizations focus primarily on the measurement and reporting of systematized assets or processes, for both tangible (digitized) assets, and intangible but process-driven knowledge seeking (e.g., communities of practice, networks, subject matter expert (SME) identifications, single points of contact). For example, decisions regarding funding for a community of practice may be tied to how many white papers are produced, or contact with a SME might be systematized through a ticketing process where the SME is rewarded with a bonus if he or she has a certain number of tickets closed.

In the drive to systematize, the strategic importance of localized knowledge-seeking practices that are inherently tied to communication and are used to respond to unanticipated, indeterminate needs gets minimized. In particular, the *inimitable* and *non-substitutable* aspects of knowledge as a strategic asset are supported by the ways in which indeterminate situations are responded to, usually through highly localized practices. These situations can trigger valuable results in emergent knowledge, ensuring the continued expansion of the organization's capabilities and advantages. Localized practices often exist only within the context of the organization and the individual executing them, making them difficult, if not impossible, for a competitor to imitate. The actions and their results are dependent on the environment in which they are executed, making them non-substitutable, meaning that competitors cannot use something different to create equal results. An environment with the structures to strike the right balance between centralized resources to respond to highly determinate needs with localized resources that can respond to highly indeterminate needs attends to all dimensions of a strategic advantage for an organization.

In considering the "7C" model (McPhee, 2008), we suggest that it most easily foregrounds the managerial processes, in which the approach to knowledge management centralizes the creation of a tangible asset to capture and track as a centralized event or process. A practice-based view of knowledge processes shifts the cause/event/consequence focus to the communicative interactions that support both explicit and implicit knowledge development. Extending Glaser's (1978) model to accommodate this, we can centralize the action that happens around knowledge needs, with a strong emphasis on context, covariance, and causal factors. Documentation and development of assets becomes a constituent subprocess, while the communicative processes by which knowledge is discovered and applied move to a more central position. Context becomes more important, as do covariances including indeterminate processes by which knowledge comes to be known. The managerial lens emphasizes asset creation, which may be accomplished in a variety of ways – individually, collaboratively, automatically, and so forth. This lens aligns with Glaser's input/action/output flow in the foreground. As a resource or an asset, the consequence is that the asset or process is documented in a retrievable way, and it is reduced to a replicable, commonplace item that may be broadly available within the firm. It may be removed from its original context and applied in ways that were not considered when the primary event took place. The resource-based view of the firm does not heavily weigh covariance or context, focusing more on the cause/effect/consequence chain of events, with some attention to the conditions (availability of systems and tools) under which they occur. A combined view recognizes especially the cause – the impetus for the knowledge-seeking activities that drives the choices made regarding what knowledge assets to utilize. From the cause, the context and cultural influences become important, driving to consequences that may include maintaining a competitive advantage as well as creating new knowledge for the organization.

Our combined perspective acknowledges the value of digitized knowledge assets and orderly processes, but makes clear that maintaining knowledge as a strategic asset requires an environment that supports indeterminate and emergent practices as well. Without these dimensions, knowledge is still an asset, but it is not strategic and it does not support a strong competitive advantage. In application, this is important when it comes to decisions regarding funding for KM initiatives and business cases for systems and tools versus cultural or social efforts. In theory development, this has implications regarding what we privilege, how we understand organizational choices, and methodological choices for researching knowledge in organizational settings.

Combining Perspectives: Methodological Challenges

In addition to understanding the penetration of systems and tools through traditional quantitative measures, a combined perspective would include examination of other ways to understand how knowledge practices are enacted in the workplace, when and how choices are made to engage determinate or indeterminate activities, and how different activities are privileged in the organizational context. This includes the ways in which power and control are associated with knowledge management, making decisions regarding prioritization, funding, and exposure. This requires qualitative analysis in addition to the common quantitative analysis used to evaluate systematized assets. Practice-based qualitative analysis has been used effectively to evaluate and understand cultural dimensions that might remain hidden with different research agendas. Practice-based methods have been used to uncover and define the context in which organizations are successful at ambiguous, difficult-to-define practices (Orlikowski, 2002), and the implementation of processes that support knowledge development and transfer through groups like communities of practice (Saint-Onge & Wallace, 2003; Wenger, 1998; Wenger, McDermott, & Snyder, 2002) have been systematized to the point that they are often measured in terms of assets developed, participation, and/or group satisfaction. Various approaches to primarily qualitative network analysis have been actively explored as KM has grown as a field (see, for example, Hansen, 2002; Leonard & Swap, 2005; Monge & Contractor, 1998). These methods provide useful ways to explore knowledge-sharing practices, but still do not fully help organizations to understand knowledge as a strategic asset, meeting all of the VRIN attributes. They lack a defined approach to understanding the impetus of the knowledge-seeking activity, together with a way to see the choices made by the knowledge seeker, and how those choices influence the result and contribute to ongoing knowledge development in the organization.

Recently, Kuhn and Jackson (2008) suggested an "episodic" framework that examines discursive moves in problem-solving episodes and evaluates them based on determinacy as a function of identification, legitimacy, and accountability. This framework is a useful way to build an understanding of how various knowledge assets support scenarios with different levels of determinacy. In one of their examples, a call-center representative assists a new staff member in finding and implementing a documented process. This episode of a combination of localized and centralized knowledge seeking and sharing can be seen as an example of the full value of the strategic nature of knowledge in the organization. There is a systematized asset that is made available to someone because of the practice of assisting new staff members through the sharing of practices. Extending this framework to understand how enactment reflects systematized or practice-based activities to support the knowledge seeker's capacity to act – the central versus local dimension – would allow for a robust evaluation of an organization's knowledge base as a strategic asset, or simply an organizational resource. It provides a framework within which organizational knowledge can be seen as valuable, rare, inimitable, and/or non-substitutable, and how it can meet a range of organizational needs. Recalling the VRIN attributes in the call-center example, the process documentation is valuable because it supports the representative in providing service to the customer, thereby supporting revenue. It is rare because the information it contains is not readily available to be offered in the same way by an external organization. The practice of helping new representatives by showing them the process when it is needed (as opposed to formal training) is inimitable – only an experienced representative in that context could have recognized the need and provided the knowledge – and it is non-substitutable – the same representative in a different context would not have been able to engage in the knowledge-sharing activity.

Conclusion

The promise of both the IT and HR tools and systems that have been developed to support KM is that the complexity of individual experience and know-how can be reduced to a manageable asset that can be routinely replicated, effectively ending the messiness that comes from knowledge that has not been catalogued. However, this promise has rarely been kept. As Pollard (2006) noted,

> The story of KM (knowledge management) so far has been, for the most part, a failure – failure to articulate, to imagine, and to implement. We allowed the bold vision of knowledge sharing to be diminished and appropriated by those who saw it is merely an exercise in automating the acquisition, storage and dissemination of documents.... Most executives saw it as a means to speed up and reduce the cost of the back office, the same way the assembly line had reduced manufacturing times and costs.

In the scenario cited in the introduction, knowledge found in a repository may be suitable for certain situations, especially when the client has a predictable request. However, the contextualization available when the seeker goes to "the source" provides additional value that sets the knowledge gained as a strategic asset to the firm. An organization that only has one or the other – systems or unidentified practices – does not have a strategic asset in its knowledge base. Looking only at the systematized assets and their application does not fully meet the VRIN attributes, but neither does a pure practice-based view. Only by bringing them together do we see the strategic value of knowledge in a way that can be fully valued by an organization, especially one that requires return on investment in order to validate future investments.

A systematic approach to knowledge management that focuses on building reservoirs of knowledge assets is quantitatively measurable in management terms. It can be understood as valuable and rare relative to generating revenue, maintaining a margin advantage, and supporting a competitive advantage. However, it does not afford a complete picture of the strategic nature of knowledge assets of an organization, because it neglects the inde-terminate processes, or seeks to marginalize or eliminate them. This limits an organization's ability to leverage the power of emergence, the moments of serendipity that occur in communication that underpin indeterminate knowledge-seeking practices. A culture and environment in which these moments can occur naturally and frequently creates a significant competit-ive advantage by virtue of knowledge-seeking practices that are inimitable and non-substitutable. KM environments must be able to respond to a full range of determinate and indeterminate needs to fully satisfy the RBV stra-tegic asset requirements.

We maintain that systemization and categorization efforts of the last two decades are useful ways of understanding certain forms of explicit knowledge as an organizational asset. The more indeterminate practices around knowledge-seeking practices provide the additional dimensions that make knowledge a strategic asset to an organization. Researchers and practitioners alike can benefit from models that cut through the reduction-ist impulse and value the processes of knowing, rather than focusing on what is known. Doing this requires overcoming methodological challenges as well as balancing the very different impulses of systems versus practice-based values. By utilizing the RBV theory together with the practice-based communicative theory, this balance may be achieved in useful ways that extend our understanding of both knowledge as a tangible resource and knowledge as an ambiguous resource.

Implications for Practice

There are practical implications to this approach. The managerial empha-sis on systemization impacts perceptions of value in an organization. Spira's concern quoted earlier regarding the cost of time spent searching may be misplaced in a more robust definition of knowledge as a strategic asset – perhaps the time spent searching isn't a cost, but rather an invest-ment, in the development of knowledge-seeking skills. If the practices of knowledge seeking are an integral component of knowledge as a strategic asset, maybe the estimated $25M isn't "lost;" rather, it is an investment in developing the knowledge asset. This shift in perspective has practical implications regarding funding allocations, management commitment, and employee engagement in the practices of knowing, as well as the tracking of knowledge as assets to the organization. For example, investing in col-laboration networks that help people funnel their search efforts to targeted groups of people may be more productive than investing in systems that make it seem unnecessary to connect with peers and other experts. Rather than tracking only contributions of documents to a knowledge database, management evaluations could also consider contributions to peer efforts, including peer reviews, discussion participation, and formalized job shad-owing or experiential learning opportunities with associated budgets and plans. This would also shift the focus to the practices of knowledge sharing, as highlighted by Spender (2008) in his call to be more attentive to the actual work of organizational knowledge and the managerial practices that surround it.

Finding ways to value the indeterminate practices without forcing them into a systematized structure is necessary in protecting the strategic dimension of knowledge in a firm. At this time there are few robust frameworks for understanding the value of localized activities in response to indeterminate needs. We have suggested here an approach that focuses on observing episodes of knowledge seeking, drawing out the ways in which both systems and practices work together to create strategic value. Continuing with this line of inquiry will assist organizations in better understanding how to best leverage organizational knowledge in a competitive environment. Additionally, it will further our understanding of the vital role knowledge plays in organizational design, and role of communication in fostering the ongoing development of organizational knowledge over time in a way that effectively attends to knowledge needs and maintains a competitive advantage.

References

Bollinger, A., & Smith, R. (2001). Managing organizational knowledge as a strategic asset. *Journal of Knowledge Management, 5*, 8–18.

Bowman, C. (2006). A strategy overview and competitive strategy. In D. O. Faulkner & A. Campbell (Eds.), *Oxford handbook of strategy* (pp. 410–442). Oxford, UK: Oxford University Press.

Collison, C., & Parcell, G. (2004). *Learning to fly: Practical knowledge management from leading and learning organizations* [Kindle Digital version]. Chichester, UK: Capstone Publishing.

Glaser, B. (1978). *Theoretical sensitivity: Advances in the methodology of grounded theory*. Mill Valley, CA: Sociology Press.

Hansen, M. (2002). Knowledge networks: Explaining effective knowledge sharing in multiunit companies. *Organization Science, 13*, 232–248.

Hickson, D. J., Hinings, C. R., Lee, C. A., Schneck, R. E., & Pennings, J. M. (1971). A strategic contingencies' theory of interorganizational power. *Administrative Science Quarterly, 16*, 216–229.

Jones, R. (2003). Measuring the benefits of knowledge management at the Financial Services Authority: A case study. *Journal of Information Science, 29*, 475.

Kuhn, T., & Jackson, M. H. (2008). Accomplishing knowledge: A framework for investigating knowledge in organizations. *Management Communication Quarterly, 21*, 454–485.

Leonard, D., & Swap, W. (2005). *Deep smarts: How to cultivate and transfer enduring business wisdom*. Boston, MA: Harvard Business School Press.

Maier, R., & Remus, U. (2003). Implementing process-oriented knowledge management strategies. *Journal of Knowledge Management, 7*, 62–74.

McPhee, R. D. (2008). *Revision of Glaser's 6C model*. Unpublished paper.

Monge, P., & Contractor, N. (1999). Emergence of communication networks.

In F. Jablin & L. Putnam (Eds.), *The new handbook of organizational communication: Advances in theory, research, and methods* (pp. 440–502). Thousand Oaks: CA: Sage.

Orlikowski, W. J. (2002). Knowing in practice: Enacting a collective capability in distributed organizing. *Organization Science, 13*, 249–273.

Pollard, D. (2006). The PKM-enabled organization. *Salon*, retrieved August 15, 2008, from www.blogs.salon.com.

Rockley, A. (2006). 2006: Content management market year in review. Downloaded August 15, 2008: www.cmswire.com.

Saint-Onge, H., & Wallace, D. (2003). *Leveraging communities of practice for strategic advantage*. New York, NY: Butterworth Heinemann.

Spender, J. C. (2008). Organizational learning and knowledge management: Whence and whither? *Management Learning, 39*, 159–176.

Spira, J. (2005). In praise of knowledge workers. *KMWorld*. Downloaded August 15, 2008: www.kmworld.com/Articles/News/News-Analysis/In-praise-of-knowledge-workers-9605.aspx.

Swan, J., Newell, S., Scarbrough, H., & Hislop, D. (1999). Knowledge management and innovation: Networks and networking. *Journal of Knowledge Management, 3*, 262–275.

Wenger, E. (1998). *Communities of practice: Learning, meaning, and identity*. New York, NY: Cambridge University Press.

Wenger, E., McDermott, R., & Snyder, W. (2002). *Cultivating communities of practice* (pp. 161–185). Boston, MA: Harvard Business School Press.

Chapter 5

The Politics of Knowledge

A Critical Perspective on Organizational Knowledge

Alexander Lyon and Joseph L. Chesebro

We recently heard a story about a married couple that moved to the US. In their former country, the husband, who was an engineer, had a higher professional status than his wife, who was a physician. Most readers would likely agree that physicians in the US enjoy higher status. When the couple moved to the US this reversal of fortune strained their marriage, so the wife quit her job as a physician and became a nurse – a job with less prestige. While the patriarchal nature of these choices is troubling, the example also illustrates the ambiguous, contestable value of knowledge. From an American viewpoint, one could assume the couple's occupational problems stem from a historic overvaluing of engineering knowledge or the undervaluing of medical knowledge in their home country. We may even feel that their perceptions were "corrected" to see it our way. This interpretation, however, begs the question, how did we come to see the physician as the more naturally valuable occupation?

This example illustrates the assumption held by most approaches to knowledge in organizations – that is, knowledge has inherent value. The critical perspective on knowledge takes a different viewpoint. It sees knowledge as "an explicit social formation arrived at through value-laden social processes" (Deetz, 1995, p. 136). Knowledge is not automatically valuable, nor are certain types of knowledge more naturally valuable than others. The perceived value of some types of knowledge over others often results from participants' practices and organizational cultural struggles. This chapter argues that the political side to organizational knowledge and its management has consequences for the relative health of organizations.

Knowledge as a Resource, Process, and Power Struggle

The vast majority of extant research on knowledge in organizations thus far handles knowledge as either a resource or a process.[1] The most traditional perspective conceptualizes knowledge *resource*, asset or otherwise, "as an objectively definable commodity" (Empson, 2001a, p. 812). This approach to knowledge sees it as "something to be acquired, measured, and distributed" (Pfeffer & Sutton, 1999, p. 89). The knowledge-as-an-asset perspective seeks to tame members' otherwise intangible knowledge, objectify its form, and "develop mechanisms for managing it effectively" (Empson, 2001a, p. 812). As Nonanka (1991, p. 96) argues, the most traditional streams of research insist "the only useful knowledge is formal and systematic – hard [quantifiable] data, codified procedures, universal principles." More recently, researchers and practitioners have developed a *process* or communicative view of knowledge in organizations. As Pfeffer and Sutton (1999, p. 90) note, "Knowledge management systems rarely reflect the fact that essential knowledge, including technical knowledge, is often transferred between people by stories, gossip, and by watching one another work. This is a process in which social interaction is often crucial." From the process view, knowledge is socially constructed, transmitted, and sustained through numerous situated social interactions. For example, Pfeffer and Sutton (1999, p. 90) argue that "Informal learning occurs in dozens of daily activities, including participating in meetings, interacting with customers, supervising or being supervised, mentoring others, communicating informally with peers, and training others on the job." Rather than viewing knowledge as a commodity, the process approach focuses more on how we construct knowledge and arrive at shared meanings.

The resource and process views of knowledge, however, share some practical problems. That is, they both take for granted that knowledge is inherently valuable, and do not explore deeply the real-world power struggles that knowledge and its management often involve. As Alvesson (1993, p. 998) points out, the word *knowledge* "contains such a strong symbolic value that it can easily create biases when discussed." In fact, knowledge or expertise is often handled interchangeably with "intellectual capital" (see, for example, Zorn & Taylor, 2004) as a way to substantiate the value of knowledge. Thus, the way we label, interpret, and position our activities shapes the perception of our work. The other approaches to knowledge notwithstanding, we argue in this chapter that there is a political or ideological side to knowledge in organizations. First, we explore the historic roots of the critical perspective on knowledge and power, examine the "politics" of knowledge, and introduce concerns of research in these areas. Next, we examine some actual struggles faced by members in a knowledge-driven organization. Finally, we offer practical suggestions for practitioners and researchers who share these concerns.

Knowledge and Power

Critical studies of organizations are primarily concerned with issues of power, particularly the connection of knowledge and power. Critical researchers handle the term "power" as a covert and difficult-to-pinpoint social process in contrast with traditional approaches that locate power in the organizational hierarchy and official authority relationships. A critical approach to power asks questions such as: Whose version of organizational reality becomes normalized? Whose values guide our decisions? Whose priorities do organizational members pursue? In whose voice or interests are members speaking? Who benefits the most by an organization's taken-for-granted views and practices? This approach has its roots in classical critical theorists' work. Clegg and Dunkerly (1979) review this work as falling into two categories: "radical humanism" (explaining organizational power and knowledge as subjective ideology), and radical structuralism (explaining organizational power and knowledge materialistically as superstructural results of the organization of relations of production).

Foucault (1972, 1980) is the most frequently mentioned researcher who argues that knowledge and power are inseparable. A common misunderstanding of the "knowledge-is-power" connection is that those with the most education, knowledge, or expertise have a personal advantage over those with less of it. While this may be the case in some circumstances, it is not the concern of the critical approach. Further, the critical view of knowledge does not see the world as if it is run by a conspiracy of powerful individuals who actively control knowledge. Rather, critical researchers of knowledge see the historical development of *meaning* as a central concern. That is, critical theorists focus on the situated historical processes that led to certain interests, values, and norms emerging as society's unquestioned knowledge. In that sense, we ask how preferred types of knowledge in particular organizations become established as such. Townley (1993, p. 521), for instance, argues that organizational formation of knowledge is not random. Instead, it involves particular "mechanisms for inscription, recording, and calculation: ways of coding (e.g., in balance sheets, audits, population tables, censuses)." These knowledge micro-practices have the appearance of neutrality. We often forget that norms and procedures were designed by and for particular people, often for some advantageous purpose. For this reason, Alvesson and Karreman (2001, p. 1000) argue that "knowledge is not an innocent or neutral tool for accomplishing something socially valuable, but is closely related to power. Knowledge creates rather than reveals truths. It imprints standards for being that discipline and subordinate the individual." The apparent impartiality of mundane practices masks the interests, priorities, and human effort used to construct them in the first place.

This perspective on knowledge underscores that most societies and organizations wrestle over control in situated, micro-political ways. People engage in small, in-the-moment practices that influence decisions, shape rules, and pass policies. Over time, these situated practices accumulate and tend to benefit those already in power. As Bourdieu (1998) argued, those who occupy influential positions in society are likely to use that influence in ways that help them maintain or increase their influence and voice. That is, power is not simply located in a particular position. However, power relationships are perpetuated by those who are positioned with the most voice and influence. Power, knowledge, and communication, then, tend to reproduce dominant–subordinate relationships. Habermas (1970) described this reproduction of routinely one-sided communication as systematically distorted communication. Deetz (1990, 1992) develops this idea for organizational settings, and shows how communication often becomes lopsided and routinized in ways that favor certain types of expertise, knowledge, and ways of knowing over other potentially valuable perspectives. If left unchecked, routinely distorted, one-sided communication can quickly create unhealthy organizations that are at great risk of losing competitiveness, increasing their exposure to crisis, and even failing completely (Heath, 1990; Lyon, 2007; Seeger & Ulmer, 2003).

The "Politics" of Knowledge and Power

"Politics" describes activities that subvert or reinforce formalized authority structures. As Mumby (2000, p. 586) defined, "Politics is power enacted and resisted." Political activity manifests at all levels of our organizational experience, from one-on-one interactions to the organizational cultural level. We suggest that knowledge and knowledge management is political in at least three intersecting ways.

First, people in organizations frequently play obvious political games. Mintzberg (1983, p. 188) characterizes a variety of power games meant to resist authority, counter the resistance to authority, build power bases, and defeat rivals. Similarly, Frost (1987, p. 527) suggests that power games can be fairly complex and involve "interpretive strategies that specify the rules, data, and successful outcomes of the game." People commonly describe these games as "office politics" that are aimed at grabbing power. Some tactics are blunt and others more nuanced. Bourdieu (1998) explains, however, that our strategic activities have deeper roots – that is, people's strategic calculations are likely engaging historic, embodied commitments that merely surface explicitly upon reflection. For instance, if a customer service employee argues for improving customer service at the organization, he or she might be making a self-interested move that will likely result in more responsibilities and professional benefits, or might be making what feels like an authentic argument for better customer service. In the heat of the situation, it is thus often difficult to tell if people are arguing merely from their genuinely felt passions or with at least the implicit awareness that arguing in such a way helps them professionally.

Second, knowledge and its management are also political, in that knowledge itself is a social product and differs according to each organization. Lazega (1992), for instance, explains that knowledge is constructed in epistemic communities – that is, groups produce and reinforce their own favored types of knowledge and interpretation about it. He states that knowledge is "organized by categories socially approved, and differently legitimated in different groups" (Lazega, 1992, p. 26). The social negotiation of knowledge has obvious stakes, and dominant groups tend to perpetuate knowledge priorities that preserve their privileged status. When viewed from the inside of organizations, employees often accept the legitimacy of socially constructed preferences even when such norms subordinate their own contributions. In contrast, newcomers often question the sensibility of existing arrangements because they did not live through the contentious processes that positioned some groups' knowledge above others.

Third, organizational processes and structures are infused with an already present set of beliefs, commitments, and priorities that were themselves socially constructed. Deetz (1992) explains that politics are "already *in* the experience at hand, the person and the perception produced.... It is in the habit, the routine, and the thoughtlessness that [politics] is reproduced" (Deetz, 1992, p. 128). That is, we enter organization settings that were formed through the accumulated history of battles won and choices made. The politics of the day gets solidified and becomes the organization's routine way of doing things. Organizational realities are framed for us in ways that make certain actions and decisions seem like natural choices, even if these same choices would not make sense in any other context. Similarly, the formation of our own interests has its own forgotten history. In organizations, therefore, we often take action but rarely question how we came to believe that action was important (Deetz, 1992).

Communication, Knowledge, and Power

Within the general framework of a critical approach to knowledge, power, and politics, certain practical issues have emerged in recent studies of knowledge-laden organizations such as law, consulting, engineering, and high-technology firms. Such knowledge-intensive organizations are susceptible to particular types of overlapping struggles involving ambiguity, rhetorical representation, power and control, and identity.

Ambiguity of Knowledge

The term "knowledge" is itself contested and inherently ambiguous. Without doubt, each author in this book presents a slightly different view of what counts as knowledge. Alvesson and Karreman (2001) describe the various concepts of knowledge in current research as inconsistent, vague, broad, two-faced, and unreliable. We add to this view that researchers are not wrong in their collective imprecision. The diversity of academic approaches to knowledge reflects the complex issues that knowledge-centric organizations confront. The ambiguity of knowledge presents a real problem in that it makes it difficult for those who don't share a knowledge base to evaluate the work of others. Few of us, for instance, can evaluate the work of engineers, consultants, software developers, or physicians. In contrast, we do not need to be a professional chef to judge the quality of a cheeseburger, or a craftsman to test the comfort of a chair. We can touch, taste, and smell the quality of many kinds of work. The ambiguity of knowledge, however, amplifies the opportunity for power struggles.

Knowledge Rhetoric

The ambiguity of knowledge highlights the rhetorical dimensions to knowledge work. As Alvesson (1993, p. 1008) stated, "As a socially constructed phenomenon [knowledge] is in a sense interaction, dependent on recognition – without being recognized by others that 'knowledge' is, for all practical matters, nothing." Knowledge work does not speak for itself. Employees rhetorically represent their work to others. From Alvesson's view, organizations are driven by the perceived usefulness and relevance of their particular types of knowledge. Employees may thus use their rhetorical skills for personal advantage to various degrees. They may use communication merely to highlight certain facts, or use it to conceal other facts and convince others of the undue importance of their work (Zorn & Taylor, 2004).

Power and Control

Most knowledge-driven, new-economy organizations consider members' knowledge the most valuable asset (see Chapter 4 in this volume). In fact, much of the early work on knowledge management focused on ways to gain some type of control over employees' knowledge. Zorn and May (2002), for example, argue that knowledge management often attempts to extract, capture, harvest, and otherwise "commodify that part of the employee that is valued (his or her knowledge), thus making the organization less vulnerable to the employee's loss and making the employee more expendable" (p. 239). Leaders' attempts at extracting employees' knowledge shows that employees possess a valuable asset. Further, peer-level experts may find themselves in power struggles with each other for the same reason. For instance, Alvesson (1993) explains the interdependence of peer-level experts: "Only insiders can by definition evaluate who is very knowledgeable. Insiders are dependent on each others' recognition. The play within a relatively restricted field then becomes important" (Alvesson, 1993, p. 1008). The battle over perception, prestige, power, and control among *peers* is thus an important part of knowledge work.

Identity

At the most personal level, knowledge-intensive work can play a crucial role in sustaining workers' identities. The intangible nature of knowledge prompts workers to do identity work. As Deetz (1998) explains, workers may define themselves in high-end ways such as "consultants," "engineers," or other labels that promote the expertise and prestige inherent to their work. Deetz (1994, p. 35) demonstrated, "Personal identity is often as invested in [employees'] profession and professional groups as in their particular role in the workplace." This is not as possible in cases where one's work is more concrete. For example, defining oneself as a "garbalogist," as an acquaintance recently joked, did not hide for long that he worked on a garbage truck. Such work is easy to observe. For some knowledge workers, "Being perceived as an expert is then more crucial [to workers] than being one" (Alvesson, 1993, p. 1004). For this reason, organizations may reinforce desired identities as a management strategy (see, for example, Kunda, 1992). The prestige and esteem we accept from rhetorically elevated organizational identities is thus not free.

Ambiguity, rhetorical representation, power and control, and identity are best understood as interdependent features of knowledge in organizations, rather than compartmentalized issues. Many of these concerns are demonstrated in the following case.

Knowledge Politics: The Case of Virtual-Learn

We turn now to the case of Virtual-Learn (VL), an e-learning organization that made online courses for medical professionals. VL's clients were hospitals who employed nurses and other medical professionals who needed to take continuing education credits to maintain their professional status. The company was started in the late 1990s, and closed down in late 2003. VL employed about 120 people who were hired for their respective areas of expertise. Software application developers, web programmers, physicians, nurses, instructional designers, editors, and digital animators all worked together to create interactive online courses. Almost all members had bachelor's degrees, and numerous members had MAs, PhDs, or MDs. The company's offices consisted of little more than desktop computers, hip décor, and Birkenstock sandals. In every way, VL represented a knowledge-driven, new-economy organization in that the organization's collective assets were in and among its members.

VL existed at "the nexus of education and technology," as one employee said. They depended heavily upon two groups: (1) employees who helped with the educational side, and (2) employees who helped with the technology end of the courses. The education employees included instructional designers, content researchers, physicians and nurses, and editors. The technology employees included the application developers, web programmers, and digital illustrators. As a former college professor, the founding CEO was an academic at heart. He framed the organization as primarily educators who used the Internet and technologies to deliver that education in a convenient way. Under this leadership team, most members regularly proclaimed "we're educators," and discussed "learning objectives," "learner-centered courses," and "context-based learning" as priorities.

Most of the company's money came from their largest client, a hospital chain which also bought a majority share of the company. A few years before starting VL, the founder had sold a similar company. As he had done before, at the highpoint of VL's growth, the founder abruptly resigned with a generous severance package. VL's majority owner and largest client replaced him with one of its own executives. These changes increased uncertainty at VL. Employees' power struggles that had arguably already existed below the surface became more acute as the new CEO tried to steer the company in a different direction. In other instances, VL employees willingly collaborated and shared their knowledge. As the case below shows, however, strings were attached to their generosity. Ultimately, members became overly concerned with the internal knowledge politics of the organization, were unable to create online courses that satisfied their clients, and hastened the company toward ruin. Most of the power struggles directly or indirectly involved people's knowledge. These struggles surfaced (1) between and among peer-level employees, (2) between employees and managers, and (3) within the organization's changing culture. Issues of ambiguity, rhetorical representation, power and control, and identity are evident at each level in varying degrees.

Employee Level Experts: Attaching and Defending Knowledge Territory

At VL, peer-level employees often clashed in ways that had little to do with the managers' and organization's activities more broadly. This usually occurred between departments with similar knowledge areas. For example, the online-course editors often clashed with the instructional designers. Although the latter were hired to design and write the courses, the editors, who were responsible for editing content to ensure consistent style across the courses, thought they wrote better, and tried to wrestle away the responsibility of the writing from the instructional designers. The following excerpt was taken from an interdepartmental meeting of six people that was supposed to increase collaboration between departments by moving away from an assembly-line style of course development. Instead, one of the editors, Helen (pseudonym), used the meeting as a chance to devalue the instructional designers.

RYAN (researcher): The problem I see happening is that it's too [departmentalized] right now. Where all the skills are "Oh, it's a *writing* issue, send it to the instructional design department or to edit." So, what we end up doing is trying to put all the [separate] pieces together as opposed to developing all as more of an organic or holistic effort.

HELEN (editor): Well, I would love it to be like that, but I've found that a lot of the instructional designers don't write well. So, there's no way that it can happen. And I don't mean that as a criticism but the instructional designers aren't expected to write like that. (*There was a long pause and people exchanged uncomfortable glances*)

TUCKER (instructional designer): Well, they are actually expected to write.

HELEN: What we've been told is that they're responsible for organizing and designing the courses and not necessarily for *(pause)* the writing is not a big thing. They're not hired for their writing skills! They're hired for their design skills.

TUCKER: Well, they are. Anyway. *(awkward silence)*

RYAN: Well we have to have somebody who can handle it all, who can recognize where all the deficiencies lie and not say "okay, let's send it over there." You know? If the instructional designers can't write, then we need someone who can.

Officially, Helen's statement that instructional designers were "not hired for their writing skills!" is not accurate. Writing was part of their job description, and they spent much of their day writing. Thus, the meeting shows Helen criticizing and devaluing the instructional designers' writing in an in-the-moment power struggle over whose expertise on writing counted more. At the time, the editors were one of the smallest departments at VL and enjoyed little status. By constantly devaluing the writing skills of the instructional designers, they were positioning themselves as the experts on writing and increasing their perceived importance. Ryan, a researcher who was not part of either department, unwittingly enforced this perception by concluding, "If the instructional designers can't write, then we need someone who can." Helen's criticisms opened a discursive space for the editors' expertise.

This type of power struggle is possible because the issue of writing "quality" is inherently ambiguous and has clear rhetorical dimensions. In many ways, VL implicitly left it up to the experts, or editors, to evaluate quality. As Alvesson (1993, p. 1008) explained, knowledge is "dependent on recognition – without being recognized by others that 'knowledge' is, for all practical matters, nothing." That is, without the editors' recognition of the instructional designers' writing expertise, the value of the instructional designers' knowledge contributions remained questionable. One of the main ways people jostled for power at VL, thus, was to attempt to take over the historic knowledge territory of a competing group.

Similarly, the application developers often clashed with the web programmers, both of whom handled various onscreen and technical aspects of the courses. The software application development department seemed to do everything it could to maintain the exclusivity of its small and "elite" department. The employees were most concerned with members of the web programming department who had ambitions to do application development. Most computer-savvy readers know that these two jobs entail different sets of knowledge. What was striking at VL, however, was the continuous effort application developers put forth to maintain their perceived superiority and keep the web programmers in their place. Below, an application developer explains what he saw as a need to keep his department exclusive despite the growing skills of many web programmers.

They've [web programmers] been increasing their skills and a lot of them now are ready to move on [to application development]....
[However] it's rare [for web programmers to move into the application development department]. But in the near future, I think [the business] is going to expand. And so some of the web programmers are taking on new tasks and – not necessarily that they're moving into application development – but they are beginning to do some application development in [the web] programming [department but] ... it doesn't mean that all programmers are going to move into [the] application programming [department] because, at the same time, we're now redefining what application programming [is and] the skills it takes to get in there. We just need to redefine now what it means to be an application developer and what it means to be a programmer.

By his admission, many of the web programmers were quite capable of doing application development. At the same time, he and the other developers did not want them joining their small elite club of about five employees. They did numerous things to "redefine now what it means to be an application developer" and keep others from joining their department. For instance, the application developers decided to require any hypothetical new members to pass external certification tests in the applications they currently used. In an embarrassing turn, some of the current application developers failed to pass the tests themselves. They also required any new members to possess an ambitious list of different prerequisite application skills. Again, some current departmental members did not themselves possess all of skills on the list and instead had one or two specialties. Application developers' tactics were meant to secure their place as the organization's most expert members. However, once they became known, these failed tactics unintentionally displayed the contrived nature of their reputation, and wasted inordinate amounts of time.

The closer one listened to the application developers, the less their explanations had to do with employees' respective levels of talent. Instead, these struggles were directly related to issues of employees' power, control, and their desired identities within the organization. As Empson (2001b, p. 856) explains, "Professionals therefore risk diminishing the perceived value of their service offering if they allow their image to be called into question by association with apparently 'downmarket' colleagues." Application developers clearly saw the web programmers as "downmarket." Further, these power struggles played out between peer-level employees who sometimes jockeyed for perceived positions by attacking and defending knowledge territory.

Managers and Employees: Sharing Knowledge with Strings Attached

Divisions between employees and managers still exist at knowledge-intensive organizations. At VL, some struggles occurred along this traditional division. The nature of the struggles at VL, however, had mainly to do with knowledge. In general, the managers wanted employees to share their knowledge and expertise as much as possible. Employees sometimes resisted. At other times they happily obliged, with certain strings attached. The web programming manager, Dave, explained his view on the benefits of sharing knowledge, mentoring, and spreading expertise widely.

> If everybody knew what I know all of a sudden, it makes my job easier. If I show people how to do something in HTML, or whatever, then they know it. That means they can do it over and over again, and they can teach other people how to do it, and that's easier for me. Because if people know how to do their job at my level – or whatever level, as long as they're getting to a higher level – that means it's going to be easier for me because they know what they're doing. It's going to be easier for them because they know what they're doing, and they can do things faster and … you want everybody to move forward and sometimes people pass [you]. I've seen Jess learn ASP right before my eyes, and he started learning it after me and he knows way more than me. I guarantee it.

Managers like Dave wanted everybody to improve their skills and encouraged the sharing of knowledge whenever possible.

Sometimes, managers encouraged the use of teams. In one case, for instance, some managers thought it would be useful to use a cross-functional team to create an online course instead of sending the course from one department to the next in a quasi-assembly line. Employees who volunteered for the team saw this as a great opportunity to diversify their skills by working with others who brought different expertise to the project. Melissa, an editor, "loved the collaboration … and less linear" relationship. Tim and Hal, two other members of the team, echoed Melissa's feelings, and commented on the increased quality of the work as a result of the team approach.

HAL: I think the improved communication is also going to help with innovation too as far as coming up with new activities and things like that…. That was something brand new. I think there's a lot of room for, you know, if people are collaborating in the beginning, and these ideas are coming out right before the course is even really written or whatever, there's a lot of opportunity for cool things like that to happen.

TIM: Yeah, and in that type of collaboration, new ideas come up that never would.

To be sure, this type of knowledge sharing and collaboration helped the company. As Tim put it, "new ideas come up that never would." At the same time, the employees were not being entirely altruistic in their approach. Aside from helping the organization, most employees were open to sharing their knowledge and collaborating when it included two conditions: (1) it was face-to-face sharing of knowledge; and (2) they personally gained something from the collaboration. Employees' seemingly prosocial activities had political dimensions that increased their own power and influence. Further, employees who were most willing to share their knowledge tended to be the company's lower-status employees who had the most to gain by doing so. High-status members routinely resisted sharing.

In contrast, employees' least favorite way to share knowledge was through the organization's knowledge management system (KMS). VL invested thousands of dollars in their KMS, and pushed employees aggressively to use it. Employees were supposed to post anything from quick tips to robust content on the KMS that would help others increase their skills and improve their work. For instance, if an employee discovered a way to automate a mundane task, he or she was supposed to post these instructions and remind peers about the innovation. In other cases, VL would fully fund employees' travel to the latest workshops and conferences. In return, managers expected a compulsory posting of any useful content to the in-house KMS (see Chapter 4). The managers' goal was to create a collection of resources and best practices that all employees could contribute to and access at any time.

Employees almost never complied with these requirements. They delayed posting to the KMS, claimed to be too busy, or acted confused about how to do it. Not surprisingly, VL employees preferred to share their knowledge one-on-one. In one employee's words, "It doesn't make sense to just post these ideas. It's better to walk by and see them working on something and say, 'You know what? Why don't you try it like this.'" Employees saw the KMS as a clumsy, ineffectual, and impersonal way to handle their knowledge. Hence, the overall reason for employees' resistance was simple: they received little in return when they distributed their knowledge freely on the KMS. In many ways, employees saw posting to the KMS as handing over their knowledge to the management for nothing in return.

In contrast, when they shared and collaborated face-to-face, they received complementary skills in return, or the prestige of expert and informal leader status among their peers. They either deepened their existing skills through sharing ideas, or they diversified their skills by collaborating across departmental lines. One employee explained the need to be thoughtful about sharing knowledge and collaborating: "At a certain point, you're not going to [help people]. They need to be at a certain level.... But, if people have similar skills in different areas, it's a nice sharing of knowledge that can go on." Thus, working in teams and collaborating one-on-one helped employees gain various skills. As an employee said, "It's all about increasing your skills. There's nothing higher than skills." Employees mentioned the need for increasing skills to "keep up with peers" in other organizations to "remain marketable."

Thus, when managers attempted to manage employees' knowledge, employees resisted. When employees managed their own knowledge, they did so in ways that preserved or enhanced their status. Even collaborating and working in teams hence had political stakes. As Bourdieu (1998) explains, it is not always clear if people are consciously acting in calculated, self-beneficial ways or if they are merely acting out of their own deeply held commitment. Neither was it clear at VL. What was clear, however, was that VL members tended to act in ways that helped themselves the most. Employees' secondary concern was helping the company through their collaboration, teamwork, or use of the knowledge management system.

Organizational Cultural Level: Knowledge and Collective Direction

VL's culture sometimes gravitated toward unwise knowledge priorities. Under the founding CEO's leadership, the educational members of the organization enjoyed the most prestige. He routinely called the instructional designers "the heart of the company," "the backbone," and "the architects." The instructional designers, the biggest educational department, worked in semi-private offices they shared with just one or two other people. Almost all instructional designers had window views on the top floor of the building near the executives' offices. The instructional designers regularly interacted with the executives, and their voices were influential in shaping the direction in which the online courses were developing.

In contrast, many of the technology members were moved to the "garden level" when the company outgrew its original space. None of the education members moved to the less prestigious area downstairs. Further, no executive offices were near the technology members, and most of them were in a large open space that provided no privacy. As one executive put it, "When we expanded, the move was tough. There were a lot of bad feelings. It was very political. There are favorites groups and you can tell which ones by looking at where everybody ended up." The contrast of prestige and influence was easy to detect. As Deetz (1992) reminds us, organizational contexts, processes, and structures are the result of the forgotten political battles won and lost.

When the founder left abruptly, however, he was replaced by a CEO who favored technology over education. He quickly hired other likeminded executives to surround him, and they reframed what VL was all about. Many education employees noticed the difference immediately, and complained that the company was drifting away from its core purpose. An executive explained the new direction by reflecting on what the new chief technology officer (CTO) stated at a previous meeting:

> Dale [CTO] made a point in the executive meeting the other day, you know, "What kind of company are we?" And his answer to the question is that "We're a services company, not a technical company. A services company."

The absence of "education" from the company's description was striking to the education employees. The executive's phrasing, "not a technical company," was disingenuous and likely meant to placate an anxious group of education employees. The company quickly became focused almost entirely on technological priorities under his leadership. Phrases such as "the need for innovation," "technology solutions," "users," "platforms," and "course templates" replaced educational discourse.

Importantly, these changes did not correspond to things happening outside of the organization in the marketplace or with VL's clients. The changes in the organization's direction were driven directly by the new executives inside of VL. This disconnection from the outside marketplace was striking. For example, some midlevel managers traveled out of state to test-market some of the organization's new courses with nurses in hospitals. The nurses reacted negatively. They hated the presentation of the material, and the computers themselves repelled them. "I'm not touching that 'mouse.' That's disgusting. As long as you call it a mouse, I won't touch it. Call it something else and I might," one nurse complained. At the same demonstration, another nurse attempted repeatedly to move the cursor arrow on the screen by picking up the mouse and rubbing it directly on the computer screen itself. They were not accustomed to using computers as an educational tool. Additionally, the nurses were overwhelmed by the overly complex presentation of the course content. They complained about "too many bells and whistles" or onscreen options. They expected a more straightforward presentation of the material. Executives' prioritization of technology was completely out of touch with what VL's clients were saying.

Though executives were surprised by this feedback, most of the problems with the courses could have easily been handled by the instructional designers and other education members. The instructional designers suggested simplifying the courses' readability and content. In contrast, however, technology members rebuffed such solutions. Technology members seemed unwilling or unable to understand the incompatibility between their own love for technology and the clients' explicit distaste for it. In the end, technology members argued that the nurses could not understand their own needs. Executives decided that VL could solve the problem by focusing even more on technology. Executives allocated almost all of their efforts to building an expensive and time-consuming course-delivery system to which the client would have to adapt.

Unfortunately, VL lost its main client within a year of this decision because the company's courses never improved in ways that satisfied the client's needs. As Lazega (1992) might have predicted, knowledge at VL was political in that it was constructed in ways that reflected the organizational members' preferred types of knowledge and favored interpretations. Technology executives and employees essentially became the audience of their own rhetoric (Heath, 1990). Executives at VL, for instance, won their short-term battles and enforced their personal-knowledge priorities. Their activities, however, shaped the organization's culture in inevitably harmful ways, and contributed to the failure of the company about 18 months later.

Contributions of the Critical Perspective

The case of VL demonstrates the important political features of organizational knowledge. This case highlights the ambiguous, rhetorical, power-laden identity issues noted by critical-knowledge researchers. We draw four implications from the case for researchers and practitioners interested in organizational knowledge.

First, a critical approach to organizational knowledge can help researchers and practitioners see costly political dynamics that they otherwise may not notice. It can be difficult to understand why people sometimes spend a great deal of time clashing over matters that seem to have little personal consequence, to the harm of the organization. At VL, executives wasted enormous amounts of time and money on a knowledge-management system that most members rejected precisely because employees perceived that it robbed them of their worth to the company. Employees most likely avoided using the knowledge-management system because doing so commodified the "part of the employee that is valued (his or her knowledge)" (Zorn & May, 2002, p. 239). A critical approach to knowledge identifies with precision the often-overlooked stakes that drive these interactions and can guide organizations to make more reflective decisions.

Second, organizational leaders and members should not assume that their knowledge and expertise have automatic value to those inside or outside of the organization. Knowledge-driven organizations function as epistemic communities that produce, reproduce, and then defer to their own knowledge in myopic fashion. Our concern about cultural blind spots should not be limited to critical approaches to knowledge, but should be a central issue for anybody interested in taking organizational knowledge seriously. Collective experiences and interpretations can normalize or enforce *the* way of seeing things (Weick, 1995). As a result, practices that become sensible in an organization may appear irrational or incomprehensible to those who were not present in the organization when those knowledge practices and processes were developed. Power struggles may result in knowledge norms and values that are difficult to appreciate from the outside.

Third, members of knowledge-driven organizations should be prepared to engage in and evaluate highly communicative processes about their own and their peers' work. That is, knowledge does not speak for itself. The connection between knowledge and ambiguity creates an interesting dynamic: we should expect that the more dependent an organization is on its members' knowledge, the more subject its culture will be to rhetorical influence. A considerable amount of advocacy, positioning, and interpretation is needed to establish and gauge the significance of various types of knowledge. Knowledge work thus depends upon rhetorical processes.

Fourth, we suggest that organizational leaders should foster collaborative knowledge sharing that helps members to gain something in return. From our view, political activity is not automatically harmful to organizations. That is, both collaboration and competition at VL had political motivations and stakes, but one was more harmful. For instance, some employees collaborated with an implicit agenda of sharing their knowledge to gain prestige, make their job easier, or learn different knowledge. Collaboration helped the employees and the organization. Researchers who emphasize the social and interaction features of knowledge (e.g., Pfeffe & Sutton, 1999) are the most sympathetic to collaborative and mutually beneficial approaches to managing knowledge. In contrast, VL employees who adopted a competitive or guarded posture did not contribute to the organization's overall health. We suggest that employees and managers who are preoccupied with jockeying for symbolic or real positions are not likely to produce innovative organizations as a result.

In conclusion, organizational knowledge has political features which some research approaches do not address. We argue that knowledge is not inherently valuable. Instead, the perceived value of knowledge and expertise requires ongoing communicative work. The fact that certain types of knowledge become viewed as more naturally valuable than others in organizational settings is the result of deeply political processes. Such processes are often lopsided to favor routinely some group's contributions over others. To avoid the darker side of knowledge politics, we suggest that organizational leaders nurture environments that value all knowledge contributions aligned with companies' collective goals.

Note

1. There are many other equally useful ways to categorize this literature explained in other chapters of this book.

References

Alvesson, M. (1993). Organizations as rhetoric: Knowledge-intensive firms and the struggle with ambiguity. *Journal of Management Studies, 30,* 997–1015.

Alvesson, M., & Karreman, D. (2001). Odd couple: Making sense of the curious concept of knowledge management. *Journal of Management Studies, 38,* 995–1018.

Bourdieu, P. (1998). *Practical reason.* Stanford, CA: Stanford University Press.

Clegg, S., & Dunkerley, D. (1979). *Organization, class and control.* London, UK: Heinemann.

Deetz, S. (1990). Reclaiming the subject matter as a guide to mutual understanding: Effectiveness and ethics in interpersonal interaction. *Communication Quarterly, 38,* 226–246.

Deetz, S. (1992). *Democracy in the age of corporate colonization.* Albany, NY: State University of New York.

Deetz, S. (1994). The micro-politics of identity formation in the workplace: The case of a knowledge-intensive firm. *Human Studies, 17,* 23–44.

Deetz, S. (1995). *Transforming communication, transforming business: Building responsive and responsible workplaces.* Cresskill, NJ: Hampton.

Deetz, S. (1998). Discursive formations, strategized subordination, and self-surveillance: An empirical case. In A. McKinlay & K. Starkey (Eds.), *Foucault, management and organizational theory* (pp. 151–172). London, UK: Sage.

Empson, L. (2001a). Introduction: Knowledge management in professional service firms. *Human Relations, 54,* 811–817.

Empson, L. (2001b). Fear of exploitation and fear of contamination: Impediments to knowledge transfer in mergers between professional service firms. *Human Relations, 54,* 839–862.

Foucault, M. (1972). *The archeology of knowledge and the discourse on language.* New York, NY: Pantheon.

Foucault, M. (1980). *Power/knowledge: Selected interviews and other writings.* New York, NY: Pantheon.

Frost, P. J. (1987). Power, politics and influence. In F. M. Jablin, L. L. Putnam, K. H. Roberts, & L. W. Porter (Eds.), *Handbook of organizational communication* (pp. 503–548). Beverly Hills, CA: Sage.

Habermas, J. (1970). On systematically distorted communication. *Inquiry, 13,* 205–218.

Heath, B. (1990). Effects of internal rhetoric on management response to external issues: How corporate culture failed the asbestos industry. *Journal of Applied Communication Research, 18,* 153–167.

Kunda, G. (1992). *Engineering culture: Control and commitment in a high-tech corporation.* Philadelphia, PA: Temple University Press.

Lazega, E. (1992). *Micropolitics of knowledge: Communication and indirect control in work groups.* New York, NY: Aldine de Gruyter.

Lyon, A. (2007). "Putting Patients First": Systematically distorted communication and Merck's marketing of Vioxx. *Journal of Applied Communication Research*, *35*, 376–398.

Mintzberg, H. (1983). *Power in and around organizations*. Englewood Cliffs, NJ: Prentice-Hall.

Mumby, D. K. (2000). Power and politics. In F. M. Jablin & L. L. Putnam (Eds.), *The new handbook of organizational communication: Advances in theory, research, and methods* (pp. 440–502). Thousand Oaks, CA: Sage.

Nonaka, I. (1991). The knowledge-creating company. *Harvard Business Review*, *69*, 96–104.

Pfeffer, J., & Sutton, R. I. (1999). Knowing "what" to do is not enough: Turning knowledge into action. *California Management Review*, *42*, 83–108.

Seeger, M. W., & Ulmer, R. R. (2003). Explaining Enron: Communication and responsible leadership. *Management Communication Quarterly*, *17*, 58–84.

Townley, B. (1993). Foucault, power/knowledge, and its relevance for human resource management. *Academy of Management Review*, *18*, 518–545.

Weick, K. (1995). *Sensemaking in organizations*. Thousand Oaks, CA: Sage.

Zorn, T. E., & May, S. K. (2002). Forum introduction. *Management Communication Quarterly*, *16*, 237–241.

Zorn, T. E., & Taylor, J. R. (2004). Knowledge management and/as organizational communication. In D. Tourish & O. Hargie (Eds.), *Key issues in organizational communication* (pp. 96–112). London, UK: Routledge.

Part II

The Communicative *Connections* of Organizational Knowledge

Chapter 6

Information, Technology, and Knowledge Sharing in Global Organizations

Cultural Differences in Perceptions of Where Knowledge Lies

Paul M. Leonardi

By all accounts, the trend toward using information and communication technologies (ICTs) for the global expansion of organizations is growing swiftly. Many organizations have moved into global operations through captive offshoring (offshoring work to a branch office or wholly owned subsidiary in another country). In fact, a 2005 report by the McKinsey Global Institute has predicted that, by the decade's end, US companies will employ more than 2.3 million offshore knowledge-intensive workers (Farrell & Rosenfeld, 2005). From the perspective of organizational communication research, increases in the captive offshoring of knowledge-intensive tasks that rely heavily on the use of ICTs are hardly surprising. Recent studies have consistently shown that technologies enable the global distribution of knowledge-intensive work by providing individuals access to crucial information (Sakthivel, 2005; Tractinsky & Jarvenpaa, 1995), improving knowledge transfer capabilities among corporate units in different countries (Bhagat, Kedia, Harveston, & Triandis, 2002; Werner, 2002), and permitting new organizational forms that more effectively handle spatial and temporal dispersion (Boudreau, Loch, Robey, & Straub, 1998; Monge & Fulk, 1999).

A good number of authors who study organizations in which people in different parts of the world are working on highly interdependent tasks have concluded that global knowledge sharing is fraught with difficulties (Jarvenpaa & Leidner, 1999; Maznevski & Chudoba, 2000). The problem, as they often argue, is circular in nature. ICT infrastructure, such as telephone lines and the Internet, and software applications that run on them, like groupware, group decision support systems, and even complex computer simulation technologies, enable organizations to internationalize; they create the conditions that make it possible to offshore interdependent knowledge-intensive tasks. But those same technologies also pose major obstacles for global knowledge sharing.

This circular problem is often implicitly understood in terms provided by the transmission metaphor of communication. ICTs create an easily accessible channel for information to flow through space and time. Channels are always limited in their carrying capacity. Only a small extract from the entire body of knowledge necessary to perform a task can flow at a given time. Further, as the knowledge leaves its source (a sender) it becomes de-contextualized and uprooted from the practical space that defines the contours of its meaning, and can best be termed "information." Consequently, when such information arrives at its terminus (a receiver) it appears only in bits and pieces, and is abstracted from its original context and key referents.

Because channels are limited in the types of content they can transmit, some amount of information must be left behind. Researchers of computer-mediated communication have long suggested that because the channels created by ICTs support text and voice predominantly, non-verbal cues are often omitted from transmission (Cornelius & Boos, 2003; Walther, 1994). The omission of non-verbal cues has been shown to impede mutual under-standing by reducing personal self-disclosure and increasing conflict (Cramton, 2001; Hinds & Weisband, 2003). Further, channel limitations can preclude the transfer of entire spaces of knowledge. Knowledge gained from touch, smell, taste, or lived experience cannot be transferred through most ICTs available for use in today's global organizations. A good deal of knowledge is acquired through these sensory stimuli, and when senders attempt to translate this knowledge into text and voice, receivers are not often able to acquire the contextual understanding necessary to use that knowledge in meaningful ways.

Limitations of the transmission metaphor also direct our attention to problems that arise when knowledge is, at one time, encoded into a channel by someone with a particular constellation of socio-cultural under-standings and later decoded by someone who does not share those same orientations. A persistent concern is that a sender from one culture might encode knowledge in a way that will not be decodable by someone from another culture (Gibson & Manuel, 2003; Zakaria, Amelinckw, & Wilemon, 2004). If such cultural misalignment occurs, knowledge is not transferred. A related concern is that culture shapes the way individuals cognitively process information (Markus & Kitayama, 1991; Nisbett, Peng, Choi, & Norenzayan, 2001). As a consequence, individuals who encode or decode information will sample it in different ways, assign dif-ferent weights to what is sampled, and make distinct associations between different pieces of knowledge (Bhagat et al., 2002). The result is that the entirety of knowledge sent from one shore via ICTs may not be received on the other. Such a practically grounded and communicatively situated con-ceptualization helps us to explain why so many problems arise when knowledge is extracted from the context that defines it, forced into an ICT that mutates it, and decoded by someone who has neither the practical nor cultural experience to apprehend it.

It is striking that, despite the subtlety with which these accounts are constructed, few researchers seem to consider that people who are attempting to transfer knowledge and share it with others may not even agree on what knowledge is. Imagine the following (and heretofore entirely unrealistic) scenario. Person A wants to transmit a dog (metaphor for knowledge) to person B. Person A finds a teleporter that breaks the dog down into subatomic particles, which are sent across space and time and reassembled on the other side. He puts the dog in the transporter and presses the "send" button. In our current conceptualization of knowledge transfer, we say that a problem of transmission occurs if person B receives the dog but it has only three legs, it has no tail, or it has two heads. Indeed, our theories can explain, in intricate and varied ways, why the dog that went into the transporter is not as complete as the dog that came out on the other end. But what if person B receives a monkey? She calls person A and says, "I thought you were going to send a dog, but I got a monkey." Person A responds, "I did send a dog, check it again." She checks. The monkey is the same weight, the same size, and the same color as the dog person A says he sent – but it's a monkey. In this scenario, the problem is not with the transfer process; no content was atrophied in the transmission. The problem is that persons A and B do not agree on what constitutes a dog. If they continue to have different ideas of what a dog is, no amount of refinement or improvement in the transfer process that eliminates channel noise (e.g., more advanced technology, more description of the dog's characteristics, etc.) will help. Where one person sees a dog, the other person will see a monkey.

The knowledge-sharing problem that this metaphor raises is one of semantic incompatibility. It comes as no shock to most that people from different cultures often have markedly distinct understandings of concepts like family, fidelity, faith, and friendship. So why wouldn't people from different cultures also have divergent understandings about what counts as knowledge? If people have unique understandings of what knowledge is, an important attending concern is that they will have different perceptions of where knowledge lies. Just as dogs lie on the ground and monkeys (the arboreal ones, at least) lie on branches, thing X, which is considered to be knowledge by person A, is likely to lie in a different place than thing Y, which is understood to be knowledge by person B. The issue of where knowledge lies is of great importance for theories of knowledge sharing in global organizations, particularly those engaged in offshoring. In most offshoring arrangements (even those that are captive), there is little direct interpersonal exchange of knowledge. Instead, people on one shore simply point each other to locations where they are likely to find the knowledge they need to do their tasks (Dibbern, Goles, Hirschheim, & Jayatilaka, 2004). Research shows that people variously point to images or models (Leonardi & Bailey, 2008), knowledge management systems (Carmel & Agarwal, 2002), or written documentation and contracts (Gopal, Sivaramakrishnan, Krishnan, & Mukhopadhyay, 2003) as loci for knowledge. But if people from different cultures have distinct conceptualizations of what counts as knowledge, and, consequently, unique beliefs about where knowledge lies, one person may look in a location designated by another and find nothing there that she considers knowledge. Or worse, when pointed toward a particular location by a colleague on a different shore, she might grow frustrated, thinking "of course there is no knowledge here," and form disparaging opinions about that colleague's competence, which, consequently, can cause her to question the soundness of the organization's offshoring plan altogether.

The goal of this chapter is to explore how cultural differences in perceptions of where knowledge lies can have adverse effects on global knowledge sharing in organizations. Rather than take for granted that people on different shores each conceptualize knowledge similarly and look for it in the same places, I begin with the assumption that cultural differences may compel workers in the same company to think of knowledge in distinct ways and to look for it in diverse places. This approach focuses attention on how people within the same organization come to think about knowledge in varied ways. Drawing on empirical examples from a large automotive engineering firm, I explore how different conceptualizations held by engineers in the US, Mexico, and India about what knowledge is and where it lies stifled sharing, impeded learning, and led to general animosity among members of the organization who needed to work collaboratively to design and test vehicles. I conclude this chapter by discussing the implications of these findings for theories of technology, knowledge sharing, and organizational communication.

Information Technology and Offshoring in Automotive Engineering

The International Automobile Corporation (IAC)[1] is a large automobile manufacturer headquartered in the United States. IAC is one of a growing number of companies, such as Intel, Dell, General Electric, Microsoft, and others, who have formed captive offshore facilities in a number of countries around the world. In contrast to offshoring-sourcing (see, for example, Kotabe & Swan, 1994), a captive offshore arrangement is a company-owned offshore operation in which the individuals who work at the offshore sites are full-time salaried employees of the focal organization.

In this chapter, I focus on the work of performance engineers (PEs) who are responsible for using simulation tools to validate and test parts as they are assembled into complete vehicles. Performance engineering work is comprised of two major tasks: model building and model analysis. To build simulation models, PEs convert computer-aided drawings (CAD) into finite element models by dividing the geometry of a part into a collection of discrete portions called finite elements. The elements are joined together by shared nodes. Nodes are the locations where values of certain load cases will later be approximated. The collection of nodes and finite elements together is known as the "mesh." This mesh is programmed to contain the material and structural properties which define how the structure will react to certain loading conditions (i.e., heat, stress, etc.). Once a mathematical finite element model is built, PEs begin to analyze it by submitting the model to a solver – a software package that performs computational analyses on the finite element models.

I chose to study the work of PEs because they are the engineers who are most active in using information technologies that permit the offshoring of tasks to foreign locations. In the eyes of IAC managers, the mathematical nature of model building and analysis, paired with the availability of advanced technology applications, VOIP, FTP sites, instant messaging, collaboration tools, and networked databases, means that PEs should be able to easily share work over geographic distance. As one senior manager commented:

> We've paid lots of money to get technologies in place to help support our global work. We've got very expensive infrastructures that are among the best in the world. So we shouldn't see many problems with transferring work back and forth. The tools are all in place to share work, knowledge, and learning. In other words, we've been careful to get the right technologies in place so now all people need to do is use them to collaborate effectively across the globe.

As IAC managers regularly noted, offshoring is made possible, in large part, by the move away from using physical (steel) models for analyzing vehicle dynamics and toward the use of mathematically-based simulation technologies and the use of advanced ICTs.[2]

This chapter focuses on the ways that PEs at IAC engineering centers in the US and Mexico offshored work to engineers in India. Apart from their size, the US and Mexican centers were quite similar. Both locations were responsible for the development of vehicle platforms. A vehicle platform is a common architecture upon which different models (called programs) for various automotive brands can be based. PEs at both engineering centers were grouped into identical functional organizations that were responsible for various aspects of vehicle performance. In 2003, IAC decided to begin its own captive offshoring operation in India. The India center was explicitly created by IAC to be a captive offshore service provider for engineering centers that worked on their own vehicle programs. The India center had neither its own vehicle platforms nor production facilities.

As program-based engineering centers, both the US and Mexico centers sent tasks offshore to the India center. This relationship is illustrated by the flow following the solid arrows in Figure 6.1. Although the task assignment was unidirectional, knowledge sharing was not. To complete work successfully, the India center had to obtain knowledge from either the US or the Mexico center. In addition to the knowledge they acquired from

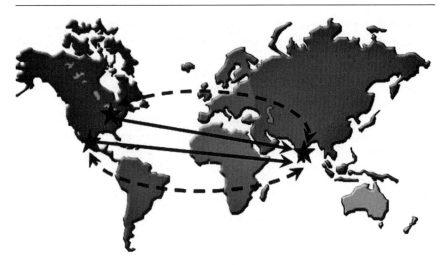

Figure 6.1 Global transfer of tasks and sharing of knowledge at IAC.

Note
Straight solid lines represent sharing of tasks (unidirectional) and curved dashed lines represent sharing of knowledge (bidirectional).

these two centers on how to do the task, the India center gained important knowledge about the vehicle's performance in the context of actually conducting the task. This knowledge had to be sent back onshore along with the completed task so that the engineers in the US or Mexico could make recommendations for improved vehicle design. This meant that the flow of knowledge was bidirectional (illustrated in Figure 6.1 by the dashed lines).

In the following sections, I demonstrate that each of the three engineering centers had a unique understanding of what constituted knowledge and, consequently, where that knowledge could be found. I explore how cultural norms for communication and interaction helped to shape these conceptualizations of knowledge and where it lies, and I then consider how these differences among the sites made difficult the collaboration between these globally distributed centers.

Cultural Differences in Perceptions of Where Knowledge Lies

US Center: Knowledge Lies in the Head

Over the years, many scholars in the organizational sciences have given prominence to the individualism–collectivism distinction between national cultures (Early & Singh, 2000; Triandis, 1995). Individualism can be defined as a communicative pattern that consists of loosely linked individuals who view themselves as independent of collectives, and who are motivated by their own preferences. Collectivism, by contrast, is often defined as a communicative pattern that consists of closely linked individuals who see themselves as belonging to collectives, and who are motivated by the norms imposed by those collectives. Following the work of Hofstede (1980), scholars have argued that the individualism–collectivism dimension of cultural variation is the major distinguishing characteristic in the way that various societies of the world analyze social behavior and process information.

Scholars frequently characterize the US as a highly individualistic national culture (Gudykunst et al., 1996; Triandis, 1995). At IAC, one need only walk around the offices occupied by PEs to see vestiges of this individualistic orientation toward knowledge. A good number of PEs display diplomas from undergraduate and graduate studies, and many more proudly exhibit certificates earned for the completion of in-house training courses. There are also many signs hung in jest on the walls of people's cube that read "Weld Guru" or "Brake Booster Boss." When asked why PEs were so eager to display these indicators of individual accomplishment, one informant responded:

> You know, this stuff just tells other people what you know. It's all sort of like displaying your credentials so other people know if you have some knowledge or some kind of expertise that other people need. I mean, no one really says that, but if you see someone got their [mechanical engineering degree] from MIT and you know that he's got lots of experience in vehicle dynamics, you might say, "hey, I'll go to him if I need to learn something about a problem I'm having." It's all subtle, but it helps to just point out who knows what.

As this PE (and many more like him) regularly observed, engineers at the US center were very clear in their understanding that knowledge was something that belonged to people.

Banal though this observation may seem, PEs' belief that knowledge existed in the heads of people who were experts directly influenced the way they went about acquiring knowledge. PEs often sought knowledge from other people through both face-to-face and mediated communication. In most instances, PEs were working on solving a vehicle analysis problem alone at their workstations. When PEs grew frustrated enough to seek help, they would often turn to me (sitting quietly behind them documenting their every action) and say something like the statements made, at separate times, by three PEs:

> "I can't figure this out. I better go find someone who knows it."

> "The file has some penetrations[3] in it. I need to talk to [the DE]. He probably knows why this is happening."

"The last three iterations of the model haven't produced any better results. I'm going to talk to [another PE] because he might know how to fix it. He's really knowledgeable about this."

In each case, the PE was certain that the knowledge he or she was seeking lay in some other PE's head, as opposed to a book, a set of routines, or a communal data repository.

To build and analyze a complex simulation model required a considerable amount of technical (how to use the software) and domain (how to do the engineering analysis) knowledge. Once a model was complete (either a physical or a mathematical one), the technical knowledge that was used to produce the model remained with the PE who built it. However, the domain knowledge used to produce the model became embedded in the model itself. To give a concrete example, a knowledgeable PE might know from his training and experience (domain knowledge) that to build an effective frontal crash model he needed to use a dense finite element mesh.[4] The technical knowledge he used to build the model with a software program (which commands to use, what order to use them in) could not be deciphered by dissecting the model later on, but the domain knowledge that the model should have a dense finite element mesh could be seen by examining the model.

For this reason, one might expect that PEs who wanted to gain the domain knowledge possessed by someone else might not have to talk with them directly, but could instead look at the models they built. But due to the strongly individualistic culture of the US center, PEs were very territorial about their models. As one PE commented:

> When I build a model it's like my intellectual property. Ok, ultimately it belongs to IAC. But I'm the one that built it. I don't want anyone just being able to go and look at it and use it how they want. I mean, I'm happy to share and explain it but they just need to come and talk to me.

Institutional IT policies at the US center reinforced this individualistic orientation that favored individual ownership of models. Each PE was assigned a unique user name and password, and was required to store his models in password secure drives. PEs were strictly forbidden from sharing their passwords with one another, and IT policy precluded the creation of group-level passwords such that any one member of a workgroup could log in to any other member's files. Thus, if one PE wanted to look at another PE's model, he would have to ask him or her to fetch the model and then send it to him by e-mail or FTP server. Obviously, this policy and its attending practices encouraged PEs to talk directly to others and, for all intents and purposes, make fact out of the belief that knowledge only existed and was accessible by extracting it from someone else's head.

Mexico Center: Knowledge Lies in the Output

In contrast to the US, Mexico is often considered to be a prime example of a country whose culture is defined by a strong collectivist orientation (Buriel, 1993; Shkodriani & Gibbons, 1995). Studies have also shown that workplace cultures in Mexico carry strong overt preferences for collectivist action (Hodge & Coronodo, 2006; Lindsley, 1999). PEs at IAC's Mexico center were acutely aware that anthropologists, psychologists, and communication theorists viewed them as members of a communally-based society. As one informant commented on my first visit, after he learned that I had spent time observing engineers at the US center:

> I bet you'll find that we're much closer and more group-centered than the engineers in the US. All of the studies say that about us, right? We'll I think they're true. You'll find that there is much more talking going on here and we're all a lot closer and more friendly than if you are in the office in Michigan.

At first glance, the evidence seemed to corroborate this bold proclamation by the Mexican informant. The data reveal that PEs at the Mexico center did actively share knowledge with one another. However, unlike their US counterparts, they had a strong understanding that knowledge lay not in people's heads, but in the outputs of their labor. For PEs working on vehicle analysis, the outputs that they normally referenced were simulation results and finite element models. Informants commented that they could typically gather greater domain-specific knowledge by examining the models a colleague had built as opposed to talking with that colleague directly:

> If you want to learn something it's best to look at someone's work. Find out someone who did something similar to what you need to do and go look at his model. You can examine the model and that is going to be more effective and more efficient. For example, if someone tells you that they found that some certain shape of a part gave the best performance that's helpful. But maybe your problem is a bit different. So if you can look at their models and see the steps they went through – I mean the different iterations of the test – then you can start to pick up some trends that will help you to design your parts better.

In addition to the perceived advantage of following a particular design solution through a series of iterations, Mexican PEs also believed that knowledge had a comparative basis. In other words, if one talked to another PE directly, that PE was likely to tell you what worked for her. Another PE would discuss what sorts of solutions had met her needs. But without direct comparison of these described solutions to performance metrics, Mexican PEs felt that they could not tell which engineer's knowledge was better, or whose was most pertinent to the problem at hand:

> It's like everyone can tell you a different answer and everyone can seem to be very knowledgeable. But if you don't look at their results, you can't tell who is really the most knowledgeable. So it is better to look at their models than to talk to them. Get a model from person one, and a model from person two, and compare them side by side. See whose solution gave you better performance given the parameters you've set and then you can really tell. The knowledge that is in the models is more objective than the knowledge you get by talking to people.

This strong statement underscored a common distinction made by PEs at the Mexico center between what they called "espoused knowledge" and "demonstrated knowledge." To be sure, PEs valued demonstrated knowledge over espoused knowledge, and believed that the former lay in the output of people's work and it is there that one should go to uncover it.

The collectivist orientation permeating the Mexico center had, over time, diffused into a number of shared practices and policies. Among the most important for knowledge sharing was open access to others' models. It was a strong norm at the center for PEs to enter each other's files without permission and review each other's simulation results. Although PEs had their own unique user names and passwords to protect their documents, it was common practice for informants to store the results of their simulation analyses on a shared drive. The IT department at the Mexico center provided common passwords to these directories so that they could be accessed by anyone at any time. Indeed, PEs espoused a very different relationship with their models and the results of their analysis than did their compatriots at the US center:

> When you build and analyze a model it's an opportunity for you and for other people to learn what works and what doesn't. You should share your model around if other people want it. But most of the time we're too busy to do that so you can just put it in the [common directory] and then if someone needs it they can look at it later.

Thus, a common collectivist belief in the value of sharing work and the notion that models belonged to the group rather than to any individual encouraged and was reinforced by IT policies that made it easy for PEs to share the outputs of their simulations. The chatter and informal talk that took place in the office provided a useful venue for PEs to learn about who had done what kinds of jobs in the past, even if they didn't learn any specific domain knowledge from those conversations. But knowing who did what allowed PEs to form a mental directory that later helped them to navigate the electronic directories to find a person's output and examine it.

During my tenure at the Mexico center, I routinely observed PEs opening each other's models and studying their outputs. On occasion, PEs would add documentation to their output in anticipation of others examining it later and wanting to learn from it. Together, the collectivist orientation prevalent at the Mexico center encouraged and endorsed an understanding that knowledge lay in the products of people's work. As one PE put it so succinctly: "If you look, all the things you see are arrangements of knowledge in some form or another. You just have to look at them to learn yourself what the builder knew. Knowledge belongs to a community."

India Center: Knowledge Lies in the Position

While India is often viewed to tilt in the direction of a collectivist culture (Perlow & Weeks, 2002), most observers agree that the cultural dimension that most strongly pervades everyday life, whether on the street, in the home, or at the workplace, is the ingrained respect for social hierarchy (Parish, 1996; Zakaria, 2006). As Mines (1994, p. 317) notes: "In India, hierarchy structures all relationships and proscribes autonomy." Research conducted in Indian organizations has described, for more than half a century now, the pervasive effects that the cultural inscription of hierarchical thinking has on working relations (Rice, 1953; Sahay, 1998; Walsham, 2002). Such a cultural sensitivity toward and respect for hierarchy is enabled and perpetuated by a deeply seated Hindu caste system, which has been shown to lead Indian nationals to be cognizant and respectful of the status differences inherent in any social relationship (Srinivas, 1984).

At IAC's India center, PEs were acutely aware of where they stood in the center's status hierarchy. During my two months at the India center, I often encountered PEs running into problems building or analyzing simulation models. The reasons for these problems were varied. In some cases, the Indian PEs simply did not have enough information from the requesting engineer (either in the US or in Mexico) in order to complete the assigned task. In other cases, the Indian PE did not have enough domain knowledge (in crashworthiness or aerodynamics, for example) to effectively build or analyze the model. If this were the case, it was often because the engineer in India had never seen or worked with the kind of analysis that the engineer in the US or in Mexico was requesting.

When Indian PEs found themselves in a situation where they did not have the domain knowledge to solve a particular problem, they were often quite candid with me, the observer. They would say things like, "I don't know how to do this," or "this problem seems to be more complex than I can know how to solve." I would often ask them who they believed did have the knowledge to solve the problem. Consider the following responses:

> "Oh, my manager will know the answer to this."

> "It's definitely my manager. I will talk to him about this."

> "My manager will be able to figure this out."

> "I will have a conference with my manager. He can give me some knowledge about how to do this."

Such statements contain an unwavering belief that someone of a higher status position will have the knowledge to solve the particular problem at hand. After conducting research at the US and Mexico centers, I was quite surprised to hear this type of response. It was a norm, rather than an exception, for PEs in the US and in Mexico to verbally denigrate the skills and knowledge of their managers. In India, by contrast, PEs seemed quite assured that their managers could solve most engineering problems, and that they were key holders of important domain knowledge.

This tendency to believe that knowledge lay in one's position had consequences for PEs' daily work. For example, I spent time observing a PE in the HVAC group who was conducting an airflow analysis. The analysis used a simulation to determine whether the force of air emanating from the vents on the dashboard was sufficient to cool the driver and the front passenger. After running the simulation, the PE opened a 3D rendering of the mathematical model, which depicted air flowing out of the dashboard vents and through the passenger compartment. After spending some time looking at the 3D rendering, the PE turned to me and commented:

> Basically, these are the flow lines. What happens is that when the flow comes it will go through the ducts and from the outlet it will come out. But we need for people to be at certain angles so that the air either it hits chest, face or lap position which are our target points. So, to cool it effectively, rotation of the vent should meet the target – that is head, chest and lap. So if it's not meeting the target it won't hit you on the face or lap, you won't get cold air, so that is the reason. So we cannot run the analysis with just this vent, because what will happen is the place where this is happening it will show regulation of the temperature because when you, this is just for the flow when you do it with the temperature, see, the velocity here it is very high. So this is a problem.

The problem that the PE referred to is that the model was run by simulating airflow from only one vent in the center of the dashboard. As the PE observed, this particular model would not give an accurate representation of the force of airflow because it omitted an analysis with the other vents. The implication of such an omission on the model was that if a decision about the force of the airflow was made on this analysis alone it would be incorrect, because it failed to consider the alternate sources of airflow in the passenger compartment. The PE copied the 3D rendering into a Power-Point presentation and wrote several notes in the margin indicating that the analysis was run with only airflow from one vent modeled. He sent the PowerPoint deck via e-mail to his manager.

The next day, the PE and his manager sat down to review the results of the airflow analysis. They began by opening the PowerPoint that the PE had created the day before. The manager looked at the image and commented:

MANAGER: Why was this run done with only the vent in the center stack operating?

PE: This vent was the only one included in the geometry that was sent from the US center.

MANAGER: It is not a sufficient analysis because it is missing the other dash vents, so this model of the airflow will not be accurate.

PE: Yes, I see.

MANAGER: Did you notice this when you were running the analysis?

PE: Yes

MANAGER: Why didn't you fix it then?

PE: Yes sir. I thought I should review it with you before I made any changes.

MANAGER: But you knew it was a problem?

PE: Yes.

MANAGER: So now we've lost a day because you did not repair the model before running it.

PE: I just thought it was best to ask you because you might be knowing better whether this should be adjusted instead of me just doing it without asking.

What is striking about this interchange, and the many more like it that I observed, was that the PE indicated just the day before that he knew the model was inaccurate and that it needed to be fixed. Despite this know-ledge, he was reluctant to make any changes without the explicit consent and recommendation of his manager. The PE felt that because his manager had a higher status position, he would be more knowledgeable about the analysis and would be in a better position to determine whether or not the model needed to be changed. The interchange, however, shows the tension that can arise when a PE has sufficient domain knowledge to complete the task but does not believe that he is as knowledgeable as someone with a higher status position. To wit, we see the manager growing frustrated that the PE did not take more initiative to complete the task on his own. This problem was common, even between PEs and managers who were both Indian nationals. The hierarchical nature of the work at the India center led to very clear culturally-bound understandings that knowledge was not the province of individuals (e.g., some were brighter, more informed, or more recently educated than others), but that knowledge lay in one's position in a status-driven hierarchy of relations.

Problems Arising When Attempting To Share Knowledge Across Cultures

US and India

The task-based relationship between PEs in the US and India normally began when an engineer in the US sent a statement of requirements (SOR) offshore to the India center. Typically, this SOR was a one-page standardized format that included a brief summary of the task that was to be completed, a list of parameters that the India PE should follow when completing the task, a list of the files that were needed to conduct the analysis and their locations, and the date upon which the task should be completed. US PEs sent the SOR form to India, and the Indian PE would read it. If she did not know how to do the task, she would seek knowledge from someone in a higher status position within the India center. This person was usually a manager.

The PEs at the India center rarely sought knowledge from PEs in the US, opting instead to discuss problems with their immediate managers. Indian PEs perceived (and often commented) that, as the newest engineering center in IAC's network, and as the only center without its own vehicle program, their center was the lowest status of all of IAC's centers. Although PEs recognized that, despite sharing their same title, the US PEs were higher status by virtue of working at the US center, they often chose to seek knowledge from their immediate managers in India because they held a higher status position in the IAC hierarchy. Thus, PEs would often seek knowledge about how to complete a task from their managers instead of PEs in the US, and would only contact the US PE when it came time to share the knowledge gained from the analysis of the simulation model.

As one might imagine, this knowledge-sharing process was not often smooth. Indian PEs were tasked by US PEs to run an analysis and share the knowledge gained from that analysis with the engineer who requested it. But the Indian PEs perceived that they were in a lower status position than the US PEs, and, because knowledge lay in positions rather than in people, that it was, as many said, "not my place" to pass knowledge to them. Consequently, Indian PEs often tried to convince their managers to report the results of an analysis or to make suggestions for vehicle design. But the managers were too busy to do this work, and normally did not have a deep enough understanding of the task request or the work that the Indian PE did in order to make it. Thus, the job of passing knowledge to the US center often fell squarely on the Indian PE.

The following example illustrates this difficulty. An Indian PE received a SOR from the US center requesting that he analyze the crashworthiness of the front end of a cross-over vehicle. The Indian PE read through the SOR and everything looked straightforward. Upon reviewing the results, he noticed that too much of the energy generated during the crash was being passed into the occupant compartment. By examining the load curves and reviewing the animations of the simulation, he determined that one of the primary causes of the poor performance was that a bracket that affixed the radiator to the chassis bent during the impact, causing the radiator to separate and intrude on the firewall, which in turn intruded into the occupant compartment. As the PE was analyzing these results, he turned to me and said:

> The problem here is the bracket is failing. I think that the problem is the design. There was a bracket like this that failed on [another project he had worked on in the past] and the US PE eventually fixed it by removing the holes in it and changing the geometry so it couldn't bend. I think this is the same problem.

Clearly, the PE knew the cause of the problem and had a direct design solution that would solve it. For two hours he tried to talk to his manager, hoping that his manager would corroborate his assessment of the situation. After several e-mails to the manager and after stopping by his desk three times, the PE decided that he would not be able to talk with him before the report was due to the engineer at the US center. So, the PE spent the remainder of the afternoon writing a report of his findings, which indicated that the crash test did not produce the desired performance because the bracket failed. I asked him why he hadn't recommended the design change to the bracket that he mentioned to me. He responded:

> Oh, that is not my place to make that recommendation. I tried to talk to my manager to verify if that was a good solution so he could make the recommendation, but I could not reach him before the deadline came. It's OK. He [the PE from the US center] requested that we were finding if the test met the performance objectives. I am telling him it did not. He is knowing more about this analysis than me because he is a higher position so he would know better what the correct change should be.

The PE believed that the knowledge about whether the design change of the bracket was a good idea lay in a position that was higher than his own. Because his attempts to cull this knowledge from his immediate manager (a higher status position) failed, he felt it was "not his place" to make this recommendation to the US PE (who he perceived was also of higher status), and thus opted to only report the results of the simulation.

One month after this incident, I had the opportunity to return to the US center and talk with the PE who received the results from India indicating the bracket failure. He expressed his frustration at the work of the Indian PE:

> I got this result back from him that showed a failure in the bracket. Great. That's wonderful [said sarcastically]. But it's like, if you see that the bracket failed, why don't you fix it? I mean it's pretty basic. I thought he would call me up or send an e-mail telling me what kind of design change to make ... We're sending work over to people who aren't that bright or who just don't have the ability to do this kind of work. I mean, this is simple, but he couldn't even figure out how to change it. He just told me what was wrong. If he didn't know, he should get the knowledge he needs by talking with me...

What happened here? The Indian PE understood that the bracket had to be redesigned, and even had an idea about how to do the redesign. But because he believed that the authority to possess this knowledge lay in a position that was superior to his own, he would not make the recommendation to the US PE who he perceived to have more status. The US PE did not see the locus of knowledge similarly. He was surprised that the Indian PE would not make a recommendation to him. Instead, he took the lack of a recommendation as evidence that the Indian PE didn't have the knowledge (in his own head) about how to do the redesign. However, as we've seen, the Indian PE did indeed have the knowledge, but didn't recognize it as authoritative enough to share with the US PE.

In short, neither PE questioned whether the other had the same understanding of where knowledge lay. There was no technology problem – the files were all transferred correctly, the information was not lost in the channel, the two engineers could talk easily by phone or e-mail if they decided to do so – and there was no encoding or decoding problem – a PE on one end didn't see knowledge sent by the PE on the other end and misinterpret its contents. Instead, each engineer expected knowledge to be in a different place, and when they looked in that place they didn't find it. Consequently, the US PE became frustrated and formed a perception that the Indian PE "wasn't that bright" and "didn't have the ability" to do the work, and, based on this perception, became disenchanted with the off-shoring arrangement and declined to send future work to India. The Indian PE was also frustrated. He didn't understand why he never received more work from the US PE.

Mexico and India

Mexican PEs rarely used any formal SOR form when sending work to the India center. A typical request for work was made in an e-mail. The Mexican PE would ask an Indian PE to perform a certain task, and would indicate what files she needed to download to do it. In the e-mail, the Mexican PE would also indicate a location where the Indian PE could download reference models. A reference model was simply a model that the Mexican PE had built or analyzed at an earlier time in a way that was very similar to what he was requesting that the Indian PE do in the current e-mail. Mexican PEs believed that the knowledge the Indian PEs needed to complete the task lay in the output of previously completed tasks:

> I always send over a reference model when I send the work. That way the Indian PE can just open it up and take a look at it and see what we did. It is just an example like a template that they can follow. I think the reference models are very helpful.

Indian PEs, on the whole, appreciated the reference models; they were helpful guides from which much information could be gleaned. But because the Indian PEs were not as highly skilled as the Mexican PEs, they could not always easily extract the knowledge that was implicitly coded into the reference models. For example, the Indian PE might observe from the reference model that the Mexican PE used welds spaced at 15-mm intervals along the side of a flange. The Indian PE might interpret that this wide interval was chosen to reduce vehicle mass (more welds result in more vehicle weight, which reduces fuel economy). Upon making this interpretation, she might decide in the future that if she needed to add more welds to strengthen the attachment of this flange stronger, she could indeed do so as long as she recognized the costs associated with adding mass to the vehicle. What she would not be able to know from looking at the reference model, though, was that the reason the Mexican PE spaced the welds at this interval was that, due to the flange's placement in the vehicle, the welding gun could not fit in between other parts to make the welds at any smaller intervals. Whereas a Mexican PE who was seeking knowledge from the reference model would have seen the weld spacing and known that the interval was chosen for manufacturing concerns, an Indian PE would likely not be able to make this interpretation. Thus, much of the knowledge embedded in the reference model was lost.

Although some amount of information could be learned from the reference models, Indian PEs, because of both their culturally shaped perceptions of knowledge and their inability to decipher information presented in an output, did not often perceive them to be locations where knowledge lay. Instead, Indian PEs often expressed frustration that they could not learn directly from their higher status Mexican counterparts:

PEs at the Mexico center are good engineers and have higher positions than us, so they know more normally. We want to learn from them. But many times they only send their models to us to look at. It is good to get details from the model, but how can you get the knowledge you need? They are in a position to teach us, so we would like to learn more by discussing directly with them. So we try to call them instead of looking at the models.

As this PE indicates, engineers at the India center did not perceive that knowledge lay in the reference models received from Mexico. For this reason, the Indian PEs would often call Mexican PEs directly on the phone during hours that they overlapped in their offices to ask for clarification and to request knowledge directly from them.

The following example illustrates the problems that these differential beliefs in the location of knowledge brought to the collaborative relationship between Mexico and India. On a Thursday morning, an Indian PE arrived at the office to find an e-mail request from a Mexican engineer. The Mexican PE asked the Indian PE to do an analysis of whether the fuel tank on a sports car would crack and leak its contents in the event of a rear-impact collision. The Mexican PE included several reference models, and their related graphs, which had been constructed for a similar test on a compact sedan several years earlier. The Indian PE opened the models and graphs and spent nearly an hour examining them. He then turned to me and said, "One thing I don't know is what angle the fuel tank can be placed at. I will call him later today for clarification." The Indian PE waited until 6:30 p.m. (when it was 8 a.m. in Mexico) to call the Mexican PE via phone. After two minutes of pleasantries, the conversation turned toward the model:

INDIAN PE: I am not sure what angles are acceptable for placement of the tank?
MEXICAN PE: Did you look at the models I sent you?
INDIAN PE: Yes, but they are not showing it.
MEXICAN PE: All the information you need is in those models.
INDIAN PE: I did look into them.
MEXICAN PE: If you compare the angles across iterations 4, 5, and 6, the acceptable parameters should be there?
INDIAN PE: Yes.
MEXICAN PE: Can you find them?
INDIAN PE: I will look more.

After hanging up the phone, the Indian PE expressed his frustration with the call:

The model is not so helpful, I don't think. What can you learn from it? I think he is knowing what the correct angle is so he could only tell it to me or put it in the e-mail. I think he is knowing this because he has been working on this job before for a different vehicle and he is an experienced engineer.

Later, the Mexican PE expressed his own frustration:

> This problem is very common. They [the Indian PEs] don't look at the models. All of the information is right there for them to learn. We've put all the knowledge in there and we are sharing it with them. They like to call and are very needy. So it takes a lot of our time to talk with them and it is frustrating. I have other things to do. I want them just to do the work, that is why I sent it. I don't want to be teaching them all the time. They should look to the model to learn.

Mexican PEs continually voiced their dissatisfaction with the offshoring arrangement, indicating that they spent more time teaching and communicating with engineers from India on how to build and analyze models than it would take for them simply to do the task themselves.

As this example makes clear, differences in perceptions of where knowledge lay often went unnoticed in interactions between the engineering centers. Engineers on both sides became frustrated; Mexican PEs were frustrated because Indian PEs were not finding the knowledge in the output they sent, while Indian PEs were frustrated because they were continually told to look for knowledge in the reference models, a place where they thought knowledge could not be found. Consequently, they believed that Mexican PEs were not taking their concerns seriously or dismissing them by not taking the time to pass knowledge from their superior status position to the lower status position of the Indian PEs.

Conclusion: Toward a Location-based Understanding of Knowledge

I began this chapter by suggesting that most perspectives on global knowledge sharing within organizations highlight the difficulty that arises when knowledge is miscommunicated, when it atrophies in a communication channel, or when people on the receiving end can't decode the knowledge in the same way that it was encoded by the sender. The common assumption upon which these perspectives are based is that people agree on what counts as knowledge and where that knowledge is to be found. The empirical examples drawn from the daily lives of IAC workers question this assumption. Engineers in the US, Mexico, and India each had different culturally shaped perceptions about where knowledge lay. Engineers at one site believed that engineers at the other site agreed that knowledge could be found in the same place. What they did not recognize was that engineers at different sites looked for knowledge in different places. Consequently, engineers on both shores were frustrated. Engineers onshore who sent knowledge thought that people on the other side just didn't get it and began to think of them as incompetent, while engineers offshore felt that their counterparts onshore didn't send them knowledge and were not interested in helping them to learn.

The problems that arose at IAC were not technological. As discussed above, IAC had a very sophisticated technological infrastructure, and spent a great deal of money on ICTs and other technologies to help engineers around the world talk with one another and share their work. Yet as it became evident that engineers in all three locations were becoming frustrated with the offshoring arrangement, IAC management responded by spending more money on the technological infrastructure. As one manager commented:

> People aren't as happy working with India as we'd like. A large part of that seems to be that they can't communicate effectively across the time difference and the geographical difference. So we'll get better tools, better FPT sites, better software for instant messaging and to find people's contact information so they can communicate better and share information and knowledge with one another better.

Even engineers themselves viewed the problems of knowledge sharing to be technological in nature. They proclaimed the usefulness of video-conferencing and real-time groupware tools, and encouraged their managers to invest in these technological solutions. Indeed, certain upgrades in the hardware and software that IAC used to connect the engineering centers would have been beneficial. But the central problem was not that knowledge was lost in the channel because the current ICTs didn't have features to support its transfer, or that cues were filtered out during communication events such that people on the other end could not accurately convey their message. Rather, the problem was that engineers in each location looked in the traditional places where they believed knowledge to lie, and found no knowledge placed there by colleagues on a different shore. Even if more advanced technologies help to increase the fidelity of a message sent from one shore to the other, if the sender and receiver are not looking in the same place for it, even the most perfectly transmitted message will be of little use.

The findings presented herein suggest that researchers of organizational knowledge may have much to gain by including the location of knowledge in theories of knowledge transfer. Currently, there is little attention paid to the idea that knowledge transfer problems may arise as frequently because of differences in perceptions of where knowledge lies as they do because of misinterpretations, technological constraints, or lack of context-specific cues to decode it. This chapter has shown that cultural orientations are one important factor determining how people come to believe that knowledge can be found in a certain location. Researchers should work to discover whether there are other factors, perhaps institutional or structural, that influence perceptions of where knowledge lies.

These findings also have a number of implications for managers of global organizations. First, managers should recognize that problems of knowledge transfer cannot be mitigated simply by implementing new information and communication technologies. As these findings have shown, even in an organization possessing the most state-of-the-art communication tools, knowledge-sharing problems abound because people have differences in their understanding of where knowledge lies. To combat this problem, managers should help their workers to make explicit their knowledge-search practices. At the very least, recognition that someone in a different country may search for knowledge in a different place may help to alleviate some of the tensions documented in this study. Second, managers should also recognize that although the digital artifacts with which people work may appear quite robust, they require some domain knowledge to extract the assumptions embedded in them. Thus, organizations should invest in creating environments in which individuals can discuss and debrief one another about the artifacts that they send back and forth, instead of relying solely on the artifacts themselves to convey important task-related information. Third, managers should recognize that even though the people to whom work is offshored might have adequate computer and analytical skills, their understandings of the product and the tasks needed to produce it may initially be quite limited. Thus, attending to the overall imbalance in knowledge in the work system is an important first step to improving the flow of work amongst geographically distributed locations.

Effective knowledge sharing is essential for global organizations. Without it, units operating on different shores would not be able to collaborate and the organization would miss many opportunities to leverage the unique leanings generated by individuals with different orientations, perspectives, and experiences. Certainly, ICTs are critical to global knowledge sharing; they provide the infrastructure that makes transfer possible and enables the distribution of tasks and responsibilities across space and time. But even the best technological infrastructures will fail to bring about effective knowledge sharing if the people who use them do not agree on what knowledge is or where it lies. This chapter provides a call for researchers and practitioners to develop theories and strategies that assure that what is sent as a dog from one side doesn't arrive looking like a monkey on the other.

Notes

1. For details on the procedures used to collect and analyze these data, please see Leonardi and Bailey (2008).
2. This situation is not unique for performance engineering work at IAC. A recent

report by the McKinsey Global Institute predicts that up to 42 percent of all automotive engineering jobs could theoretically be offshored due to the increasing move toward mathematical models that are tested via information technologies instead of physical models that require expensive testing facilities and are not easily transportable (Pascal & Rosenfeld, 2005).

3. A penetration occurs when the mathematical representations of two parts intersect one another – occupy overlapping vehicle coordinates. Penetrations can exist in mathematical models but not in physical parts because two pieces of matter cannot occupy the same space at the same time. Penetrations in math models must be fixed if the model is to accurately represent the physical vehicle.

4. The elements in a finite element model are connected at defined nodes (corner and mid-segment points), and the entire connected system composes a defined structure called a "mesh." Dense meshes (with smaller element sizes) give more accurate simulations of vehicle dynamics than course meshes, but they take longer for the simulation software to solve. Typically, engineers strive to find a balance between mesh size and processing time.

References

Bhagat, R. S., Kedia, B. L., Harveston, P. D., & Triandis, H. C. (2002). Cultural variations in the cross-border transfer of organizational knowledge: An integrative framework. *Academy of Management Review, 27(2)*, 204–221.

Boudreau, M.-C., Loch, K. D., Robey, D., & Straub, D. W. (1998). Going global: Using information technology to advance the competitiveness of the virtual transnational organization. *Academy of Management Executive, 12(4)*, 120–128.

Buriel, R. (1993). Acculturation, respect for cultural differences, and biculturalism among three generations of Mexican American and Euro American school children. *Journal of Genetic Psychology, 154(4)*, 531–543.

Carmel, E., & Agarwal, E. (2002). The maturation of offshore sourcing of informaiton technology work. *MIS Quarterly Executive, 1(2)*, 65–77.

Cornelius, C., & Boos, M. (2003). Enhancing mutual understanding in synchronous computer-mediated communication by training: trade-offs in judgmental tasks. *Communication Research, 30(2)*, 147–177.

Cramton, C. D. (2001). The mutual knowledge problem and its consequences for dispersed collaboration. *Organization Science, 12(3)*, 346–371.

Dibbern, J., Goles, T., Hirschheim, R., & Jayatilaka, B. (2004). Information systems outsourcing: a survey and analysis of the literature. *The DATA BASE for Advances in Information Sciences, 35(4)*, 6–102.

Early, P. C., & Singh, H. (Eds.) (2000). *Innovations in international and cross-cultural management.* Thousand Oaks, CA: Sage.

Farrell, D., & Rosenfeld, J. (2005). *US Offshoring: Rethinking the response.* Washington, DC: McKinsey Global Institute.

Gibson, C. B., & Manuel, J. (2003). Building trust: Effective multi-cultural communication processes in virtual teams. In C. B. Gibson & S. G. Cohen (Eds.), *Virtual teams that work: Creating conditions for virtual team effectiveness* (pp. 59–86). San Francisco, CA: Jossey-Bass.

Gopal, A., Sivaramakrishnan, K., Krishnan, M. S., & Mukhopadhyay, T. (2003). Contracts in offshore software development: an empirical analysis. *Management Science, 49(12)*, 1671–1683.

Gudykunst, W. B., Matsumoto, Y., Ting-Tommey, S., Nishida, T., Kim, K., & Heyman, S. (1996). The influence of cultural individualism-collectivism, self construals, and individual values on communication styles across cultures. *Human Communication Research*, 22(4), 510–543.

Hinds, P. J., & Weisband, S. (2003). Knowledge sharing and shared understanding in virtual teams. In C. Gibson & S. Cohen (Eds.), *Creating conditions for effective virtual teams* (pp. 21–36). San Francisco, CA: Jossey-Bass.

Hodge, B., & Coronodo, G. (2006). Mexico Inc.? Discourse analysis and the triumph of managerialism. *Organization*, 13(4), 529–547.

Hofstede, G. (1980). *Cultures consequences: International differences in work-related values*. Beverly Hills, CA: Sage.

Jarvenpaa, S. L., & Leidner, D. E. (1999). Communication and trust in global virtual teams. *Organization Science*, 10(6), 791–815.

Kotabe, M., & Swan, K. S. (1994). Offshore sourcing: Reaction, maturation, and consolidation of US multinationals. *Journal of International Business Studies*, 25(1), 115–140.

Leonardi, P. M., & Bailey, D. E. (2008). Transformational technologies and the creation of new work practices: Making implicit knowledge explicit in task-based offshoring. *MIS Quarterly*, 32(2), 411–436.

Lindsley, S. L. (1999). Communication and "the Mexican way": stability and trust as core symbols in maquiladoras. *Western Journal of Communication*, 63(1), 1–31.

Markus, H. R., & Kitayama, S. (1991). Culture and self: Implications for cognition, emotion, and motivation. *Psychological Review*, 98, 224–253.

Maznevski, M. L., & Chudoba, K. M. (2000). Bridging space over time: Global virtual team dynamics and effectiveness. *Organization Science*, 11(5), 473–492.

Mines, M. (1994). Conceptualizaing the person: Hierarchical society and individual autonomy in India. In R. T. Ames, W. Dissanayake, & T. P. Kasulis (Eds.), *Self as person in Asian theory and practice* (pp. 314–334). Albany, NY: SUNY Press.

Monge, P., & Fulk, J. (1999). Communication technology for global network organizations. In G. DeSanctis & J. Fulk (Eds.), *Shaping organization form: Communication, connection, and community* (pp. 71–100). Thousand Oaks, CA: Sage.

Nisbett, R. E., Peng, K., Choi, I., & Norenzayan, A. (2001). Culture and systems of thought: Holistic versus analytic cognition. *Psychological Review*, 108, 291–310.

Parish, S. M. (1996). *Hierarchy and its discontents: Culture and the politics of consciousness in caste society*. Philadelphia, PA: University of Pennsylvania Press.

Pascal, R., & Rosenfeld, J. (2005). *The emerging global labor market: Part I – The demand for offshore talent in services*. Washington, DC: McKinsey Global Institute.

Perlow, L., & Weeks, J. (2002). Who's helping whom? Layers of culture and workplace behavior. *Journal of Organizational Behavior*, 23, 345–361.

Rice, A. K. (1953). Productivity and social organization in an Indian weaving shed: An examination of some aspects of the socio-technical system of an experimental automatic loom shed. *Human Relations*, 6(4), 297–329.

Sahay, S. (1998). Implementing GIS technology in India: Issues of time and space. *Accounting, Management, and Information Technologies*, 8(2–3), 147–188.

Sakthivel, S. (2005). Virtual workgroups in offshore systems development. *Information and software technology*, 47(5), 305–318.

Shkodriani, G. M., & Gibbons, J. L. (1995). Individualism and collectivism among university students in Mexico and the United States. *Journal of Social Psychology*, *135(6)*, 765–772.

Srinivas, M. N. (1984). Some reflections on the nature of caste hierarchy. *Contributions to Indian Sociology*, *18(2)*, 151–167.

Tractinsky, N., & Jarvenpaa, S. L. (1995). Information systems design decisions in a global versus domestic context. *MIS Quarterly*, *19(4)*, 507–534.

Triandis, H. C. (1995). *Individualism & collectivism*. Boulder, CO: Westview Press.

Walsham, G. (2002). Cross-cultural software production and use: a structuration analysis. [Article]. *MIS Quarterly*, *26(4)*, 359–380.

Walther, J. B. (1994). Anticipated ongoing interaction versus channel effects on relational communication in computer-mediated interaction. *Human Communication Research*, *20(4)*, 473–501.

Werner, S. (2002). Recent developments in international management research: a review of 20 top management journals. *Journal of Management*, *28(3)*, 277–305.

Zakaria, F. (2006, March 6). India rising. *Newsweek*, *167*, 18–30.

Zakaria, N., Amelinckw, A., & Wilemon, D. (2004). Working together apart? Building a knowledge-sharing culture for global virtual teams. *Creativity and Innovation Management*, *13(1)*, 15–29.

Chapter 7

Transactive Memory and Organizational Knowledge

Edward T. Palazzolo

Transactive memory (TM) theory provides a useful framework for understanding how organizational members manage their knowledge. As knowledge is one of the most important assets an organization has, understanding how it manages that asset is crucial. The framework provided by TM theory includes mechanisms regarding how knowledge enters the team, what, if anything, is done with that information, and how members get the required knowledge they need, when they need it.

Although TM theory was originally conceived as a model for understanding knowledge sharing between intimate partners, the usefulness of the theory for other contexts quickly became apparent, particularly for organizational work teams. Previously, working within a strict hierarchical organization lessened the need to develop a TM system because employees could rely on the hierarchy for locating necessary knowledge (or responsible individuals). On the other hand, much work accomplished in organizations today is done by emergent work teams rather than hierarchies. Emergent teams rely heavily on each other's knowledge to complete their work. Thus, TM theory provides an excellent framework for understanding how newly formed or existing teams manage their knowledge base.

TM theory describes how two or more individual memories can operate as a system with one larger memory. It describes how people in interdependent relationships (e.g., work teams) gain, store, and utilize their collective knowledge. That is, a TM system is made up of two or more memories, and the communication between the people to access knowledge as needed.

TM System Benefits to Organizations

There are two main benefits to teams and organizations for developing their TM systems: (1) a reduction in cognitive load for all members, and (2) collectively, the team can store and access a greater amount of knowledge. The reduced cognitive load comes from members being required to learn only information within a small number of knowledge domains. Further, these knowledge domains are easier for individuals to work with because they have already developed the cognitive processes required to understand and integrate information within this domain. Likewise, they are not required to learn information regarding the domain about which they are not knowledgeable.

The second benefit, access to a greater amount of knowledge, is also a function of the knowledge specialization of the team members. That is, as individuals focus on the knowledge they are best equipped to learn, they are likely to learn more in that domain than they could if they were responsible for all knowledge domains. Thus, by each person focusing on a smaller set of domains, they actually build a larger knowledge base collectively. Then, as becomes necessary, the team members have access to this larger body of knowledge and utilize it through the process of communication to retrieve information.

The focus of this chapter is to overview the work on TM theory and to provide future directions for those interested in conducting TM research, as well as those looking to learn from the work being performed. The chapter begins by providing a brief review and typology of the research conducted on TM theory. The second section explains the three core processes of TM systems, including the role of communication for knowledge management, and concludes by highlighting the organizational benefits for following these processes. Following that review is a discussion of my current TM research agenda, ending with a discussion of the contributions from my research (present and future) to both the understanding of organizational knowledge and its usefulness in contemporary organizations.

Brief Review and Typology of Transactive Memory Research

Research on TM can be classified into four general categories: (1) theoretical development, (2) laboratory studies, (3) fieldwork, and (4) computational modeling and simulations. Naturally, TM research overlaps between these categories, but having the categories provides an organizational structure to the growing body of work. Conveniently, these categories also identify the evolutionary process of TM research. While each category seems to have evolved into the next, there is currently considerable activity within each category. The sections below provide an overview of these four types of TM research (see Palazzolo (2005) and Peltokorpi (2008) for detailed reviews of TM literature).

Theoretical Development

TM theory was conceptualized by Daniel Wegner as a means to explain how one person can access stored knowledge in another person's memory (Wegner, 1987; Wegner, Giuliano, & Hertel, 1985; Wegner, Erber, & Raymond, 1991). Since those early papers, much research has been undertaken to further understand how people work together to store, encode, and retrieve information. Some additional noteworthy theoretical articles include Wegner (1995), which provided a computer network model of TM systems leading to multiple network-centric TM articles (cf. Borgatti & Cross, 2003; Rulke & Galaskiewicz, 2000), and Brandon and Hollingshead (2004), who defined the 1:1:1 relationship between tasks, expertise, and person, called TEP units, stating that teams need to maintain this relationship to perform successfully as a TM system (see Chapter 8 in this volume for more information about TEP units).

Laboratory Studies

Once the theory was reasonably well explained and understood, researchers worked to test the fundamentals of the theory through multiple series of experimentally designed research studies. At this point, TM systems were being articulated for couples and triads with the assumption that the properties would scale to teams and organizations (Hollingshead, 1998a; Moreland, 1999). One of the primary researchers to study TM systems through interactions in experimental lab studies is Hollingshead. Focusing on dyads, Hollingshead tested the relationships between TM systems and familiarity (1998a, 1998b), as well as the effects of various forms of communication on both the development and performance of TM systems (Hollingshead, 1998b). These lab studies proved to be quite influential in the further development of TM theory in that they demonstrated the importance of communication for the successful development, maintenance, and usability of TM systems.

In another example, Moreland and colleagues tested three-person teams of undergraduates by tasking them with learning how to build an AM radio and then having the team actually build the radio from memory (Liang, Moreland, & Argote, 1995; Moreland, 1999). They demonstrated the benefit gained by having people learn together for something that is complex and requires team performance (Moreland, Argote, & Krishnan, 1996). Additionally, Moreland and Myaskovsky (2000) demonstrated the detriment of membership turnover on a team's ability to perform. Further, they showed these effects can be mitigated by providing a newly formed team with a list of each member's areas of expertise.

Moving beyond the laboratory (but not quite into the field), researchers started working with teams of MBA students and their projects (cf. Lewis, 2004; Lewis, Belliveau, Herndon, & Keller, 2007; Rulke & Galaskiewicz, 2000). Rulke and Galaskiewicz's work focused on multiple teams' network structures, the extent of their knowledge distribution, and how variations of structure and distribution affected the teams' performance. Their study furthered TM research by incorporating the concepts of social networks to TM systems, as well as studying five-person teams who interacted for the duration of a semester.

Fieldwork

Much of the theoretical and experimental research on TM systems speculates that the processes identified and tested with two or three people should hold for larger teams. In particular, they argue teams within organizations should exhibit the properties of TM systems – namely, teams will identify and develop domain-specific experts, and teams will use communication between their members to develop and utilize those experts as needed. Based on these arguments and building on the solid theoretical foundation, researchers moved to the field to study TM systems in organizations (Austin, 2000, 2003; Lewis, 2000, 2003; Palazzolo, 2005; Yuan et al., 2005). Such speculation may seem accurate at first; however, when more closely scrutinized, some of the processes seem to break down in larger teams. For example, Palazzolo (2005) found a fair number of teams in which there was no exclusively referenced team expert for information retrieval. Given that, and other inconsistencies, much more research on intact TM systems needs to be conducted to discern the TM properties that are and are not scalable, as well as to identify the properties unique to larger, organizational-based TM systems.

Computational Modeling and Simulations

The last, and most recent, type of social science research involves the use of computational modeling (Lazer et al., 2009) to run simulations of TM systems (Palazzolo, Serb, She, Su, & Contractor, 2006; Ren, Carley, & Argote, 2002). Such simulations allow researchers to test hypotheses with computer models of work teams as opposed to intact work teams, and therefore do not disrupt the regular workflow of actual teams. Further, these simulations allow researchers to test experimental designs (akin to the research in laboratories) that it is not practical to execute with actual teams (e.g., what happens when a team is formed with no one having any working knowledge of what is required of them but members think everyone else is an expert?).

These types of studies are not a substitute for other types of research. Rather, computational models are an additional tool available to researchers which complement their other methodologies. Moreover, computational modeling can help researchers identify the critical components or processes in systems and then focus their effort and resources in a more limited manner. More details regarding the use of computational modeling are provided later in the chapter.

Processes of Transactive Memories

A TM has three principle processes: (1) directory updating; (2) communication to allocate information; and (3) communication to retrieve information. Each of these is considered a process because they are ongoing throughout the duration of the team (and in some situations extend beyond the team's lifespan). Directory updating is the process used to build the TM system, communication to allocate information is the process to support the system, and communication to retrieve information is the process to utilize and benefit from the TM system. Each process is described in turn below. These processes are consistent with the process and subprocess components of Glaser's (1978) "six Cs" knowledge coding model.

Directory Updating

Directory updating is the process by which team members learn what each of the other members know. This process is referred to as directory updating, because people are only learning what knowledge domains others are knowledgeable in as opposed to learning all of the information themselves (like Glaser's subprocess of meta-knowledge development). That is, in directory updating people are learning labels, associating those labels with specific people, and, where relevant, assigning a relative value regarding how much the individual knows. So, for example, one may learn that "Bob is quite knowledgeable about structuration theory." Learning these three pieces of information is most likely a lot easier for people than learning structuration theory.

There are multiple ways for directory updating to occur. One of the early forms of learning what another person knows is through stereotype information. While this information may not be accurate, people still use their stereotypes when they first learn about another person. For example, how a person is dressed may influence how educated you perceive that person to be. Naturally, a walk around a university campus quickly demonstrates that how someone dresses is not directly related to how educated he or she is. Thus, people's directories can vary with regard to how accurate they are. Ideally, through the ongoing process of directory updating, a person's directory would become more accurate over time.

The next means by which a person learns what another knows is through communication. While communicating with someone, people have the opportunity to learn more about the domains others do and do not know. Further, the communication does not have to be explicitly regarding an individual's directory and knowledge base. Such information can be gleaned from a conversation simply by being observant about what is discussed, and then people can update their directory information for this particular individual.

Another way for a person to update his or her directory is to talk to other people who know something about an individual. That is, it is not necessary to have direct contact with someone in order to know something about him or her. Lastly, a person can learn what another knows through research – that is, by looking up and reading prior work by an individual (e.g., academic articles), people can update their directory. Additionally, if available, a person can use an organization's knowledge management system to look up any topics or work the individual has submitted to the database. Finally (and a common place for many to start), people can always Google others to learn what is publicly available about them.

Identification of Team Experts

The process of directory updating allows individuals to identify whom they perceive as team experts. That is, of all the people on the team, the expert is the person perceived as knowing the most. Naturally, a person could perceive herself as the expert if she believes she knows more than everybody else on the team. This concept of team expert is applicable to all knowledge domains the team utilizes – in other words, a team can have different members as experts for different knowledge domains relevant to their work. Further, TM theory argues that teams should have different members as experts across the different knowledge domains as a means of specializing. This process allows a team to benefit with a reduced cognitive load because the specialists are better equipped to learn new information in their knowledge domain, since the directory frees up their need to learn information in other domains.

Clarification and Correction of Directory Errors

As previously mentioned, mental directories are not always accurate. Often a directory is created by assumptions and, therefore, not explicitly discussed amongst team members. Without discussion areas, members on the team may incorrectly assign the label of expert to a person. Further, if everyone assumes someone else to be the team expert, then no one will take responsibility for encoding incoming information, and the team risks losing the new information (Wegner, 1987, 1995). Clearly, such losses are highly problematic for teams (see Chapter 8 in this volume for more information about types of errors possible in TM systems). Fortunately, short discussions between team members are sufficient to correct many errors in people's directories. Likewise, such discussions can be used to clarify and reinforce existing perceptions of expertise. Thus, while the directory is a knowledge resource, the process of directory updating is primarily communicative. The next two processes discussed are also communication focused.

Communication to Allocate Information

Communication to allocate information is the process whereby members of a team help develop and support the teams' knowledge structure. First, a member must receive new information from the environment. This information may come in many forms, including a phone call, an e-mail, or a personal conversation. Second, upon receiving the new information, the person must identify what knowledge domain it belongs to and then reference her directory of expertise to identify whom she perceives as the expert for that knowledge domain. Once these two conditions are met, she must then communicate this new information to the identified team expert. A strong benefit of going through the process of communicating to allocate information is that she is no longer responsible for maintaining the new information; she can trust her team expert to store and best utilize the information. Thus, information is passed from someone less qualified to the most qualified. That is, the expert is also the one who is most capable of successfully storing the information as well as converting information into usable knowledge.

Communication to Retrieve Information

The third process central to TM theory is communication to retrieve information. This process is the point where the benefits of building and developing a team's TM come to fruition. Like communication to allocate information, communication to retrieve information is related to a person's perceptions of other team members' expertise. First, as opposed to receiving new information, a team member has a task to accomplish, and this task requires knowledge from a domain in which he is not an expert. As an alternative to quickly learning the required knowledge, he can utilize a team member's expertise. To do this, this person must reference his mental directory of who knows what to identify the team expert for the required knowledge domain. Having satisfied these two conditions, he may then contact the perceived expert and request information to help him complete his task.

Communication to allocate information and communication to retrieve information provide growth opportunities for people to update their knowledge directories. For example, when allocating information to the perceived expert, the perceived expert may refuse to accept the information, claiming it is not part of his job, and point to another person on the team he believes to be the team expert. Faced with this situation, a person would downgrade the perceived knowledge of the targeted person and, perhaps, upgrade the perceived knowledge of the person to whom he was referred. Likewise, when a team member seeks another to retrieve information, he can use that experience to update his directory.

Contemporary Trends in TM Research

Although there has been a great deal of research to date about TM systems, there is still much to be done – especially with respect to TM

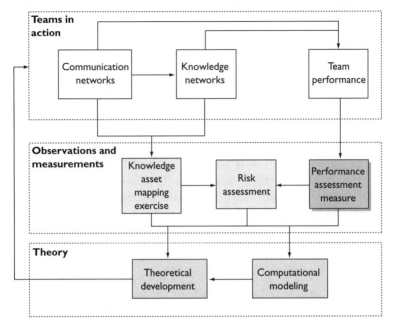

Figure 7.1 Research program.

systems in organizations. Thus, my research centers on understanding information and knowledge management in organizational work teams. Towards that end, I am currently focusing on four aspects of TM theory: (1) teams in action, (2) developing measurement instruments, (3) computational models, and (4) theoretical development. The relationships between these aspects are shown in Figure 7.1.

Teams in Action

The first area of focus is the study of teams in action to capture their activities and knowledge processes in their natural environment. As my objective is to best understand organizational work teams, it is necessary to study intact work teams from a variety of industries. Of particular interest in this area is the role of social networks. That is, how do people create, maintain, dissolve, and reconstitute connections with co-workers in communication, knowledge, and performance networks? As previously discussed, communication networks are the means by which co-workers locate and retrieve information as well as directory updating by learning who knows what. Here, knowledge networks have two parts. First, they represent where the knowledge actually is (or is not) on the team. Second, which is explicitly detailed in TM theory, is the perceptions of who knows what. That is, while the first part may represent the actual location of knowledge, people will only act on their perceptions, thus making the second part crucial for understanding TM systems.

The last network type of interest is team performance networks. Here, the network is a function of the team's performance. That is, do the members perceive the same team goals? Do they work together to try to reach those goals? To what extent do individuals impact the team performance (for better or worse)? The goal of understanding teams in action leads to the second research goal: to design and develop better measurement instruments for the study of TM theory in the workplace.

Development of Measurement Instruments

To date, TM theory has been tested via the sets of surveys or measurement processes unique to the research team performing the study. That is, there is presently no standard of measurement for TM systems. Although helpful and perhaps necessary during the formative time of theory development, the use of unique measurement systems prevents the ability to compare research findings across studies and between research teams. Thus, my second research goal is to design and develop a measurement instrument that can be adopted by anyone involved in TM research doing field research with intact work teams. That is not to say they can no longer use their unique measurements; rather, these proposed instruments can be combined with theirs as appropriate and useful. Currently, my work is focused on creating and developing three different instruments which are informative for three different, but overlapping, dimensions of TM systems and research.

Identification of Knowledge Assets

The first instrument is a subset of the Knowledge Asset Mapping Exercise (KAME) designed under a National Science Foundation grant for the study of distributed knowledge systems (NSF Grant No. IIS-9980109). The KAME is an elaborate survey designed to get an as complete as possible map of the knowledge that exists in work teams. It includes both human and non-human (i.e., computers, servers, books, etc.) locations as knowledge storage repositories. The subset consists of questions about the team's membership, tasks, knowledge requirements, interdependence, and communication patterns. These questions were chosen for their direct connection with TM theory and appropriateness for studying professional work teams.

Measuring Team Performance

The second instrument is the Performance Assessment Measure (PAM) designed to study the performance levels of work teams (Palazzolo &

Simunich, 2006). The emphasis of the PAM is to study a team's performance regardless of the type of team being studied. That is, past TM research has studied team performance unique to the team being studied. For example, Moreland, Argote, and Krishnan (1996) studied radio assembly errors, and Hollingshead (1998a, 2000) studied word recall errors. Although such measures were quite useful for the research at the time, they fail to allow for comparisons across studies and over time. Thus, it is my intention for the PAM to be incorporated into future TM research such that we may explore the various tenants of the theory with comparable measurements.

Given the goal of applicability to a wide range of teams, the primary questions of the PAM were derived from a review of the literature in communication and business journals. From that review, four dimensions repeatedly appeared as important to the study of team performance and have been incorporated into the PAM: (1) time for task completion; (2) quality of task completion; (3) satisfaction with task completion; and (4) satisfaction with team members after task completion.

Textual Analysis

The third component of observation and measurement is textual analysis. Textual analysis can be applied to a variety of sources and may be used to supplement interview and survey data. A few examples of texts appropriate for analysis are e-mail archives, discussion boards or forums, and transcripts from team meetings (see Chapter 9 in this volume).

Analyzing the text from these sources may provide insights into the team's knowledge structure and communication patterns that may go unreported because of what is happening directly around them. Another benefit of textual analysis is its access to actual behaviors and interactions between team members. That is, surveys are typically subject to recall issues that may degrade the quality of data. Captured text avoids recall problems; however, like surveys, we must assume the participants are honest in their transactions.

The third benefit of textual analysis is the ability to analyze team interactions over time. Naturally, the timeframe is limited to the available data (e.g., some people save all e-mails while others delete old e-mails). Such longitudinal data allow for network analysis of team development, and can provide insights into the ongoing development of TM systems. Lastly, this data can be punctuated by significant team landmarks. For example, the initial data regarding the team formation, task assignments, task due dates, and team member turnover are all events with an impact on the TM system. Including these dates in longitudinal analyses will help account for events which may appear anomalous without the appropriate context. Likewise, having such context for analyses will help researchers develop TM theory with respect to particular events in a team's lifecycle.

Computational Models

The next component of this research agenda is the use of computational models to simulate work teams' communication and knowledge systems. Computational modeling is an important tool to utilize for the advancement of theory. If built well, these models can provide a close approximation of human interaction.

A computational model is a computer program that allows the researcher to specify, with considerable detail, every aspect of a team to be studied. This type of modeling is used extensively in the physical sciences. For example, NASA will model a space mission long before the creation of a satellite or its launch date, to assure the mission is feasible. Computational modeling has not been utilized as much in the social sciences and for the study of social systems, but it has been used more in recent years (cf. Carley & Prietula, 1994; Palazzolo et al., 2006; Tutzauer & Palazzolo, 2005), as computing power has increased and cross-disciplinary teams have flourished.

Computational models allow a researcher to input a set of initial conditions (i.e., the state of the system at the onset of interactions), observe as the system evolves, and obtain the output data upon completion of the simulation for analysis. These properties make computational modeling well suited for the study of organizational systems and, more specifically, TM systems. For example, Palazzolo and colleagues (2006) tested TM theory by varying three critical components of a TM system (i.e., initial knowledge level of team members, the members' accuracy in recognizing what others on the team know, and team size), letting the system evolve via a simulation, and studying the end state of the system to understand better the impact of these different initial conditions on the development of the transactive memory system. To account for the natural variations in team development, this model was built with stochastic components (i.e., interactions were based on probabilities as opposed to being deterministic). Therefore, that research was based on the simulations of 3200 teams. The study just described is but one example of studying TM systems with computational models. This approach offers many benefits, with the principle ones described next.

The first benefit to using computational models for the study of TM systems is the ability to run multiple "What if...?" scenarios without the disruption to actual work teams. A "What if...?" scenario is any situation in which a researcher wants to know what effect a change in the system would have on the development of the system. For example, what if the smartest person on the team left, as in a turnover situation? These "What if...?" scenarios are limited only by the researcher's creativity in asking good questions and programming these questions into the model. The ability to run so many different situations in a computational model is a huge benefit to researchers in that they can study such effects and variations in team composition without having to manipulate intact work teams.

Further, computational modeling provides for considerable savings of both time and money. Running a virtual experiment via modeling allows for the testing of team development in a compressed time period – for example, a month's worth of human interaction can be modeled in minutes on the computer. Thus, much time is saved by not having to wait out the actual time. Moreover, if a model shows a desired manipulation to have no effect on the team, the researcher can save actual time that would be wasted in conducting an experiment only to get non-significant findings in the end. Naturally, saving large amounts of time leads to the saving of money as well. That is, the financial expenses associated with running experiments and conducting field research can be spent more judiciously by using models to test a multitude of research questions, and only going to intact teams for a limited number of questions. Likewise, modeling would save the social and political capital required to gain access to organizations.

The third principle benefit from computational modeling is the ability to identify the key or critical processes in the system and then study these processes with the intact work teams. These critical processes may be unintuitive because of the complex nature of systems and the human mind's limitation to process so many different components at once. By using these models to identify critical parts, much time and money can be saved.

Theoretical Development

Collectively, the study of teams in action, the development of standard measurement instruments, and the use of computational modeling culminate in the fourth research agenda item, which is theoretical development. Each of the three aforementioned items contributes unique information for developing TM theory. For example, working with intact professional teams provides the grounding information that drives the need for theoretical development.

Further, designing a standard measurement instrument allows for comparison between studies and can increase researcher confidence that we are all looking at the same thing when we refer to a collection of people as a TM system. Lastly, computational modeling provides useful tools for zoning in on important system aspects which provides the additional bonus of saving time and money. In conclusion, all of the work described above is done with the intent of better understanding work teams, and to inform such teams of the lessons learned and how theory has advanced. That is, this program of research is cyclical in nature: practice informs theory, and theory informs practice.

Contributions of Research for Theory and Practice

The cyclic nature of the research program detailed above allows for the mutual and continual influence on both TM theory and organizational practice. The contributions to each one are discussed, in turn, below.

Contributions to Understanding of Organizational Knowledge and Organizations

The theoretical contributions of my work to the field of organizational knowledge are based on the advancement of TM theory. To date, there has been only a relatively small amount of research on the role of TM systems in organizations. Much of the formative work on TM theory was done in research labs with small, ad hoc teams. That foundational work was critical to the development of TM theory, but it does not provide sufficient information to accurately generalize to professional teams. By grounding my research within the study of intact work teams, my research should help further our understanding of how teams negotiate and manage their information.

Communication Networks

More specifically, my research should contribute to TM theory in terms of communication networks, knowledge networks, and team performance. With respect to communication networks, I am focusing on the specific communication patterns team members create for: (1) the allocation of information; (2) the retrieval of information; and (3) social communication. By separating people's communication into these categories, different patterns emerge. For example, teams are much more active in the retrieval of information than they are in the allocation of information. Further, such a separation allows for research to be designed around the different functions each of these communicative processes has in TM systems.

In the study of team communication, I use a social network paradigm for both data collection and analysis. Therefore, my work provides an increased level of specification with respect to who talks to whom and about what. Further, through the use of the latest social network analysis techniques (e.g., exponential random graph models), I am working towards the identification of probabilities of any two team members to create a communication tie given other conditions, or properties, of the network. Likewise, I am also working to identify the probabilities of team members to have specific perceptions of who knows what on their teams. These probabilities will then become parameter estimates used in computational models to more accurately model work team interactions.

Knowledge Networks

As done with communication networks, my research has also pushed forward theoretical definitions for the four components of a TM system's knowledge network. By describing these components in network terms, I have provided a higher level of specificity to their definitions. Further, by defining these parts in a computational model of TM systems, my colleagues and I have provided definitions with mathematical specificity to these components of TM theory.

The process of converting a verbal theory into a computational model can be quite illuminating. In particular, many of the gaps in the verbal descriptions become much more obvious. For example, the network attribute of an individual's knowledge is described verbally as what or how much an individual knows on a particular topic. However, such a description does not provide boundary details necessary to fully grasp what is being conveyed. In trying to comprehend "how much" an individual knows about a specific topic, a person must have an understanding of a zero point (i.e., the person knows nothing) ranging to an absolute high end, assuming a limit to the amount of available information that exists (i.e. the person knows everything).

Next, a person must also consider the boundaries to the "specific" topic. In the research lab, the researcher has much control over the topic areas utilized for the study; however, professional work teams have organically built their knowledge and the research works to codify the existing system. Lastly, computational models, which attempt to map the actual system, require an exact specification of how many knowledge areas are utilized and how much information each one can contain before assigning different people (i.e., agents) their knowledge levels. Thus, this work on designing such models has helped to identify and, in some cases, to fill in the gaps in theories' verbal descriptions.

Team Performance

The third part of TM theory where my work has made a contribution is in the study of a TM system's performance. The measurement tools I developed with my graduate students allow researchers to test team performance in a consistent and comparable manner. In doing so, we move from general claims about people working as a TM system having benefits, to making specific and quantifiable claims about a team's performance. This is not to say prior work did not have quantifiable measures of performance; rather, those measures were suitable to the lab and specific studies conducted, whereas my work continues the move to how we study TM systems in the field.

Relationships

The fourth contribution of my work to organizational knowledge is in the study of the relationships between the first three groups: communication networks, knowledge networks, and team performance. In particular, my current research efforts focus on the relationships between team performance and communication networks, and the relationships between team performance and knowledge networks. I am focusing my research in this area because improved team performance is a central claim of TM theory, yet, to date, has not received much attention with intact work teams. That is, prior research has shown considerable evidence to support the claim that an established TM system in a research lab environment outperformed groups of strangers (Hollingshead, 1998b, 2004), or disrupted TM systems (Moreland & Myaskovsky, 2000). However, such studies are based on two- and three-person teams, and not the larger teams commonly used in organizational setting. Thus, it is necessary to follow up lab research with field research to identify the ideal (or at least preferred) conditions associated with performance.

Contributions of Research to Practice

There are three specific contributions I would like my work to make to organizational professionals: first, to help organizational leaders consciously develop their organizational knowledge; second, to teach organizational members about TM systems and how such systems are supported through the members' communication patterns; and third, to demonstrate to organizational leaders the importance and benefits of viewing their organization's communication and knowledge networks as assets and resources for investment. Each of these contributions is described, in turn, below.

Conscious Development of Organizational Knowledge

This first application of my work is necessary for the other two contributions to be fruitful. The primary benefit here comes from an adjusted mindset: rather than letting an organization's organizational knowledge naturally develop and then manage what has emerged, this perspective argues for leaders to take a proactive role in the design of the organization's knowledge components. Although this argument, per se, is not new (cf. Weick & Ashford, 2001; Wenger, 1998), its focus is on developing organizational knowledge as a TM system. That is, there are specific benefits to a well-developed TM system (as previously discussed), and consciously designing the organization's organizational knowledge as a TM system increases its ability to gain these benefits.

Some specific steps can be followed to help with the conscious development of organizational knowledge, especially for newly developed project teams. Prior to team formation, the person responsible for putting the team together should do the following four things:

1   Identify all knowledge domains useful to the project. These should include both general competencies, such as use of virtual meting technologies, as well as higher level, task-specific knowledge domains, such as high-power engineering.

2   Identify a pool of potential team members and their expertise levels in each of the knowledge domains identified in step (1), as well as any complementary knowledge domains.

3   To the best extent possible, form the teams with those members who have expertise in the relevant knowledge domains. All members should have a good working knowledge of the domains identified as general competencies (i.e., integrative knowledge domains (Hollingshead, 2001; Wegner, 1987; Wegner et al., 1985)), and there should be at least one member on the team per task-specific knowledge domain. As mentioned at the start of this chapter, Brandon and Hollingshead (2004) call this a TEP unit.

4   Educate the team about this process and why each member was specifically chosen to be on the team. By evaluating team members in this fashion, it will make each member's expertise salient to the team; a process shown to expedite TM system development (Moreland & Myaskovsky, 2000).

As an excellent example of these steps, NASA's Team X, its extreme design team at the Jet Propulsion Laboratory, utilizes team member expertise quite well. "Team X is a cross-functional multidisciplinary team of engineers that utilizes concurrent engineering methodologies to complete rapid design, analysis and evaluation of mission concept designs" (Jet Propulsion Laboratory, 2009). Team X's objective is to take a potential space mission and create a prototype design, mission timetable, and approximate budget – all within one week – to assess the mission's viability. To accomplish this incredibly complex process, Team X relies on clearly identified experts in 30 unique knowledge domains, such as Power, Thermal, Propulsion, and Telecommunications. They go so far as to clearly label each workstation with the knowledge domain so that those in the room can quickly find the person responsible for topic-specific knowledge. Furthermore, Team X members are referenced by their knowledge domain as opposed to their personal names. This process makes the system fluid, especially when the second- or third-chair individual attends the design session in lieu of the primary knowledge domain expert. That is, it reduces their susceptibility to slowdown from turnover.

Members' Communication Patterns

By expressing the components of TM systems as processes, it is my intention to highlight the ongoing developmental changes to TM systems. That is, a TM system is not something that is built once and then used; rather, TM systems are in a constant state of flux requiring active maintenance by members. Some contributing factors to the changes in a TM system are training, whereby some or all members acquire new knowledge; turnover, when people leave and take their expertise with them, leaving a hole in the

TM system's knowledge structure; and temporary changes such as employee travel, vacations, holidays, or sickness, which create temporary holes in the knowledge structure.

Two communication processes can be used to help support the team's TM system. Communication to retrieve information encounters can be used not only to acquire information, but also to update a person's directory of who knows what on the team. More specifically, with an understanding that the system will change, conscious awareness of people's responses to requests for information can be quite fruitful in learning a person's expertise levels for various knowledge domains, as well as in learning what that person thinks others on the team know for the same knowledge domains. For example, a request for information resulting in a response of "I don't know" can be followed up with the question, "Who do you think might know the answer?" These responses can then be integrated into a person's knowledge directory for later use. Likewise, the person who is being asked to provide information also has an opportunity to update his or her knowledge directory about what the seeker knows, or in this case, does not know. Communication to allocate information can similarly be used to help team members learn who knows what. Interestingly, my research has shown teams utilize their TM system for the retrieval of information much more so than they support their TM system by allocating topic-specific information to team experts. Thus, teams need to more actively work to support their TM systems by more freely sharing information with one another in a targeted manner.

Asset and Resource of Communication and Knowledge Networks

The third contribution I would like to make to practice is to help work teams to see their communication networks and knowledge networks as assets in the same way they view other assets, such as real estate, equipment, product inventory, and human resources. This may be a shift in their thinking, because assets are usually tangible things and these networks are intangible. Still, based on the International Accounting Standards Board's definition, "an asset is a resource controlled by the entity as a result of past events and from which future economic benefits are expected to flow to the entity" (IAS Board, 2005); TM networks are consistent with the economic role of other organizational assets. I hope to further assist organizations, through the research I have undertaken, to understand the relationship between TM systems and team performance by finding better ways to assess the value of communication and knowledge networks.

Conclusion

As organizations continue to rely on information resources and organizational knowledge as their means of revenue generation, combined with the ever increasing complexity in organizational tasks and endeavors, it is evident that considerable effort needs to go into understanding just how people manage the information and knowledge they have. And although much TM research has been conducted already, considerably more is needed. In particular, research focusing on the connection between TM systems and team performance is critical in that it will allow for a deeper understanding of the benefits of knowledge management to teams and organizations. Further, such research will allow for organizational leaders to be more effective, to design and manage their workforce better in an effort to maximize the available resources, and to achieve the most creative and successful outcomes possible.

References

Austin, J. R. (2000). *Knowing what and whom other people know: Linking transactive memory with external connections in organizational groups.* Paper presented at the 16th Annual Meeting of the Academy of Management, Toronto.

Austin, J. R. (2003). Transactive memory in organizational groups: The effects of content, consensus, specialization, and accuracy on group performance. *Journal of Applied Psychology, 88(5),* 866–878.

Borgatti, S. P., & Cross, R. (2003). A relational view of information seeking and learning in social networks. *Management Science, 49(4),* 432–445.

Brandon, D. P., & Hollingshead, A. B. (2004). Transactive memory systems in organizations: Matching tasks, expertise, and people. *Organization Science, 15(6),* 633–644.

Carley, K. M., & Prietula, M. J. (Eds.) (1994). *Computational organization theory.* Hillsdale, NJ: Lawrence Erlbaum Associates.

Glaser, B. G. (1978). *Theoretical sensitivity: Advances in the methodology of grounded theory.* Mill Valley, CA: Sociology Press.

Hollingshead, A. B. (1998a). Communication, learning, and retrieval in transactive memory systems. *Journal of Experimental Social Psychology, 34(5),* 423–442.

Hollingshead, A. B. (1998b). Retrieval processes in transactive memory systems. *Journal of Personality and Social Psychology, 74(3),* 659–671.

Hollingshead, A. B. (2000). Perceptions of expertise and transactive memory in work relationships. *Group Processes & Intergroup Relations, 3(3),* 257–267.

Hollingshead, A. B. (2001). Cognitive interdependence and convergent expectations in transactive memory. *Journal of Personality and Social Psychology, 81(6),* 1080–1089.

Hollingshead, A. B. (2004). Communication technologies, the Internet, and group research. In M. B. Brewer & M. Hewstone (Eds.), *Applied social psychology: Perspectives on social psychology* (pp. 301–317). Malden, MA: Blackwell Publishing.

IAS (International Accounting Standards) Board (2005). Framework for the Preparation and Presentation of Financial Statements. Retrieved July 1, 2009, from www.iasplus.com/standard/framewk.htm.

Jet Propulsion Laboratory. (2009). JPL Team X. Retrieved July 1, 2009, from http://jplteamx.jpl.nasa.gov.

Lazer, D., Pentland, A., Adamic, L., Aral, S., Barabasi, A.-L., Brewer, D., et al. (2009). Computational Social Science. *Science, 323(5915)*, 721–723.

Lewis, K. (2000, August). *Transactive memory and performance of management consulting teams: Examining construct and predictive validity of a new scale.* Paper presented at the Academy of Management, Toronto.

Lewis, K. (2003). Measuring transactive memory systems in the field: Scale development and validation. *Journal of Applied Psychology, 88,* 587–604.

Lewis, K. (2004). Knowledge and performance in knowledge-worker teams: A longitudinal study of transactive memory systems. *Management Science, 50,* 1519–1533.

Lewis, K., Belliveau, M., Herndon, B., & Keller, J. (2007). Group cognition, membership change, and performance: Investigating the benefits and detriments of collective knowledge. *Organizational Behavior and Human Decision Processes, 103(2),* 159–178.

Liang, D. W., Moreland, R., & Argote, L. (1995). Group versus individual training and group performance: The mediating role of transactive memory. *Personality and Social Psychology Bulletin, 21(4),* 384–393.

Moreland, R. (1999). Transactive memory: Learning who knows what in work groups and organizations. In L. Thompson, D. Messick & J. Levine (Eds.), *Sharing knowledge in organizations* (pp. 3–31). Hillsdale, NJ: Lawrence Erlbaum.

Moreland, R., & Myaskovsky, L. (2000). Exploring the performance benefits of group training: transactive memory or improved communication? *Organizational Behavior & Human Decision Processes, 82(1),* 117–133.

Moreland, R., Argote, L., & Krishnan, R. (1996). Socially shared cognition and work: Transactive memory and group performance. In J. L. Nye & A. M. Brower (Eds.), *What's social about social cognition? Research on socially shared cognition in small groups* (pp. 57–84). Thousand Oaks, CA: Sage.

Palazzolo, E. T. (2005). Organizing for information retrieval in transactive memory systems. *Communication Research, 32(6),* 726–761.

Palazzolo, E. T., & Simunich, B. A. (2006, November). *Understanding Team Performance in Transactive Memory Systems: The Development of the Performance Assessment Measure.* Paper presented at the National Communication Association, San Antonio, TX.

Palazzolo, E. T., Serb, D., She, Y., Su, C., & Contractor, N. S. (2006). Co-evolution of communication and knowledge networks as transactive memory systems: Using computational models for theoretical development. *Communication Theory, 16(2),* 223–250.

Peltokorpi, V. (2008). Transactive memory systems. *Review of General Psychology, 12(4),* 378–394.

Ren, Y., Carley, K. M., & Argote, L. (2002). *The contingency effects of transactive memory.* Paper presented at the Computational Analysis of Social and Organizational Systems, Carnegie Mellon University, Pittsburgh, PA.

Rulke, D. L., & Galaskiewicz, J. (2000). Distribution of knowledge, group network structure, and group performance. *Management Science, 46(5),* 612–625.

Tutzauer, F., & Palazzolo, E. T. (2005). Self-organization in the infinite-choice prisoner's dilemma. In G. Barnett & R. Houston (Eds.), *Advances in self-organizing systems* (pp. 89–105). Cresskill, NJ: Hampton Press.

Wegner, D. M. (1987). Transactive memory: A contemporary analysis of the group mind. In B. Mullen & G. R. Goethals (Eds.), *Theories of group behavior* (pp. 185–208). New York, NY: Springer-Verlag.

Wegner, D. M. (1995). A computer network model of human transactive memory. *Social Cognition, 13(3)*, 319–339.

Wegner, D. M., Giuliano, T., & Hertel, P. T. (1985). Cognitive interdependence in close relationships. In W. J. Ickes (Ed.), *Compatible and incompatible relationships* (pp. 253–276). New York, NY: Springer-Verlag.

Wegner, D. M., Erber, R., & Raymond, P. (1991). Transactive memory in close relationships. *Journal of Personality and Social Psychology, 61(6)*, 923–929.

Weick, K. E., & Ashford, S. J. (2001). Learning in organizations. In F. M. Jablin & L. L. Putnam (Eds.), *The new handbook of organizational communication* (pp. 704–731). Thousand Oaks, CA: Sage.

Wenger, E. (1998). The concept of practice. In *Communities of practice: Learning, meaning, and identity* (pp. 45–50). New York, NY: Cambridge University Press.

Yuan, Y., Fulk, J., Shumate, M., Monge, P. R., Bryant, J. A., & Matsaganis, M. (2005). Individual participation in organizational information commons: The impact of team-level social influence and technology-specific comments. *Human Communication Research, 31(2)*, 212–240.

Chapter 8

Communication and Knowledge-sharing Errors in Groups

A Transactive Memory Perspective

*Andrea B. Hollingshead, David P. Brandon,
Kay Yoon, and Naina Gupta*

Working in groups can be difficult. Group members must decide who knows what, coordinate who will do what, share knowledge, and accomplish their individual and collective tasks. Research indicates that groups do not often handle these tasks as well as they should, and, as a result, almost always perform worse than expected based on the sum of members' individual knowledge and abilities (Hastie, 1986). Groups composed of people who know each other well or who have worked together in the past often work together better than comparable groups of strangers (Hollingshead, 1998a, 1998b; Liang, Moreland, & Argote, 1995).

One explanation for why group performance improves over time is that experienced groups develop a transactive memory that enables them to make better use of each individual's expertise (Liang et al., 1995.) Transactive memory systems (TMS) theory, a theory of group-level cognition, explains how people in collectives learn, store, use, and coordinate their knowledge to accomplish individual, group, and organizational goals (Hollingshead, 2010). It is a theory about how people in relationships, groups, and organizations learn "who knows what " and use that knowledge to decide "who will do what," resulting in more efficient and effective individual and collective performance. Cognitive interdependence and the norm of reciprocity drive the creation of transactive memory – each member takes responsibility for different knowledge areas, and members rely on one another for information outside of their responsibility.

Although experienced groups often share knowledge more effectively and perform better than newly formed groups because of their more developed transactive memory system, they still rarely achieve their theoretical maximum (Hastie, 1986). This chapter investigates why this might be the case, and what groups can do to improve their knowledge sharing among members. It explores sources, processes, and outcomes of knowledge-sharing problems through the theoretical lens of transactive memory theory. We will present a conceptual framework for understanding knowledge-sharing errors in groups, and investigate the role of communication in creating, correcting, and reinforcing errors.

It is important to note the assumption that underlies this conceptualization: namely that, taken together, members have sufficient knowledge, skills, and resources to perform group tasks. In addition, we will focus our attention on the organizational context, but these concepts could also apply to groups in other contexts, such as families, friendship groups, support groups, etc.

Transactive Memory

As originally formulated, transactive memory theory (Wegner, 1987) indicates that group members utilize one another as storehouses of information, and assign information based on notions of relative expertise. The resulting system of labels (i.e., areas of knowledge) and locations (i.e., people) provides the group with access to a large body of knowledge while at the same time reducing the cognitive load for remembering information across group members. Brandon and Hollingshead (2004) extended Wegner's (1987) initial conceptualization in a paper describing the development of transactive memory systems in organizations by adding task to labels and locations as a defining element of the cognitive representation of the system. That is, task is viewed as a macro-organizing feature defining the overall structure of transactive memory, and as a micro-element defining the connections between expertise and people, in the form of task–expertise–person (TEP) units.

Transactive Memory Development and TEP Units

Brandon and Hollingshead (2004) argued that transactive memory evolves from three iterative, independently operating, but reciprocally influential cyclical processes: (1) satisfaction of conditions leading to perceived cognitive interdependence among group members, (2) TEP unit and individual mental model development, and (3) shared mental model development – i.e., reconciling perceptions across group members (Figure 8.1). At the very

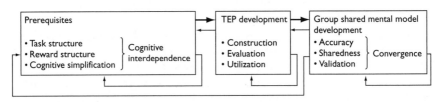

Figure 8.1 Development of transactive memory in organizations.

Note
Reprinted, by permission, from David P. Brandon & Andrea B. Hollingshead, Transactive memory in organizations: Matching tasks, expertise and people, *Organization Science*, 15(6), 2004, 633–644. Copyright 2009, the Institute for Operations Research and the Management Sciences, 7240 Parkway Drive, Suite 300, Hanover, MD 21076 USA.

beginning of transactive memory development, groups are likely to proceed linearly through the model; however, the model is dynamic and can be non-linear. Group activities at later points in the model may induce changes in all three processes. We will revisit the dynamic aspects of the model later in the chapter.

Conditions Favoring Transactive Memory Development

Perceived cognitive interdependence is a prerequisite for the development of transactive memory, as it motivates members to attend to what other members know in the group, and to begin developing a conceptual map regarding "who knows what." Without it, a transactive memory system is not likely to develop. Perceived cognitive interdependence occurs when members perceive that each member's outcomes are dependent on the knowledge or information held by other members of the group (Hollingshead, 2001). It can be stimulated by group reward structures, divisible task structures, a general need for cognitive simplicity, a close relationship, or some combination of these factors. Some examples of conditions that might foster perceived cognitive interdependence include: (1) a team must divide up a large project into subparts and assign each part to a different team member; (2) members of a project team are rewarded based on overall team performance rather than on each member's individual contribution to the project; and (3) co-workers who also have a close personal relationship may rely on one another for information, advice, and help. It is important to note that perceptions of cognitive interdependence are more important than the reality of it, although they are likely to be positively associated.

Construction and Organization of TEP Units

Once members perceive cognitive interdependence, the group is likely to move into the next phase of transactive memory development – the creation of TEP units. The addition of TEP units to transactive memory theory evolves from a general view that task perceptions are fundamental to the transactive memory system. Understanding that the task of building a home requires areas of expertise such as architectural design, plumbing, etc., helps the construction team identify the subtasks, the expertise, or information needed for each subtask, and the responsible person. Further, the perceived structure of the task will likely define the major labels and locations of the transactive memory system – for example, architecture, plumbing, electrical, and carpentry will likely be the top-level hierarchical labels for expertise.

What TEP units provide are connections between the hierarchically organized domains of knowledge (i.e., expertise) and locations (i.e., group members) to a conception of the group task. Brandon and Hollingshead

(2004) suggest that task perceptions link easily to labels and locations because task perceptions also have an easy-to-use hierarchical organization of simplified labels for task components (McGrath, 1991) to provide a basic reference system for the task. A complete reference for transactive memory then results by knowing, for example, that installing the hot water system in a house (task) requires a plumber (expertise) named Hakuho (person). Partial TEP units – where task, expertise, or person information is missing – are less useful. It is not that helpful to know that Asashoryu is a fine chef (an E-P unit) when the task is building a house, or to know that the design of the home requires design blueprints (T-E) until one knows that group member Akebono is an architect. While TEP units therefore provide a complete reference for transactive memory, task perceptions can also be a source of error for a group if task representations are a poor fit to the actual task, or if there is disagreement among group members about the structure of the task.

Brandon and Hollingshead (2004) describe TEP units as constructed via an ongoing, iterative process of three related cycles: *construction, evaluation*, and *utilization*. In the *construction* cycle, full or partial TEP units evolve from each member's notions about task, expertise, and people. Once constructed, full or partial TEP units do not represent certainty, but rather hypotheses a group member has about the distribution of task-relevant information within the group. Wegner (1995) states that one quality of transactive memory systems is the modification of crude notions of expertise via group communication to more refined and accurate conceptions, which suggests a dynamic quality to TEP units. Thus, in the second cycle of TEP development, hypothesized full TEP units, components of TEP units, or partial TEP units are tested, confirmed, and/or revised using available information in the *evaluation* phase.

After construction and evaluation cycles are satisfied, group members make use of TEP units for transactive memory tasks in the utilization cycle, such as requesting or passing along information. Results from the utilization feed back to the earlier cycles for further TEP development, as needed. For example, a group building a home may initially construct a TEP unit that links carpentry to Kitanoumi, due to his certification as a master carpenter. However, when Kitanoumi repeatedly fails to remember information related to the home's wall framing, group members will begin to reassess their TEP units, and perhaps start to allocate information related to carpentry elsewhere (i.e., the next most related TEP units). Over time, ongoing iterations of TEP development cycles will produce more accurate representations of who knows what about the group task.

The TEP units and their labeled reference systems and representations comprise the individual's mental model of the transactive memory system. Such a structure meets definitions of mental models as organized structures of (perceptual or abstract) objects and their relations (Staggers & Norcio, 1993), and as an individual's view of a system that is dynamic, system specific, and gained through experience.

Mental Model Development

In the third phase of transactive memory development, group members begin to form similar mental models and arrange their TEP units in a similar fashion. Blickensderfer, Cannon-Bowers, and Salas (1997, p. 252) define shared mental models as "the extent to which individual team members' mental models overlap – the extent to which team members share the same understanding of the task and the team," which in the case of transactive memory means not only similar TEP units, but also similar macro-organization of those units. While some differences in representations among group members are likely (Poole, 1985), a premise of transactive memory theory, and a tenet of mental model research, is that groups will seek to reduce these differences via communication and negotiation (Derry, DuRussel, & O'Donnell, 1998; Hinsz, 1995; Wegner, 1995). We expect that mental models will be most similar between group members who interact frequently.

Ultimately, transactive memory functions best when mental models are (1) accurate in their representations of expertise, (2) shared across group members, and (3) validated – that is, group members' actions meet members' expectations about their areas of expertise and responsibility. When all these factors are high, the group has an effective or convergent transactive memory system (Brandon & Hollingshead, 2004). One concept that may seem notably absent in our figure is team performance. Although the presence of a transactive memory has been positively linked with team performance in previous research, knowledge-sharing errors can sometimes produce positive outcomes. We will discuss the complex relations between knowledge-sharing errors and performance at the end of the chapter.

Dimensions of Transactive Memory Errors

The conceptual framework we propose for understanding errors is adapted from Brandon and Hollingshead's (2004) dimensions of transactive memory effectiveness. Transactive memory systems can vary in terms of accuracy (the degree to which group members' perceptions about other members' task-related expertise are accurate), sharedness (the degree to which members have a shared representation of the transactive memory system), and validation (the degree to which group members participate in the transactive memory system.) Transactive memory systems will be most effective when knowledge assignments are based on group members' actual abilities, when all group members have similar representations of the system, and when members fulfill expectations. It is important to note that each of these dimensions should be thought of as a continuum rather than a dichotomy.

Accuracy Errors

Effectiveness of transactive memory depends on the extent to which group members recognize one another's expertise accurately. Inaccurate recognition of expertise directly affects the expertise–person relations in the TEP unit (Brandon & Hollingshead, 2004). Accuracy errors occur when members are unaware of one another's expertise or inaccurate in their judgments of expertise. Actual expertise can be different from people's stereotypes about relative knowledge based on diffuse characteristics such as gender, race, or age (Bunderson, 2003; Hollingshead & Fraidin, 2003; Yoon & Hollingshead, 2010) and communication behavior such as talkativeness and frequency of speech (Littlepage & Mueller, 1997; Littlepage, Schmidt, Whisler, & Frost, 1995).

Inconsistency between actual and inferred expertise can result in: (1) *unexpected ignorance* of a group member who was initially assumed to be an expert but turned out to be a non-expert (e.g., a male team member who doesn't know about tools) or (2) *unexpected expertise* which can be discovered later in a member who was not perceived as an expert initially (e.g., a female team member who is a tool expert). Changes in team environment, such as instability of membership and task structures, can increase the likelihood of accuracy errors (Lewis, Belliveau, Herndon, & Keller, 2007; Majchrzak, Jarvenpaa, & Hollingshead, 2007).

Sources of Accuracy Errors

When a team meets for the first time, it is challenging for group members to identify one another's knowledge, skills, and abilities accurately without direct experience on which to base their judgments. Therefore, people often rely on various signals to form perceptions of expertise. Those signals include diffuse characteristics such as gender, race, and age (Berger, Cohen, & Zelditch, 1972). Diffuse characteristics often carry social status and are associated with beliefs that a high status person (e.g., male, older person) is expected to be more competent than a low status person (female, younger person) even when there is no evidence to support the expectation (Berger et al., 1972). Some social stereotypes include expectations about domains of expertise. For instance, female members are expected to be more knowledgeable about cooking than male members (Hollingshead & Fraidin, 2003), and Asian members are assumed to be better at math than white American members (Yoon & Hollingshead, 2010). The effects of diffuse characteristics tend to be smaller for groups that have longer tenure and equal distribution of power (Bunderson, 2003).

Communication behaviors can also serve as indicators of expertise. Speaking forcefully without hesitation, a greater frequency and longer duration of talking, and a high proportion of group participation are positively associated with perceptions of expertise (Littlepage & Mueller, 1997; Littlepage et al., 1995; Pearsall & Ellis, 2006). However, such communication behavior may not be closely related with true expertise. For example, individual members with expertise may hesitate to participate and display a lack of assertiveness when speaking with a higher status person. This may be especially true in vertical cultures, which value hierarchy (Singelis, Triandis, Bhawuk, & Gelfand, 1995). Many Asian cultures value modesty, and may view explicitly communicating one's competence as egregious self-promotion (Kurman, 2003).

In certain situations, experts may not want to let their expertise be known to their group – to avoid additional work assignments, for example. Self-censorship may further exacerbate knowledge-sharing problems (Thomas-Hunt & Phillips, 2003). Another way that communication can influence accuracy errors is through third parties. Valued colleagues and friends often provide opinions, experiences, and insights about other people. Sometimes these insights can lead to inaccurate perceptions about relative knowledge.

Sharedness Errors

Some degree of sharedness errors – a lack of agreement among members about "who knows what," "who is to remember what," and "who is doing what" – seems an inevitable part of transactive memory development. Whatever the origin of the error(s), the consequence for the group in part or whole is reduced efficiency in the allocation and retrieval of information, often with subsequent impacts on group processes and outcomes.

Sharedness errors fall into one of three categories: omission, redundancy, and expediency. Failure to complete tasks due to group members assuming that others are doing the work is an example of an omission error. Such errors arise when the "person" component of a TEP unit is faulty – i.e., there is failure to connect notions of task and expertise notions to a specific group member. Two related categories of errors, each involving self-assignment into TEP units, are redundancy and expediency. Redundancy errors involve group member(s) repeating tasks already completed by another group member(s). Redundancy errors can result when there are multiple members who have expertise in the same area, and failure to clarify the "person" component of the TEP unit leads to duplicated work. In expediency errors, group members take on tasks, regardless of their level of expertise, out of perceived urgency to complete the work.

Shared micro- and macro-organization of TEP units are critical to the development of an effective transactive memory system. The notion of similarity in memory organization is common across transactive memory research, although under a variety of terms such as "shared representations," "shared mental models," or "convergent expectations" (see, for example, Hollingshead 1998a, 2001; Levine & Moreland 1999; Moreland, Argote, & Krishnan, 1996a, 1998). While variation in mental models across group members is expected for newly formed groups, over time those differences can be reduced via group interaction (Hinsz, Tindale, & Vollrath, 1997). In terms of measurement, mental model sharedness will range along a continuum described by completely idiosyncratic (no overlap in mental models) to completely shared (total overlap in mental models).

Sources of Sharedness Errors

Few if any groups will tread an idealized path to completely shared mental models and, subsequently, a convergent transactive memory system; all groups will tread in the waters of idiosyncrasy for at least some time. New groups, particularly where tasks are unfamiliar and members are not acquainted, are likely to have low sharedness. Mental models will be transferred more quickly when newcomers are already familiar with their new group and demonstrate adaptability and commitment to the group, and when old-timers socialize newcomers via direct and indirect feedback (Levine & Moreland, 1999).

Regarding group factors most likely to influence sharedness, the quality and frequency of communication is likely the most critical element. Transactive memory research has already indicated the importance of communication-related variables on transactive memory, such as communication channels and interpersonal training (cf. Hollingshead 1998b, 1998c, 1998d; Hollingshead & Brandon, 2003; Prichard and Ashleigh, 2007). In general, low levels of communication and feedback from other group members can prevent individual members from generating or revising TEP units.

Validation Errors

Validation errors occur when group members fail to take responsibility for actions in their perceived areas of expertise and, as a result, fail to participate in the transactive memory system (Brandon & Hollingshead, 2004). Examples include a group member not providing an answer to a question, or failing to execute a task in an area of perceived expertise. Validation errors can sometimes be made unintentionally. For instance, group members interacting electronically may fail to contribute because of an undetected technological glitch in the network.

A single validation error is not likely to completely invalidate the transactive memory system. For instance, when a group member fails to contribute on one occasion, others may attribute that failure to factors outside the control of the group member and thus continue to perceive the group member as the relative expert if there are high levels of trust in the group. Complete invalidation of the system would occur when *all* group members fail to take responsibility on *every* occasion that they are asked questions on their perceived expertise or are required to execute a task in their area of expertise.

Sources of Validation Errors

Validation errors arise from many sources that can be grouped into two broad categories – motivational and contextual sources. Group members may not be *motivated* to contribute to a team because they place a low priority on their team membership, because they do not receive any incentives for contributing to that team, or because other members are not contributing or have not in the past.

There are also features of the work, communication, and team context that can lead to validation errors. For example, team members may fail to take responsibility because they are experiencing work overload. This is most likely to occur when work responsibilities are unevenly divided in the group. Work overload can result from attending to one's own work, or from backing-up an overloaded co-worker (cf. Barnes et al., 2009.) Validation errors can be caused by problems imposed by the communication environment: failures in the communication network, misinterpretations of group members' messages due to the lack of richness offered by electronic communication, or time zone differences. Members may not contribute because of status differences among members of the group, and the evaluation apprehension that can accompany it (cf. Hollingshead, 1996).

It is important to note that inaccurate attributions about why a member is not contributing can exacerbate validation errors (cf. Cramton, 2001). For example, a team member may attribute the consistently delayed responses of a member in another time zone to personal characteristics (lazy or disengaged) rather than to the situation (it's 1:00 a.m. in the other team member's location). This, in turn, can lead to resentment and a negative group climate.

Other Precursors of Knowledge-sharing Errors

Knowledge-sharing errors can also stem from characteristics of the task, team, or team members as well as from the team's external environment.

Task Volatility

Tasks can change over time either because they are not well structured at the onset or because of changes in the task specifications by the client or customer. The performance benefits of a transactive memory system can materialize only if there is a match between task knowledge available within the team and the requirements of the task. In addition, some tasks, such as disaster relief work, are by nature volatile. The impromptu teams that respond to such events (Majchrzak et al., 2007) are also likely to experience transactive memory errors of sharedness and validation, as the expertise required by the task may not be available, and members may lack the time to develop a shared understanding of the task and the expertise required; even when the expertise is known and available, team members may lack resources to take action based on their expertise.

Membership Change

Many organizational groups experience dynamic membership changes due to turnover, transfers, and change of organizational roles (Moreland &

Argote, 2003). While a newcomer's novel areas of expertise could potentially contribute new knowledge to the transactive memory system, such membership changes can sometimes have a negative effect on group performance, at least in the short run. When newcomers join a group, they often fill predetermined roles by adapting their specialization to preserve the stability of the original group structure (Lewis et al., 2007). Without deliberate examination of the newcomer's area of expertise, the emphasis on the maintenance of the old structure may override the need to assimilate the newcomer's expertise into the system.

Group Size and Work Allocations

There is much evidence that large groups may be more likely to suffer from knowledge-sharing errors than small groups. A review of the literature on the effects of group size by Moreland, Levine, and Wingert (1996b) indicates that large groups experience more coordination problems, including confusion about task assignments, miscommunication, and scheduling difficulties. They are more likely to have motivational problems with social loafing, free-riding, and efforts to avoid exploitation. Cooperation is less likely in large groups, and negative behaviors such as stealing, cheating, and not helping people in need are more likely. Members in large groups tend to participate less, and are less satisfied with their group. Of course, these are just generalizations, and there are many exceptions. All of these factors can contribute to the likelihood of accuracy, sharedness, and/or validation errors.

Lack of Teamwork Skills

Lack of teamwork skills can lead to an increase in knowledge-sharing errors. Pritchard and Ashleigh (2007) found that team skills training in problem-solving, interpersonal relationships, goal setting, and role allocation were positively associated with many aspects of transactive memory development. For instance, it is likely that a lack of teamwork skills such as goal setting and role allocation increases the incidence of sharedness errors, as they are important in reaching agreement on who is doing what.

Group Climate and Stress

Group climate can influence the frequency and severity of knowledge-sharing errors. Acute stress in the group has been positively associated with breakdowns in the transactive memory system (Ellis, 2006). High levels of relationship conflict negatively influence the relation between group agreement on where the expertise is located in the team, and performance (Rau, 2005). Thus, even in situations of high sharedness, relationship conflict can increase the incidence of validation errors. Group members can refuse to participate in the transactive memory system by intentionally withholding their knowledge (Hollingshead, Fulk, & Monge, 2002). Further, a competitive climate may lead to knowledge hoarding in that group members only complete their part of the task but do not verbalize their expertise while doing so. Nor do they answer questions related to their expertise once their part of the work is complete.

Outcomes of Errors

In the previous sections, we have argued that accuracy, sharedness, and validation errors present unique obstacles to reaching convergence of transactive memory in groups. In this section, we discuss consequences of these errors at the individual, group, and organizational levels, and how the errors affect transactive memory development and group outcomes.

Many empirical research findings on the positive relations between transactive memory systems and group performance imply that transactive memory errors would negatively affect the quality of performance at the group level (Hollingshead, 1998c, 2000; Liang et al., 1995; Moreland & Myaskovsky, 2000). Our previous discussion on the three dimensions of transactive memory errors specify the mechanisms through which those errors can negatively affect group performance: (1) accuracy errors create ambiguity about the content, reliability, and depth of group members' expertise and reduce use of available knowledge resources (Liang et al., 1995); (2) sharedness errors increase coordination costs, omission, and redundancy of some tasks (Hollingshead, 2001); and (3) validation errors lead to the lack of group members' participation in the memory system. Each type of error (or combinations of more than one type) is likely to lead to performance losses (Austin, 2003).

At the individual level, group members may experience negative emotions and interpersonal conflicts due to transactive memory errors. When group members find that their expertise was not accurately assessed by fellow members, they may feel that their expertise and contributions are unnoticed, devalued, and minimized, which in turn lowers their level of trust toward other members and satisfaction about their group processes. Also, when there is no agreement on who knows what and who is responsible for what, group members may experience role conflicts, and much time may be spent trying to reach consensus about subtask assignments. These coordination problems may negatively affect the group members' perceptions about their group effectiveness.

Transactive memory errors may also lead to both performance and financial loss at the organizational level. Validation errors in particular are directly related to and reflective of knowledge management processes in organizations. The lack of participation in maintaining and contributing to a knowledge repository (e.g., intranet) costs organizations a loss of time, effort, and money (Fulk, Monge, & Hollingshead, 2005; Moreland &

Argote, 2003). When organizational members foresee the transactive memory system failing in the future, they may be more likely to pursue working alone as opposed to actively participating in sharing knowledge.

While the consequences we have addressed so far are pessimistic, transactive memory errors may not always lead to catastrophic outcomes in the long term. When we consider that transactive memory systems constantly change over time until the system approaches full convergence, errors are a natural part of the process of constantly updating the system. For instance, there may be unexpected gains when a new expert is discovered in a group and that expert can contribute to the group task in a more meaningful way. By aligning the new expert's roles more accurately with the person's expertise, the group is better able to update the TEP units, redefine member roles, and get closer to the fully converged transactive memory system.

The dynamic nature of transactive memory systems is important when considering changes in group membership, member learning, task types, and structures over time. Positive outcomes from knowledge-sharing errors can occur, but may not be common. Because of such changes, an error at one point may not be an error at a different point. For instance, when a group member is incorrectly assessed as an expert in computer programming at an early stage, it would be an incidence of accuracy error. However, that member, who was initially not an expert in computer programming, is likely to acquire knowledge and become an expert over time as task experience accumulates (Fraidin & Hollingshead, 2005). Similarly, while membership changes increase the likelihood of accuracy and sharedness errors, having a new member in some cases may help the entire group reassess relative expertise of all group members and reconfigure areas of responsibilities. When errors go undetected and the transactive memory system is not updated by the group, errors may be harmful to group process, group performance, or the individual members who are trying to repair the damage done by those errors.

Error Prevention

As mentioned earlier, transactive memory systems are unlikely to develop unless members perceive that they are interdependent with other members in the group. This motivates members to attend to other members' knowledge and abilities, and to participate in the system. The team leader and team members must do their part to make everyone feel that they are valuable, everyone's contributions matter, they can rely on others for information and assistance, and they are accountable to others for their actions. Team-based rewards can also help create feelings of cognitive interdependence among group members.

The likelihood of using transactive memory errors to change and update the system may be higher when group members are vigilant in identifying potential sources of errors. This is likely to be easier to do when there is frequent task-related communication and interpersonal trust among members. Training members in groups and cross-training in different jobs gives group members an opportunity to learn about others' knowledge, abilities, and job requirements (Hollingshead, 1998d; Moreland et al., 1998).

Previous research has considered two interrelated factors to improve accuracy of transactive memory: time and communication. Team tenure seems to be positively related to minimizing the errors, because time allows extensive social relationships, socialization processes, mutual learning, and continuous observation of each other's performance (Bunderson, 2003; Littlepage, Robison, & Reddington, 1997; Rico, Sanchez-Manzanares, Gill, & Gibson, 2008). Communication facilitates familiarity with group members and their expertise over time (Hollingshead, 1998; Lewis, 2004; Rulke & Rau, 2000).

Although communication in general is critical to mitigate accuracy errors, group members are not always diligent or motivated to communicate their expertise or learn others' expertise, especially in autonomous and short-term groups (Yoon & Hollingshead, in press). Therefore, specific communication procedures that facilitate the expertise recognition will likely reduce accuracy errors. Self-disclosure and feedback in the early stage of group development can facilitate group learning, through which group members introduce themselves and explicitly exchange their areas of expertise to better align their roles to their expertise (London, Polzer, & Omoregie, 2005; Rulke & Rau, 2000; Yoo & Kanawattanachai, 2001). This process can be even more beneficial for heterogeneous groups because early verifications of each member's unique characteristics may help the group to better leverage them, especially when they reflect unexpected expertise. In situations where errors can have grave impacts, such as air traffic control, team familiarity and experience are especially important, as they increase the likelihood that members will request and accept back-up when needed (Smith-Jentsch, Kraiger, Cannon-Bowers, & Salas, 2009).

Conclusion and Connections

We conclude by reorganizing our framework of knowledge-sharing errors to fit the 7C model introduced in Chapter 1 (McPhee, 2008; Figure 8.2). Consistent with some other chapters in this book, the norm of reciprocity is the "*cause*" or mechanism that leads to the development of transactive memory. Team-based rewards, divisible tasks, close relationships, and a cooperative group climate are conditions of a *supportive climate* that gives rise to perceived cognitive interdependence, the *condition* necessary to jumpstart the transactive *processes* of evaluating members' knowledge and capabilities, delegating knowledge responsibilities, and information processing, which involve learning, storing, and sharing knowledge. The *subprocesses* of creating, testing, and revising TEP units and of individual

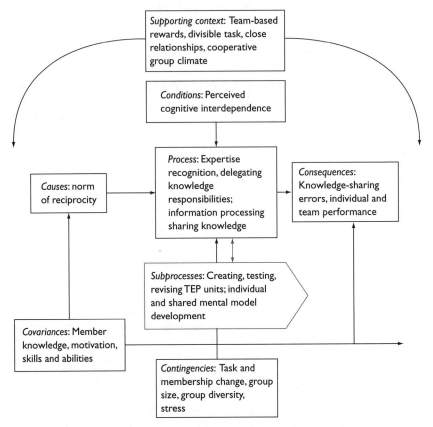

Figure 8.2 Model of knowledge-sharing errors based upon McPhee's (2008) amended diagram of Glaser's (1978) six coding families.

and shared mental model development influence how members evaluate other members' knowledge, delegate knowledge responsibilities, and process information. Member knowledge, motivation skills, and abilities are important to measure and control as *covariances*, as these aspects of group composition naturally have a strong and significant impact on the fidelity of the transactive memory system. *Contingencies* such as task and membership change, group size, group diversity, and acute stress can lead to *consequences* such as knowledge-sharing errors, which in the short term may have a negative impact on individual and team performance. In the long term, these knowledge-sharing errors may lead to improved performance under some conditions.

   Knowledge-sharing errors are a natural and unavoidable process as team members learn and adjust to one another's capabilities. Managers, team leaders, and team members themselves can reduce the negative impacts of these errors by creating conditions that facilitate effective knowledge sharing, and through vigilance. However, these steps alone do not guarantee that knowledge-sharing errors will be corrected, let alone detected (Edmondson, 2004.) What leads some teams to learn from their mistakes, and others to continue down the same ill-advised path? Future research should address this important issue.

References

Austin, J. R. (2003). Transactive memory in organizational groups: The effects of content, consensus, specialization, and accuracy on group performance. *Journal of Applied Psychology, 88*, 866–878.

Barnes, C. M., Hollenbeck, J. R., Wagner, D. T., DeRue, D. S., Nahrgang, J. D., & Schwind, K. M. (2008). Harmful help: The costs of backing-up behavior in teams. *Journal of Applied Psychology, 93*, 529–538.

Berger, J., Cohen, B. P., & Zelditch, M. (1972). Status characteristics and social interaction. *American Sociological Review, 37*, 241–255.

Blickensderfer, E., Cannon-Bowers, J. A., & Salas, E. (1997). Theoretical bases for team self-correction: Fostering shared mental models. In M. M. Beyerlein, D. A. Johnson, & S. T. Beyerlein (Eds.), *Advances in interdisciplinary studies of work teams: Team implementation issues*, Vol. 4 (pp. 249–279). London, UK: JAI Press.

Brandon, D. P., & Hollingshead, A. B. (2004). Transactive memory systems in organizations: Matching tasks, expertise, and people. *Organization Science, 15(6)*, 633–644.

Bunderson, J. S. (2003). Recognizing the utilizing expertise in work groups: A status characteristics perspective. *Administrative Science Quarterly, 48*, 557–591.

Cramton, C. D. (2001). Mutual knowledge problem and its consequences for dispersed collaboration. *Organization Science, 12(3)*, 346–371.

Derry, S. J., DuRussel, L. A., & O'Donnell, A. (1998). Individual and distributed cognitions in interdisciplinary teamwork: a developing case study and emerging theory. *Educational Psychology Review, 10*, 25–57.

Edmondson, A. C. (2004). Learning from mistakes is easier said than done: Group and organizational influences on the detection and correction of human error. *Journal of Applied Behavioral Science, 40*, 66–90.

Ellis, A. P. J. (2006). System breakdown: The role of mental models and transactive memory in the relationship between acute stress and team performance. *Academy of Management Journal, 49*, 576–589.

Fraidin, S. N., & Hollingshead, A. B. (2005). "I know what I'm doing": The impact of gender stereotypes about expertise on task assignments in groups. In M. Neale, E. Mannix, & M. Thomas-Hunt (Eds.), *Managing groups and teams*, Vol. 7, *Status* (pp. 121–141). Greenwich, CT: JAI Press

Fulk, J., Monge, P., & Hollingshead, A. B. (2005). Knowledge resource sharing in dispersed multinational teams: Three theoretical lenses. In D. L. Shapiro, M. A. von Glinow, & J. L. C. Cheng (Eds.), *Managing multinational teams: Global perspectives* (pp. 155–188). Oxford, UK: Elsevier.

Hastie, R. (1986). Experimental evidence on group accuracy. In B. Grofman & G. Owen (Eds.), *Decision research* (Vol. 2., pp. 120–157). Greenwich, CT: JAI Press.

Hinsz, V. B. (1995). Mental models of groups as social systems. *Small Group Research, 26(2)*, 200–233.

Hinsz, V. B., Tindale, R. S., & Vollrath, D. A. (1997). The emerging conceptualization of groups as information processors. *Psychological Bulletin, 121*, 43–64.

Hollingshead, A. B. (1996). Information suppression and status persistence in group decision making: The effects of communication media. *Human Communication Research, 23*, 193–219.

Hollingshead, A. B. (1998a). Communication, learning, and retrieval in transactive memory systems. *Journal of Experimental Social Psychology, 34*, 423–442.

Hollingshead, A. B. (1998b). Retrieval processes in transactive memory systems. *Journal of Personality and Social Psychology, 74*, 659–671.

Hollingshead, A. B. (1998c). Distributed expertise and communication processes in groups. In E. A. Mannix, M. A. Neale, & D. H Gruenfeld (Eds.), *Research on managing groups and teams*, Vol. 1 (pp. 105–125). Greenwich, CT: JAI Press.

Hollingshead, A. B. (1998d). Group and individual training: The impact of practice on performance. *Small Group Research, 29*, 254–280.

Hollingshead, A. B. (2000). Perceptions of expertise and transactive memory in work relationships. *Group Processes and Intergroup Relations, 3*, 257–267.

Hollingshead, A. B. (2001). Cognitive interdependence and convergent expectations in transactive memory. *Journal of Personality and Social Psychology, 81*, 1080–1089.

Hollingshead, A. B. (2010). Transactive memory. In J. Levine & M. Hogg (Eds.), *Encyclopedia of group processes and intergroup relations* (in press). Thousand Oaks, CA: Sage.

Hollingshead, A. B., & Brandon, D. P. (2003). Potential benefits of communication in transactive memory systems. *Human Communication Research, 29*, 607–615.

Hollingshead, A. B., & Fraidin, S. N. (2003). Gender stereotypes and assumptions about expertise in transactive memory. *Journal of Experimental Social Psychology, 39*, 355–363.

Hollingshead, A. B., Fulk, J., & Monge, P. (2002). Fostering Intranet knowledge sharing: An integration of transactive memory and public goods approaches. In P. Hinds & S. Kiesler (Eds.), *Distributed work: New research on working across distance using technology* (pp. 335–355). Cambridge, MA: MIT Press.

Kurman, J. (2003). Why is self-enhancement low in certain collectivist cultures? An investigation of two competing explanations. *Journal of Cross Cultural Psychology, 34*, 496–510.

Levine, J. M., & Moreland, R. L. (1999). Knowledge transmission in work groups: Helping newcomers to succeed. In L. Thompson, J. Levine, & D. Messick (Eds.), *Shared cognition in organizations: The management of knowledge* (pp. 267–296). Mahwah, NJ: Lawrence Erlbaum.

Lewis, K. (2004). Knowledge and performance in knowledge-worker teams: A longitudinal study of transactive memory systems. *Management Science, 50*, 1519–1533.

Lewis, K., Belliveau, M., Herndon, B., & Keller, J. (2007). Group cognition, membership change, and performance: Investigating the benefits and detriments of collective knowledge. *Organizational Behavior and Human Decision Processes, 103(2)*, 159–178.

Liang, D. W., Moreland, R., & Argote, L. (1995). Group versus individual training and group performance: The mediating role of transactive memory. *Personality and Social Psychology Bulletin, 21,* 384–393.

Littlepage, G. E., & Mueller, A. L. (1997). Recognition and utilization of expertise in problem-solving groups: Expert characteristics and behavior. *Group Dynamics: Theory, Research, and Practice, 1,* 324–328.

Littlepage, G. E., Schmidt, G. W., Whisler, E. W., & Frost, A. G. (1995). An input–process–output analysis of influence and performance in problem-solving groups. *Journal of Personality and Social Psychology, 69,* 877–889.

Littlepage, G. E., Robison, W., & Reddington, K. (1997). Effects of task experience and group experience on group performance, member ability and recognition of expertise. *Organizational Behavior and Human Decision Processes, 69,* 133–147.

London, M., Polzer, J. T., & Omoregie, H. (2005). Interpersonal congruence, transactive memory, and feedback processes: An integrative model of group learning. *Human Resource Development Review, 4,* 2005.

Majchrzak, A., Jarvenpaa, S. L., & Hollingshead, A. B. (2007). Coordinating expertise among emergent groups responding to disasters. *Organization Science, 18(1),* 147–161.

McGrath, J. E. (1991). Time, interaction, and performance (TIP): A theory of groups. *Small Group Research, 22(2),* 147–174.

McPhee, R. D. (2008). *7C model of theoretical constructs.* Unpublished manuscript.

Moreland, R. L., & Argote, L. (2003). Transactive memory in dynamic organizations. In R. S. Peterson & E. A. Mannix (Eds.), *Leading and managing people in the dynamic organization* (pp. 135–162). Mahwah, NJ: Lawrence Erlbaum Associates, Inc.

Moreland, R. L., & Myaskovsky, L. (2000). Exploring the performance benefits of group training: Transactive memory or improved communication? *Organizational Behavior and Human Decision Processes, 82,* 117–133.

Moreland, R. L., Argote, L., & Krishnan, R. (1996a). Socially shared cognition at work: Transactive memory and group performance. In J. L. Nye & A. M. Brower (Eds.), *What's social about social cognition? Research on socially shared cognition in small groups* (pp. 57–84). Thousand Oaks, CA: Sage.

Moreland, R. L., Levine, J. M., & Wingert, M. L. (1996b). Creating the ideal group: Composition effects at work. In J. Davis & E. Witte (Eds.), *Understanding group behavior,* Vol. 2 (pp. 11–35). Mahwah, NJ: Erlbaum.

Moreland, R., Argote, L. L., & Krishnan, R. (1998). Training people to work in groups. In R. S. Tindale et al. (Eds.), *Theory and research on small groups* (pp. 37–60). New York, NY: Plenum Press.

Pearsall, M. J., & Ellis, A. P. J. (2006). The effects of critical team member assertiveness on team performance and satisfaction. *Journal of Management, 32,* 575–594.

Poole, M. S. (1985). Task and interaction sequences: A theory of coherence in group decision making interaction. In R. Streed & J. Capella (Eds.), *Sequence and pattern in communicative behavior* (pp. 206–224). London, UK: Edward Arnold.

Prichard, J. S., & Ashleigh, M. J. (2007). The effects of team-skills training on transactive memory and performance. *Small Group Research, 38,* 696–726.

Rau, D. (2005). The influence of relationship conflict and trust on transactive memory: Performance relation in top management teams. *Small Group Research*, *36*, 746–771.

Rico, R., Sanchez-Manzanares, M., Gil, F., & Gibson, C. (2008). Team implicit coordination processes: A team knowledge-based approach. *Academy of Management Review*, *33*, 163–184.

Rulke, D. L., & Rau, D. (2000). Investigating the encoding process of transactive memory development in group training. *Group and Organizational Management*, *25*, 373–396.

Singelis, T. M., Triandis, H. C., Bhawuk, D. P. S., & Gelfand, M. J. (1995). Horizontal and vertical dimensions of individualism and collectivism: A theoretical and measurement refinement. *Cross-Cultural Research*, *29*, 240–275.

Smith-Jentsch, K.A., Kraiger, K., Cannon-Bowers, J. A., & Salas, E. (2009). Do familiar teammates request and accept more backup? Transactive memory in air traffic control. *Human Factors*, *51*, 181–192.

Staggers, N., & Norcio, A. F. (1993). Mental models: Concepts for human–computer interaction research. *International Journal of Man–Machine Studies*, *38*, 587–605.

Thomas-Hunt, M. C., & Phillips, K. W. (2003). Managing teams in the dynamic organization: The effects of revolving membership and changing task demands on expertise and status in groups. In R. S. Peterson & E. A. Mannix (Eds.), *Leading and managing people in the dynamic organization* (pp. 115–133). Mahwah, NJ: Lawrence Erlbaum.

Wegner, D. M. (1987). Transactive memory: A contemporary analysis of the group mind. In B. Mullen & G. R. Goethals (Eds.), *Theories of group behavior* (pp. 185–205). New York, NY: Springer-Verlag.

Wegner, D. M. (1995). A computer network model of human transactive memory. *Social Cognition*, *13*, 319–339.

Yoo, Y., & Kanawattanachai, P. (2001). Developments of transactive memory systems and collective mind in virtual teams. *International Journal of Organizational Analysis*, *9*, 187–208.

Yoon, K., & Hollingshead, A. B. (in press). Cultural stereotyping, convergent expectations, and performance in cross-cultural collaborations. *Social Psychology and Personality Science*.

Chapter 9

Problems and Promises of Managing Explicit Knowledge

The Ideal Case of University Research

Steven R. Corman and Kevin J. Dooley

In the field of knowledge management there is a classic distinction, introduced by Polanyi (1967), between *explicit* knowledge and *tacit* knowledge. Explicit knowledge is formal, and can be recorded and expressed directly in discourse. Tacit knowledge is more implicit and intuitive. It is fragmentary, held internally, and is not expressed directly in discourse: "We know more than we can tell" (Polanyi, 1967, p. 4). The distinction introduced by Polanyi is itself an example of explicit knowledge; understanding how the tacit/explicit distinction fits into the universe of discourse about knowledge management is an example of tacit knowledge.

Many researchers and practitioners believe that tacit knowledge is the most valuable kind, since it is least imitable and typically more complex than explicit knowledge. Thus, much effort has been allocated to determining how to convert tacit knowledge into explicit knowledge, which can be readily managed and exploited. Polanyi believed that this transformation is at work when scientists propose a new explanation or theory. In a more practical example, Nonaka and Takeuchi (1995) tell a story about a group of engineers tasked with making a bread machine, who studied a master baker to unravel the secrets of dough manipulation. Through a laborious process of observation they determined that a special kind of twisting motion seemed to be the key to good bread-making. In another applied domain, Bogue (2006) explains why it is worth the effort for software developers to battle through the tacit-to-explicit conversion process:

> If expert food testers can quantify the differences in jams with no real difference in the outcome, so too can we convert tacit knowledge of how software can and should be developed into the explicit knowledge that we need to be able to communicate with the entire development team – or the entire organization.

Codification takes tacit knowledge out of the mind and makes it communicable. Still, there are limits to what this process can achieve, and many question whether codification is always a worthwhile goal (see, for example, Johnson, Lorenz, & Lundvall, 2002).

We believe that this current orientation towards focusing on tacit over explicit knowledge is problematic in two ways. First, plenty of useful and complex explicit knowledge already exists – some professions routinely create explicit knowledge through writing and publication. Engineering, law, and journalism are three examples. In these cases, even if a good deal of knowledge remains implicit, there is still a substantial body of explicit knowledge that could be managed for the benefit of the organization, but typically is not. Second, it assumes that the management of explicit knowledge is straightforward, at least compared to the problem of making tacit knowledge explicit. Yet the distributed nature of explicit knowledge in the kinds of organizations that are likely to produce it – what Mintzberg (1979) called "adhocracies" – is a problem in itself. Finding and organizing explicit knowledge wherever it is deposited is a significant challenge, even in cases where it is digitally stored. Third, a knowledge management system based on explicit knowledge helps mitigate the errors of sharedness and accuracy that can impede the organization's transactional memory systems (see Chapter 8 in this volume).

In order to explore the potential of managing an organization's explicit knowledge, we undertook development of a demonstration knowledge management system for a large research university. The benefits of management of university knowledge are potentially enormous. Modern research universities are large organizations that employ thousands of scholars and researchers. Poor awareness of what researchers in other parts of the organization are doing creates opportunity costs for universities that want to promote interdisciplinary collaboration. Yet traditional disciplinary structures tend to isolate such knowledge in "stovepipes" of local departments and colleges. Here the problem is not lack of explicit knowledge, which is abundant; the challenge is finding it, organizing it, and communicating it to specific others who could benefit.

The setting for the case is the College of Liberal Arts and Sciences (LAS) within a large, research-intensive university located in the US Southwest. A university setting is ideal to study the potential of systematic knowledge management. First, explicit artifacts representing knowledge domains are readily available via journal and conference papers, and other academic works. Second, an existing knowledge structure, evolved in a different era, exists in the form of organizational structure. Third, because the product of a research university is knowledge, a knowledge management system should provide ample opportunity for improved institution-wide performance through, for example, matching faculty to other faculty, and matching faculty to research opportunities (Dooley, Corman, & McPhee, 2002).

Within this chapter we focus on four important research questions related to the acquisition and use of explicit faculty knowledge artifacts:

1   What challenges exist with regard to locating and getting access to explicit knowledge artifacts? In the context of this case study, we study

the objections faculty might have to participating in a knowledge management project, and how easy or hard it is to obtain faculty publications without the direct involvement of the faculty themselves.

2   How do different representations of explicit knowledge differ in their information content? For this case, we examine whether the titles of academic papers contain different information than their abstracts. This is relevant as titles are easier to capture, but obviously contain less textual information. Thus, the practical side of this question is: What do we lose by only collecting data concerning the titles of faculty works, rather than collecting a more complete representation of the artifact (e.g., abstract, full paper)?

3   How different would an organization look if it organized according to knowledge areas? In our case, this general question translates to: How different would a college look if it were organized around clusters of existing research areas? Colleges and schools within universities tend to be structured according to traditional disciplines, for both institutional and market reasons (Abbott, 1988). Given the rapidly changing nature of research today, and its increasingly interdisciplinary nature (Bammer, 2008), it is relevant to ask how different an academic organization would look if it were organized according to emergent knowledge clusters.

4   If members of an organization have common areas of knowledge, does it make them more likely to know of one another and work together? We examine to the extent to which faculty within the same college who have common interests know of one another and collaborate. This is important because it addresses whether departmental structures are a significant barrier to faculty collaboration.

In the remainder of this chapter, we describe how we collected and analyzed data, discuss key insights derived from our analysis, and conclude by discussing the broader implications of our study.

Data Collection and Analysis Methods

A knowledge management system consists of three components: data that represent knowledge, a structured database to store the knowledge artifacts, and analytical functions that mine and organize the database in various ways. In this case, LAS had implemented a pilot standardized activity reporting system (SARS) for annual evaluation of faculty beginning two years before our project, so by the start of our project the system contained two years of entries for every researcher in the LAS. The entire database encompassed 826 faculty. Of these, 740 participants had at least one publication (identified) between 2002 and 2004. Most faculty (776) were spread between 30 different departments or centers, and represented all ranks.

The SARS contained the title and date of each participant's publications over the two years the system had been running. These corresponded to journal papers, book chapters, conference proceedings and presentations, and other presented works. However, the data in the SARS system was inadequate for two reasons. First, the system was still in "pilot" mode and was still not mandatory for use in performance evaluations. There was therefore no particular incentive for users to be exhaustive or accurate in the information they posted to SARS. Second, the database was updated once a year during the performance evaluation period. Our study was launched mid-year, meaning new articles published since the last performance evaluation period were not included.

In order to accurately test the research questions above, we supplemented the SARS data with a manual search for additional items. We employed approximately a dozen research assistants for two months to find work not recorded in the SARS. These assistants searched department and personal web pages, research indexes such as ABI Inform, Google Scholar, and ISI to find title and abstract data, and went to individual faculty to request specific data as needed. At the end of this process, we had titles and abstracts for 13,274 publications.

The titles and abstracts were combined into one "meta" text for each researcher being studied. Levels of productivity varied greatly among faculty; Figure 9.1 shows a histogram of the number of publications for

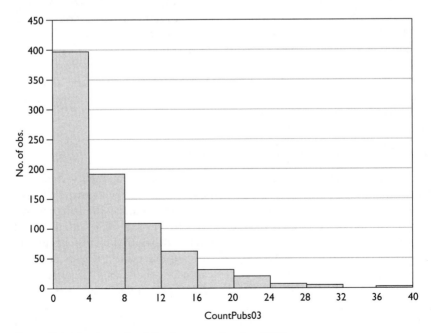

Figure 9.1 Number of publications per faculty, 2003.

each researcher in 2003. Approximately half had four or fewer publications, 70 percent had eight or fewer, and approximately 7 percent had 20 or more publications. If we assume omissions in the database system are more likely the more publications one has to report, then reporting systems like the one used at this university will probably be accurate for the bulk of the people reporting.

In order to analyze the qualitative data (compiled publication titles, abstracts) we used computerized text analysis, a form of manifest content analysis. Traditional content analysis (Krippendorff, 2004) would have been impractical, given the number of texts to be analyzed. It also has the disadvantage of having less than perfect reliability, given its reliance on human coders. Analysis of manifest content has the benefit of being completely reliable, and it is able to analyze large amounts of data in a short period of time. Manifest methods can suffer from validity problems if they are used to answer questions about the latent content of texts (e.g., what they mean); however, in our case the research questions address manifest content, so there is no validity risk.

Centering Resonance Analysis (CRA; Corman, Kuhn, McPhee, & Dooley, 2002), is a method for manifest content analysis of text using network models. CRA has been used by a variety of management and communication researchers (Canary & Jennings, 2008; Lee & James, 2007; Lichtenstein, Dooley, and Lumpkin, 2006). CRA is based on centering theory that posits that speakers and writers create coherence in a text by forming "centers" (noun phrases) that are backward- and forward-looking. Thus, centering theory places importance on words that occur within noun phrases, and words that occur in sequence. These structures are used to create a set of words and their centering-based connections that represents the text as a network. The representation is then analyzed using typical network analysis methods to measure the importance (influence) of words based on their network position. It also allows measurement of the similarity of texts based on the similarity of their networks, and other features of interest to researchers.

Using Crawdad 2.0 software (Corman & Dooley, 2006), texts representing the researchers were parsed, analyzed into noun phrases, then converted into networks – one representing each researcher. The network measure of betweenness centrality (Freeman, 1979) was then used to assess the importance, or "influence" of words within a text. Words that are frequent usually tend to have high influence, but infrequent words may also be influential because the way they are used gives them a central position in the CRA network.

CRA uses "resonance" as a measure of discursive (structural) similarity between two texts. It is computed as a correlation of the word and word-pair influence vectors of two networks, calculated using a cosine similarity metric (Baeza-Yates & Ribeiro-Neto, 1999). Such a statistic can be interpreted as a distance. A matrix of these distances between the networks of all 740 researchers in the study was used as input for spatial analysis techniques, like the multivariate clustering described below.

Lessons Learned from the Data Collection Effort

The first important lesson learned was that the SARS database was not particularly timely in making explicit knowledge resources available for a management effort. The system was used for performance evaluations that take place on a yearly basis. Accordingly, records were only brought up to date around the time evaluations were performed. This is a less than optimal arrangement for facilitating research collaborations in real time. In the most extreme case, valuable knowledge connections might not be discovered until a year after they become relevant. While after-the-fact connections might be interesting from a research point of view, they could occur too late to perform a valuable management function of creating connections that could support a project or meet a grant application deadline.

Second, because data in the system was entered by humans, it did an imperfect job of making explicit knowledge visible. There was a distinct difference between the average publication count per faculty in 2002, 2003, and 2004. Our data for 2002 corresponded to what could be found via manual search, while our data for 2003 and 2004 corresponded to what was found in the SARS database. Assuming that differences in the number of publications from 2003 and 2004 (7.2 per faculty per year, via SARS database) and 2002 (0.7 per faculty per year, via student search) are due to differences in access (not productivity), we conclude that the SARS database increased publication visibility by 10-fold. In other words, the presence of a structured process with appropriate technology increased the visibility of the faculty's work to anyone (internal administrator, other faculty, external stakeholders) by an order of magnitude.

Additionally, the difference between 2003 (5.7 publications per faculty) and 2004 (8.7 publications per faculty) may be attributable to increased "conformance" by faculty. Thus, increased conformance may have enhanced the visible publication count by 50 percent. The student researchers found abstracts for 23 percent of the publications, but this varied greatly across the years: They found 78 percent in 2002, but only 19 percent in 2003 and 2004. Thus, most publications that can be found via Internet search also have easily-found abstracts, and, conversely, most publications that cannot be found via web search do not have (easily-found) abstracts.

Third, political considerations played an unexpected role in our efforts to collect data, and these factors seem to present potential challenges for designing and deploying a system to manage the knowledge artifacts. For example, in this case study, we experienced reluctance of administrators to share data concerning research proposal abstracts sent by faculty members to federal, state, and corporate sponsors. Academic managers already have access to this data, and grants submitted to public agencies are available to the public in varying forms. However, proposals that are submitted and pending or not accepted are not publicly available. The same can be said for articles, chapters, and books that are in preparation or under review. Faculty are reluctant to have these proposals made visible in a system where other researchers (both within the university and at other universities) could use them for competitive advantage.

When we contacted certain faculty for papers not found in the library or online, some of the faculty, upon hearing about the project, were concerned that there could be negative consequences of making their work too visible. One concern was with possibly increasing their internal workload. Some researchers worried that if such data were made available within the university it might result in their being flooded with students or other people seeking help. Many faculty are careful to guard against too much "access," as they view ad hoc inquiries and meeting requests as a disruption to their time allocated to research and service tasks. They felt that by making it easier for students (for example) to find the "right" faculty member, that certain faculty would become inordinately burdened with requests for support. While those who stated concern were in the minority, this is a challenge that any university implementing such a system will have to grapple with; analogous external requests might concern any knowledge-intensive organization.

Another group of faculty feared that the data would be used for evaluation purposes. A research knowledge base gives university managers a holistic view of the university's knowledge production system. There are two risks associated with this. First, simple metrics, such as number of faculty publications, can be used to make judgments about the productivity across units, yet such comparisons may not be valid. A five-page research report in the proceedings of a computer science conference is not comparable to a 30-page article in a history journal, yet entries in a database tend to elide the difference. Second, the data may fly in the face of pre-existing beliefs about the place of certain units. Such results might be attacked simply because they do not conform to traditional structures or a desired storyline based on them. This fear of retribution or negative judgment would be even greater in a setting where there was not the safety of job security (i.e., tenure).

An unexpected consequence of our study was that our data were appropriated to argue against the closing/merging of a particular department. We had included a slide showing the publications per faculty member in each department, and the particular department slated for elimination had one of the highest rates of publication, challenging administrators' arguments that the department was unproductive. Others argued that publications in this area were of lesser quality, and therefore a simple count of quantity was not valid. For some participants, the existence of a knowledge management system threatened to separate data about productivity from narratives they would normally provide to put it in context. Clearly, care must be used in selecting any metrics and incorporating them into a decision-making process.

Comparative Value of Knowledge Artifacts

Because explicit knowledge about a topic or associated with a human agent can exist in multiple forms, any knowledge management system has to make design trade-offs between information value and the cost of obtaining, storing, and analyzing that data. If we use text to represent these knowledge artifacts, then a key methodological question is how the unit of analysis is defined. In our case of using academic publications as texts, there are three possibilities: to define the text as the title, as the abstract, or as the whole body of the text. The whole text provides the broadest representation of knowledge, but it is difficult to obtain full texts in a reliable manner for all active faculty. Titles are the easiest to collect, as titles are typically easily extracted from faculty vitae, which are typically collected annually for performance evaluations. The shortness of titles, and their potential to be used rhetorically, causes some concern from a validity standpoint – is a paper title a valid and complete manifestation of the underlying knowledge area? Abstracts represent a compromise in that they contain significantly more information than the title, and yet are easier to collect than full texts. Our pilot implementation allowed us to study results using titles and abstracts as knowledge artifacts, in order to see if they contained different information.

Table 9.1 shows the words with the highest average influence across all LAS publications in 2003 and 2004, using publication titles as data; Table 9.2 shows the same using abstract text as data. The overlap in content between the compiled titles versus the compiled abstracts appears to be moderate, but not strong:

- In constructing two lists of words, the most influential 30 words from *titles*, and then from *abstracts*, about half of the words occur on both lists.
- Words on both lists: analysis, child, communication, development, effect, electron, family, method, model, new, protein, social, structure, student, study, system.
- Words only in *abstracts* list: behavior, change, data, gene, group, high, human, large, process, program, relationship, research, species, theory.
- Words only in *titles* list: adolescent, American, dynamics, gender, history, influence, language, political, reaction, review, role, woman.

A possible interpretation is that individual words are perhaps used in three ways within the academic text. First, both the title and the abstract contain

Table 9.1 Highest average influence, 2003–04, using titles

Word	Average influence	Word	Average influence
American	0.0118	method	0.0045
child	0.0115	family	0.0044
study	0.0096	adolescent	0.0043
analysis	0.0092	student	0.0043
effect	0.0080	development	0.0042
woman	0.0079	gender	0.0039
model	0.0077	use	0.0038
history	0.0074	political	0.0038
communication	0.0067	role	0.0038
system	0.0064	influence	0.0038
electron	0.0064	DNA	0.0038
reaction	0.0058	null	0.0038
social	0.0056	Latino	0.0037
protein	0.0053	gene	0.0037
research	0.0051	data	0.0036
structure	0.0051	Arizona	0.0036
review	0.0050	relationship	0.0032
new	0.0048	population	0.0032
language	0.0047	human	0.0032
dynamics	0.0045	property	0.0032

Table 9.2 Highest average influence, 2003–04, using abstracts

Word	Average influence	Word	Average influence
study	0.0248	human	0.0103
research	0.0221	large	0.0102
data	0.0218	relationship	0.0101
child	0.0207	program	0.0101
model	0.0200	electron	0.0100
system	0.0191	change	0.0099
analysis	0.0177	group	0.0098
high	0.0127	process	0.0096
social	0.0126	theory	0.0091
communication	0.0120	gene	0.0090
protein	0.0119	field	0.0087
method	0.0119	cell	0.0086
student	0.0115	problem	0.0083
structure	0.0114	region	0.0083
effect	0.0114	community	0.0082
species	0.0113	plant	0.0082
development	0.0112	conflict	0.0080
new	0.0107	response	0.0076
behavior	0.0105	sample	0.0075
family	0.0103	population	0.0075

explicit references to the phenomena being studied (e.g., child, communication, protein). Second, the text may refer to information about the research process (e.g., behavior, process, theory); such references are more likely to occur in the abstract than the title because of the extended length available in the abstract. Third, text may act as a frame to attract attention and signify position within the research community (e.g., American, dynamics, political, role, woman). This type of market-oriented usage is more likely to occur in the title than the abstract because titles are typically the first thing a potential reader looks at in order to determine interest and intent to read.

While we did not collect enough longitudinal data to make claims of how these textual, explicit themes may change over time, we believe that there may be more commonality over time and across researchers in abstract-based texts. The research process is relatively stable and shared, and this should be reflected in abstractions. On the other hand, the framing of research is more dynamic and idiosyncratic, meaning titles should tend to change with intellectual trends. We caution that these interpretations are limited by the fact that only 20 percent of the titles had an accompanying abstract for comparison.

Uncovering Research Clusters

Colleges tend to be organized along traditional disciplines: psychology, sociology, language arts, physics, etc. These disciplinary boundaries are an efficient market mechanism to recruit and train students, vet and disseminate research knowledge, and reward accomplishment. However, areas in which faculty are currently working may or may not correspond to those disciplinary boundaries, in part because there is not a one-to-one correspondence between what is taught and what is researched. In any given department, faculty may teach topics that they do not research and they may do research on topics they do not teach in the department/school. Whereas traditional department structures may still be useful ways to organize for universities' teaching missions, they may not yield the most effective research results at an institutional level. In order to examine this question, we used the SARS database to cluster faculty according to their knowledge domains, and compare those clusters to existing departmental structure. In order to do this, we formed a single text for each faculty, where the text was made up of all of the titles of their respective publications.

We used a measure of similarity between CRA networks described above – resonance – to identify clusters of faculty. Resonance between two participants is high if their CRA networks use similar words that are connected in similar ways. In some cases resonance occurs because people have co-authored and thus have some of the same paper titles in their text, but it can also occur in cases where people have published independently on similar topics. We computed resonance for all possible pairs of the 590 personnel in the set, using combined titles for both 2003 and 2004.

Combining all pair-wise resonance values into a matrix produces a "similarity" matrix that can be analyzed by hierarchical clustering. This is a bottom-up method that begins by combining the two most similar cases into a cluster, treating them as a combined case. It then repeats this process, combining the next two most similar cases, and so on. The result is a pyramid with the individual cases at the bottom, a progression of growing clusters at various steps in the middle, and one cluster containing all the cases at the end. An analyst interprets this structure to select a level somewhere in the middle where the clustering "makes sense." In our case, this means it distinguishes coherent topic sets without combining too many unlike cases. The structure above the selected level of clusters shows how they combine into higher-order groupings.

Figure 9.2 depicts how the 25 low-level clusters we identified are organized at higher levels. Clusters within a given branch are more similar to each other than clusters in other branches. The main division is between

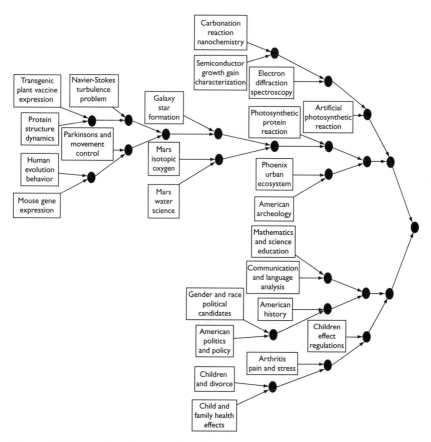

Figure 9.2 Hierarchy of knowledge clusters.

natural sciences in the top half and social sciences in the bottom half. This is what one would expect in a college of liberal arts, providing face validation of our analysis. The natural science branch contains 20 fewer researchers but almost twice as many clusters, indicating more fragmentation. This may indicate that more specialized and compartmentalized knowledge exists in the physical than social sciences. It may also reflect that more knowledge (or at least language) sharing goes on in the social sciences. Two clusters near the top right contain "photosynthetic" and "reaction" in different sub-branches, one dealing with electronic systems and the other with natural systems. This is an example of a possible collaboration opportunity that university managers could strategically target for development.

An alternate way of looking at similarity (resonance) scores is to set some threshold resonance value (e.g., 0.01) and treat a pair of people as being *linked* if their resonance is at or above the threshold, then show these links as a network of shared interests. We conducted such an analysis to examine differences between the within- vs cross-department shared interests, whatever they might be. We found some interesting features of the cross-disciplinary connections in the college. Many of the within-department links were in groups that were disconnected from the rest of the network. This supports our contention above that while traditional department-based structures may be good for organizing teachers under a particular broad academic topic, they do a rather poor job of connecting researchers with similar specific interests. By contrast, few of the cross-department links are of this isolated nature. Instead, the connections form several dense clusters. This means that there is considerable potential for making these people aware of one another's interests if they are not already (a subject we discuss below).

Our analysis also indicated that cross-department clusters were joined by *bridges*, who connected two groups by co-membership in both; and/or *liaisons*, who connected groups without belonging to them. Researchers who occupy these "choke points" play a disproportionate role in integrating the system of research interests. They are good candidates for leadership on efforts like grant projects that cross disciplinary boundaries, because they have knowledge in each of two domains. They are also especially good candidates for retention efforts, since losing them would entail fragmentation of different parts of the network.

We also collapsed similar-interest data across researchers according to department memberships to see which departments were most closely related from a knowledge perspective. Figure 9.3 shows this structure. It is shaded to reflect *factions* (de Amorim, Barthélemy, & Ribeiro, 1990), which partition network nodes into k groups that maximize within- versus between-group connections. Here $k = 3$ because the departments in question represent humanities, social science, and natural science divisions in the college.

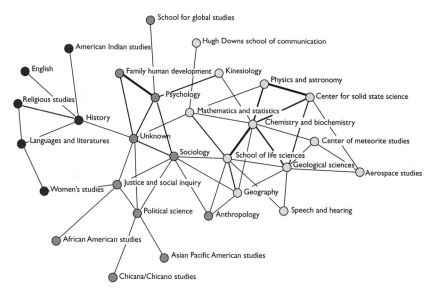

Figure 9.3 Common interest network, departments.

Of particular interest here is the fact that the social science faction forms a bridge between the humanities and natural sciences cluster – no connections exist between the humanities and natural sciences. Surprisingly, there are also many more connections between the social and natural sciences than between social science and humanities. A diagram like this shows both where existing connections between departments might be best exploited (say, to create new research centers), and where effort could be made to create connections (for example between the humanities and natural sciences).

In examining the overall and detailed results of the clustering, we can make the following observations:

- Overall, there is a large web of common interests in LAS.
- One large component is vulnerable to single points of disconnection. This means particular, individual faculty act as boundary spanners between knowledge factions. In discussions with university management, some of these boundary-spanning activities were known to them and others were not.
- Individual large components offer opportunities for focusing collaboration and grant getting.
- Connections between departments based on resonance links suggest three factions based on humanities, social sciences, and natural sciences.
- Connections between social sciences and natural sciences are stronger than those between social sciences and humanities.

Potential for an Intellectual "Dating Service"

University structures group faculty with similar disciplinary interests into departments. Because they occupy common physical office space, they are more likely to come into contact and share interests. Likewise, departments with similar subject matter are often located in the same building or area of campus; for example, humanities units might be located in one building, physical sciences in another, and so on. This arrangement promotes patterns based on a traditional conceptual mapping of disciplines. However, this same arrangement tends to create barriers to the development of communication relationships (Corman, 1990) among "unlike" disciplines, and these are precisely the kinds of relationships envisioned by the push for more interdisciplinary scholarship.

As demonstrated above, the methods applied in this study can be used to detect similarity between the interests of two researchers regardless of their location in the disciplinary structure or their proximity in physical space. This provides the potential for an "intellectual data service" that connects researchers to one another based on common interests. The value of such a service would depend on how it would supplement the existing relational network among scholars. Despite the tendency of university structure to reproduce traditional connections between disciplines, researchers do get to know people in other fields. They might have met them working on a university committee, for example, and know about their professional work in this way.

Therefore the potential value of matching faculty based on similarity of their texts would depend not just on the extent to which there are similarities, but also on the status of existing relationships, as shown in Table 9.3. If such a system revealed links within a researcher's own department, it would likely do little to supplement the existing physical proximity mechanisms for creating these connections. Probably, if someone is doing similar work in a researcher's own department, he or she knows about it or collaborates with that person. Outside the "home" department, there might already be some existing collaborations. Here, a match might indicate new connections between the researchers' work, but would not create any new relationships. The scale continues to the best-case scenario for an intellectual dating service, that in which it would connect two people who have similar interests who do not know one another at all.

To determine the likely value of such a service, we recruited a convenience sample of 10 researchers from a social science unit participating in the study. For each volunteer, we obtained the top 30 similarity (resonance) matches of other researchers in the university – in other words, we identified the people most similar to them in research interests. We asked participants to review these matches and indicate for each (1) if they know the person identified; (2) if they have co-authored with the person; and (3) if they could describe their common research interests. Since we already

Table 9.3 "Dating service" conditions and impact

Condition		Impact	Comment
In own department		Lowest	Can already collaborate using local networks
In other department and...	already co-authored with	Low	Relationship exists; could show new connections
	no co-authoring but can describe shared interests	Mod	Could show additional shared interest or give better picture
	know them but nothing else	High	Potential to add collaboration to an existing relationship
	don't know them at all	Highest	Potential to create new relationships *and* promote collaboration

Table 9.4 Distribution of cases across impact categories

Condition		Average (%)
In own department		29.0
In other department and...	already co-authored with	0.7
	no co-authoring but can describe shared interests	2.0
	know them but nothing else	7.7
	don't know them at all	60.7

knew the departmental affiliations of those matched, we were able to classify these 300 cases into the categories of Table 9.3.

The results are shown in Table 9.4. Only 29 percent of the matches were with people in the researchers' own departments, with approximately seven in 10 cases flagging links to potential collaborators in other departments. In nearly all of these cases the links are to other researchers the participants do not know at all. Only in a small number of cases have they co-authored with the matches or do they know anything about their common interests.

Granted, this was a small convenience sample and it focused on a single department. Perhaps the dynamics of that department make it particularly insular. However, if it is typical, then there is enormous potential in using a system like this to connect researchers with those in other disciplines who have common interests. Even if few of the relationships bore fruit, the numbers involved make it an attractive proposition. In this study we have 740 researchers. If we identify 30 good matches for each of them and 69 percent are either unknown or only casual acquaintances, then if just 1 percent of those make research connections that is more than 75 interdisciplinary connections that could be created through this method.

Implications

This case study demonstrates, first, that, despite the existence of a large supply of explicit knowledge artifacts, development of an effective management system presents a challenge. There is no technical barrier to analyzing the texts, but making them usable is hampered by practical, social, and political challenges. These barriers have to be dealt with before the considerable benefits of a management system can be realized.

Practically, there is a difference between the existence of information and it being visible to a management system. In an organization like a university, production of explicit knowledge artifacts is a routine but decentralized effort. Researchers produce articles, applications, papers, and books, but they are published in cooperation with external organizations like publishers, granting agencies, and professional associations. There is no mechanism that guarantees that the university will be aware of them.

As we learned in this case, the structure of a submission system can place limits on the timeliness of the data collected. If it only collects data on completed work (rather than work in progress) and does so only in conjunction with a yearly evaluation process, then the data may not be timely enough to make valuable connections between researchers. Even putting that problem aside, a system that depends on humans to provide it with data suffers from limitations of memory, diligence, and so on, that can constrain its completeness. An effort like the one undertaken here to supplement the SARS system with manual data collection is not practical in "production" use, and automated means of gathering data from publication outlets, granting agencies, and so on, would be needed.

An explicit knowledge management system also has unintended social and political consequences that may cause participants to question its value (see Chapter 5 in this volume). In our case, researchers worried that their work might become *too* visible, causing them extra work, providing their competitors with an advantage, and/or taking their work out of its proper evaluation context. Management may also be threatened by too-available information, as in this case where it was used to resist reorganization plans. To mitigate these concerns, it would be possible to designate certain types of data in the knowledge base as only accessible to certain groups of users, as is done in other enterprise data management systems.

While the system described here faced challenges, working those out seems clearly justified by the value it could provide. The researchers who had concerns about the system were a rather small minority. Conversely, most faculty appeared intrigued with the idea of being able to find other appropriate faculty when needed, and our "dating service" experiment bears out that such a capability is likely to yield novel and useful (i.e., creative) connections. Van Rijnsoever, Hesselsand, and Vandeberg (2008) found that academics who network extensively within research communities were more likely to have a greater number of publications and patents. From their resource-based perspective, faculty–faculty networks provide

> access to expertise, cross fertilization across disciplines, improving access to funds, obtaining prestige or visibility, learning tacit knowledge about a technique, pooling knowledge for tackling large and complex problems, enhancing productivity, educating a student, increasing specialization of science and for fun and pleasure.
> (Van Rijnsoever et al., 2008, p. 1257).

Thus, while we suspect that faculty would begrudgingly accept a knowledge base used by administrators, and potentially skeptical of one open to the public, they would probably value having access to such search services themselves.

The knowledge networks identified in this case are of tremendous potential value to a university. There is ever-increasing importance placed in cross-disciplinary collaboration, yet traditional structures do little to promote it. Designed for grouping teachers together under broad disciplinary headings, they do little to reflect specific scholarly interests that may cut across these disciplines. Analyzing explicit knowledge artifacts has the potential to show where points of connection already exist, and where effort is needed to create them. It also identifies key players who maintain connections across different fields of interest.

As much as this project demonstrated that value could be realized by identifying knowledge networks within a university, even more benefit could be gained by using this approach across universities. Professional societies and their journals serve as the primary mechanism by which academics in a particular domain aggregate and self-identify, but they are an imperfect way to identify a knowledge network because any single individual may decide not to be part of a society, or publish in its journals, for any number of reasons. Having a multi-university or even national or international knowledge base could identify connections based on actual content of work. It would not require active faculty involvement, and could be dynamic over time. Given the rapidly changing face of academic research, knowledge networks will also be dynamic, and so a knowledge base should enable such dynamism.

Our results beg the question: Are universities optimally organized today? Most universities still retain structures based on traditional disciplinary divisions. Our example showed that a structure based on research foci would have little relationship to the existing department structure, save for the split between the physical and social sciences. Thus, we might conclude that existing organizational structures facilitate the support of educational programs more so than the execution of research programs. If true, it suggests that universities may wish to move more explicitly to matrix styles of management, where a faculty member belongs to one (or more) units based on teaching responsibilities, and one (or more) orthogonal units based on research responsibilities. The emergence of interdisciplinary research centers and the increasing number of faculty with joint appointments suggests this trend has already begun.

Still, it is an open question whether there is more potential in connecting intellectually dissimilar researchers (what we might call a genesis strategy) or in connecting researchers with probable intellectual similarities (what we could call a facilitation strategy). Though resolving that question is beyond the scope of this study, it is safe to say that both strategies are potentially valuable, and that a system like the one demonstrated here is useful in either case. An explicit knowledge management system contains little information to help decide whether disparate intellectual domains – for example, American history and Mars water science – would benefit from being connected. That kind of judgment can only be made creatively and in the abstract. On the other hand, such an exercise benefits from knowing what the existing intellectual structure really is (as in Figure 9.2) and where cross-department links do not already exist. So our system could at least play a supporting role, showing where genesis could potentially take place. It could play a much more direct role in the facilitation strategy, however, as demonstrated in the intellectual dating service exercise. Given the recent emphasis on interdisciplinary development in research and education, it seems clear that this would be of enough benefit by itself to justify maintaining a knowledge management system.

Finally, we conclude with some conjectures about what our study implies regarding developing knowledge management systems in general. If we step outside of the university context and look instead at organizations where explicit knowledge also exists – for example, consulting, medicine, or law – both the challenges and the potential may be greater. Academics naturally publish their knowledge in a public manner as part of their job. In professional organizations, such knowledge might be considered proprietary and not shared, or else it might never be written into formal text simply because it is not a priority to do so. Additionally, texts that exist in such organizations may not be readily identifiable with particular individuals – many corporate reports are without authorship, for a variety of reasons. This does not keep the texts from being useful, but it does limit the ability to reason down to the individual level. In such cases, it might be more logical to associate knowledge artifacts with teams or business units. Third, job security may be an issue. Professional workers may be concerned about the type of judgments that might be made on the basis of such analytics.

That said, the opportunity for sharing explicit knowledge may be even greater outside academia. A university is typically geographically bound, thus proximity may facilitate the transactional memory system (see Chapters 7 and 8 in this volume) of the organization. Many corporations have workers distributed across the globe, thus there is very little chance that one person will meet and get to know a relevant colleague down the hallway. Systems that facilitate knowing "who knows what" can help professional organizations staff projects properly and look for knowledge-sharing opportunities.

Professional organizations also have a much greater capability to act strategically and collectively around insights gained from a knowledge management system. Whereas a university, upon finding faculty with shared interests, might facilitate them at least meeting one another, a professional organization can reorganize and assign work tasks in such a manner that the connection is made more tangibly. Future research should examine the implementation-related similarities and differences between these two contexts in order to better understand the barriers to effective implementation.

References

Abbott, A. (1988). *The system of professions: An essay on the division of Expert Labor*. Chicago, IL: University of Chicago Press.

Baeza-Yates, R., & Ribeiro-Neto, B. (1999). *Modern information retrieval*. New York, NY: ACM Press, Addison-Wesley.

Bammer, G. (2008). Enhancing research collaborations: Three key management challenges. *Research Policy, 37(5)*, 875–887.

Bogue, R. L. (2006, September 16). *Convert tacit knowledge into explicit knowledge to ensure better application development*. TechRepublic. Retrieved from: http://articles.techrepublic.com.com/5100–10878_11–6117372.html.

Canary, H., & Jennings, M. (2008). Principles and influence in codes of ethics: A centering resonance analysis comparing pre- and post-Sarbanes–Oxley codes of ethics. *Journal of Business Ethics, 80(2)*, 263–278.

Corman, S. R. (1990). A model of perceived communication in collective networks. *Human Communication Research, 16*, 582–602.

Corman, S., & Dooley, K. (2006). *Crawdad Text Analysis System 2.0*. Chandler, AZ: Crawdad Technologies, LLC.

Corman, S., Kuhn, T., McPhee, R., & Dooley, K. (2002). Studying complex discursive systems: Centering resonance analysis of organizational communication. *Human Communication Research, 28(2)*, 157–206.

de Amorim, S. G., Barthélemy, J., & Ribeiro, B. (1990). *Clustering and Clique Partitioning: Simulated Annealing and Tabu Search Approaches*. Research report from Groupe d'études et de recherche en analyse des décisions. Ecole des Hautes Etudes Commerciales, Ecole Polytechnique, Université McGill.

Dooley, K., Corman, S., & McPhee, R. (2002). A knowledge directory for identifying experts and areas of expertise. *Human Systems Management, 21(4)*. 217–228.

Freeman, L. C. (1979). Centrality in social networks: conceptual clarification. *Social Networks, 1,* 215–239.

Johnson, B., Lorenz, E., & Lundvall, B. (2002). Why all this fuss about codified and tacit knowledge? *Industrial and Corporate Change, 11(2),* 245–262.

Krippendorff, K. (2004). *Content Analysis: An Introduction to Its Methodology.* New York, NY: Sage.

Lee, P., & James, E. (2007). She EOs: Gender effects and investor reactions to the announcements of top executive appointments. *Strategic Management Journal, 28,* 227–241.

Lichtenstein, B., Dooley, K., & Lumpkin, T. (2006). An emergence event in new venture creation: Measuring the dynamics of nascent entrepreneurship. *Journal of Business Venturing, 21(2),* 153–175.

Mintzberg, H. (1979). *The structuring of organizations: A synthesis of the research.* Englewood Cliffs, NJ: Prentice-Hall.

Nonaka, I., & Takeuchi, H. (1995). *The knowledge-creating company: How Japanese companies create the dynamics of innovation.* Oxford, UK: Oxford University Press.

Polanyi, M. (1967). *The tacit dimension.* New York, NY: Anchor Books.

Van Rijnsoever, F., Hesselsand, L., & Vandeberg, R. (2008). A resource-based view on the interactions of university researchers. *Research Policy, 37(8),* 1255–1266.

Part III

The Communicative *Technologies* of Organizational Knowledge

Chapter 10

The Utility of Information and Communication Technologies in Organizational Knowledge Management

Andrew J. Flanagin and Melissa Bator

By virtue of their tremendous capacity to capture, store, transmit, and process information, electronic technologies have become critical information management tools in the last several decades. A wide range of information and communication technologies (ICTs) – ranging from simple tools like calendar systems and e-mail to more complex group support and data-mining technologies – has ushered in substantial organizational efficiency gains. Yet, in many instances, the advantages conferred by ICTs are primarily first- or second-order improvements of "substitution" or "enlargement" (see Malone & Rockart, 1991), whereby existing tasks are performed more efficiently, though often by several orders of magnitude. These efficiency gains are for the most part firmly rooted in the *processing of information*, rather than in the generation, support, and transmission of organization *knowledge*. Thus, and depending on the definition of knowledge adopted, one view is that though they are immensely important for information processing, ICTs often fail to alter organizational knowledge creation and management today in any fundamental way.

Yet, contemporary ICTs can also go well beyond substitution and enlargement of existing practices, and are in many cases being used to "reconfigure" (Malone & Rockart, 1991) social, economic, and political structures. The Internet, for example, by positioning discrimination and processing functions primarily in the hands of individuals, privileges interactivity among users through a dynamic system where people play roles of both information consumer and information provider. One consequence of this structure is wide-scale, sustained collaboration among individuals, which can support instances of collective problem-solving that reconfigure existing social relations. Indeed, this capacity to promote, support, and sustain collective endeavors among dispersed individuals is a core feature of contemporary technologies that can readily contribute to organizational knowledge creation and sharing. Nonetheless, this capacity remains largely unexamined as a form of organizational knowledge management today, particularly in its most prevalent web-based and "non-organizational" instantiations.

Thus, the utility of ICTs in organizational knowledge management to date has been both exaggerated and understated. The role of ICTs is exaggerated when their information processing features are viewed as equivalent to knowledge creation, transfer, and learning. The role of ICTs is understated when their remarkable potential for supporting situated practice – which we argue is the core feature of organizational knowledge – is not recognized, appreciated, or exploited for organizational knowledge management.

In this chapter we address these issues by first discussing the nature of knowledge (as distinct from information), and the implied requirements for organizational knowledge management (as distinct from information processing). In the process, we distinguish between "content" and "relational" perspectives on knowledge management and advocate for a view of knowledge that accommodates its communicative nature. We next discuss the circumstances under which ICTs are and are not well-suited to support knowledge management, and identify current instances of technology use that (1) are said to be used for knowledge management but are not; (2) are being used for knowledge management but are not identified as such; or (3) have potential to be used more fully for organizational knowledge processes. To this discussion we bring a focus on contemporary web-based tools that have traditionally been viewed as outside the purview of organizational knowledge and knowledge management. We then identify the kinds of social and organizational issues that arise with the use of ICTs for knowledge management processes, and suggest theoretical and practical directions for future inquiry based on these observations.

Communication and Organizational Knowledge

During the mid-1990s there emerged a growing sentiment that an organization's stock of knowledge and how it is sustained, managed, and grown is a critical part of a wider movement toward a knowledge society (Drucker, 1994; Nonaka & Takeuchi, 1995; Spender, 1996). The concept of a knowledge society stands in contrast to industrial society, where workers need neither an education nor specialized skill in order to obtain work in most industrial firms. Industrial workers could be taught their craft on the job. A knowledge society, however, requires workers with formal education, and the ability and drive to seek out continuous opportunities for learning (Drucker, 1994). Knowledge workers make use of reflective practices in order to accomplish their work, such as actively managing a network of contacts and resources that enables the worker to accomplish his or her job. This emphasis on knowledge generally, and organizational knowledge specifically, is attributed to the emergence of globalized economies, highly competitive business environments, and the advancement of information and communication technologies (Alavi, 2000; David & Foray, 2002; Zorn & May, 2002).

Organizational knowledge is enabled by the interrelation of organizational members who each possess individual stocks of knowledge, but who interact within the shared context of the firm (Nonaka, 2005). Formal organizations serve to integrate the disparate knowledge of individuals in order to accomplish larger goals, such as achieving competitive advantage (Chakravarthy, McEvily, Doz, & Rau, 2003), and knowledge takes on its organizational status when individuals "draw distinctions in the courses of their work by taking into account the contextuality of their actions" (Tsoukas & Vladimirou, 2001, p. 979). Although it is most often assumed that knowledge resides in the individual, other perspectives emphasize knowledge as socially embedded (Lundvall & Johnson, 1994), as a collective resource that is greater than individual inputs (Wegner, 1995), as a network phenomenon (Contractor & Monge, 2002), or as a social property of communities of practice (Brown & Duguid, 1998; see also Iverson & McPhee, 2002).

Boundaries demarcating where knowledge resides are not always clear in a knowledge society where free markets allow greater flows of materials and information, information and communication technologies contribute to a dramatic increase in and improved accessibility of knowledge, and competitive business environments force organizations to innovate in order to establish or maintain competitive advantage. In addition, how knowledge differs from information is sometimes ambiguous when electronic communication tools enable immediate access to a wealth of resources, both within and between organizations. Issues of where knowledge resides and how it differs from information are particularly salient to firms that seek to understand and manage the public knowledge generated by consumers, professional groups, advocates, and others that affect a business's operations on a daily basis. In this fashion, organizational knowledge is critical, yet sometimes ill-defined and indistinct, in the context of a knowledge society.

Knowledge and its Communicative Nature

There is disagreement about the nature of information and knowledge, and the distinction between the two. Traditional information processing perspectives, for example, distinguish between data (raw numbers and facts), information (processed or analyzed data that takes on relevance), and knowledge (applied information endowed by experience). A further distinction is often made between "explicit" and "tacit" knowledge (see, for example, Nonaka, 1994): explicit knowledge can be codified and communicated in the form of symbols, such as operation manuals and written procedures, whereas tacit knowledge is gained only through experience in a specific context, and is therefore obtained through mechanisms such as apprenticeship training. Thus, although explicit knowledge is "transmittable in formal, systematic language," tacit knowledge "has a personal quality, which makes it hard to formalize and communicate" (Nonaka, 1994, p. 16). The distinction between explicit and tacit knowledge is sometimes supplemented by a consideration of "cultural" knowledge, or the shared beliefs and assumptions about an organization's goals, identity, capabilities, and the like (Choo, 2006).

Yet some argue that tacit knowledge is required to make sense of explicit knowledge, since a particular personal understanding is necessary to interpret and process explicit information (Polanyi, 1966, 1969). Absent this indispensable personal component, explicit information cannot be understood, and cannot contribute to the formation of new tacit knowledge. Knowledge thus has an "irreducibly social, value-laden, and personal character" (Tsoukas & Mylonopoulos, 2004, p. 7; see also Brown & Duguid, 2000) that distinguishes it from information, which some accordingly define as knowing *about* something, as distinct from knowledge, or knowing *of* something (Tsoukas & Mylonopoulos, 2004). Seen this way, knowledge is "socially embedded and inseparable from practice" (Hayes & Walsham, 2003, p. 73), whereas information serves as an input that is contextualized and understood through complex and situated processes of knowledge creation.

Consistent with this perspective, Hayes and Walsham (2003) note two fundamentally different epistemological views underlying knowledge and knowledge management. "Content" perspectives argue that knowledge is codifiable, and can be readily and accurately stored and retrieved. This content view emphasizes knowledge as an economic asset that can be obtained, held, and exchanged among individuals. Knowledge itself is thus seen as capable of being stored in databases and other repositories, which enables it to endure beyond the tenure of any single organizational member. By contrast, "relational" perspectives argue that knowledge is relative, specific to a particular context, and reflects esoteric viewpoints that may or may not be understood beyond the specific locations in which they are embedded. From the relational perspective, the focus is on the processes by which knowledge is gained and shared. In this context, the use of ICTs as knowledge transfer tools can be problematic, unless they can accommodate the rich processes required to support sensemaking activities (Walsham, 2002).

Taken together, this suggests a definition of knowledge as *situated practice, problem-solving, and thinking*. Knowledge involves judgments within a domain that are guided by the particular context in question (Tsoukas & Vladimirou, 2001). According to Tsoukas and Mylonopoulos (2004, p. 7):

> Viewing organizations as knowledge systems makes us realize that the locus of individual understanding is not so much in the head as in *situated practice*: the individual understands and acts in the world through drawing on sets of socially defined values, beliefs, and cognitive categories within particular material and social circumstances.

Kuhn and Jackson (2008) similarly argue that knowledge is fundamentally social, and extends beyond cognition to include emergent social practices within specific contexts. They thus view knowing as "situated problem solving" (p. 457), and propose that researchers consider the "knowledge-accomplishing activities" that occur in organizational practice.

Defining knowledge as situated practice, problem-solving, and thinking suggests its fundamentally *communicative* nature. Because it is necessarily situated in practice and a specific context, knowledge requires communication among individuals in order to make sense of it, to exchange it, and therefore to derive benefit from it. These processes are all rooted in human communication, and require an understanding of communicative processes. That said, knowledge is not a commodity that can be transferred simply and unproblematically from person to person. Rather, it requires situated understanding achieved in context. As Walsham (2002, p. 272) argues, this requires a shift in current thinking about knowledge processes:

> I would like to see a change of language from the use of terms such as "knowledge repositories," "knowledge transfer," and "knowledge sharing" to more human communication-oriented terms such as "supporting sense-reading and sense-giving processes," "facilitating knowledgeable action," and "enabling effective interaction."

This change is not trivial, suggesting as it does a shift from a transmission model of communication to a more deeply relational view. Moreover, this perspective on information, knowledge, and their differences suggests particular features, roles, and capabilities of ICTs in the support of organizational knowledge, as discussed next.

The Use of ICTs for Knowledge Management

Several, often incompatible, perspectives exist regarding the applicability of ICTs to organizational knowledge management processes. Some among these are more true to the view of knowledge as a situated communicative process (as articulated above), while others rely on a more traditional information processing view. In addition, important socio-technical developments, such as the rise of social computing processes on the web, suggest compelling new directions in contemporary organizational knowledge management.

ICTs, Information Processing, and Knowledge Management

The advent of networked computing and the ability to store large amounts of information has prompted many attempts to capture organizational knowledge, using tools like information databases, expert yellow pages, or best practice directories (McDermott, 1999; Tsoukas & Vladimirou, 2001; Walsham, 2001). It is not uncommon, for example, for organizations to take a stockpile approach toward knowledge management, using ICT tools as information repositories (Huysman & de Wit, 2004) rather than as tools that foster knowledge generation and facilitate its transfer. Such efforts, however, have met with mixed success, and have spawned a number of debates regarding the use of ICTs in knowledge management.

As noted earlier, "content" perspectives on knowledge management (see Hayes & Walsham, 2003) argue that knowledge is codifiable, can be readily and accurately stored and retrieved, and therefore lends itself naturally to support from ICTs. Consistent with this view, ICTs have been heralded as critical in the development, sustenance, and creation of organizational knowledge by virtue of their capacity to capture, store, transmit, and process information. Indeed, a wide range of ICTs, ranging from e-mail to calendaring systems to group support technologies, has ushered in critical efficiencies in organizational information capture, processing, and transfer. This approach, however, has often resulted in "information junkyards" (McDermott, 1999, p. 104) or "data warehouses that nobody visits" (Walsham, 2001, p. 601), due to a misperception that knowledge can be readily and simply commoditized. For the most part, affordances of ICTs in this context either augment current capabilities or merely facilitate existing ones. Put another way, the application of ICTs in this domain appears to largely facilitate changes in scale, not kind.

Moreover, the use of ICTs for organizational knowledge management appears in many instances to be the province of information processing (i.e., the capture, storage, transmission, and processing of analyzed data) rather than organizational knowledge management. To some degree this is reflective of the predominant information technology emphasis of many organizational knowledge management initiatives, which are often seen as "technical projects" (Hayes & Walsham, 2003, p. 73) rather than social endeavors. This is further reflected in the fact that information technology specialists comprise 70 percent of the authorship for knowledge-management related publications (Easterby-Smith, Crossan, & Nicolini, 2000). As a consequence, there appears to be a propensity to "artificially reduce knowledge complexity with the use of technologies for knowledge management. In essence, the trend in knowledge management has been to condense knowledge to less than it is, in order to increase the capacity to process it efficiently" (Flanagin, 2002, p. 244). Indeed, there is considerable controversy about the appropriate use of ICTs to capture and share knowledge, which requires high levels of shared understanding (Flanagin, 2002; Walsham, 2002). As Tsoukas and Mylonopoulos (2004, p. 3) note:

> The electronic storage, processing, and retrieval, and the instant communication of information, manifested most impressively in the Internet, have made it so tempting ... to view *all* knowledge in terms of information. This leads to *information reductionism*: we believe we get to know the world through layers of abstract representations about the world.

Yet, to bring meaningful technological support to organizational knowledge processes requires acknowledgment of the core features of knowledge, as distinct from information, and a means to accommodate these features with ICTs. To truly take advantage of ICTs to support knowledge processes requires consideration of its "processual, provisional, and highly context dependent" nature (Hayes & Walsham, 2003, p. 54). Consistent with the relational perspective noted earlier, to foster organizational knowledge ICTs must accommodate the rich processes required to support shared understanding, sensemaking activities, contextual judgments, and situated practice. To date, this appears to be the exceptional application of ICTs, rather than the rule.

To effectively support organizational knowledge ICTs must not only (1) provide effective means of communication; (2) support information sharing; and (3) coordinate individual contributions among participants when collaboration is required, but also provide effective means to form and maintain rich, unambiguous communication across diverse participants, to sustain viable communities of practice, and to fortify the social context that is critical for the situated practice, problem-solving, and thinking that define organizational knowledge. Accordingly, Walsham (2002) proposes several "opportunities" for ICTs to support knowledge management. For example, he notes their capacity to provide a structure to data that can support thinking. Google, for instance, via its algorithms that impose order on otherwise unwieldy data sources, serves to organize data in a manner that renders them manageable. Next, he argues that ICTs provide a means of information sharing and interpretation, via communication. Ideally, they provide a means of "sense-reading and sense-giving activities" that aid in the transfer and sharing of knowledge. Finally, he argues that ICTs can serve as guides to action by providing order and social arrangements that can augment decision-making and activity. Zuboff (1988) makes a similar distinction between the capacity of new technologies to "automate" and "informate." When a technology automates, it replaces human tasks with machine technology, taking over continuity and control. The same machinery, however, can informate as well, which supersedes automating by generating new processes and abilities for human knowledge.

In spite of this potential, the success of ICTs in these pursuits has been mixed. As already noted, in many instances ICTs are actually used to process information rather than to support knowledge management. Additionally, ICTs have the potential to be used more fully for organizational knowledge processes than they currently are, and cases can be identified where ICTs are indeed being used for knowledge management but are not identified as such. To explore these possibilities, we next advocate a relatively novel focus on lessons learned from contemporary web-based tools that are typically viewed as outside the purview of organizational knowledge and knowledge management.

The Application of Emergent, Web-based Technologies to Knowledge Management Practices

Until recently, the enormous cost and complexity involved in producing and disseminating information on a large scale limited the number of information providers, who generally had substantial investment either in the information itself or in the apparatus required to deliver it. In recent years, however, web-based technologies have blossomed in their capacity to support sustained collaborative efforts among individuals working toward shared goals, across myriad domains. Digital network technologies associated with the Internet and the web have lowered the cost of information production and dissemination, thus increasing the sheer amount of information and the number of information sources available. Potential contributions from a wide variety of users can be sustained over long periods of time and across geographic, cultural, and even interest domains. The proliferation of user-generated content – ranging from the coordination of political protests to aggregations of movie ratings to the creation of complex software – and the rise of far-reaching collaborative efforts that require coordination among large numbers of people are by-products of this environment.

This fundamental shift in connective capacity represents significant new benefits to organizations, given the enormous knowledge assets that reside in collectives and which until recently remained largely untapped due to insurmountable communication and coordination costs. The essential premise of this new environment is that, given efficient means of information sharing and participation, knowledge assets can more readily be fostered, shared, and maintained.

The open-source movement serves as an example. For more than a decade now, software development efforts among independent computer programmers, often numbering in the hundreds or thousands, have thrived, based on the simple principle that the collective efforts of a diversity of software developers produce superior products (see Raymond, 2001; Weber, 2004). It is notable that prior to the open-source movement, software development was a largely isolated, proprietary activity that took place among relatively small groups of workers, who typically enjoyed high levels of personal contact with one another. Yet the open-source movement has shown that widescale, complex collaboration among disaggregated individuals can take place successfully online, and can produce freely distributed, collectively authored, viable software. Indeed, a recent survey indicates that more than half of IT professionals supplement their use of proprietary software with open-source applications in their organizations (a figure that climbs to two-thirds if those who report they plan to use it soon are included) (Schindler, 2008).

From a knowledge management perspective, the open-source movement illustrates that sustained, situated problem-solving and practice – precisely the kinds of activities achieved through the relational interaction that is required to produce software, and the heart of organizational knowledge – can be successfully supported almost exclusively through the use of ICTs. Open-source community members are guided by standards and rules, adhere to particular procedures for decision-making, and are subject to specific sanctioning mechanisms as they share and produce knowledge. Open-source collaborators epitomize the mutual engagement, shared repertoire, and joint enterprise critical for communities of practice in the pursuit of organizational knowledge (Wenger, 1998). Moreover, such communities of practice can be viewed as constitutive not only of organizational practices, but also of organizations themselves (Iverson & McPhee, 2002).

These same types of knowledge-based activities can be supported by ICTs within more traditional organizational frameworks as well. For instance, electronic procurement (e-procurement) technologies provide a rich web-based interface that connects corporations to their system of suppliers. E-procurement systems allow purchasers "to (1) formulate supplier selection criteria (2) rank potential suppliers (3) choose a subset of ranked suppliers and (4) monitor supplier performances" (Massa & Testa, 2007, p. 29). Through the system, requests for bids may be made, new searches for more competitive suppliers may be initiated, and bid histories are archived. The e-procurement tool facilitates knowledge management that crosses organizational boundaries by offering interactive features through which multiple purchasers from different parts of an organization can aggregate their individual perceptions of suppliers and information regarding previous transactions, alongside information provided by suppliers. Although the e-procurement system requires tremendous codification of organizational knowledge before it can be considered a suitable substitution for manual purchasing routines (Massa & Testa, 2007), this codification exercise itself can stimulate substantial knowledge production because it requires employees to reflect upon the processes used during a purchasing activity (Tsoukas & Vladimirou, 2001). Moreover, this knowledge creation continues after the system is implemented, because the dynamic, interactive nature of the system keeps it highly relevant and historically accurate.

The e-procurement system may be a typical organizational response to the use of ICTs in organizational knowledge management inasmuch as it allows an organization to continue to manage knowledge processes, while allowing employees wider access to the resources needed to make better decisions. Yet, there are additional lessons to be learned from the power afforded to individuals in an interactive online environment. For example, Cho, Lee, Stefanone, and Gay (2005) describe the research and development process of a distributed community where people worked together for a year in an effort to design a portion of an aerospace system. Distributed teams with different skill sets participated in this highly interdependent task, which required the ability to communicate verbally and visually in order to collaborate. Using a web-based ICT, team members were able to create simulations, share their applications, communicate with each other in a variety of ways (i.e., via audio/video conferencing, chat, instant messaging, e-mail, and discussion boards), network, retrieve information within the system, create custom information storage, and participate in conference calls with NASA scientists. These ICTs produced a knowledge management environment through their storage, retrieval, and creation mechanisms that supported the development of relationships based on expertise. In this instance, ICTs provided users the ability to customize and manage their information sharing and communication, and gave them the ability to provide structure to shared data and information. This decentralized approach gave users the means to access, interrogate, and collaboratively create new knowledge and organizational products.

Considering knowledge-sharing and knowledge-creation processes from this user-oriented point of view exposes a control bias inherent in most top-down knowledge management efforts (Huysman & de Wit, 2004), which appears to privilege ICTs as tools for information processing over knowledge management. Upper management control of centralized data repositories can result in content deemed unhelpful by those who attempt to use these static tools, which often lack context that allows integration with employees' unique knowledge sets (Newell, Bresnen, Edelman, Scarbrough, & Swan, 2006). Moreover, the pressure that upper management can put on employees to document their processes and record their insight into a static directory inhibits effective knowledge integration (Grant, 1999). However, shifting the locus of control by offering employees tools that allow them to learn and build upon others' input (similar to the open source movement, for example) may enable knowledge workers to participate more fully in knowledge creation and management, which may generate new opportunities for innovation. This more fully relational strategy acknowledges the communicative nature of organizational knowledge. Accordingly, social media tools such as RSS, social ranking, and wikis can offer users the ability to manage information, build relationships, and provide opportunities for feedback, which are key knowledge creation and sharing processes. These tools offer promise as the newest instantiation of ICTs supporting knowledge management.

The use of social media for organizational knowledge management even extends beyond an organization's boundaries. Many companies now realize that individual technology users external to an organization create public knowledge about an organization by sharing information and comments about products and services, through product ratings, social networking groups and connections, and RSS feeds, to name only a few possibilities. In response to individuals' new role in the information environment, some companies are working to actively manage external knowledge channels. For example, Dell has created a "communities and conversation team," where employees reach out to customers on Twitter and blogs in order to provide proactive customer service and actively seek out customer-driven innovation. Southwest Airlines has a similar team, ready to respond to anything related to Southwest that appears in cyberspace (Johnson, 2008). Monitoring tweets, understanding what is being talked about in the blogosphere, and seeing which news stories are rising to the top of consumer rated news (e.g., digg.com) allows organizations to partially control, or at least be aware of and potentially manage, what circulates about topics of concern. In this manner, knowledge is shared and created by cutting across organizational boundaries.

Embracing this user-oriented perspective for employees can also have profound knowledge creation effects. Pfizer, for example, advocates the use of blogs, wikis, and RSS for all of its employees. Blogs enable a more informal and personal way to share what employees are currently working on or are interested in. RSS helps employees organize the different streams of information that are important to them, while wikis encourage the production of active stocks of knowledge. Pfizerpedia currently boasts over 10,000 wiki entries, including "how to" videos created by employees (McDougall, 2008). Similarly, in order to create a wider dialogue around product innovation, Dell launched a social ranking website, Dell Idea Storm, to its employees in order to encourage them to offer product suggestions and to comment on and rank suggestions offered by others. Extending this functionality beyond its organizational boundaries, Dellideastorm.com now exists as a public site where anyone can participate in this innovation tool. Finally, IBM is migrating from information management to knowledge sharing by offering and using ICT tools that facilitate knowledge-sharing processes. On any given day, for example, over 22,000 IBM employees are logged into Facebook, allowing employees to actively maintain their social networks and stay up to date regarding what their peers are working on (Lewis, 2008).

Such tools provide the situated, context-dependent interface crucial to knowledge processes while offering a means for others to build upon such experiences through feedback mechanisms. When these tools are combined, the knowledge management terrain of an organization can become much richer. For example, wiki tools can facilitate the knowledge-sharing processes of communities of practice by making a space available where the members can impart their knowledge and build upon that of their peers. Blogs offer employees a more personal space to log their organizational activity and interact around specific topics. Social ranking can be employed on any set of organizational information deemed worthy of organizational, or even wider, debate. Existing social networking tools such as Facebook enable the formation and maintenance of organizational relationships, recognizing that such relationships can extend beyond the boundaries of a company. In order to stay on top of the newest conversations emanating from these tools, employees customize RSS feeds that stay active on their desktop. To tie it all together, aggregating applications such as semantic web tools have the ability to search through the various channels and compile specific relationships that exist between the channels, such as the 10 people commenting on or involved in a particular product launch (Drucker, 1994; Feigenbaum, Herman, Hongsermeier, Neumann, & Stephens, 2007). Going one step further, IBM offers Atlas, a tool that unveils employees' social networks by analyzing the various ties (e.g., e-mails received/sent, friends on Facebook, links on blog, feedback on social ranking posts) employees accumulate through their social media tools in relation to the rest of the company (Ehrlich & Lin, nd). The most intriguing aspect of Atlas is its ability to reveal people to whom one is connected by two degrees, creating a more permeable knowledge-sharing system through a more open organizational network.

ICTs, however, are not always well-suited for knowledge management efforts. Because they are user-centered, a hierarchically managed knowledge management system can impede participation and use of these decentralized tools. In fact, the open-source movement suggests that traditional conceptions of knowledge management that utilize ICTs in a hierarchical manner can actually *detract* from knowledge sharing and production capabilities. Downing (2004), for example, describes a failed attempt at the implementation of knowledge management tools for call-center employees. This knowledge management initiative introduced a data repository designed to lead the call-center staff through a series of questions in order to prompt each caller to adequately explain his or her technical problem. This system, however, lacked any sort of interactive feature, and ultimately failed to reduce overall call times and improper diagnoses, even though the repository was fully searchable and filled with a major cross-section of known issues. Without an interactive feature, the repository actually impeded the knowledge creation process by reducing the amount of informal interaction on the call-center floor and turning the call-center employees' jobs into a keyword guessing game in order to access the required information. Those who used the knowledge management tool increased, rather than decreased, their average call length, because searching the database was a slower process than simply asking their neighbor. In this case, codifying technical problems appears to have changed a knowledge creation process into an information processing task.

Implications of ICT-supported Organizational Knowledge Management

Our discussion of the use of ICTs for organizational knowledge management suggests several organizational directions, issues, and concerns. For instance, one implication is that organizational boundaries are, or should be, more permeable and fluid. Taking advantage of knowledge that lies beyond the organization's border, for example, requires sharing ideas and collaborating with others, about whom little is sometimes known. Indeed, a feature of the contemporary media environment is the relative anonymity of information and individuals, suggesting problems of source and information credibility, potential conflicts of interest, and the complex dynamics of securing and maintaining competitive advantage. In extreme cases, information sharing and the co-production of knowledge can even take place unwittingly or unknowingly, for instance when information and knowledge artifacts are stored and subsequently accessed in publicly available forums, such as discussion boards, web sites, blog entries, and other repositories that endure long after their "contribution," which can itself be unintended, since in many instances it has become more effortful to secure information than to share it (see Bimber, Flanagin, & Stohl, 2005).

Indeed, the Internet's open-access information environment fosters the notion of information as a "public good," readily available to all regardless of organizational affiliation or individual contribution. The public nature of web pages, tweets, blogs, discussion groups, and wikis, and the endurance of these information artifacts over time, raise questions regarding the extent to which an organization should support the public posting of organizational work and the costs and benefits of knowledge creation processes in an open, inter-organizational environment. In this environment, organizations must confront a new type of knowledge production that cannot always be supervised by the organization.

An implication of this potential boundary permeability is that it is necessary in many instances to look beyond "the organization" toward *processes of organizing* as a more appropriate frame for organizational knowledge management. The very notion of knowledge as communicative and relational, for example, emphasizes the processes of knowledge creation, sharing, and maintenance. These processes are often not linear, nor can they be easily codified (e.g., as a business practice) or represented (e.g., on an organizational chart). Instead, these processes more closely resemble patterns of organizing, which enact the organization through "the actions and conversations that occur on behalf of the presumed organization and in the texts of the activities that are preserved in social structures" (Weick, Sutcliffe, & Obstfeld, 2005, p. 413). From this perspective, organizations should not be concentrating their efforts on managing knowledge, but rather on managing knowledge processes. ICTs are critical in this endeavor, and should be viewed not as static tools to capture, store, or process information (i.e., an information processing view), but as dynamic tools capable of supporting the rich and situated practice of co-creation required to generate knowledge and manage it within and across organizations. Toward this end, we have chosen to emphasize current web-based applications of ICTs that tend to highlight the capacity of technologies to support organizational knowledge management processes.

However, social media tools likely require a different kind of management than past knowledge management efforts. Organizations that lack a collaborative, knowledge-sharing spirit are unlikely to realize the full potential of these tools. For instance, organizational practices such as knowledge hoarding can seriously detract from organizational knowledge management efforts that reward individual achievements over collaborative activities (Walsham, 2001). Therefore, an organization's culture figures strongly in the success or failure of a knowledge management initiative. Larger cultural issues, such as the communicative style of a particular group (e.g., high context versus low context cultures), also play a part in the acceptance of ICTs as suitable tools for knowledge creation, storage, and sharing actions. Hence, the tools introduced here must be considered in light of these and other organizational constraints.

The notion of more fluid and flexible organizational boundaries also suggests a reconsideration of interrelated features such as organizational definition, commitment, ownership, and identity. The relational perspective on organizational knowledge evokes a more fluid definition of the organization that can encompass processes, and therefore assets and resources, outside of an organization's traditional boundaries. Similar to the mutual technological dependence that occurs among firms who search beyond their boundaries for sources of innovation (see, for example, Jaffe, Fogarty, & Banks, 1998), many knowledge workers engage in boundary-spanning activities to stay up to date in their field, complete their everyday tasks, and/or find new opportunities for innovation that create a kind of knowledge dependence. The effects of this dependence on organizational commitment should not be overlooked. When knowledge processes occur at a community or professional level instead of at the organizational level, this may impact knowledge workers' organizational commitment. In turn, concerns over knowledge ownership could potentially lead an organization to attempt to control employee movement within an industry for fear of losing competitive advantage through employee turnover. Yet, such manipulation of employees' portability within an industry can also negatively affect an industry's knowledge growth.

Our focus on organizing processes and the management of knowledge processes, instead of organizational knowledge management, also brings to light theoretical and practical directions for future inquiry. Research will need to consider literature on organizational forms and new forms of organizing to better understand the structural impediments organizations must overcome as they shift to a relational view of knowledge management through ICTs. For example, research should consider (1) how the decentralized nature of ICTs may affect workflows, worker relations, and worker commitment, as organizational knowledge is produced; (2) the role of management in shaping employee use of ICTs, and whether such use might simply reify existing structures or facilitate truly new forms of organizing; and (3) the implications of and for privacy policies in organizational implementations of ICTs that facilitate knowledge processes and make many organizational conversations public.

In addition, evolving notions of organizational definition, commitment, and knowledge ownership implicate a new understanding of organizational identity. The concept of identity is both relational and comparative (Tajfel & Turner, 1985). Therefore, the provision of tools that increase relationally-driven knowledge processes is sure to affect multiple levels of identity. Open issues include questions of what kinds of identity (e.g., individual, group, organizational, industry level) are fostered through knowledge and organizing processes that cross organizational borders, and whether these new identities are empowering and beneficial to an organization, or detract from an organization's cohesiveness and constrain its ability to bring incongruent identities together through an overarching goal.

Finally, when the interactive features of knowledge creation are privileged, the informational component of knowledge is not what distinguishes organizations. Rather, as they become more comfortable with a facilitative role in the management and development of organizational knowledge, the successful use of ICTs for knowledge management is what provides organizations with competitive advantages. In this case, a communicative understanding of organizing processes and knowledge will provide greater insight into the characteristics of competitive advantage in a knowledge economy where trust, reputation, and credibility are assessed and assigned through a complex mix of sources and media.

Conclusion

The use of ICTs has increased organizational efficiency and scope by exploiting the scalability that technology affords. The focus, however, has traditionally been on the informational use of ICTs, rather than their capacity for rich communication and the situated practice, problem-solving, and thinking they support. This focus has in turn bled over into knowledge management efforts that have largely created static tools for organizational knowledge. However, current, often web-based, applications make the most of the communicative ends of ICTs by drawing attention to knowledge management processes. These communicative features give organizations the tools to facilitate knowledge creation, sharing, and maintenance by supporting the relational nature of knowledge. As ICTs continue to evolve, their ability to contextualize interactions has the potential to enhance their appropriateness and desirability for inclusion in efforts to manage organizational knowledge processes.

References

Alavi, M. (2000). Managing organizational knowledge. In R. W. Zmud (Ed.), *Framing the domains of IT management.* Cincinnati, OH: Pinneflex Educational Resources.

Bimber, B., Flanagin, A. J., & Stohl, C. (2005). Reconceptualizing collective action in the contemporary media environment. *Communication Theory, 15,* 365–388.

Brown, J. S., & Duguid, P. (1998). Organizing knowledge. *California Management Review, 40,* 90–111.

Brown, J. S., & Duguid, P. (2000). *The social life of information.* Boston, MA: Harvard Business School Press.

Chakravarthy, B., McEvily, S., Doz, Y., & Rau, D. (2003). Knowledge management and competitive advantage. In M. Easterby-Smith & M. A. Lyles (Eds.), *The Blackwell handbook of organizational learning and knowledge management* (pp. 305–323). Malden, MA: Blackwell.

Cho, H., Lee, J.-S., Stefanone, M., & Gay, G. (2005). Development of computer-supported collaborative social networks in a distributed learning community. *Behaviour & Information Technology, 24(6),* 435–447.

Choo, C. W. (2006). *The knowing organization* (2nd Ed.). New York, NY: Oxford University Press.

Contractor, N. S., & Monge, P. R. (2002). Managing knowledge networks. *Management Communication Quarterly, 16(2),* 249–258.

David, P., & Foray, D. (2002). An introduction to the economy of the knowledge society. *International Social Science Journal, 54(171),* 9–23.

Downing, J. R. (2004). "It's easier to ask someone I know": Call center technicians' adoption of knowledge management tools. *Journal of Business Communication, 41(2),* 166–191.

Drucker, P. (1994). The age of social transformation. *The Atlantic Monthly, 274(5),* 53–80. Retrieved from www.theatlantic.com/politics/ecbig/soctrans.htm.

Easterby-Smith, M., Crossan, M., & Nicolini, D. (2000). Organizational learning: Debates past, present and future. *Journal of Strategic Management, 37(6),* 783–796.

Ehrlich, K., & Lin, C. (nd). IBM Watson Research Center: Project Small Blue. Retrieved October 2, 2008, from http://domino.watson.ibm.com/cambridge/research.nsf/99751d8eb5a20c1f852568db004efc90/d78a63b90871a4aa852573d1005d390a?OpenDocument.

Feigenbaum, L., Herman, I., Hongsermeier, T., Neumann, E., & Stephens, S. (2007, Dec.). The semantic web in action, *Scientific American, 297,* 90–97. Retrieved from http://thefigtrees.net/lee/sw/sciam/semantic-web-in-action.

Flanagin, A. J. (2002). The elusive benefits of the technological suppport of knowledge management. *Management Communication Quarterly, 16,* 242–248.

Grant, R. (1999). Prospering in dynamically-competitive environments: Organizational capability as knowledge integration. In M. Zack (Ed.), *Knowledge and strategy* (pp. 133–156). Woburn, MA: Butterworth-Heineman.

Hayes, N., & Walsham, G. (2003). Knowledge sharing and ICTs: A relational perspective. In M. Easterby-Smith & M. A. Lyles (Eds.), *The Blackwell handbook of organizational learning and knowledge management* (pp. 54–77). Malden, MA: Blackwell.

Huysman, M., & de Wit, D. (2004). Practices of managing knowledge sharing: towards a second wave of knowledge management. *Knowledge and Process Management, 11(2),* 81–92.

Iverson, J. O., & McPhee, R. D. (2002). Knowledge management in communities of practice: Being true to the communicative nature of knowledge. *Management Communication Quarterly, 16,* 259–266.

Jaffe, A. B., Fogarty, M. S., & Banks, B. A. (1998). Evidence from patents and patent citations on the impact of NASA and other federal labs on commercial innovation. *Journal of Industrial Economics, 46*(2), 183–205.

Johnson, C. Y. (2008, July 7). Hurry up, the customer has a complaint. *The Boston Globe.* Retrieved from www.boston.com/business/technology/articles/2008/07/07/hurry_up_the_customer_has_a_complaint/.

Kuhn, T., & Jackson, M. H. (2008). Accomplishing knowledge – A framework for investigating knowing in organizations. *Management Communication Quarterly, 21(4)*, 454–485.

Lewis, R. (2008, Feb. 6). *NEW* IBM gambles on a shift from the KM model: Into the big blue yonder.* Retrieved October 4, 208 from www.knowledgeboard.com/item/2860/23/5/3.

Lundvall, B., & Johnson, B. (1994). The learning economy. *Journal of Industry Studies, 1,* 23–42.

Malone, T. W., & Rockart, J. F. (1991). Computers, networks, and the corporation. *Scientific American, 265,* 128–136.

Massa, S., & Testa, S. (2007). ICTs adoption and knowledge management: the case of an e-procurement system. *Knowledge and Process Management, 14,* 26–36.

McDermott, R. (1999). Why information technology inspired but cannot deliver knowledge management. *California Management Review, 41(4),* 103–117.

McDougall, P. (2008, June 11). Enterprise 2.0: Pfizer's cyberpunks drive social computing at drugmaker. *InformationWeek.* Retrieved from www.informationweek.com/news/internet/web2.0/showArticle.jhtml?articleID=208403394.

Newell, S., Bresnen, M., Edelman, L., Scarbrough, H., & Swan, J. (2006). Sharing knowledge across projects – Limits to ICT-led project review practices. *Management Learning, 37(2),* 167–185.

Nonaka, I. (1994). A dynamic theory of organizational knowledge creation. *Organization Science, 5,* 14–37.

Nonaka, I. (2005). *Knowledge management.* New York, NY: Routledge.

Nonaka, I., & Takeuchi, H. (1995). *The knowledge creating company.* NY: Oxford University Press.

Polanyi, M. (1966). *The tacit dimension.* Garden City, NY: Doubleday.

Polanyi, M. (1969). *Knowing and being.* London, UK: Routledge & Kegan Paul.

Raymond, E. S. (2001). *The cathedral and the bazaar: Musings on Linux and open source by an accidental revolutionary.* Cambridge, MA: O'Reilly.

Schindler, E. (2008). *Open source is entering the enterprise mainstream, survey shows.* Retrieved October 3, 2008, from www.cio.com/article/375916/Open_Source_is_Entering_the_Enterprise_Mainstream_Survey_Shows.

Spender, J. C. (1996). Making knowledge the basis of a dynamic theory of the firm. *Strategic Management Journal, 17,* 45–62.

Tajfel, H., & Turner, J. (1985). The social identity theory of intergroup behaviour. In S. Worchel & W. G. Austin (Eds.), *Psychology of intergroup relations.* Chicago, IL: Nelson-Hall.

Tsoukas, H., & Mylonopoulos, N. (2004). Introduction: What does it mean to view organizations as knowledge systems? In H. Tsoukas & N. Mylonopoulos (Eds.), *Organizations as knowledge systems: Knowledge, learning, and dynamic capabilities* (pp. 1–26). New York, NY: Palgrave Macmillan.

Tsoukas, H., & Vladimirou, E. (2001). What is organizational knowledge? *Journal of Management Studies, 38(7),* 973–993.

Walsham, G. (2001). Knowledge management: The benefits and limitations of computer systems. *European Management Journal, 19(6)*, 599–608.

Walsham, G. (2002). What can knowledge management systems deliver? *Management Communication Quarterly, 16*, 267–273.

Weber, S. (2004). *The success of open source.* Cambridge, MA: Harvard University Press.

Weick, K. E., Sutcliffe, K., & Obstfeld, D. (2005). Organizing and the process of sensemaking. *Organization Science, 16(4)*, 409–421.

Wegner, D. M. (1995). A computer network model of human transactive memory. *Social Cognition, 13*, 319–339.

Wenger, E. (1998). *Communities of practice: Learning, meaning, and identity.* Cambridge, UK: Cambridge University Press.

Zorn, T. E., & May, S. K. (2002). Forum introduction. *Management Communication Quarterly, 16(2)*, 237–241.

Zuboff, S. (1988). *In the age of the smart machine.* New York, NY: Basic Books.

Chapter 11

Knowledge Management Systems and Work Teams

Michelle Shumate

Modern work teams face challenges that make the use of technology to manage information and knowledge particularly attractive. Geographic dispersion (O'Leary & Cummings, 2007), dramatic membership changes (Lewis, Belliveau, Herndon, & Keller, 2007), and the use of contract and part-time workers (Kalleberg, 2000) each present challenges to non-mediated knowledge management. Knowledge management systems (KMSs), or "a class of information systems applied to managing organization knowledge" (Alavi & Leidner, 2001, p. 114), are one solution used to manage these new work complexities. While knowledge flows are important throughout the knowledge life cycle (Nissen, 2002; Nonaka, 1994), knowledge management systems have been primarily developed to enable the organization, formalization, and distribution of information.

The purpose of this chapter is to set forth a network model of knowledge flows among agents in a work team that accounts for both trends in KMSs and work teams. Work teams, for the purposes of this chapter, will be defined broadly as individuals working together to achieve a common goal. The chapter focuses primarily on the organization, formalization, and distribution of information, and embraces the information-processing approach to knowledge management (see Chapter 10 in this volume for a relational approach). First, this chapter reviews the current communication theory and research that examines knowledge sharing among work teams, then it suggests that new models of organizing and modern KMSs require a shift in research trajectory and proposes several networks likely to influence the use of such systems.

Role of Communication

While some researchers have suggested network and repository models of knowledge management represent competing traditions (Kankanhalli, Tan, & Kwok-Kee, 2005), communication scholars have combined both models to understand the contextual use of both direct exchange and group-generalized exchange among team members (Child & Shumate, 2007; Heaton & Taylor, 2002; Hollingshead, Fulk, & Monge, 2002; Yuan, Fulk,

& Monge, 2007). The integrated communication-based theory of transactive memory and public goods, hereafter referred to as the integrated model, explains the level of knowledge flow among actors in a work team, including team members and knowledge repositories (Hollingshead et al., 2002). The integrated model combines elements of transactive memory theory, including knowledge specialization, recognition of experts, and task interdependence, with the recognition that geographic dispersion makes the use of repositories necessary. In this model, KMSs help individuals in work teams to identify the expertise that they seek. Individuals are more likely to participate in these KMSs when knowledge is distributed, individuals perceive their knowledge to be unique, and others are perceived as both contributing and retrieving knowledge from the same KMS. If individuals in distributed teams use the KMSs and gain a better cognitive schema of the expertise in their team, they will be more likely to specialize, leading to greater benefits for the team, including more effective and efficient task performance.

Three constitutive subprocesses underlie the model: (1) encoding, (2) retrieving, and (3) allocating knowledge (Hollingshead & Brandon, 2003). Encoding, or the codification of information/experience, represents the primary cost in contributing to knowledge repositories and sharing information directly (Kankanhalli et al., 2005). Some knowledge management scholars describe this process as knowledge conversion (Nonaka, 1994). Knowledge conversion is especially challenging for the transition from tacit knowledge, or "know-how," to explicit knowledge, which is codified (see Polanyi, 1966, for the distinction); this process, however, is key for individual knowledge to become organizational knowledge (Herschel, Nemati, & Steiger, 2001).

Communication to retrieve information is a subprocess in both the direct exchange of information (Hollingshead & Brandon, 2003) and the use of KMSs (Fulk, Flanagin, Kalman, Monge, & Ryan, 1996). Individuals can either directly retrieve information that they need, or they may seek out referrals regarding from which individuals to retrieve the needed information. This is a process described as a transactive information search (Hollingshead, 1998), and can occur both via direct exchange and via KMSs.

The third subprocess is information allocation, the communication of incoming information to specific individuals or to knowledge repositories (Wegner, 1995). In well-functioning transactive memory systems, information allocation follows the pattern of knowledge requirements (Brandon & Hollingshead, 2004). When individuals acquire information in knowledge areas for which they do not personally have knowledge requirements, they will reallocate that information to persons who do have those requirements. Additionally, individuals may allocate information to knowledge repositories (Fulk et al., 1996; Fulk, Heino, Flanagin, Monge, & Bar, 2004). A knowledge repository is more valuable as the amount of information and the timeliness of that information increases (Fulk et al., 1996).

In order for these subprocesses to occur with any frequency, a series of *conditions* must be met. For favorable direct exchange among team members, the primary prerequisite is cognitive interdependence (Brandon & Hollingshead, 2004). Cognitive interdependence is induced when a team's knowledge-intensive tasks require team members to work together and the rewards depend upon each team member's success. Conditions for contributing to a KMS include task interdependence, centralization of resources, and geographic dispersion (Fulk et al., 1996; Markus, 1990). Further, public goods theory suggests that individuals tend to contribute more to the system as their personal gain increases (Fulk et al., 2004; Marwell & Oliver, 1993).

While the integrated model presents a parsimonious picture of the factors that influence the level of knowledge flow among actors in a work team, including team members and knowledge repositories, the empirical results have been inconsistent. Fulk and colleagues' (2004) test of the individual action model of contribution to communal goods was supported in two of the three organizations that they examined. Palazzolo's (2005) test of the transactive memory processes for retrieval among individuals across work teams found mixed results that varied both by knowledge area and by team.

These inconsistent findings have led researchers to amend and extend both public goods and transactive memory theories in order to explain the level of knowledge flow. Yuan and colleagues (2005) expanded the individual action model to include both technology-specific competence and perceived level of provision by others. Further, Yuan and colleagues (2005) found that individuals do not distinguish contributing to and retrieving information from KMSs. In addition, the relationship between gain and the level of use of the KMS is reversed; the revised model predicts that perceived gain is the result rather than the cause of increased KMS use (Yuan et al., 2005). Palazzolo, Serb, She, Su, and Contractor (2006), using a computational modeling approach, suggest that direct exchange models of information sharing should include the level of initial knowledge held by the team, the initial accuracy of expertise recognition, and group size. In computational models, each of these factors was important in predicting the level of communication among team members.

A Trajectory for Future Knowledge Management Systems and Work Teams

Drawing from the amendments to the integrated model of transactive memory and public goods theories, I suggest a network model of knowledge flows between and among various agents, including KMSs and human actors. This model is depicted in Figure 11.1. The model, as do many of the chapters in this volume, draws from Glaser's (1978) six coding

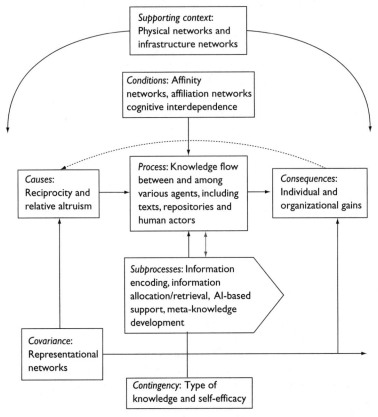

Figure 11.1 Network model of knowledge flows. This model utilizes McPhee's (2008) 7C model, an extension of Glaser's (1978) six coding families.

families. The focal process of the model is the knowledge flow between and among various agents, including KMSs and human actors; however, only human actors have agency.

Two factors necessitate the development of a network model of knowledge flow among work teams: (1) the changing nature of workgroups, and (2) the changing nature of enabling conditions. First, in many new organizational forms, the boundaries of both organizations and teams are blurred and dynamic (Badaracco, 1991; Child & McGrath, 2001; Fulk & DeSanctis, 1999; Hirschhorn & Gilmore, 1992). Such change in organizational form necessitates a dynamic perspective on knowledge flows (see Nonaka, 1994). Prior research has assumed that team members who shared knowledge were linked through task interdependence and group rewards (Brandon & Hollingshead, 2004). As such, the research has focused on teams with clear boundaries and futures.

Rejecting the assumption of static boundaries, affinity and affiliation networks play a greater role in determining who is working with whom, and for what purpose. Affinity and/or affiliation ties are *conditions* for knowledge flow to occur. Both networks are conceptualized as whole networks, not egocentric networks. Thus, both networks represent conditions because they provide a shared context for information flow (see Nonaka & Konno (1998) for the importance of shared context). Affinity networks represent the various evaluations people make of one another, including friendship, liking, respect (Wasserman & Faust, 1994) and trust (Kankanhalli et al., 2005). Even before organizational boundaries are formed, affinity ties among individuals can serve as the condition for knowledge sharing. For example, Shumate's social entrepreneurship research demonstrates that individuals with experience forming similar organizations often share knowledge with social entrepreneurs, acting as an ad hoc work team in the founding of a non-profit organization (Shumate, forthcoming). These individuals act together to form organizational boundaries and structures and, as such, they do not have the joint task interdependence and group rewards suggested as a prerequisite for knowledge sharing in prior research. Instead, their affinity bonds with one another serve as the basis for knowledge sharing. Interdependencies may develop over time, and eventually result in the formation of team or organizational boundaries.

Once organizational boundaries are established, affiliation networks can serve as a condition of knowledge flow. Affiliation networks describe the relationship between people and organizations and/or groups (Wasserman & Faust, 1994), allowing for multiple members in various organizations to facilitate knowledge transfer across organizational boundaries. Affiliations can represent formal membership or identification (Scott, 1997). Formal membership and identification serve as conditions for transfer of knowledge both through direct exchange and via KMSs. For example, Kankanhalli and colleagues (2005) have found that such organizational identification is an important contextual factor explaining the level of contribution to KMSs. Through positing that affiliation networks, rather than organizational boundaries, represent conditions, theorizing about inter-organizational knowledge sharing can be described by the network model of knowledge flows. In addition, by allowing individuals to become affiliated through identification, knowledge sharing among customers and interested publics can be explained by the model (see Chapter 10 in this volume for more on inter-organizational knowledge sharing through e-procurement, and incorporating knowledge sharing beyond traditional employees through social media). As with affinity networks, repeated knowledge sharing among the same individuals for a common goal may lead to cognitive interdependence.

Second, the *supporting contexts* of modern work are changing, including physical and infrastructure networks. As noted by Brandon and

Hollingshead (2004), geographic proximity aids in the development of a transactive memory system where individuals know who knows what and delegate tasks responsibility accordingly. As work increasingly becomes more global and more geographically-dispersed (Gibson & Manuel, 2003; Hinds & Weisband, 2003), communication models of knowledge flow need to account for the physical factors that influence knowledge flow networks. O'Leary and Cummings (2007) suggest that physical dispersion has five characteristics: spatial, temporal, site configuration, isolation configuration, and imbalance configuration. Spatial dispersion refers to the physical distance among team members, while temporal dispersion refers to time-zone differences among members. Site configuration refers to the number of locations of team members. Isolation configuration describes the locations where individuals on the team work alone. Finally, imbalance identifies locations with a greater number of team members than others. Drawing from Brandon and Hollingshead (2004), greater geographic proximity may increase the amount of direct exchange among work-team members. Some communication research has suggested that physical distance, even within the same building, may influence the likelihood of two individuals communicating (Monge, Rothman, Eisenberg, Miller, & Kirste, 1985). However, as geographic proximity decreases, technologically mediated knowledge flow patterns become more likely and KMSs may play a more significant role (Fulk et al., 1996; Hollingshead et al., 2002). Similarly, work-team members that operate in isolation must exclusively rely upon technologically mediated knowledge flow patterns, while team members who are co-located may use a mix of direct exchange and technologically mediated flows. Finally, temporal dispersion makes synchronous knowledge flows difficult, encouraging the use of asynchronous communication. Such asynchronous communication via technology is likely to inhibit tacit knowledge sharing (see Chapter 12 in this volume).

In addition to the changing physical networks, infrastructure networks, or relationships among various connective and communal repositories, have also evolved. Communal repositories describe the parts of KMSs in which "members jointly hold a single body of information" (Fulk et al., 1996, p. 7), and connective repositories describe parts of KMSs that directly connect members to one another based upon their identified expertise or interest. When the first KMSs were developed, they did little more than document storage. In KMS evolution, the next wave involved the development of best practices databases. Such databases documented what appear to be the best ways of addressing complex problems or workflows (O'Leary, 1998). Incorporating data into such systems requires considerable effort, since the evaluation of practices requires the evaluation and codification of tacit knowledge. In spite of the high knowledge conversion costs, best practices databases remain one of the most common applications in the modern business environment, and provide important internal benchmarking functions for teams (Alavi & Leidner, 2001).

More recent KMSs differ from these predecessors in several ways. First, they are *searchable* in ways that were not previously available. Better search algorithms and the ability to search across multiple knowledge repositories in a single KMS reduces individuals' costs when locating information. Second, modern KMSs are *accessible* from geographically dispersed locations. The use of encryption, remote access, and virtual private networks has made systems that were previously only available when hard-wired into the company's network accessible from any number of devices. Third, most modern knowledge repositories are *distributed*. The use of open standards, such as XML (Extensible Markup Language) and object-oriented databases, have made it possible for information to be stored in multiple repositories that are distributed across the network (Bouwman, van de Wijngaert, Van Den Hooff, & Van Dijk, 2005). Fourth, the use of KMS is *traceable*, providing more information about the usefulness of various types of information. Managers can use the logs of KMS use to reconfigure the system, or track how knowledge ontologies are evolving in their organization (Maedche, Motik, Stojanovic, Studer, & Volz, 2003). Fifth, increasingly modern KMSs include both *push* and *pull* information technologies. Pull information technologies require the user to initiate the search for new information. In contrast, push information technologies initiate or facilitate the location of information. Finally, KMSs are often characterized by *blended connective and communal properties*, connecting information seekers to both people and information.

One class of such KMSs is customer relationship management systems, which coordinate information about customers and related knowledge across all points of interaction and all business functions (see Bose & Sugumaran, 2003). Such systems draw from multiple knowledge repositories including customer profiles, customer transactions, domain knowledge, and policies and procedures. Modern customer relationship management systems seamlessly integrate data entered from e-mail programs, customer service call logs, and transactions. Some systems go a step forward, pulling information from public databases and from websites to map the social network of potential contacts. Sales agents can visualize who at their company went to school with, sits on a board of directors with, or is a personal friend of a potential or current customer.

Such systems demonstrate each of the characteristics highlighted above. Information about each potential contact is searchable, immediately available within a few keystrokes. Additionally, information is available anywhere. Modern systems are accessible even through hand-held devices. Information from multiple sources is linked in the system, seamlessly tying together multiple databases. Who accessed what information about what customer is traceable. Information does not have to be added manually to the system, but is pulled from databases. That information is easily pushed to employees, such as call-center operators when the system recognizes the phone number of an incoming caller. Finally, information about customers has both communal and connective dimensions. Codified information about transactions and policies from communal knowledge repositories is integrated with information about who knows this customer from connective knowledge repositories.

Next-generation KMSs go further. Such technologies are designed to allow geographically dispersed teams to work synchronously on a project, with all the information needed at their fingertips. For example, some KMSs on the market today combine project management, groupware, and document management into a single platform.

Most KMSs, whether large customized mammoth systems or systems designed on Service Oriented Architecture principles, are customized to each organization. As such, the particular infrastructure network, including the way that data are coupled across database systems and the degree to which the system enables connections among individuals, is likely to influence the knowledge flow within and among work teams. As in adaptive structuration theory (Desanctis & Poole, 1994), the effect of the infrastructure network is not deterministic, but enables particular types of interactions.

Given changes in assumptions about the nature of the organizational connections that bring people together, and in the supportive contexts necessary to enable some types of knowledge flow, the subprocesses that account for the knowledge flows among agents must also be amended. Following Shumate and Lipp (2008) and Sohn and Leckenby (2007), I suggest that information sharing occurs through a group-generalized exchange or network-generalized exchange mechanisms. The left pane in Figure 11.2 depicts a communal public goods structure; in this knowledge flow, the communal knowledge repository becomes part of the knowledge network (Hollingshead et al., 2002). The communal knowledge repository functions successfully if a group-generalized exchange model operates, where

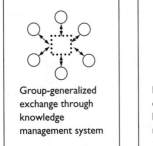 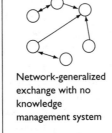 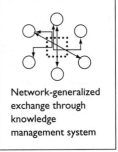

| Group-generalized exchange through knowledge management system | Network-generalized exchange with no knowledge management system | Network-generalized exchange through knowledge management system |

Figure 11.2 Three patterns of knowledge flow.

Notes
Circles represent individuals in the knowledge management system. Dotted rectangles represent a knowledge management system.

the system has centrality in the network. In the middle pane, there is no knowledge repository present. In this case, team members exchange information through an unmediated network-generalized exchange. In the right pane, a connective knowledge repository directs individuals to one another. In this case, the knowledge repository strengthens and/or may reconfigure the existing knowledge network, but does not become a node in the network. The connective knowledge repository functions successfully if individuals connect to experts. While these three ideal types demonstrate that knowledge flows may take several routes, in work teams with modern KMSs a hybrid of these three knowledge flow patterns likely exists. The centrality of the KMSs and the network structure of group member interactions are important elements in determining the outcomes of knowledge sharing (see Chapter 12 in this volume).

Further, modern KMSs change two additional subprocesses related to information flow; encoding and information retrieval from KMSs. First, some KMSs now automatically encode information to be stored in the system. For example, some systems scrape information from websites, input information from external databases, and automatically encode employee e-mails and calendars. While encoding for unmediated network-generalized exchange and some mediated group-generalized exchange, such as best practices databases, remains unchanged, automated encoding challenges many assumptions about the nature of contributions to KMSs. Further, artificial intelligence-based knowledge management (Edwards, Shaw, & Collier, 2005), including the use of intelligent agents (Bose & Sugumaran, 2003), automated data mining, and knowledge discovery techniques (Liebowitz, 2001), are a growing part of KMSs. These systems help to push information to individuals rather than requiring them to pull the information out of systems. Thus, the system allocates information to individuals, rather than acting as a passive repository from which individuals must retrieve information.

Finally, the presence of KMSs also has the potential to amend the meta-knowledge of work teams. Meta-knowledge describes both the knowledge of whom and what system has particular information (Hollingshead et al., 2002) and the ontologies team members use to categorize information (O'Leary, 1998). Connective repositories allow individuals to search for experts, more quickly identifying who knows what (Hollingshead et al., 2002). Further, AI-based KMSs have the ability to track what sets of information individuals access, allowing for new classifications of knowledge managed by these systems to be made (O'Leary, 1998).

Each of these subprocesses contributes to the overall pattern of knowledge flow. For the processes initiated by human actors, two *causes* explain variations in individuals' levels of knowledge sharing: reciprocity and relative altruism. Reciprocity and relative altruism are conceptualized as individual-level variables that are likely to vary across team members. To begin, reciprocity is one of the most basic human communication tendencies, occurring often above any individual effect (Guerrero & Burgoon, 1996). As such, any model of knowledge flow among humans should include the effect of reciprocity, especially when the flow is based upon network-generalized exchange (Sohn & Leckenby, 2007). In network-generalized exchange, reciprocity is characterized by dyads sharing information with one another. For example, Palazzolo (2005) demonstrated in a study of 12 work teams that information retrieval patterns demonstrated a structural tendency for reciprocity. Similarly, collective action theory suggests that contributions to discretionary databases, or communal knowledge repositories, are motivated by the norm of reciprocity (Connolly & Thorn, 1990). In this case, individuals expect reciprocity from a set of team members in making contributions to a knowledge repository.

Relative altruism describes when individuals are motivated more by the desire to benefit others than by their own self-interest, and represents an additional cause of information sharing. Relative altruism stems from a desire either to help others for their benefit, or to help others for the benefit of the team or organization. In the first case, information sharing is related to a personal relationship or affinity tie. Prior research has demonstrated that a degree of enjoyment felt by helping others was positively and significantly related to the use of a knowledge repository (Kankanhalli et al., 2005). In the second case, information sharing is motivated by an affiliation with the work team or organization. For example, in an overtime network case study, Shumate, Ibrahim, and Levitt (2010) found that individuals who were leaving a work team in the midst of a continuing workflow tended to allocate information to those who would be continuing in that same workflow. As such, these team members could not be motivated by the norms of reciprocity within the team, since they were leaving the team. Instead, they were motivated to share information for the team's benefit.

While the causes of knowledge flows between and among various agents, including KMSs and human actors, are the same, type of knowledge is an important *contingency* in the level and pattern of knowledge flows. Further, type of knowledge is likely to influence whether information is exchanged via group-generalized exchange or network-generalized exchange patterns. Tacit knowledge can not be easily communicated (Polanyi, 1966). While explicit knowledge may be stored in communal repositories, tacit knowledge is more difficult and costly to transfer (Grant, 1996). As such, tacit knowledge may be better exchanged via network-generalized exchange (Child & Shumate, 2007; Shumate et al., 2010). Further, some knowledge types are formally regulated by federal, state, or local regulations. For example, project developers must keep architectural drawings up to date and submit the paperwork to local authorities. These drawings then become important repositories from which various subcontractors retrieve information. While that information could have passed to these subcontractors in other ways, legal regulations related to particular knowledge types are an important contingency in determining the path of the knowledge flow.

A second contingency in the knowledge flow among agents is perceived knowledge self-efficacy. Perceived self-efficacy "refers to beliefs in one's capability to organize and execute the courses of action required to produce given attainments" (Bandura, 1997, p. 3). Kankanhalli and colleagues (2005) found that individuals who had higher knowledge self-efficacy were more likely to contribute to knowledge repositories than individuals with lower knowledge self-efficacy. Similarly, Yuan and colleagues (2005) found that perceived competence using a knowledge repository was positively related to the use of that repository. Thus, knowledge self-efficacy is a necessary contingency for individuals to contribute, even if norms of reciprocity and/or relative altruism are present.

Group size is a third contingency in the network model of knowledge flow. Both transactive memory theory (Palazzolo et al., 2006) and public goods theory (Fulk et al., 2004; Markus, 1990) suggest that as group size increases, knowledge flow changes among individuals. In transactive memory theory, group size is negatively related to the amount of communication and accuracy of expertise recognition (Palazzolo et al., 2006). In public goods theory, larger group size increases the tendency for individuals to free-ride, or to retrieve information from the system while not contributing information to the system (Markus, 1990). In both cases, reciprocity is undermined by large group size.

Representational networks are an important *covariate* that may influence knowledge flow. Representational networks, or what Bender-deMoll (2008) refers to as attributional networks, are technologically mediated networks where individuals and organizations publicly state their relationships (Shumate & Lipp, 2008). Representational networks include hyperlink networks, social networks created on social networking websites like Facebook or MySpace, and any connective network that allows individual or group connections to be represented to others. Such networks are often characterized by strong popularity effects, sometimes referred to as power law effects (Barabasi, 2003). In these networks, a few individuals or nodes have significantly more connections than most of the nodes in the network. Representational networks are about public association, not knowledge flow. The links in the network suggest that by associating with a more popular or well-known person, the individual gains legitimacy (see Stewart, Denton, & Smith (1989) for an explanation of the rhetorical functions of association). For example, in customer relationship management systems, individuals may contribute significant information about their contacts with "important" people to enhance their prestige within the organization.

Similarly, in modern KMSs, representational links can be created that link expertise, tasks, and individuals (Brandon & Hollingshead, 2004).

For example, in open-source software development, it is often the peer recognition of the individual's expertise in completing a particularly difficult section of code that serves as the reward for the effort (Raymond, 2001). The "signature" of the programmer in the code itself is a representational link between the code and the programmer. Similarly, Leonardi and Treem (2009) have demonstrated that representational networks within KMSs are often the result of the strategic presentation of information in order to influence others' attributions. In their studies, the length and "meatiness" of an explanation in an IT ticketing system was being used to determine who the experts on particular problems were. Once the technicians realized this representational network was influencing the assignment of tasks, they began to "game the system" by entering lengthy documentation about problems on which they wanted to spend more time working. In short, the technicians used the system to amend the representational network regarding what type of information they knew. Thus, the representational network may create an important covariance in the knowledge flow network.

Finally, the model specifies that the consequences of knowledge flow include various degrees of both individual gain and gains for the workgroup/organization. The various types of gains experienced by members of the workgroup depend upon the knowledge flow pattern resembling a group or network-generalized exchange pattern. In group-generalized exchange, an individual's gain is related to both the individual's level of provision and the perceived provision of others into the knowledge repository (Connolly & Thorn, 1990). Yuan and colleagues (2007) found that individuals who used the communal repository and who reported their teammates also used the knowledge repositories were more likely to report that they had sufficient access to the information they needed. In group-generalized exchange, individuals need to know how to use the KMSs to both contribute and retrieve information. However, in network-generalized exchange, individuals need to know who knows what, and share information with individuals within the network. In such network-generalized exchange systems, the public good and its value are specialized (Kaul, Grunberg, & Stern, 1999). This means that while each individual receives gains, each of those gains is different. Child and Shumate (2007) found that knowing how to retrieve knowledge information through unmediated network-generalized exchange was linked with perceptions of team effectiveness, while retrieving knowledge through group-generalized exchange was not. Thus, specialization of gains through network-generalized exchange may be of particular value.

Organizational gain occurs when people assigned to a task have the information that they need. When teams have developed an accurate cognitive map of who knows what, transactive memory research demonstrates that they complete tasks more effectively (Faraj & Sproull, 2000; Lewis, 2004; Moreland, 1999; Moreland & Myaskovsky, 2000), have better team goal performance, and have higher external and internal team evaluations (Austin, 2003). The use of KMSs has also been linked with organizational gains, including organizational performance (Lai, 2001) and socializing newcomers during organizational transitions (Empson, 2001).

Finally, following Yuan and colleagues (2005), the network flow model recognizes that individual and organizational gains also influence the contributions that individuals make. Individuals who have personally gained through information exchange are likely to reciprocate that knowledge sharing in the future. The presence of a critical mass of information in a knowledge management system can inspire individuals to contribute to a communal knowledge repository (Marwell & Oliver, 1993). Inversely, if individuals do not personally gain from knowledge flows, or knowledge flows do not produce positive organizational gains, individuals may be less motivated to use the system and contribute to network-generalized knowledge flows. Thus, the network flow model allows for the possibilities of both positive and negative feedback.

Contributions of Network Flow Model

The network model of knowledge flow departs from the work of prior communication scholars in its assumptions about the nature of the organizational connections that bring people together, the supportive contexts that enable some types of knowledge flow, and the inclusion of the representational networks enabled by Web 2.0 technologies as a covariate. As such, the model of knowledge flows makes three contributions to understanding organizational knowledge and organizations. First, the model highlights the important enabling (and constraining) functions that both physical and infrastructure networks have. The features draw attention to the ways that tangible structures influence symbolic processes.

Second, the model draws attention to the boundary-blurring composition of modern work teams. By problematizing group membership through the inclusion of affinity and affiliation networks, the model recognizes the complexities of modern membership in organizations, and is inclusive of organizing that has yet to form organizational boundaries (Aldrich & Ruef, 2006).

Third, the model draws attention to the way that networks represented in Web 2.0 technologies influence knowledge flows. Individuals and organizations often associate themselves publicly with others in order to gain legitimacy (Stewart et al., 1989). Similarly, individuals may attempt to publicly associate themselves with people, knowledge, or tasks in order to change others' cognitive map of who knows who, who knows what, and who should do what kind of work respectively.

The network model of knowledge flow also contributes to practice. First, the model draws attention to the various ways in which physical and infrastructure configurations may enable or constrain communication. While business processes or convenience may suggest a particular geographic configuration for a work team, there are important implications of those configurations for knowledge sharing that cannot be easily overcome via technology.

Second, the model draws attention to the various ways in which KMSs might be designed, contingent on various types of knowledge that should be shared. KMSs based upon connective knowledge repositories may serve to enhance the flow of knowledge through a network-generalized exchange process. Thus, turnover, dynamic membership, and geographic distribution may be managed with these systems, but not by them.

Conclusions

The network model of knowledge flows focuses on the ways that information flows among and through people and technology. Defining a work team broadly, the model encompasses knowledge sharing that occurs among individuals who have affinity and affiliation network ties. While the model is based broadly on prior communication research and the integrated model (Hollingshead et al., 2002), many of the elements set forth require empirical investigation. In particular, research is needed to better understand how the subprocesses interact with the supporting context, conditions, contingencies, and covariances that are set forth in the model.

As new organizational forms and advances in KMS simultaneously challenge our assumptions about why individuals work together and reduce the cost of information sharing, research and practice must adapt to these changes. Knowledge management practice and research should encompass a variety of informal and network organizing that occurs both within and beyond traditional organizational boundaries and structures. Further, research and practice should pay attention to the ways in which new AI-based systems are eliminating the choice to share knowledge by capturing inputs from a variety of sources. Finally, as Web 2.0 brings representational networks of various forms to the forefront of network-based KMSs, both research and practice must distinguish between representation and flow of information.

Each of these changes represents opportunities for the practice of collaboration across organizational boundaries. As Mancur Olson once said, "the biggest gains in society cannot be picked up through uncoordinated individual action." Whether through advanced KMSs or direct exchange, individuals, organizations, and in some cases broader publics have much to gain by learning how to best share information with those seeking to achieve a common goal.

References

Alavi, M., & Leidner, D. E. (2001). Review: Knowledge management and knowledge management systems: Conceptual foundations and research issues. *MIS Quarterly, 25*, 107–136.

Aldrich, H., & Ruef, M. (2006). *Organizations evolving* (2nd Ed.). Thousand Oaks, CA: Sage.

Austin, J. R. (2003). Transactive memory in organizational groups: The effects of content, consensus, specialization, and accuracy on group performance. *Journal of Applied Psychology, 88*, 866–878.

Badaracco, J. L. J. (1991). The boundaries of the firm. In A. Etzioni (Ed.), *Socioeconomics: Toward a new synthesis* (pp. 293–327). New York, NY: M. E. Sharpe.

Bandura, A. (1997). *Self-efficacy: The exercise of control.* New York, NY: W. H. Freeman and Company.

Barabasi, A.-L. (2003). *Linked: How everything is connected to everything else and what it means.* New York, NY: Plume.

Bender-deMoll, S. (2008). *Potential human rights uses of network analysis and mapping.* Washington, DC: Science and Human Rights American Association for the Advancement of Science.

Bose, R., & Sugumaran, V. (2003). Application of knowledge management technology in customer relationship management. *Knowledge & Process Management, 10*, 3–17.

Bouwman, H., van de Wijngaert, L., Van Den Hooff, B., & Van Dijk, J. (2005). *Information communication technology in organizations: Adoption, implementation, use and effects.* Thousand Oaks, CA: Sage.

Brandon, D. P., & Hollingshead, A. B. (2004). Transactive memory systems in organizations: Matching tasks, expertise, and people. *Organization Science, 15*, 633–644.

Child, J., & McGrath, R. G. (2001). Organizations unfettered: Organizational form in an information-intensive economy. *Academy of Management Journal, 44*, 1135–1148.

Child, J. T., & Shumate, M. (2007). The impact of communal knowledge repositories and people-based knowledge management on perceptions of team effectiveness. *Management Communication Quarterly, 21*, 29–54.

Connolly, T., & Thorn, B. (1990). Discretionary databases: Theory, data, and implications. In J. Fulk & C. Steinfeld (Eds.), *Organizations and communication technology* (pp. 219–233). Newbury Park, CA: Sage.

Desanctis, G., & Poole, M. S. (1994). Capturing the complexity in advanced technology use – adaptive structuration theory. *Organization Science, 5*, 121–147.

Edwards, J. S., Shaw, D., & Collier, P. M. (2005). Knowledge management systems: Finding a way with technology. *Journal of Knowledge Management, 9*, 113.

Empson, L. (2001). Fear of exploitation and fear of contamination: Impediments to knowledge transfer in mergers between professional service firms. *Human Relations, 54*, 839–862.

Faraj, S., & Sproull, L. (2000). Coordinating expertise in software development teams. *Management Science, 46*, 1554–1568.

Fulk, J., & DeSanctis, G. (Eds.) (1999). *Shaping organization form: Communication, connection, and community.* Thousand Oaks, CA: Sage.

Fulk, J., Flanagin, A. J., Kalman, M. E., Monge, P. R., & Ryan, T. (1996). Connective and communal public goods in interactive communication systems. *Communication Theory, 6*, 60–87.

Fulk, J., Heino, R., Flanagin, A. J., Monge, P. R., & Bar, F. O. (2004). A test of the individual action model for organizational information commons. *Organization Science, 15*, 569–585.

Gibson, C., & Manuel, J. (2003). Building trust: Effective multi-cultural communication processes in virtual teams. In S. G. Cohen & C. Gibson (Eds.), *Virtual teams that work* (pp. 59–86). San Francisco, CA: John Wiley & Sons.

Glaser, B. G. (1978). *Theoretical sensitivity*. Mill Valley, CA: Sociology Press.

Grant, R. M. (1996). Toward a knowledge-based theory of the firm. *Strategic Management Journal, 17*, 109–112.

Guerrero, L. K., & Burgoon, J. K. (1996). Attachment styles and reactions to nonverbal involvement change in romantic dyads patterns of reciprocity and compensation. *Human Communication Research, 22*, 335–370.

Heaton, L., & Taylor, J. R. (2002). Knowledge management and professional work: A communication perspective on knowledge-based organizations. *Management Communication Quarterly, 16*, 210–236.

Herschel, R. T., Nemati, H., & Steiger, D. (2001). Tacit to explicit knowledge conversion: Knowledge exchange protocols. *Journal of Knowledge Management, 5*, 107–116.

Hinds, P., & Weisband, S. (2003). Knowledge sharing and shared understanding in virtual teams. In S. G. Cohen & C. Gibson (Eds.), *Virtual teams that work* (pp. 21–36). San Francisco, CA: John Wiley & Sons.

Hirschhorn, L., & Gilmore, T. (1992). The new boundaries of the "boundaryless" company. *Harvard Business Review, May–June*, 104–115.

Hollingshead, A. B. (1998). Distributed knowledge and transactive processes in decision-making groups. *Research on Managing Groups and Teams, 1*, 103–123.

Hollingshead, A. B., & Brandon, D. P. (2003). Potential benefits of communication in transactive memory systems. *Human Communication Research, 29*, 607–615.

Hollingshead, A. B., Fulk, J., & Monge, P. (2002). Fostering intranet knowledge-sharing: An integration of transactive memory and public goods approaches. In P. J. Hinds & S. Keisler (Eds.), *Distributed work: New research on working across distance using technology*. Cambridge, MA: MIT Press.

Kalleberg, A. L. (2000). Nonstandard employment relations: Part-time, temporary and contract work. *Annual Review of Sociology, 26*, 341–365.

Kankanhalli, A., Tan, B. C. Y., & Kwok-Kee, W. (2005). Contributing knowledge to electronic knowledge repositories: An empirical investigation. *MIS Quarterly, 29*, 113–143.

Kaul, I., Grunberg, I., & Stern, M. A. (Eds.). (1999). *Global public goods: International cooperation in the 21st century* (Peace Ed.). New York, NY: Oxford University Press.

Lai, V. S. (2001). Intraorganizational communication with intranets. *Association for Computing Machinery, 44*, 95–100.

Leonardi, P. M., & Treem, J. W. (2010). Technology, Information Visibility, and the Social Construction of Expertise. Paper presented at the International Communication Association Conference, Chicago, IL.

Lewis, K. (2004). Knowledge and performance in knowledge-worker teams: A longitudinal study of transactive memory systems. *Management Science, 50,* 1519–1533.

Lewis, K., Belliveau, M., Herndon, B., & Keller, J. (2007). Group cognition, membership change, and performance: Investigating the benefits and detriments of collective knowledge. *Organizational Behavior and Human Decision Processes, 103,* 159–178.

Liebowitz, J. (2001). Knowledge management and its link to artificial intelligence. *Expert systems with applications, 20,* 1–6.

Maedche, A., Motik, B., Stojanovic, L., Studer, R., & Volz, R. (2003). Ontologies for enterprise knowledge management. *IEEE Intelligent Systems, 18,* 26–33.

Markus, M. L. (1990). Toward a "Critical mass" Theory of interactive media. In J. Fulk & C. Steinfeld (Eds.), *Organizations and communication technology* (pp. 194–219). Newbury Park, CA: Sage.

Marwell, G., & Oliver, P. E. (1993). *The critical mass in collective action: A microsocial theory.* New York, NY: Cambridge University Press.

Monge, P. R., Rothman, L. W., Eisenberg, E. M., Miller, K. I., & Kirste, K. K. (1985). The dynamics of organizational proximity. *Management Science, 31,* 1129–1141.

Moreland, R. L. (1999). Transactive memory: Learning who knows what in work groups and organizations. In L. L. Thompson, J. M. Levine, & D. M. Messick (Eds.), *Shared cognition in organizations: The management of knowledge* (pp. 3–31). Mahwah, NJ: Lawrence Erlbaum Associates.

Moreland, R. L., & Myaskovsky, L. (2000). Exploring the performance benefits of group training: Transactive memory or improved communication? *Organizational Behavior and Human Processes, 82,* 117–133.

Nissen, M. E. (2002). *Harnessing knowledge dynamics: Principled organizational knowing and learning.* Hershey, PA: Idea Team, Inc.

Nonaka, I. (1994). A dynamic theory of organizational knowledge creation. *Organization Science, 5,* 14–37.

Nonaka, I., & Konno, N. (1998). The concept of "Ba": Building a foundation for knowledge creation. *California Management Review, 40,* 40–54.

O'Leary, D. E. (1998). Using AI in knowledge management: Knowledge bases and ontologies. *IEEE Intelligent Systems, 13,* 34–39.

O'Leary, M. B., & Cummings, J. N. (2007). The spatial, temporal, and configurational characteristics of geographic dispersion in teams. *MIS Quarterly, 31,* 433–452.

Palazzolo, E. T. (2005). Organizing for information retrieval in transactive memory systems. *Communication Research, 32,* 726–761.

Palazzolo, E. T., Serb, D. A., She, Y., Su, C., & Contractor, N. S. (2006). Coevolution of communication and knowledge networks in transactive memory systems: Using computational models for theoretical development. *Communication Theory, 16,* 223–250.

Polanyi, M. (1966). *The tacit dimensions.* Garden City, NY: Doubleday.

Raymond, E. S. (2001). *The cathedral and the bazaar: Musing on Linux and open source by an accidental revolutionary.* Sebastopol, CA: O'Reilly & Associates, Inc.

Scott, C. R. (1997). Identification with multiple targets in a geographically dispersed organization. *Management Communication Quarterly, 10,* 491–522.

Shumate, M. (forthcoming). The networks of social entrepreneurship: The ties that give birth.

Shumate, M., & Lipp, J. (2008). Connective collective action online: An examination of the hyperlink network structure of an NGO issue network. *Journal of Computer Mediated Communication, 14,* 178–201.

Shumate, M., Ibrahim, R., & Levitt, R. (2010). Information retrieval and allocation in project teams with discontinuous membership. *European Journal of Information Management,* in press.

Sohn, D., & Leckenby, J. D. (2007). A structural solution to communication dilemmas in a virtual community. *Journal of Communication, 57,* 435–449.

Stewart, C. J., Denton, R. E., & Smith, C. A. (1989). *Persuasion and social movements* (2nd Ed.). Prospect Heights, IL: Waveland Press.

Wasserman, S., & Faust, K. (1994). *Social network analysis: Methods and applications,* Vol. 8. Cambridge, UK: Cambridge University Press.

Wegner, D. M. (1995). A computer network model of human transactive memory. *Social Cognition, 12,* 319–339.

Yuan, Y., Fulk, J., Shumate, M., Monge, P. R., Bryant, J. A., & Matsaganis, M. (2005). Individual participation in organizational information commons: The impact of team level social influence and technology-specific competence. *Human Communication Research, 31,* 212–240.

Yuan, Y., Fulk, J., & Monge, P. R. (2007). Access to information in connective and communal transactive memory systems. *Communication Research, 34,* 131–155.

Chapter 12

Knowledge Utilization in Electronic Networks of Practice

Liqiong Deng and Marshall Scott Poole

Electronic networks of practice refer to information and communication technology (ICT)-supported social networks, similar to communities of practice. In today's business organizations, the trend toward globalization and rapid advances in ICT has spurred the emergence of numerous electronic networks of practice, which allow individuals widely distributed across time and space to help each other, work together, and share information and knowledge around a common practice. Electronic networks of practice rely on a collection of modern information and communication technologies, including e-mail, video/audio-conferencing, instant messaging and chat, listserv, newsgroup and bulletin board systems, interactive white board, and collaborative technologies. By eliminating the spatial and temporal limitations of traditional networks, electronic networks of practice provide faster access to wider sources of knowledge by bringing otherwise dissociated actors into contact and expediting information flow in the networks. However, the availability of more knowledge resources does not necessarily translate to improved knowledge utilization within electronic networks of practice. This chapter focuses on the development of electronic networks of practice to promote effective knowledge transfer, sharing, and utilization in business organizations. Since electronic networks of practice consist of ICT-enabled network ties among individuals, this chapter aims to answer the following research questions: (1) How do the characteristics of ICT used for an electronic network of practice influence knowledge utilization within the network?; (2) How do the structural properties of an electronic network of practice affect knowledge utilization within the network?

Literature Review

Knowledge Utilization as a Social Interaction Process

For the purpose of this chapter, knowledge utilization refers to the dissemination and use of knowledge within electronic networks of practice. The theory of community of practice (Brown & Duguid, 1991) assumes that knowledge utilization emerges from the interactions/collaborations among individuals engaged in a joint enterprise (Borgatti & Foster, 2003). Knowledge sharing and utilization occur more easily and quickly when actors form a community that consults about a practice or problem (Brown & Duguid, 1991). Members of communities of practice are aware of each other's perspectives and tendencies. They value one another's views, and may even implicitly take others' perspectives into account when facing an uncertain situation. A community of practice is a public good to its members. Its members know that they obtain value from the community, and are willing to contribute their own questions, expertise, and insights in a system of generalized exchange. Once a community of practice is recognized as a public good, it acquires a momentum of its own. Members are drawn to contribute to the community, and interaction within the community is self-sustaining.

The transactive memory research suggests that knowledge is distributed in the minds of different individuals (Borgatti & Foster, 2003). To utilize and integrate distributed knowledge in solving problems and creating new knowledge, individuals must "know who knows what" and interact with each other to access knowledge. Factors that influence knowledge utilization include (1) the extent to which a person knows and values the expertise of another, (2) the accessibility of that person, and (3) the potential costs incurred in seeking information from this person (Borgatti & Cross, 2003). Although transactive memory research differs from community of practice research in its view of knowledge as remaining distributed in individuals' heads even after being accessed (Borgatti & Foster, 2003), both assume that knowledge sharing and utilization is fundamentally a social interaction process (Wenger, 1998).

The practice perspective of knowledge management considers knowledge as an inherent aspect of action (Cook & Brown, 1999; Orlikowski, 2002). The focus is on "knowing," which is an ongoing social accomplishment, constituted and reconstituted in everyday practice (Orlikowski, 2002). The major role of knowledge is that it may be employed as a "tool at the service of knowing" (Cook & Brown, 1999). Knowledge utilization thus refers to bringing the knowledge in individuals' heads into use in actual situations in order to go forward in what we know (Haythornthwaite, Lunsford, Kazmer, Robins, & Nazarova, 2003). The attentions are toward actions and interactions as well as artifacts and languages used in these social interactions (Hustad, 2007).

These research streams imply the potential of an electronic network of practice to be an ongoing, interactive learning system for knowledge sharing and utilization. Electronic networks of practice are essentially self-organizing, open-activity systems in which participants dispersed across time and space are engaged in a shared practice or common topic of interest through ICT-mediated communication (Wasko & Teigland, 2004). They provide ways for individuals to collectively share, integrate, and use knowledge, through ICT-mediated connectivity and interaction with others, related to their activities and work practices.

Communication plays a critical role in knowledge utilization within electronic networks of practice because knowledge utilization is essentially a social interaction process. To achieve successful knowledge utilization within an electronic network of practice, it is important that the network be developed so as to provide and sustain the proper context for facilitating the exchange of information and knowledge, complex interactions, and collaboration that are all crucial to knowledge sharing and utilization. Two conditions are important for knowledge utilization: (1) creating awareness of the opportunities of utilizing knowledge embedded within the network; and (2) developing a shared understanding that helps to apply knowledge in different contexts (Galunic & Rodan, 1998). While these conditions largely determine the occurrence of knowledge utilization, to examine the nature of knowledge utilization occurring in electronic networks of practice we also need to understand the different types and contents of knowledge utilization processes.

Knowledge Exploitation and Exploration

Knowledge utilization entails two distinct knowledge processes – knowledge exploitation and knowledge exploration. Knowledge exploitation is concerned with the transfer and use of existing knowledge, with a focus on incremental improvements and efficiency, while knowledge exploration refers to the development of new knowledge through an innovative combination of knowledge with an emphasis on radical change and innovation (March, 1991). Knowledge exploitation and exploration require different approaches to knowledge utilization. Knowledge exploitation requires the storage and reuse of available knowledge in an efficient way whenever possible, while knowledge exploration involves creating opportunities for the combination of existing knowledge in new ways (Galunic & Rodan, 1998).

Electronic networks of practice involve diverse forms of knowledge, both explicit and tacit, in various areas of practice. While knowledge exploitation and knowledge exploration pertain to different approaches to knowledge utilization, explicit knowledge and tacit knowledge are two different forms of knowledge that are concerned with the content of knowledge utilization. Explicit knowledge, as the term implies, is knowledge that has been articulated and can be easily captured or codified in the form of text, diagrams, etc. It is easily transferred through less interactive media, such as written communication. Transactive knowledge – the knowledge of who knows what and who knows who – is a type of explicit knowledge, which is readily captured and transmitted in the form of hard data. In contrast, tacit knowledge cannot be articulated, which makes it hard to formalize, encode, and communicate. Tacit knowledge includes know-how, expertise, and context-specific skills, which are gained from experience and high-level interaction with people. The transmission and cultivation of tacit knowledge requires a more interactive system, such as video-conferencing.

Characteristics of ICT

While there are a variety of factors that may influence knowledge utilization within electronic networks of practice, such as the knowledge-receiver's absorptive capacity, the knowledge-giver's willingness to contribute knowledge, and the characteristics of communication infrastructure, here we focus on the effects of the characteristics of ICT used for the network. Each electronic network of practice is built on a particular suite of ICT technologies, which enables and constrains social interactions for knowledge sharing and utilization among network members. Knowledge utilization is made possible by the ICT-mediated communication and coordination activities.

Swan and colleagues identified two approaches of using ICT for knowledge management: the cognitive model of knowledge management systems, and the network model of knowledge management systems (Swan, Newell, Scarborough, & Hislop, 1999). The cognitive model assumes knowledge can be extracted, codified, stored, and transferred using ICT, while the network model views knowledge as socially constructed and largely tacit, which can only be shared through joint practices or experiences. The cognitive model of knowledge emphasizes the development of searchable information-system based knowledge repositories where explicit knowledge can be stored and searched. This approach to knowledge utilization is impersonal in the sense that minimal direct personal contacts are involved. In contrast, the network model focuses on the development of direct personal contacts for tacit knowledge sharing and utilization through ICT with high synchronicity and interactivity. It involves the use of highly interactive ICT technologies to support direct information exchange and knowledge sharing through face-to-face contacts, discussion, dialogue, and shared practice among individuals.

Social interactions with regard to knowledge utilization not only require the use of ICT as the communication channel, but also need effective ways of knowledge representation to make the knowledge visible and accessible to all the network members (Boland & Tenkasi, 1995). Carlile and Rebentisch (2003) propose boundary objects as a central element of knowledge representation. A boundary object is an artifact that represents the specialized knowledge of one domain that is shared among all the parties involved (Star & Griesemer, 1989). Boundary objects in an electronic network of practice are mostly ICT enabled (such as knowledge repository, electronic document, prototype, simulation, etc.). Carlile (2004) suggests three approaches for managing boundary objects: syntactic, semantic, and pragmatic. The syntactic approach suggests an information processing view of knowledge transfer, which is considered as a process of sending and receiving information/knowledge among all the parties involved. It assumes that the knowledge sender and receiver share a common syntax/language, and storage and retrieval technologies, which serve as the basis for information processing. A knowledge repository is an example of a syntactic boundary object (Carlile, 2002). The semantic approach recognizes differences in the interpretations of meaning. Its focus shifts from information processing to uncover different interpretations and develop shared understanding of knowledge among the parties. The semantic approach involves not only knowledge transfer, but also knowledge translation. The semantic boundary object is required for knowledge representation when the knowledge sender and receiver use different meanings and languages, and recognize that interpretive differences exist. Examples of semantic boundary objects include unstructured digital objects with rich information (Carlile, 2002). The pragmatic approach goes beyond the semantic approach by resolving or reconciling interpretation differences through modification of existing knowledge and creation of new knowledge. Hence, it emphasizes the transformation of knowledge. The transformation of knowledge is necessary when understanding the sources of differences in knowledge and interpretation is insufficient, and the individuals have to modify their own domain-specific knowledge in a way that creates a form of "common knowledge" (Carlile, 2004). The pragmatic approach requires all the parties to engage in joint problem-solving, negotiating interests, and developing new knowledge. Virtual prototype and simulation are examples of pragmatic boundary objects (Carlile, 2002).

Network Structural Properties

While the characteristics of ICT play an important role in enabling knowledge utilization through the interactions within networks, network structural properties, such as network centralization and density, are also likely to influence knowledge utilization. Network structure is defined as "the arrangement of the differentiated elements that can be recognized as the patterned flows of information in a communication network" (Rogers & Kincaid, 1981). As implied by its definition, network structure determines information (data) flow within a network, and thus steers social interactions among network actors. Therefore, network structural properties have been considered essential for the utilization of network resources (Granovetter, 1973; Conway, 1997; Uzzi & Lancaster, 2003), including information and knowledge.

Centralization and core/periphery structures are two important network structure constructs in social network studies. Highly centralized structures, measured by the prominence of certain network members in their connectivity with all the other network members, are advocated for their efficiency in transmitting information within traditional social networks

(Koku & Wellman, 2002). The core/periphery structure is an extension of the centralization concept. It consists of two subgroups of actors; a dense, cohesive core, and a sparse or unconnected periphery (Cummings & Cross, 2003). In the cohesive subgroup (the core), actors are strongly connected to each other in some maximal sense; in the other subgroup (the periphery), actors are more weakly connected to the cohesive subgroup and each other (Borgatti & Everett, 1999). Dense core/periphery networks are very efficient at disseminating knowledge (Borgatti & Foster, 2003). However, the core/periphery structure is not good at innovation, because the conventional wisdom of the core group dominates the entire network and is not likely to be challenged by new ideas (Borgatti & Foster, 2003). In contrast to core/periphery networks, multi-hub networks are characterized by two or more subgroups that are well-connected within the group but weakly connected across groups – like a collection of islands (Borgatti & Foster, 2003).

In summary, the pervasiveness of ICT in all aspects of our work and daily life has led to a variety of electronic networks of practice. Due to the varied characteristics of ICT and network structures, they differ in the patterns and structures of social interaction among network actors, which in turn result in varied knowledge utilization processes. Whether an electronic network of knowledge entails effective knowledge utilization, what types of knowledge utilization process can occur in the network, and the content of knowledge utilization are largely determined by the environment provided by the network. Organizing our analysis around the occurrence of different types of knowledge utilization, we propose that the characteristics of ICT and structural properties of an electronic network of practice influence the occurrence, nature, and content of the knowledge utilization process.

Theoretical Framework

In an electronic network of practice, a well-developed transactive memory (knowledge of who knows what) system is necessary (Wenger, 1998) for network members to recognize opportunities for knowledge utilization (Galunic & Rodan, 1998). Due to the well-established connections of central members with other members in the network, the information/ knowledge acquisition and delivery abilities of members in the central positions are essential for the development of transactive memory in the network. In a highly centralized network, people at the center of the network usually act as information/knowledge brokers who can transfer knowledge from one person to another, or direct people seeking assistance or requesting information to the right people who can help them.

However, in the context of electronic networks of practice, which usually are characterized by larger size and greater heterogeneity than traditional networks, the members occupying the central positions of the network may be overwhelmed by the large amount of information exchange that occurs through them. In addition, the high costs of maintaining quality contacts with other members in the network may also lower the efficiency of distributing information across the network (Huang & DeSanctis, 2005). In an electronic network of practice, utilizing an information system-based knowledge repository in place of humans at the center of the network can on the one hand overcome the above-mentioned problems with humans' limited information processing and storing capabilities, and on the other hand retain the advantage of a highly centralized structure for developing transactive memory. Following Kane and Alavi's (2005) definition of information systems' centrality, here we define the centrality of an IS-based knowledge repository as the extent to which the repository is central or peripheral to all the information/knowledge exchange and sharing relationships across the network. The definition implies the following two elements for establishing IS repository centrality in an electronic network of practice: (1) any communication/interaction, either direct or indirect, one-way or two-way, is automatically stored in the repository; and (2) all the stored communication is made available to anyone in the network – for example, providing searching and sorting functions can facilitate easy and fast access to information or knowledge in the repository.

Centrality of an IS-based knowledge repository is important but not sufficient for developing an encompassing transactive memory system in an electronic network of practice. A core/periphery network structure is also needed for the development of transactive memory. The communication among members in the densely connected core lays the foundation for developing a transactive memory system by transferring the information or knowledge from individuals to the centralized IS repository, which then spreads knowledge across the network and benefits the periphery members (Huang & DeSanctis, 2005). Furthermore, through properly stored communication with their respective core group members, the periphery members, who may span the boundaries of multiple networks, can distribute their new ideas or knowledge to other core group members or periphery members. Therefore, the following proposition can be suggested:

Proposition 1: The high centrality of an IS-based knowledge repository in the core/periphery network structure leads to well-developed transactive knowledge shared among members in an electronic network of practice.

Furthermore, the high centrality of the IS-based knowledge repository in the core/periphery network structure promotes the exploitation of explicit knowledge within the network. On the one hand, explicit knowledge, which can be easily articulated and codified in the form of text, diagrams, etc., is readily captured and stored in the IS-based repository central to all the network communications. As a syntactic boundary object, a knowledge repository is most useful for knowledge transfer and utilization when there is a shared perspective among the network members. A dense core/periphery network with the dominance of strong ties in the core group breeds norms and shared perspectives (McPherson & Smith-Lovin, 1987), and thus provides a common ground for effective knowledge transfer. On the other hand, as a result of the high centrality of the IS-based knowledge repository in the core/periphery network structure, a well-developed transactive knowledge system can enhance the network members' awareness of opportunities to exploit the existing knowledge within the network. Network members hence are more likely to become aware of, access, and adopt relevant knowledge from others in the same network. Therefore, we suggest the following proposition:

Proposition 2: The high centrality of IS-based knowledge repository in the core/periphery network structure increases exploitation of explicit knowledge in an electronic network of practice.

Unlike explicit knowledge, tacit knowledge is context-specific, and can only be communicated and transferred through extensive high-level dialogue and interactions among network actors, such as through face-to-face mentoring or coaching using video-conferencing. Tacit knowledge encompasses the expertise and skills acquired through people's dynamic experiences with work practice. The context-dependent, situated nature of tacit knowledge highlights the centrality of activity or practice in knowledge utilization. The sharing and utilization of tacit knowledge requires concurrent activity performance in the current context and across all of the personal interactions. Therefore, ICT with high synchronicity (high immediacy of feedback and symbol variety) (Dennis & Valacich, 1999), which allows simultaneous practice and communication, is effective at providing the contextualization required for situated acquisition and utilization of tacit knowledge. The following proposition can be suggested:

Proposition 3: The use of high-synchronicity ICT for task-related interaction increases exploitation of tacit knowledge in an electronic network of practice.

Moreover, during the task-related interaction, the use of boundary objects at the semantic level for knowledge representation also facilitates the exploitation of tacit knowledge. Semantic boundary objects enable not simply knowledge representation, but also learning about the differences in perspective and interpretation of meaning. The semantic boundary object can reveal the sources of differences by making explicit the individual, context-specific aspects of knowledge among all the parties involved. The surfacing of the tacit aspects of knowledge thus provides a shared basis for understanding and utilizing knowledge in different contexts. Therefore, we suggest the following proposition:

Proposition 4: The use of semantic boundary objects for knowledge representation increases exploitation of tacit knowledge in an electronic network of practice.

Knowledge exploration is the pursuit of new knowledge and innovation. Knowledge exploration requires access to new or innovative ideas and/or heterogeneous sources of knowledge/information. The presence of weak ties can enable knowledge exploration, as weak ties open the network to new participants and introduce novel information. The network diversity may also facilitate knowledge exploration, because it provides the opportunity for the parties to access and combine relevant information from qualitatively different sources. The multi-hub network structure, which consists of multiple subgroups interconnected through weak ties, provides opportunities for knowledge exploration. The subgroups within the network are interdependent and serve as the sources for a diverse set of knowledge, which can be recombined into new knowledge. However, the weak ties and network diversity of a multi-hub network may also make it difficult to combine diverse knowledge and generate new ideas due to the lack of shared understanding or a common knowledge base between the knowledge senders and receivers. The use of pragmatic boundary objects, by surfacing the underlying assumptions and values of knowledge from different sources, overcomes the cognitive distances and promotes a shared understanding and integration of heterogeneous knowledge and diverging perspectives. More importantly, the pragmatic boundary object serves as a negotiation space for collaborative, cross-disciplinary problem-solving, which involves modification of existing knowledge and generation of new knowledge (Carlile, 2002). Therefore, we propose the following proposition:

Proposition 5: The use of a pragmatic boundary object for knowledge representation in the multi-hub network structure increases knowledge exploration in an electronic network of practice.

Implications and Contributions

This chapter proposes that effective knowledge utilization, such as knowledge exploitation and exploration, can be promoted in an electronic network of practice by utilizing ICT with varying media capabilities for communication channels and as boundary objects for knowledge representation at the syntactic, semantic, and pragmatic levels. Network structure also plays a crucial role in facilitating knowledge utilization. Maintaining high centrality of IS-based knowledge repositories in the core/periphery network structure will promote the development of transactive knowledge and exploitation of explicit knowledge. The use of pragmatic boundary objects in a multi-hub network will facilitate exploration of knowledge. Knowledge utilization will be improved to the extent that networks support fast and broad sharing of knowledge, enhance shared understanding of knowledge, and integrate distributed knowledge for knowledge transformation. We believe that these ideas offer several contributions to knowledge management, and to communication research and practice. From a theoretical perspective, they contribute to the understanding of how the learning environment of an electronic network of practice, consisting of ICT characteristics and network structural properties, influences knowledge utilization within the network. According to the model presented by Glaser (1978) and modified by McPhee (2008), ICT characteristics and network structural properties constitute the supportive context necessary for various types of knowledge utilization processes to occur. The different approaches and contents of knowledge utilization are important contingencies in determining the nature of knowledge utilization processes. Organizing our analysis around knowledge utilization, propositions in this chapter posit relationships between the supportive context and contingencies of knowledge utilization within an electronic network of practice. Giving prominent attention to these relationships is important to understanding the outcomes of knowledge utilization occurring within electronic networks of practice, to enhancing effectiveness of these networks, and to building new networks capable of promoting different knowledge utilization processes. Furthermore, this chapter also extends previous work on knowledge management theories by examining knowledge utilization in the new context of electronic network of practice. From a practical perspective, this chapter demonstrates how electronic networks of practice can be built to facilitate various knowledge utilization processes. It provides guidelines for developing electronic networks of practice conducive to effective knowledge utilization.

Conclusion

Understanding how and what types of knowledge utilization can occur within an electronic network of practice is a critical issue in knowledge management and communication research. The proposed model can be tested in a variety of electronic networks of practice, including open-source communities, online professional forums, and other knowledge-intensive networks. Testing the model will involve identification of the ICT used for building the network, network structural properties, and the various knowledge utilization processes within the network. Ultimately the model should be linked to outcome variables, such as the quality of the product or practice delivered through the network. Longitudinal research designs will be most appropriate for inferring the causal relationships between the supportive context of the electronic network of practice and the types and contents of knowledge utilization processes in the network. In view of the complexity of the phenomena under study, a combination of quantitative and qualitative data from multiple sources, such as surveys, documents, interviews, observations, and so on, may be needed to provide a rich description of and deep insight into the network dynamics between the contextual characteristics of the network and knowledge utilization processes.

References

Boland, R. J. J., & Tenkasi, R. V. (1995). Perspective making and perspective taking in communities of knowing. *Organization Science, 6(4)*, 350–372.

Borgatti, S. P., & Cross, R. (2003). A relational view of information seeking and learning in social networks. *Management Science, 49(4)*, 432–445.

Borgatti, S. P., & Everett, M. G. (1999). Models of core/periphery structures. *Social Networks, 21*, 375–395.

Borgatti, S. P., & Foster, P. B. (2003). The network paradigm in organizational research: A review and typology. *Journal of Management, 29(6)*, 991–1013.

Brown, J. S., & Duguid, P. (1991). Organizational learning and communities-of-practice: Toward a unified view of working, learning, and innovation. *Organizational Science, 2*, 40–57.

Carlile, P. R. (2002). A pragmatic view of knowledge and boundaries: boundary objects in new product development. *Organization Science, 13(4)*, 442–455.

Carlile, P. R. (2004). Transferring, translating, and transformation: An integrative framework for managing knowledge across bundaries. *Organization Science, 15(5)*, 555–568.

Carlile, P. R., & Rebentisch, E. S. (2003). Into the black box: The knowledge transformation cycle. *Management Science, 49(9)*, 1180–1195.

Conway, S. (1997). Strategic personal links in successful innovation: Link-pins, bridges, and liaisons. *Creativity and Innovation Management, 6*, 226–233.

Cook, S. D. N., & Brown, J. S. (1999). Bridging epistemologies: The generative dance between organizational knowledge and organizational knowing. *Organization Science, 10(4)*, 381–400.

Cummings, J., & Cross, R. (2003). Structural properties of work groups and their consequences for performance. *Social Networks, 25(3)*, 197–210.

Dennis, A. R., & Valacich, J. S. (1999). *Rethinking media richness: Towards a theory of media synchronicity*. Paper presented at The 32nd Hawaii International Conference on System Science, Maui, HI.

Galunic, D. C., & Rodan, S. (1998). Resource combinations in the firm: Knowledge structures and the potential for Schumpeterian innovation. *Strategic Management Journal, 19(12)*, 1193–1201.

Glaser, B. G. (1978). *Theoretical sensitivity*. Mill Valley, CA: Sociology Press.

Granovetter, M. S. (1973). The strength of weak ties. *American Journal of Psychology, 78(6)*, 1360–1380.

Haythornthwaite, C., Lunsford, K. J., Kazmer, M. M., Robins, J., & Nazarova, M. (2003). *The generative dance in pursuit of generative knowledge.* Paper presented at the 36th Annual Hawaii International Conference on System Sciences, Big Island, HI.

Huang, S., & DeSanctis, G. (2005). *Mobilizing information social capital in cyber space: Online social network structural properties and knowledge sharing.* Paper presented at the Proceedings of the 26th International Conference on Information Systems, Las Vegas, NV.

Hustad, E. (2007). *A conceptual framework for knowledge integration in distributed networks of practice.* Paper presented at the 40th Hawaii International Conference on System Sciences, Big Island, HI.

Kane, G. C., & Alavi, M. (2005). *Casting the net: A multimodal network perspective on knowledge management.* Paper presented at the Proceedings of the 26th International Conference on Information Systems, Las Vegas, NV.

Koku, E., & Wellman, B. (2002). Scholarly networks as learning communities: The case of Technet. In S. Barab, P. Kling, & J. Gray (Eds.), *Building online communities in the service of learning.* Cambridge, MA: Cambridge University Press.

March, J. G. (1991). Exploration and exploitation in organizational learning. *Organization Science, 2(1),* 71–87.

McPhee, R. D. (2008). *Revision of Glaser's 6C model.* Unpublished paper.

McPherson, J. M., & Smith-Lovin, L. (1987). Homophily in voluntary organizations. *American Sociology Review, 52,* 370–379.

Orlikowski, W. (2002). Knowing in practice: Enacting a collective capability in distributed organizing. *Organization Science, 13(3),* 249–273.

Rogers, E., & Kincaid, D. (1981). *Communication networks: Toward a new paradigm for research.* New York, NY: The Free Press.

Star, S. L., & Griesemer, J. R. (1989). Institutional ecology, translations and boundary objects: Amateurs and professionals in Berkeley's Museum of Vertebrate Zoology. *Social Studies of Science, 19,* 387–420.

Swan, J., Newell, S., Scarborough, H., & Hislop, D. (1999). Knowledge management and innovation: Networks and networking. *Journal of Knowledge Management, 3(4),* 262–275.

Uzzi, B., & Lancaster, R. (2003). Relational embeddedness and learning: The case of bank loan managers and their clients. *Management Science, 49(4),* 383–399.

Wasko, M. M., & Teigland, R. (2004). Public goods or virtual commons? Applying theories of public goods, social dilemmas, and collective action to electronic networks of practice. *Journal of Information Technology Theory and Application, 6(1),* 25–41.

Wenger, E. (1998). *Communities of practice: Learning, meaning, and identity.* New York, NY: Cambridge University Press.

Part IV

The Communicative *Contexts* of Organizational Knowledge

Managing Community Risks through a Community-Communication Infrastructure Approach

H. Dan O'Hair, Katherine M. Kelley, and Kathy L. Williams

The risk communication literature offers a number of commonly held assumptions about individuals' perceptions of risk, their processing of risk messages, and likely responses to communication strategies (see Covello, Peters, Wojtecki, & Hyde, 2001; Griffin, Dunwoody, & Neuwirth, 1999; Ropeik & Slovic, 2003). Not all of these assumptions have been empirically tested, especially in the context of community risk-management activities, although new advances in communication sciences are beginning to be integrated into systematic research programs designed for community-communication risk-management initiatives (Heath & O'Hair, 2009; Hobbs, Kittler, Fox, Middleton, & Bates, 2004; O'Hair, 2005; O'Hair, Heath, & Becker, 2005). A select sampling from that body of research includes: knowledge management, cultural factors, community dynamics, decision-making styles, relationship building resilience, inclusion/exclusion, information flow directions, collaborative process, media preferences, informal networking, and threat mitigators. These initiatives, when integrated with knowledge management strategies, will create a more in-depth understanding of how local communities deal with information and communication in the context of risks and crises.

A keystone to the management of risks and disasters is an understanding that these events occur at the local or community level. This chapter focuses on community risk communication by leveraging insights from these areas of research and applying them within a local community knowledge management perspective. Specifically, a community-communication infrastructure approach will take center stage as a means for increasing community resilience against a backdrop of continuing and emerging community vulnerabilities. A community-communication infrastructure is the process of placing attention on a diverse body of stakeholders who are encouraged to participate in the sharing of ideas regarding risks and threats in their communities. Collaboration is established when multiple layers of scientists, practitioners, and the public manage knowledge at levels that are accessible to most of those concerned (Heath, Palenchar, & O'Hair, 2009).

Within this context, communication processes can create awareness, educate, and coordinate and evaluate efforts toward managing community knowledge about risks (Heath & O'Hair, 2009). This chapter isolates knowledge processes involved in preparing the public, media, and risk managers for risks and threats associated with emergencies and disasters in support of a *community-based risk communication infrastructure model*. We believe that a community-communication infrastructure (Kim, Ball-Rokeach, Cohen, & Jung, 2002; Palenchar & Heath, 2002) approach stands above other ideas for conceptualizing and operationalizing risk and crisis communication in local communities. Because communities are unique and their members and organizations respond differently to communication stratagems, a model or framework such as the one proposed here assimilates the diverse knowledge bases of a community's unique profile, and recommends appropriate policies and plans (O'Hair, 2004; Rodriguez, Diaz, Santos, & Aguirre, 2006). This approach is compatible with those that emphasize a synergy of different knowledge management perspectives, as advocated by Murphy and Eisenberg in Chapter 15 of this volume.

Organizational Knowledge and Community Risks

As a means of positioning our arguments we engage the 7C model (McPhee, 2008), where knowledge in risk communities can be seen within a causal process. Figure 13.1 provides an explanation of this method (as it applies to community risks) where *process* assumes a central position, and *contexts* (and *conditions*) provide a backdrop for the problem under study. The *causes* within the framework specify challenges of the current system, and *consequences* serve to identify outcomes from knowledge management processes. To begin, by specifying community as a context for research, we aim to heighten awareness on organizational knowledge issues that contribute to community-communication infrastructure building. In marked contrast to other paradigms of research, a community science approach includes staples of inquiry that presume a multi-layered framework from which to study. Communities must be studied in their environment, encumbered with their own peculiarities that emanate from the social, cultural, political, and geographical influences in which they live. The set of circumstances or facts that surround a particular event matters, so a sub-

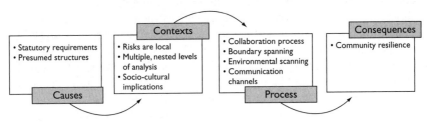

Figure 13.1 Knowledge flows in risk communities (based on McPhee, 2008).

stantial challenge for community research is finding an appropriate mechanism for examining community problems where theory and methods are applied within the context of the community framework (Barker & Pistrang, 2005). Preparedness is often linked to levels of community motivation, and research findings have offered glum reports regarding the low priority placed on a community-centered approach directed toward risk management (Peek & Mileti, 2002; Ronan & Johnston, 2005). Communities are often characterized as socio-political entities composed of multiple semi-autonomous organizations competing for scarce resources (Peacock & Ragsdale, 1997). Portraying communities in this manner signifies processes of conflict rather than consensus, and the products of these practices marginalize opportunities for resilience (Kendra & Wachtendorf, 2006). Depicting communities as compositions of self-interested networks and organizations paints a bleak picture for developing knowledge management programs that are effective and lasting. Community-communication infrastructure capacity building creates space for considerations of resource dependency issues, turf battles, and disincentives for collaborative action. It is within this infrastructure that knowledge interpretation about risk policies can transpire (see Chapter 14 in this volume for a more detailed explanation of policy knowledge processes). Media accounts of communities failing to protect residents are commonplace, and point to complexities inherent in identifying and managing risks.

An additional issue to be considered is that communities are complex systems with multiple levels of analysis begging to be measured, compared, and triangulated for generating "big picture" explanations (Luke, 2005). A systems approach to analysis involves collecting data at individual, neighborhood, organizational, network, and community levels. We are invoking "conditions" in specifying how context is better understood. Explanations for community phenomena are often elusive when investigators focus only on a certain level (behavioral) that is inextricably nested within other levels. Take the example of tornado warning research that seeks to understand sheltering behavior based only on survey responses from community members. Unknown to investigators are community norms for sheltering based on previous experiences, community warning systems, protocols, and the influence of media on community-based practices in severe weather contexts. An important consideration, then, is developing and implementing evidence-based solutions or practices within the community (Barker & Pistrang, 2005; Wandersman, 2003). In knowledge ecologies such as communities, a primary goal of research is finding mechanisms for translating research findings into practical guidelines for problem management. Communities and their stakeholder-practitioners are not empty vessels simply waiting for researchers to pour knowledge into their vacuous holding tanks. Trust and credibility play large roles in making the knowledge transition a less arduous process. Ensuring that knowledge transfers are unpacked for public consumption, and are evidence-based, are key steps that involve the collaboration of scientists, practitioners, and community members.

A second condition of the context involves community risk perceptions, the social-cultural context, and knowledge networks. Despite ongoing debates, recognition of the social and cultural dimensions of communication is now a part of the knowledge processes in communities, government, and industry. Decades of research suggests that anxieties, fears, and responses are based upon factors other than "objective" risk itself (Pidgeon, Kasperson, & Slovic, 2003). For example, Dake and Wildavsky's (1991) study of individual differences in community risk perception and risk-taking preferences found that risk perceptions have little to do with knowledge, are modestly related to personality, and are more strongly related to political orientation and cultural biases than objective risk perception. These overviews are built on economic conceptualizations of risk that distinguish uncertainty from risk, and argue that risk is an ordered application of knowledge to the unknown. From a different perceptive, anthropologist Douglas (1992) and her associates (e.g., Douglas & Wildavsky, 1982) highlight the different ways of approaching risk that are culturally defined; risk perceptions are developed through the filter of shared expectations and conventions. Making sense and making decisions are issues of culture, and culture is a principle contributor to the risk community-communication process. The perspective that emerges from this work is one in which risk issues are embedded in a "tangle" of perceptions, associations, and, sometimes, unrelated agendas. In order to make sense of such issues, people draw on shared interpretive resources (Horlick-Jones, Sime, & Pidgeon, 2003). The risk communication process is talked into existence interactively, in ways that reflect and re-form political agendas, cultural agendas, values, and power relations.

In the wake of multiple disasters in the past five years, most people assume they live in an uncertain, if not risky, environment. This phenomenon has created multiple models that integrate individual risk forecasting, information management processes, and media access (O'Hair, 2005), and demonstrated that people cope by blocking information from their awareness and strive for a "new normalcy" (Sellnow, Seeger, & Ulmer, 2005). Knowledge networks expand and contract during risk information seeking and play key roles in risk management processes, including access, veracity, and usability. For instance, when risk probability is low, risk messages are unlikely to resonate with individuals who will have little motivation to seek or process information from media sources. When risk probability is heightened, individuals become curious, process risk messages more directly, and may seek additional information from the government and media. As the threat of risk becomes more salient, individuals become more immediate in their desire for information and will intensify their media exposure. When threat seems imminent, the process of information seeking becomes acute and media access becomes vigorous, if not frantic.

Thus, a challenge to any risk communication process is to understand information that leads a knowledge network to more accurate cognitions and risk perceptions, and then to protective actions. These perceptions are not shaped only by the objective state of risk, but also by social, cultural, and political factors (Eiser, 1994; Rosa, 2003; Heath & O'Hair, 2009).

Challenges of Presumed Communication Structures

Community preparedness officials are expected to perform their responsibilities in accordance with federal mandates such as the National Incident Response System (NIMS) in the United States. NIMS is based on the classic Incident Control System (ICS), drawing heavily from the centralized and hierarchical concept of "command and control." NIMS and the command and control structure hail from a military background that is often inappropriate for those community organizations that operate in a much less hierarchical and scalar fashion in which flexibility, collaboration, and open communication are expected (Tierney, 2006). Moreover, because a typical response to an adverse event evokes a "panic" frame of mind (Perrow, 2006), centralization of authority and responsibility ensue, confirming that citizen participation is curtailed and services at the local level are usurped. This is unfortunate, since research has demonstrated that more effective response efforts result from localized units who are most familiar with the community (Clarke, 2002; Tierney, 2003). Glaser's framework component, *cause*, becomes operational in this regard (Glaser, 1978). Due to statutory requirements and years of normative behavior, many researchers challenge the notion of a top-down command and control approach to disasters (see, for example, Boin & 't Hart, 2006; Ronan & Johnston, 2005; Smith & Wegner, 2006). A notable exception to this assertion is the 9/11 Commission Report suggesting that this type of approach operated somewhat effectively at the Pentagon on that fateful day primarily due to the Incident Command System that overcame difficulties in coordinating the response efforts of local, state, and federal agencies. Beyond that example, most reports by government and independent organizations have taken issue with the command and control paradigm that pervades many response agencies, FEMA being the most visible. As a result, the top-down approach to disaster prevention, preparation, response, and mitigation faces a number of challenges that are becoming more salient each year. First, the public has expressed its concern with the ineffectiveness of command and control approaches that lack competent inter-organizational communication. This scrutiny reached a fever pitch in the United States following Hurricane Katrina. Second, media coverage and editorializing before, during, and after disasters will only become more prominent. Response organizations must engage in strategic relationship management with the media prior to disasters to develop the collaborative working relationships necessary during these catastrophic events. The command and control approach offers less of a chance of making that type of partnership work. Third, information and communication management will become more complex as advances in technology outstrip human capacity to assimilate information. Information overload is difficult to manage from a command and control perspective. Thus, there are challenges in the way the federal government is organized for dealing with disasters. The US Government Accountability Office has issued numerous reports recommending approaches that are more localized and efficient.

Although perhaps living up to the parameters for which they were originally institutionalized in the 1950s, command and control structures are no longer meeting the preparedness, response, and recovery expectations a half century later, thereby inhibiting information exchange (and the *cause* in the 7C model). It is not so much that the command and control system should be entirely supplanted by new and unproven initiatives. The command and control system, in fact, has evidenced a noteworthy record of rapidly moving federal financial resources, human resources, and materiel in emergencies in ways that remain pertinent. Governmental entities need to continue command and control activities within a more complete system of organizational knowledge. This means that in addition to a constant iterative improvement of the command and control function, the larger resilience system enables all levels of society to prepare, respond, relieve, recover, and mitigate in a massively parallel and flexible manner that cannot be accomplished by federally directed top-down command and control systems. Following Ronan and Johnston (2005), we must think more in terms of an integrated risk-crisis environment – one that recognizes and leverages local organizational knowledge assets not as unwieldy and independent phenomena, but as sources for potential interdependency. Such interdependency has the best chance of succeeding when multi-organizational response networks are recognized and legitimized through collaborating processes (Kreps & Bosworth, 2006).

Collaboration Processes and Boundary Spanning

Collaboration is a process through which autonomous stakeholders can constructively explore mutual benefits, interdependence, reciprocity, concerted action, and joint production (Wood & Gray, 1991; Gray, 1989; Rosenthal, 1995). Research has shown that the collaborative process gathers professionals from organizations that differentiate responsibilities and their orientations toward the problem. It promotes diversity in stakeholders, and embraces the natural complexities that produce a more comprehensive outcome. The process brings forth goals, values, and priorities that articulate the overall purpose of the alliance, and begins to identify knowledge resources necessary to manage a risk. All too often, however, collaboration efforts fall short, resulting in inefficient or even disastrous results (Dickson, 2005; Gupta, 1999). The tsunami disaster and Hurricane

Katrina are noteworthy illustrations of the failure of risk networks to operate conjointly.

The developmental phases for establishing inter-organizational collaboration move from selecting key stakeholders, to committing to work together, to attending to the problem domain, to finally managing implementations of ideas and recommended proposals (Gray, 1989; Bailey & Koney, 2000). Flexibility, adaptability, and ongoing information sharing are key aspects of collaboration. A process of sustained and systematic communication strategies (follow-up, inquiry, reflective listening, etc.) are enacted by relationship partners seeing themselves through collective identities where they share ownership for their relationships and the resultant knowledge structures.

Collaborative networks also evolve through the structures and relationships among organizations in communities. These networks are often structured based on statutory requirements at the federal, state, and/or local levels. In many other instances, inter-organizational networks emerge as semi-formal configurations due to common interests in risk awareness and communication issues (Weigold, 2001). For example, most disasters bring together scientists, public officials, policy analysts, and practitioners as members of risk analysis networks. Risk messages exchanged among these constituents create a communication network essential to the community infrastructure. The interdependency of their relationships is important to understand. Scientists depend on policy-makers to facilitate their work and promote their results among practitioners. Practitioners and scientists depend on public officials to fund their risk communication initiatives. Collaboration among these diverse audiences requires constant interaction between scientists, managers, and other stakeholders that improves the policy-making process and builds robust consensus (Peterson & Franks, 2006). When collaboration processes are championed and embraced by community stakeholders, multiple benefits are often observed (Lawson, 2004, p. 225):

- effectiveness gains (e.g., improved results; enhanced problem-solving competence);
- efficiency gains (e.g., eliminating redundancy);
- resource gains (e.g., more funding);
- capacity gains (e.g., weaknesses are covered; workforce retention improves);
- legitimacy gains (e.g., power and authority are enhanced; jurisdictional claims are supported);
- social development benefits (e.g., social movements are catalyzed).

Boundary spanning is a process that is highly related to collaboration, and is viewed as the coordination of experiences, values, context information, expert insight, and the actions of two or more independent organizations.

Learning organization literature offers a plentiful stream of studies related to boundary spanning, with many having a focus on knowledge management (Kogut & Zander, 1992; Larsson, Bengtsson, Henriksson, & Sparks, 1998; Rosenkopf & Nerkar, 2001). General conclusions drawn from this research indicate that boundary spanning includes working together with organizations, coordinating activities, and mobilizing resources in the community. Knowledge networks often have the responsibility to formally or informally establish and maintain communication patterns across organizations (Alexander, 1995). Not only do individual participants belong to multiple communities of practice; "their multiple memberships provide a mediating mechanism that permits the spanning of boundaries between these communities" (Wenger, 1998, p. 123). At this level, boundary-spanning information systems integrate information-flow and coordinate work across "islands" of knowledge (Lamb & Davidson, 2000; Markus, Majchrzak, & Gasser, 2002). The creation of shared knowledge is feasible when organizations share and improvise local practices through membership in the same workgroup (Gasson, 2005). By belonging to a community of organizations, mutual engagement in joint enterprise utilizes a shared repertoire of resources (Wenger, 1998).

When inter-organizational groups are formed to address community safety, boundary spanning allows for interactions with outside stakeholders, and enables members to effectively deal with ambiguities of external threats (Golden & Veiga, 2005). Knowledge is constructed across organizational groups through collaborative processes such as conversation and joint work (Brown & Duguid, 1991; Orr, 1990; Wenger, 1998). Collaboration between organizations exists in part because there is a belief in the power of many versus one in successfully addressing a shared problem among large and/or diverse organizations (Gray, 1989). Community partners who participate in boundary spanning require sensitivity to and an understanding of the dynamics of power. In order to remain autonomous yet cope with dependency relationships, partners are mindful of who benefits in the relationship, what the perceived advantages and disadvantages of the relationship are, and what the partners compete for as they collaborate (Rogers, 1995).

Environmental Scanning

Community organizations of all types would benefit from inter-organizational communication concepts related to information seeking and coordination. One of the key concepts is environmental scanning. Environmental scanning (ES) is the acquisition and use of information about events, trends, and relationships in an organization's internal and external environments (Aguilar, 1967; Auster & Choo, 1993; Voros, 2001). Assessing risks utilizing ES creates uncertainty and the need for change. However, through the search for important cues about how the world is changing, environment scanning helps inter-organizational domains create a risk management framework that will lead knowledge networks toward a strategic assessment of future events (Moen, 2003). Dutton and Jackson (1987) and Galbraith (1973) determined that scanning activity is inherent in the identification of and formation of strategic issues and the analysis of alternative courses of action.

The keys to successful scanning are active and open exploration of communities incorporating diverse sources of information and diverse viewpoints. Environmental scanning represents a process where "information seeking is seldom an end in itself, but instead is part of the processes of decision making and problem solving" (Rouse & Rouse, 1984, p. 134). The more organizations utilize a systemic approach, the more likely it is that they will avoid blind spots while scanning. Scanning is an opportunity to take an objective look at community needs by: (1) detecting important economic, social, cultural, environmental, health, technological, and political trends, situations, and events; (2) identifying the potential opportunities and threats implied by these trends, situations, and events; (3) gaining an accurate understanding of strengths and limitations; and (4) providing a basis for analysis of future strategies (Eadie, 1989; Sofranko & Khan, 1988; West, Clegg, & Black, 1988; Williams, 2007). This results in preliminary information needed to select priority issues for which specific plans will be developed.

Environmental scanning includes both looking *at* information (viewing) and looking *for* information (searching). It is through environmental scanning that organizations, and thus communities, can better plan and prepare for potential crises. Environmental scanning offers the opportunity for a more formal system of information collection and appraisal, and provides community members the mechanism to devise and implement a strategically designed risk management plan. Several studies have reported the positive influence of ES on performance (Daft, Sormunen, & Parks, 1988; Porter, 1985; Subramanian, Kumar, & Yauger, 1994; West, 1988). The most significant influencing factors are shared vision, strategic planning, and management process, which encourage people to regularly participate in face-to-face discussions on planning issues that could be used proactively to cope with external change (Choo, 2001; Ptaszynski, 1989). Collaboration processes, boundary spanning, and environmental scanning constitute mechanisms that encourage (inter-)organizational knowledge. These can readily be seen as "processes" within the 7C framework. Channels are means of understanding these efforts, and are taken up in the following section.

Risk Communication Channels

Risk communication systems, knowledge networks, organizational structures, and channels and technology serve what Pigg (2005) refers to as community information infrastructure – places and opportunities to access and exchange risk information in all formats (formal–informal, public–private). Community members have a wide variety of risk message sources to choose from, including broadcast radio and television, cellular, print, Internet, and ham radios (Heath & O'Hair, 2009; Rodriguez, Diaz, & Donner, 2005). Accordingly, our focus herein is on the most salient channels that enhance community information processes and theories that explain channel use with a specific emphasis on risk knowledge development and management. Our purpose is not exclusively on technological channels, but on identifying processes that develop pathways for knowledge management and collaboration and the support of communication infrastructure.

Diffusion of information research, a theoretical offshoot of Rogers' diffusion of innovation theory (1995), has examined how and when people have learned of major events, from the Kennedy assassination (Greenberg, 1964; Mendelsohn, 1964) to the September 11 attacks (Bracken, Jeffres, Neuendorf, Kopfman, & Moulla, 2005). This research indicates that interpersonal communication plays a larger role (and may become the most important channel) when the event is more significant. For any given event, when and how people get the news depends largely on where they are at the time of the event (Mayer, Gudykunst, Perrill, & Merrill, 1990). For example, during the Tylenol poisonings in 1984, Carrocci (1985) found that 70 percent of respondents learned the news through radio or television, but more than 70 percent reported telling others – a higher percentage than typically found in other diffusion studies. They mainly told family and close friends. Respondents also reported seeking out additional information from the news media, a process explained by media dependency theory. Media dependency theory (DeFleur & Ball-Rokeach, 1976) holds that people in modern societies increasingly rely on mass rather than interpersonal communication for information, that this reliance intensifies in times of crisis or uncertainty, and that those who are more dependent on the media will be more likely to be influenced by it. Hindman and Coyle (1999) found increased dependency on the radio after flooding in Grand Forks, North Dakota, and dependency was linked to volunteer mobilization. Lowery (2004) found Memphis residents who were more threatened by the September 11, 2001 attacks reported greater media dependency in the months after the attacks – but threat also was positively related to reliance on interpersonal communication. Group or community identification can moderate the effects of dependency on attitudes (Hindman & Coyle, 1999; Morton & Duck, 2000). These processes highlight the essential nature of knowledge transfer at informal levels within local communities. The interplay and perhaps inherent nature of interpersonal communication and media use point to the need for additional research in this area.

Online communities are an increasingly common channel of risk and crisis communication. Online communities cross geographic lines and offer additional activities that are critical for both risk and crisis communication plans. For instance, online communities serve to create awareness for community vulnerabilities and potential risks within the community, they contribute to the platform of ideas during debates over community values, and they create "gathering spaces" for community members as they sort through a host of issues attached to the emotional conditions of crises (Palen, Hiltz, & Liu, 2007, p. 55). Online community forums dedicated to risks and crises come in a variety of forms. Some are specifically dedicated to certain types of disasters, such as Scipionus (www.scipionus.com), which provides hurricane maps (visual wiki), or are communities devoted to diseases (e.g., www.newfluwiki2.com/). Participation in online forums is presumed to enhance the responsiveness of communities in the face of risks and crises. A bold initiative was advanced by Scheiderman and Preece (2007) for an online community concept called a "community response grid" (p. 944). Based on popular social network computing platforms such as Facebook and MySpace, community response grids (CRGs) would integrate multiple channels and media for linking and informing members of breaking news and up-to-date information about risks, and provide space for discussions over community issues. Designed to be both synchronous and asynchronous, CRGs offer optimal flexibility for community members' needs, and would coordinate with public and private organizations who serve as members of the risk community. Many of the challenges in making CRGs truly functional, reliable, and, perhaps most importantly, attractive involve costs (both start-up and sustained). In an increasingly congested electronic environment with many options, CRGs and similar online community risk forums must compete for the attention of a cognitively loaded target. Investments of this size, estimated in the millions of dollars per community, pose formidable challenges for champions of these communication challenges. However, done properly, the communication opportunities afforded from a CRG are virtually limitless, bringing together the advantages of interpersonal ties, network ties, and media dependence to effectively reach dispersed and diverse audiences.

More research is required regarding how the Internet can be combined with traditional media for delivering a more effective campaign (Noar, 2006). The next section takes the notion of community information structures a step further, with a discussion of community-communication infrastructures.

Community-Communication Infrastructure and Resilience

We do not take lightly the task of employing a community-based approach to risk and crisis communication. Larger perspectives such as communication infrastructures should be embraced for understanding communities (and connecting communities) as meta-systems whose component systems have become complex, autonomous, and tentative for securing interdependence as a community goal. Kim and Ball-Rokeach (Ball-Rokeach, Kim, & Matei, 2001; Kim & Ball-Rokeach, 2006a, 2006b) characterized communication infrastructure as a system of storytelling, particularly among urban residents, that is a means for understanding and supporting community resilience. Situated in a communication action context, this framework focuses on civic engagement as a mechanism for developing a sense of collective efficacy and participation within the community. Heath and colleagues have taken a different perspective on defining communication infrastructure (Heath, Palenchar, & O'Hair, 2009), where attention is placed on a diverse body of stakeholders who are encouraged (or not) to participate in the community of ideas regarding risks and threats in their communities. "Zones of meaning" (Heath et al., 2009, p. 483) are created when multiple layers of scientists, practitioners, and the public manage knowledge at levels that are accessible to most of those concerned. Although not characterized specifically as infrastructure, the Center for Disease Control and Prevention has developed a framework for their emergency communications system that resembles what others might characterize as infrastructure. Included within their communication system are stakeholders such as clinicians, veterinarians, the media, academia, health educators, businesses, and the transportation industry, as well as processes of a communication nature – for instance, the management of hotlines, press briefings, health alerts, and Web-based content.

Our own conceptualization of community-communication infrastructure borrows from previous ideas, synthesizes available research on communities, and offers new prospects for how communities can leverage important resources in order to maximize resilience. The risk environment of today requires multiple intersections among disciplines, and opportunities must be created to engage research from related fields in focusing on common community risk challenges (see Figure 13.2). Multidisciplinary research initiatives offer the potential to address social problems that extend beyond the capacity and resources of single-investigator projects. This is accomplished through infrastructure support and participation among multiple stakeholders. Knowledge accurately acquired, developed, communicated, and managed within communities with the proper stakeholders through the most appropriate and effective channels offers the promise of a more clear and supportive community-communication infrastructure, an approach to the current web-like knowledge network of community stakeholders as seen in Figure 13.2, allowing for community risks to be more adequately and efficiently managed.

Residents of communities have come to expect that adequate risk management systems are in place to protect them from adverse events, and citizen discontent is certain when prevention, response and recovery mechanisms fail to achieve their touted goals (Quarantelli, Lagadec, & Boin, 2006). In order to effectively and efficiently manage risks, a community-

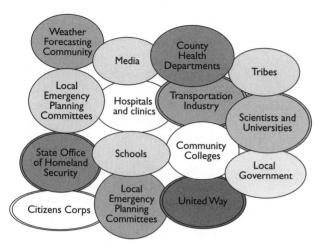

Figure 13.2 Knowledge network of community stakeholders.

communication infrastructure approach creates opportunities for information sharing and knowledge transfer. If a community has put in place communication, social, and institutional infrastructures, response time and crisis recovery should be positively affected (Davis, Cook, & Cohen, 2005). Increasing community involvement and participation in risk management spawns positive civic and social effects often referred to as resilience. *Resilience* is a community infrastructure notion, advanced by Grotberg (2002), that refers to the thoughts, feelings, and even the spirit of individuals toward their community and its members.

> It is perceived as an ideal state where communities and members possess an optimistic, pliable, and hardy perspective toward both normal and crisis conditions. Resilience is a community's level of sustainability despite the presence of risk factors (Davis et al., 2005; Guttman, 2003). Resilient communities are those that enjoy strong relationships within and outside the family, understand the need for vibrant community services (such as education, health, social, welfare), and are energetic in developing a community climate that is compassionate, empathic, respectful, and communicative.
>
> (O'Hair, Heath, & Becker, 2005, p. 313)

Resilient communities are known to exhibit four common characteristics (Grotberg, 2002): collective self-esteem, cultural identity, social humor, and collective honesty. It is through resilient acts that communities and their members construct strategies that productively approach risk and uncertainty. One of the centerpieces of understanding and building community infrastructure is enhancing community resilience. Determining community resilience levels is an essential process in developing an understanding of how members of the risk analysis network communicate with their communities. Returning to the 7C model, resilience serves as a "consequence" of the knowledge flow process.

Risk communication, trust, and community involvement are not new phenomena; previously, a National Research Council committee (Stoto, Abel, & Dievler, 1997) recommended that deliberative and participative community processes should be engaged to inform public policy choices. The committee argued that these processes lead to a more informed public and more support for decisions. *Project Impact*, established in 1997 by FEMA, was meant to actively engage communities in the process of disaster resistance. Research from *Project Impact* discovered that communities were better able to secure resources from support organizations, and were better positioned to understand their community's relative risk and plan for managing these risks. In essence, these communities became more resilient from building community infrastructure (Rodriguez, 2004). Several subsequent studies have verified the positive effect of community involvement during risk policy decision-making in a variety of contexts (Arvai, Gregory, & McDaniels, 2001; Gregory, Arvai, & McDaniels, 2001; McDaniels, Gregory, & Fields, 1999). Even community members who do not directly participate in the planning and deliberating process have more positive views of the policy decision, based on their perception that the process was fair and inclusive of community members' viewpoints (Arvai, 2003). In sum, public meetings that genuinely involve citizens in dialogue and stress the importance of interactive exchange have greater chances of success. These types of meetings not only increase perceptions of participation, but also build relationships important in the trust and credibility areas (McComas, 2003).

A community-based approach to managing risks and promoting resilience allows community members to address the ripple effect that follows a crisis. Initially, a community must deal with the physical/structural damage, such as buildings, streets, and homes. Depending on the structural issues, public health may be jeopardized as hospitals often experience surges in patients and quickly exceed capacity in a crisis. Even after a community has mobilized recovery processes, many citizens may experience psychological ramifications of the crisis, such as anxiety and fear (Woodrow, 2003). A community with a strong social network, communication infrastructure, and appropriately coordinated public and private services and institutions can not only recover from a crisis, but also move forward and develop from the experience.

Conclusion

The key to successful knowledge development among community stakeholders is active and open exploration of communities incorporating diverse sources of information and diverse viewpoints. Knowledge management is critical for capturing various forms of organizational information and data such as processes, best practices, and outcomes from benchmarking activities. Since knowledge rests within the individuals of the community, producing healthy relations is critical to sharing knowledge (see Chapter 16 in this volume). Responses to these opportunities could come in multiple forms, although we offer a prioritized set of recommendations. First, new concepts of communities must emerge that take into consideration an increasing reliance on virtual communication as a means of social interaction. Cyber-communities cannot be ignored during community planning for risks and crises (Quarantelli et al., 2006), and community leaders must recognize their omnipresence in the social lives of those who seek a sense of community through communication technology.

Future research should also focus on the coordination of community response units. How do we manage adhocracies, jurisdictional conflict, and territoriality? The key is determining how to make sense of this complex system given the multiple players involved, all with their own politics, mindsets, perspectives, goals, fears, entrenched behavior, stakeholders, and obligations. There is a need for better metrics for understanding the patterns of communication among agencies, communities, and individuals. Research should study the structure of networks responsible for managing risks/crises, and the optimal patterns of information management, and should focus on the most effective methods for coordinating actions (both planned and self-correcting). Both structural and operational strategies that lead to knowledge management models should be developed and tested, with the goal of improving inter-organizational and inter-agency cooperation and collaboration. Inherent in these processes is assessing community and organizational risk, and crisis communication programs and strategies, and developing standardized assessment tools (e.g., report cards, scorecards, communication audits) that determine areas of organizational communication vulnerability.

References

Aguilar, F. J. (1967). *Scanning the business environment*. New York, NY: Macmillan.

Alexander, E. R. (1995). *How organizations act together: Interorganizational coordination in theory and practice*. Milwaukee, TN: Gordon and Breach Publishers.

Arvai, J. L. (2003). Using risk communication to disclose the outcome of a participatory decision-making process: Effects on the perceived acceptability of risk-policy decisions. *Risk Analysis, 23(2)*, 281–289.

Arvai, J. L., Gregory, R., & McDaniels, T. L. (2001). Testing a structured decision approach: Value-focused thinking for deliberative risk communication. *Risk Analysis, 21(6)*, 1065–1076.

Auster, E., & Choo, C. W. (1993). Environmental scanning by CEOs in two

Canadian industries. *Journal of the American Society for Information Science*, *44*, 194–203.

Bailey, D., & Koney, K. M. (2000). Strategic alliances among health and human services organizations: From affiliations to consolidations. Thousand Oaks, CA: Sage.

Ball-Rokeach, S. J., Kim, Y., & Matei, S. (2001). Storytelling neighborhood: Paths to belonging in diverse urban environments. *Communication Research*, *28*, 392–428.

Barker, C., & Pistrang, N. (2005). Quality criteria under methodological pluralism: Implications for conducting and evaluating research. *American Journal of Community Psychology*, *35*, 201–212.

Boin, A., & 't Hart, P. (2006). The crisis approach. In H. Rodriguez, E. Quarantelli, & R. Dynes (Eds.), *Handbook of disaster research* (pp. 42–51). New York, NY: Springer.

Bracken, C. C., Jeffres, L.W., Neuendorf, K. A., Kopfman, J., & Moulla, F. (2005). How cosmopolites react to messages: America under attack. *Communication Research Reports*, *22(1)*, 47–58.

Brown, J. S., & Duguid, P. (1991). Organizational learning and communities-of-practice: Toward a unified view of working, learning, and innovation. *Organization Science*, *2*, 40–57.

Carrocci, N. M. (1985). Diffusion of information about cyanide-laced Tylenol. *Journalism Quarterly*, *62*, 630–633.

Choo, C. W. (2001). Environmental scanning as information seeking and organizational learning. *Information Research*, *7(1)*.

Clarke, L. (2002). Panic: Myth or reality? *Contexts*, *1*, 21–27.

Covello, V., Peters, R., Wojtecki, J., & Hyde, R. (2001). Risk communication, the West Nile Virus Epidemic, and bioterrorism: Responding to the communication challenges posed by the intentional or unintentional release of a pathogen in an urban setting. *Journal of Urban Health: Bulletin of the New York Academy of Medicine*, *78*, 382–391.

Daft, R. L., Sormunen, J., & Parks, D. (1988). Chief executive scanning, environmental characteristics, and Company Performance: An empirical study. *Strategic Management Journal*, *9*, 123–139.

Dake, K., & Wildavsky, A. (1991). *Individual differences in risk perception and risk taking preferences*. In B. J. Garrick & W. C. Gekler (Eds.), *The analysis, communication, and perception of risk* (pp. 15–24). New York, NY: Plenum Press.

Davis, R., Cook, D., & Cohen, L. (2005). A community resilience approach to reducing ethnic and racial disparities in health. *American Journal of Public Health*, *95*, 2168–2173.

DeFleur, M., & Ball-Rokeach, S. (1976). A dependency model of mass media effects. *Communication Research*, *3(1)*, 3–21.

Dickson, D. (2005). Tsunami disaster: A failure in science communication. *Science and Development Network*. Retrieved February 11, 2005 from www.scidev.net/editorials/index.cfm.

Douglas, M. (1992). *Risk and blame: Essays in cultural theory*. London, UK: Routledge.

Douglas, M., & Wildavsky, A. (1982). *Risk and Culture*. Berkeley, CA: University of California Press.

Dutton, J. E., & Jackson, S. E. (1987). Categorizing strategic issues: Links to organizational action. *Academy of Management Review, 12*, 76–90.

Eadie, D. C. (1989). Building the capacity for strategic management. In J. L. Perry (Ed.), *Handbook of public administration* (pp. 162–175). San Francisco, CA: Jossey-Bass, Inc.

Eiser, J. R. (1994). *Attitudes, chaos and the connectionist mind.* Oxford, UK: Blackwell.

Galbraith, J. R. (1973). *Designing complex organizations.* Reading, MA: Addison Wesley.

Gasson, S. (2005). The dynamics of sensemaking, knowledge, and expertise in collaborative, boundary-spanning design. *Journal of Computer-Mediated Communication, 10(4),* 1–26.

Glaser, B. G. (1978). *Theoretical sensitivity.* Mill Valley, CA: Sociology Press.

Golden, T., & Veiga, J. (2005). Spanning boundaries and borders: Toward understanding the cultural antecedents of team boundary spanning. *Journal of Managerial Issues, 17(2),* 178–197.

Gray, B. (1989). *Collaborating.* San Francisco, CA: Jossey-Bass.

Greenberg, B. S. (1964). Diffusion of news of the Kennedy assassination. *Public Opinion Quarterly, 28,* 225–231.

Gregory, R., Arvai, J., & McDaniels, T. (2001). Value-focused thinking for environmental risk consultations. In G. Böhm, J. Nerb, & T. McDaniels (Eds.), *Environmental risks: Perception, evaluation and management* (pp. 249–273). New York, NY: Elsevier.

Griffin, R. J., Dunwoody, S., & Neuwirth, K. (1999). Proposed model of the relationship of risk information seeking and processing to the development of preventative behaviors. *Environmental Research, 80(2),* 230–241.

Grotberg, E. H. (2002). From terror to triumph: The path to resilience. In C. E. Stout (Ed.), *The psychology of terrorism,* Vol. 1, *A public understanding* (pp. 185–208). Westport, CT: Praeger Publishers.

Gupta, A. K. (1999). Science, sustainability and social purpose: Barriers to effective articulation, dialogue and utilization of formal and informal science in public policy. *International Journal of Sustainable Development, 2,* 368–371.

Guttman, N. (2003). Ethics in health communication interventions. In T. L. Thompson, A. M. Dorsey, K. I. Miller, & R. Parrott (Eds.), *Handbook of health communication* (pp. 651–679). Mahwah, NJ: Erlbaum.

Heath, R. L., & O'Hair, H. D. (Eds.) (2009). *Handbook of risk and crisis communication.* New York, NY: Routledge.

Heath, R. L., Palenchar, M. J., & O'Hair, H. D. (2009). Community building through risk communication infrastructures. In R. L. Heath & H. D. O'Hair (Eds.), *Handbook of risk and crisis communication* (pp. 471–488). New York, NY: Routledge.

Hindman, D. B., & Coyle, K. (1999). Audience orientations to radio coverage of a natural disaster: A case study. *Journal of Radio Studies 6(1),* 8–26.

Hobbs, J., Kittler, A., Fox, S., Middleton, B., & Bates, D. W. (2004). Communicating health information to an alarmed public facing a threat such as a bioterrorist attack. *Journal of Health Communication, 9,* 67–75.

Horlick-Jones, T., Sime, J., & Pidgeon, N. (2003). The social dynamics of environmental risk perception: Implications for risk communication research and practice. In N. Pidgeon, R. E. Kasperson, & P. Slovic (Eds.), *The social amplification of risk* (pp. 262–285). New York, NY: Cambridge University Press.

Kendra, J. M., & Wachtendorf, T. (2006). Community innovation. In H. Rodríguez, E. L. Quarantelli, & R. Dynes (Eds.), *Handbook of disaster research* (pp. 316–334). New York, NY: Springer.

Kim, Y. C., & Ball-Rokeach, S. J. (2006a). Neighborhood storytelling resources and civic engagement: A multilevel approach. *Human Communication Research*, *32(4)*, 411–439.

Kim, Y. C., & Ball-Rokeach, S. J. (2006b). Civic engagement from a communication infrastructure perspective. *Communication Theory, 16(2)*, 173–197.

Kim, Y. C., Ball-Rokeach, S. J., Cohen, E. L., & Jung, J. Y. (2002). Communication infrastructure and civic actions in crisis. In B. S. Greenberg (Ed.), *Communication and terrorism: Public and media responses to 9/11*. Cresskill, NJ: Hampton Press.

Kogut, B., & Zander, U. (1992). Knowledge of the firm, combinative capabilities, and the replication of technology. *Organization Science*, *9*, 285–305.

Kreps, G. A., & Bosworth, S. L. (2006). Organizational adaptation to disaster. In H. Rodriguez, E. L. Quarantelli, & R. Dynes (Eds.), *Handbook of disaster research* (pp. 297–315). New York, NY: Springer.

Lamb, R., & Davidson, E. (2000). The new computing archipelago: Intranet islands of practice. *IFIP 8.2 Conference Proceedings, June*.

Larsson, R., Bengtsson, L., Henriksson, K., & Sparks, J. (1998). The interorganizational learning dilemma: Collective knowledge development in strategic alliances. *Organizational Science*, *9*, 285–305.

Lawson, H. A. (2004). The logic of collaboration in education and the human services. *Journal of Interprofessional Care*, *18*, 225–237.

Lowery, W. (2004). Media dependency during a large-scale disruption: The case of September 11. *Mass Communication and Society, 7(3)*, 334–357.

Luke, T. W. (2005). Neither sustainable nor development: Reconsidering sustainability in development. *Sustainable Development, 13(4)*, 228–238.

Markus, M. L., Majchrzak, A., & Gasser, L. (2002). A design theory for systems that support emergent knowledge processes. *Management Information Systems Quarterly, 26(3)*, 180–212.

Mayer, M. E., Gudykunst, W. B., Perrill, N. K., & Merrill, B. D. (1990). A comparison of competing models of the news diffusion process. *Western Journal of Speech Communication*, *54*, 113–123.

McComas, K. A. (2003). Citizen satisfaction with public meetings used for risk communication. *Journal of Applied Communication Research, 31(2)*, 164–184.

McDaniels, T. L., Gregory, R. S., & Fields, D. (1999). Democratizing risk management: Successful public involvement in local water management decisions. *Risk Analysis, 19(3)*, 497–510.

McPhee, R. D. (2008). *Revision of Glaser's 6C model*. Unpublished paper.

Mendelsohn, H. (1964). Broadcast vs personal sources of information in emergent public crises: The presidential assassination. *Journal of Broadcasting*, *8*, 147–156.

Moen, R. S. (2003). Environmental scanning makes planning possible. *Association Management, 55(8)*, 65–66.

Morton, T. A., & Duck, J. M. (2000). Social identity and media dependency in the gay community. *Communication Research*, *27*, 438–460.

Noar, S. (2006). A 10-year retrospective of research in health mass media campaigns: Where do we go from here? *Journal of Health Communication, 11(1)*, 21–42.

O'Hair, H. D. (2004). *Measuring risk/crisis communication: Taking strategic assessment and program evaluation to the next level. Risk and crisis communication: Building trust and explaining complexities when emergencies arise* (pp. 5–10). Washington, DC: Consortium of Social Science Associations.

O'Hair, H. D. (2005). *The complacency–curiosity–immediacy–criticality framework.* Unpublished technical report. Norman, OK: University of Oklahoma.

O'Hair, H. D., Heath, R., & Becker, J. (2005). Toward a paradigm of managing communication and terrorism. In H. D. O'Hair, R. Heath, & J. Ledlow (Eds.), *Community preparedness, deterrence, and response to terrorism: Communication and terrorism* (pp. 307–327). Westport, CT: Praeger.

Orr, J. E. (1990). Sharing knowledge, celebrating identity: Community memory in a service culture. In D. Middleton & D. Edwards (Eds.), *Collective remembering* (pp. 169–189). Thousand Oaks, CA: Sage.

Palen, L., Hiltz, S. R., & Liu, S. B. (2007). Online forums supporting grassroots participation in emergency preparedness and response. *Communications of the ACM, 50,* 54–58.

Palenchar, M. J., & Heath, R. L. (2002). Another part of the risk communication model: Analysis of communication processes and message content. *Journal of Public Relations Research, 14,* 127–158.

Peacock, W. G., & Ragsdale, A.K. (1997). Social systems, ecological networks and disasters: Towards a sociopolitical ecology of disasters. In W. G. Peacock, B. H. Morrow, & H. Gladwin (Eds.), *Hurricane Andrew: Ethnicity, gender, and the sociology of disasters.* London, UK: Routledge Press.

Peek, L. A., & Mileti, D. S. (2002). The history and future of disaster research. In R. B. Bechtel & A. Churchman (Eds.), *Handbook of environmental psychology.* New York, NY: John Wiley & Sons.

Perrow. C. (2006). The disaster after 9/11: The Department of Homeland Security and the intelligence reorganization. *Homeland Security Affairs, 2(1),* 1–32.

Peterson, T. R., & Franks, R. R. (2006). Environmental conflict communication. In J. Oetzel & S. Ting-Toomey (Eds.), *The Sage handbook of conflict communication: Integrating theory, research, and practice* (pp. 419–450). Beverly Hills, CA: Sage.

Pidgeon, N., Kasperson, R., & Slovic, P. (2003). *The social amplification of risk.* Cambridge, UK: Cambridge University Press.

Pigg, K. E. (2005). Introduction: Community informatics and community development. *Community Development, 36,* 1–8.

Porter, M. (1985). *Competitive advantage.* New York, NY: The Free Press.

Ptaszynski, J. G. (1989). *Ed Quest as an organizational development activity: Evaluating the benefits of environmental scanning.* Chapel Hill, NC: The University of North Carolina at Chapel Hill (PhD. dissertation).

Quarantelli, E. L., Lagadec, P., & Boin, A. (2006). A heuristic approach to future disasters and crises: New, old and in-between types. In R. Dynes, H. Quarantelli, & H. Rodriguez (Eds.), *Handbook of disaster research* (pp. 16–41). New York, NY: Springer.

Rodriguez, H. (2004). *The role of science, technology, and media in the communication of risk and warnings. Risk and crisis communication: Building trust and explaining complexities when emergencies arise* (pp. 11–16). Washington, DC: Consortium of Social Science Associations.

Rodriguez, H., Díaz, W., & Donner, W. (2005). *Technology, weather forecasts, and warnings: A perspective from the Oklahoma Emergency Management Organizations.* Newark, DE: University of Delaware, Disaster Research Center.

Rodriguez, H., Díaz, W., Santos, J. M., & Aguirre, B. E. (2006). Communicating risk and uncertainty: Science, technology, and disasters at the crossroads. In H. Rodriguez, E. Quarantelli, & R. Dynes (Eds.), *Handbook of disaster research* (pp. 476–488). New York, NY: Springer.

Rogers, E. M. (1995). *Diffusion of innovations* (4th Ed.). New York, NY: Free Press.

Ronan, K. R., & Johnston, D. M. (2005). *Promoting community resilience in disasters: The role for schools, youth, and families.* New York, NY: Springer.

Ropeik, D., & Slovic, P. (2003). Risk communication: A neglected tool in protecting public health. *Risk in Perspective, 11,* 1–4.

Rosa, E. A. (2003). Metatheoretical foundation. In N. Pidgeon, R. E. Kasperson, & P. Slovic (Eds.), *The social amplification of risk.* Cambridge, UK: Cambridge University Press.

Rosenkopf, L., & Nerkar, A. (2001). Beyond local search: Boundary-spanning, exploration and impact in the optical disc industry. *Strategic Management Journal, 22,* 287–306.

Rosenthal, C. S. (1998). Determinants of collaborative leadership: Civic engagement, gender, or organizational norms? *Political Research Quarterly, 51,* 847–868.

Rouse, W. B., & Rouse, S. H. (1984). Human information seeking and design information systems. *Information Processing and Management, July,* 55–62.

Scheiderman, B., & Preece, J. (2007). 911.gov. *Science, 351,* 944.

Sellnow, T., Seeger, M., & Ulmer, R. (2005). Constructing the "New Normal" through post-crisis discourse. In D. O'Hair, R. Heath, & J. Ledlow (Eds.), *Community preparedness, deterrence, and response to terrorism: Communication and terrorism* (pp. 167–190). Westport, CT: Praeger.

Smith, G. P., & Wegner, D. (2006). Sustainable disaster recovery: Operationalizing an existing agenda. In H. Rodriguez, E. Quarantelli, & R. Dynes (Eds.), *Handbook of disaster research* (pp. 234–257). New York, NY: Springer.

Sofranko, A. J., & Khan, A. (1988). It's not that simple. *Journal of Extension, 26(4).*

Staples, D. S., Greenaway, K., & McKeen, J. D. (2000). *Research opportunities relevant for managing knowledge-based enterprises.* Queen's Management Research Centre for Knowledge-Based Enterprises. Retrieved July 10, 2006, from www.business.queensu.ca/kbe

Stoto, M.A., Abel, A., & Dievler, A. (1997). *Healthy communities: New partnerships for the future of public health.* Washington, DC: National Academy Press.

Subramanian, R., Kumar, K., & Yauger, C. (1994). The scanning of task environments in hospitals: An empirical study. *Journal of Applied Business Research, 10(4),* 104–115.

Tierney, K. J. (2003). Disaster beliefs and institutional interests: Recycling disaster myths in the aftermath of 9–11. In L. Clarke (Ed.), *Terrorism and disaster: New threats, new ideas: Research in social problems and public policy* (pp. 33–51). New York, NY: Elsevier.

Tierney, K. J. (2006). Recent developments in US homeland security policies and their implications for the management of extreme events. In H. Rodriguez, E. Quarantelli, & R. Dynes (Eds.), *Handbook of disaster research* (pp. 405–412). New York, NY: Springer.

Voros, J. (2001). Reframing environmental scanning: An integral approach. *Foresight – The Journal of Future Studies, Strategic Thinking and Policy, 3(6)*, 533–552

Wandersman. A., & Florin, P. (2003). Community interventions and effective prevention. *American Psychologist, 58*, 441–448.

Weigold, M. F. (2001). Communicating science: A review of the literature. *Science Communication, 23*, 164–193.

Wenger, E. (1998). *Communities of practice: Learning, meaning, and identity.* New York, NY: Cambridge University Press.

West, D. A., Clegg, D. O., & Black, C. D. (1988). *Strategic planning: Issue identification and development for the cooperative extension system.* Extension Service, USDA.

West, J. J. (1988). *Strategy, environmental scanning, and their effect upon firm performance: An exploratory study of the food service industry.* Blacksburg, VA: Virginia Polytechnic Institute and State University (PhD dissertation).

Williams, K. L. (2007). *Maintaining a stable, safe learning environment: Interorganizational collaboration and the perception of risk.* Norman, OK: University of Oklahoma (PhD dissertation).

Wood, D. J., & Gray, B. (1991). Toward a comprehensive theory of collaboration. *Journal of Applied Behavioral Science, 27(2)*, 139–162.

Woodrow, I. (2003). N.VA. group is battling the 9/11 backlash. *Washington Post*, Nov. 16.

Chapter 14

Knowledge Types in Cross-System Policy Knowledge Construction

Heather E. Canary

It is widely recognized, and well documented within this volume, that organizational knowledge is consequential (see, for example, Chapters 5, 6, and 15 in this volume). However, those consequences also reach beyond traditional boundaries of organizations. Although most research on organizational knowledge has taken place within single organizations or with related organizational systems, little research has examined consequences of these processes beyond organizational boundaries. Many contexts exist for such examinations, and this line of research is a necessary extension of organizational knowledge theory and research.

One context for extending knowledge studies is the arena of public policy. Public policies are pervasive and consequential features of everyday life for a large number of societal members. These policies address social concerns, such as education or health care, and involve members of multiple social systems that differ in structure and purpose, including government agencies, implementing organizations, and families (Birkland, 2005). Public policy knowledge warrants careful consideration by communication researchers and organizational practitioners because the construction of such knowledge represents the nexus of policy, organizational, and epistemological processes (Canary & McPhee, 2009). Examining communication within and between policy-related systems is important for identifying knowledge resources as well as communicative strategies, language use, and features of interaction that are integral to constructing knowledge (Canary & McPhee, 2009).

Accordingly, the purpose of this chapter is to examine the communicative construction of policy knowledge within and between policy-related social systems. First, a review of previous research of organizational knowledge, policy studies, and professional–lay interactions demonstrates the value of a communication-centered approach to policy knowledge. The review is followed by a brief theoretical discussion and a description of results from an empirical study of cross-system policy knowledge. The chapter concludes with a discussion of implications for theory, research, and practice.

Organizational Knowledge in the Policy Context

A basic assumption of this chapter is that organizational knowledge is fluid and dynamic. Several chapters in this volume discuss in detail various definitions or conceptualizations of organizational knowledge, with practice-based conceptualizations offered by many contributors, such as that provided by Kuhn and Porter in Chapter 2. In line with other practice-oriented views, organizational knowledge is viewed herein as "...the symbolic and/or practical routines, resources, and affordances drawn on by organization members and social units as they maintain the institutional organization and/or coordinate their action and interaction" (McPhee, Corman, & Dooley, 1999). There are several advantages to adopting this definition. First, the definition is broad enough to include both symbolic, cognitive knowledge, and practical knowledgeability. Second, this definition also affords the inclusion of collective-level knowledge as well as individual-level knowledge. Finally, this definition indicates that policy knowledge constitutes one type of organizational knowledge because such knowledge helps coordinate action and interaction.

Research in organizational knowledge and policy studies has indicated that much remains to be learned about how policy knowledge is developed across related groups (Adams, 2004; Clases & Wehner, 2002; Gallucci, 2003; Jakubik, 2007; Spillane, Reiser, & Reimer, 2002). Parsons (2004) noted that knowledge is a central concern of policy studies, but that this concern has translated into studies of linear information-transmission processes and knowledge "utilization" rather than the value-laden process of constructing knowledge in policy contexts. Additionally, Adams (2004) argued that policy-related disciplines have largely viewed knowledge as equivalent to technical or managerial expertise, limiting what "counts" as policy knowledge and marginalizing relevant knowledge domains such as political and local domains. According to Adams, these and other knowledge domains include different ways and sites of knowing than the functional rationality privileged by expertise. In brief, policy scholars identify the need to examine policy knowledge construction in more complex ways that would recognize policy knowledge as an array of symbolic and/or practical routines, resources, and affordances used to coordinate action.

Examining the construction of knowledge involves focusing not just on what policy knowledge participants hold as a possession, but also on the knowing process itself as policy is discussed, interpreted, and implemented in practice. There is value in assessing knowledge as a possession, of course, but that value is limited by narrow operational definitions of what counts as knowledge (Adams, 2004). For example, Meyer, Cancian, and Nam (2007) studied policy knowledge among welfare recipients by asking about a specific policy provision in hypothetical situations. Knowledge levels were then assessed by "correct" and "incorrect" or "don't know" answers. This study revealed how participants interpreted one narrow part of policy text, but did not focus on how that knowledge was obtained, how policy was interpreted, or whether such textual information was valued by participants. This more nuanced understanding of the knowing process first involves recognizing the complex nature of knowledge. One way scholars have addressed this complexity is through the development of knowledge typologies (see, for example, Blackler, 1995; Collins, 1993; Cook & Brown, 1999; Spender, 1996). Typologies provide one way to better examine knowledge across different types of social systems.

Knowledge Typologies

Previous organizational knowledge research has resulted in the development of several typologies. Although typologies differ slightly, they share a common perspective that knowledge is multi-dimensional and complex. Although the theoretical roots of discerning different types or characteristics of knowledge go back to ancient philosophers (Spender, 1996), most recent theorizing about knowledge types and domains build upon Polyani's (1967) differentiation between explicit knowledge and tacit, or implicit, knowledge. Indeed, most typologies in the 1990s were variations of Polyani's concepts of explicit and tacit knowledge. Table 14.1 presents a sample of knowledge typologies offered by scholars for understanding the complex nature of organizational knowledge.

Several typologies listed in Table 14.1 were developed directly from Polyani's conceptualization. Spender (1996) summarized his view of knowledge with a grid of categories that represent combinations of individual, social, explicit, and implicit knowledge. Conscious knowledge, in this typology, is both individual and explicit, such as that knowledge one obtains from reading the newspaper. Objectified knowledge is social and explicit, such as that written in standard operating procedures and followed by organizational members. Automatic knowledge is individual and implicit, such as everyday routines one does to accomplish tasks without even noticing (for example, turning on the computer and making one's way to the coffee pot). Finally, collective knowledge is social and implicit, such as shared work routines practiced in an organization (for example, showing up for meetings five minutes early). According to Spender, these categories are not rigidly separated from one another. To the contrary, he argued that boundaries are flexible between explicit and tacit knowledge, in particular.

Typologies offered by Cook and Brown (1999) and Tywoniak (2007) (Table 14.1) use categories similar to those presented by Spender. Cook and Brown note that certain types of knowledge, such as explicit, have been given priority in theorizing and in organizational applications. In accordance with Spender's argument about porous boundaries between categories, Tywoniak (2007, p. 54) posited that tacit, explicit, personal, and common knowledge are "interdependent dimensions of knowledge

Table 14.1 Selected chronology of organizational knowledge typologies

Author	Categories
Polanyi (1967)	Explicit knowledge Tacit knowledge
Collins (1993) *Blackler (1995)	Embodied Embrained Encultured Encoded *Embedded
Spender (1996)	Conscious Objectified Automatic Collective
Cook & Brown (1999) *Tywoniak (2007)	Explicit Tacit Individual/*Personal Group/*Common
Boer (2005)	S-knowledge (subject) R-knowledge (rule) M-knowledge (mediating artifact) O-knowledge (object) A-knowledge (involved actors) D-knowledge (division of labor)

Note
*Indicates revisions to typology and author providing revisions.

that interact dynamically." That is, knowledge types shade into and influence each other. Cook and Brown contended that categories were distinct and should be viewed as functioning in different ways, but Spender's (1996) grid demonstrated how knowledge types involve different axes, so to speak, and so should not be viewed as mutually exclusive domains. This position seems most tenable, and is also supported by a completely different typology offered by Collins (1993) and elaborated by Blackler (1995).

Typologies clearly demonstrate that organizational knowledge is multifaceted, grounded in various aspects of human experience, and individual as well as collective. Like Cook and Brown (1999), Blackler (1995) criticized the tendency in research and organizations to privilege some types of knowledge over others. However, and similar to Spender (1996) and Tywoniak (2007), Blackler argued that more relationships might exist among types of knowledge than current conceptualizations recognize when focusing only on differences. Spender also recognized the limits of presenting typologies and matrices, pointing out that such categories do little in terms of explaining how knowledge types interact and how organizations specifically become contexts for knowledge development and application.

This limitation is somewhat addressed with Collins' (1993) conceptualization of knowledge types, which moved away from the use of the explicit/ tacit divide with a typology of four images of knowledge: embrained, embodied, encultured, and encoded. Blackler (1995) extended Collins' typology with a fifth image, embedded knowledge. *Embrained knowledge* is knowledge grounded in conceptual skills and cognitive abilities; it is abstract knowledge "about" things. *Embodied knowledge* is knowledge developed in action; it is knowledge "how" to go about activities. *Encultured knowledge* is grounded in shared understandings that are based in cultural meaning systems. *Embedded knowledge* resides in system rules and routines and is grounded in relations among system roles, technologies, and procedures. *Encoded knowledge* is information that is conveyed by signs and symbols; knowledge gained through books and the like (Blackler, 1995, pp. 1023–1025). Although Blackler does not treat knowledge as constituted in interaction, these images can be thought of as resources situated in social processes.

Blackler's (1995) typology of knowledge is particularly useful within the framework of structurating activity theory (SAT) used in this chapter. One theoretical foundation of SAT, structuration theory, focuses on the *knowledgeability* of actors in situated contexts (Giddens, 1984). Knowledgeability constitutes everyday, practical knowledge that guides action but might not be readily articulated. For example, individuals know how to conduct themselves in meetings at work, even though they might not articulate all the rules of engagement that they follow. Knowledgeability is inherent in social practices, and therefore is one form of knowledge that individuals draw upon in the policy process. This knowledgeability used in everyday routines corresponds with encultured and embedded knowledge, in that individuals use this knowledge as they engage in everyday activities; however, it is such a part of who they are (and where they are) that they might not be able to articulate this knowledge. Likewise, abstract, conceptual knowledge that is embrained (similar to Giddens' [1984] "discursive consciousness") is an inherent part of people who are interacting regarding policy. It is a resource for individuals and groups, and likely is influential in policy interactions. Embodied knowledge that involves how to do things is only partly explicit, and might be important in policy implementation contexts where knowledge develops through practice. More explicit knowledge that individuals can articulate, such as features of policy texts, corresponds with Blackler's encoded knowledge. Accordingly, these different knowledge types likely contribute in distinctive ways to policy-related interactions within and between social systems, and are likely involved in varying ways in policy knowledge construction across organizational boundaries.

Previous policy and organizational knowledge research indicates that these knowledge types are important. For example, Pan, Newell, Huang, and Galliers (2007) demonstrated how different phases of a new organizational process involved embrained, embodied, encultured, embedded, and encoded knowledge. Presenting only (typically privileged) encoded knowledge outcomes, according to Pan and colleagues, would have been an inaccurate and partial portrayal of the organizational knowledge process. Furthermore, Fisher and Owen (2008) noted that scholars and practitioners in the public policy arena often dismiss the experiential, embodied, knowledge of policy implementers and the relational, encultured, knowledge that develops through policy practices. As in other organizational arenas, research and practice in public policy tend to favor the explicit, encoded, knowledge of policy texts. This tendency clearly holds implications for who is seen as knowledgeable, and how knowledge processes are explained.

Knowledge typologies have been used to consider if different types of organizations produce, use, and privilege certain types of knowledge over others. Lam (2000) and Blackler (1995) both argued that various sorts of knowledge are differentially important to organizations based on their structures or functions. Although these two scholars differed in their interpretations of which knowledge types dominate which organizational types, they agreed on the idea that different organizational contexts depend on different knowledge types. For example, a hospital, which Lam would label a "professional bureaucracy" and Blackler would label an "expert-dependent organization," produces, uses, and privileges distinct types of knowledge in different ways than does an industrial factory, which Lam would call a "machine bureaucracy" and Blackler would call a "knowledge-routinized organization." Examining differences in how these types of knowledge develop, or not, in different organizational contexts constitutes a process-based empirical extension of this typology. Such an application demonstrates the potential value of typologies, in spite of limitations inherent to any static categorization scheme.

One more recent typology presented in Table 14.1 deserves mention. Boer (2005) used cultural-historical activity theory (CHAT) to propose six knowledge domains that he contended are used as resources for system participants to accomplish ongoing activity. "S-knowledge" is personal knowledge one member has of another member, such as background, interests, abilities, and such; "M-knowledge," about mediating artifacts in the system, is knowledge about what tools are available to accomplish the activity and how to use them, as well as what language to use within the system (e.g., "shop talk"); "O-knowledge" is about the collective object of activity, knowledge about the ultimate goal and motivation for the whole system; "D-knowledge," about the division of labor, is knowledge about how tasks are divided, chains of command, and such; "A-knowledge," about involved actors, is knowledge about who knows what, similar to transactive memory systems described in Chapters 7, 8, and 11 of this volume; and "R-knowledge" is about social rules, which is knowledge about appropriate behavior and relationships (Boer, 1005, pp. 311–314).

Although this typology presents another alternative to the explicit/tacit approach to organizational knowledge, it is limited by its system-specific level of analysis and emphasis on targets of knowledge rather than resources for knowledge development. Identifying these domains of knowledge does little for understanding how knowledge might be constructed between members of different activity systems.

Accordingly, the project reported in this chapter adopted Blackler's (1995) typology for examining the types of knowledge developed and used in interpreting and implementing policy in an education setting. The five images of embrained, embedded, encoded, encultured, and embodied knowledge are not limited to particular system elements, but by definition allow for analyzing the influence of such system elements on the knowledge construction process. For instance, the current environment for education systems requires highly standardized practices driven by institutional policies and routines. Such an environment might privilege encoded or embedded knowledge, but it is important to be open to other types of knowledge being used and generated, particularly in interactions that cross organizational boundaries. As Blackler noted, the nature of modern organizations – even governmental bureaucracies – is transforming. So, too, might be the nature of knowledge produced and used within them.

Family/Professional Knowledge Processes

When considering a public policy context, organizational knowledge processes extend beyond organizational boundaries. The above discussion of organizational knowledge in policy contexts necessarily leads to a discussion of how such knowledge is developed between organization members and members of related social systems, such as families that use or benefit from public policies. Most interest in organizational knowledge has been based on the recognition that knowledge processes are consequential for competitiveness, success, and viability of for-profit organizations. However, I argue that interests in these processes should be expanded by recognizing that they are consequential for more than profit and competitiveness. Indeed, applying organizational knowledge theory and research to the ubiquitous public policy arena is a "next move" in knowledge theorizing.

Previous research of lay–expert interactions regarding policy issues indicates that much remains to be known about communicative knowledge construction in lay–expert interactions. For example, Meyer et al. (2007) studied welfare and child support policy knowledge among recipients, and found there were no significant associations between recipients' level of policy knowledge (as measured), and contact with welfare staff or staff knowledge. However, there were significant positive associations between knowledge level and previous experience receiving support, as well as when recipients had specifically talked with a staff member about child support and lived in a country with highly knowledgeable staff members. These somewhat contradictory findings in one study suggest that more is going on than "knowledge transfer" through contact with professionals. Additionally, as discussed above, the way in which knowledge was operationalized could limit the ability to assess actual knowledge – of varying types – possessed by recipients. Although encoded knowledge was measured, perhaps more salient to the study sample, and to the use of welfare benefits, is embedded knowledge developed through relationships with knowledgeable staff, and embodied knowledge developed through lived experiences in the welfare system.

Previous research of parent–professional interactions regarding disability and special education policy has indicated that parents rely on professionals to interpret policy and inform parents of policy provisions that relate to them (see, for example, Canary, 2008; Canary & McPhee, 2009). When asked about how they learned about disabilities, available services, and relevant policy provisions, parent participants in these studies uniformly identified educational professionals as their main source of information. Few parents in these studies relied on policy texts to understand provisions that impact their children or their families, which would be encoded knowledge typically dependent for its meaning on embedded and even encultured knowledge. Rather, their knowledge development relied on the filter of organizational knowledge processes of professionals with whom they interacted. This dependence upon experts, and perceived expertise, comports with Adams (2004) contention that the public policy arena privileges expert knowledge domains over other domains, such as local family situations. These findings also point to a need to recognize and examine cross-system consequences of organizational knowledge processes.

Previous research also indicates that parents tend to rely on their experiences with their children in a variety of contexts in decision-making interactions with policy implementers (Harry, Rueda, & Kayanpur, 1999; Shapiro, Monzo, & Rueda, 2004; Walker, 2001). These studies suggest that policy knowledge for family members might be mediated, or influenced, by elements of their family systems, such as cultural assumptions and values, resources, roles, and priorities. In other words, constructing policy knowledge across professional and family systems cannot be separated from the embedded and encultured knowledge of policy beneficiaries. However, research also indicates that professional policy implementers, particularly in the realm of special education policy, often do not take such knowledge types or processes into account during implementation interactions that would potentially construct policy knowledge (Shapiro et al., 2004; Walker, 2001). For example, a related analysis from the larger project described below examined parent–professional interactions in special education decision-making meetings (Canary & Cantú, 2009). That analysis revealed that there were significantly more instances of professional "logistics talk" regarding procedures, documents, and testing results in these policy implementation meetings than instances of parents providing input about students' home behavior and background. In sum, these studies indicate that although public policy users, such as parents of children with disabilities or chronic health problems, might develop various types of knowledge in different ways, expert policy knowledge is privileged when professional and family systems intersect regarding policy. A question remains as to how to tap different types of knowledge to benefit policy implementers as well as policy beneficiaries.

Theoretical Framework

The above discussion indicates that organizational knowledge processes, and particularly cross-system policy knowledge construction processes, are complex. Accordingly, a communication-centered approach to organizational knowledge requires a theoretical perspective with requisite complexity. Structurating activity theory (SAT) meets this challenge by integrating foundational constructs from structuration theory and cultural-historical activity theory (CHAT) (Canary, 2010a). Although space constraints prevent a detailed explanation of this theory, a brief summary of main constructs is offered below (for detailed explanation, see Canary, 2010a). Figure 14.1 uses the 7-C model discussed in Chapter 1 to present main constructs of structurating activity theory and the explanatory connections among constructs.

First, SAT reflects structuration theory by asserting that ongoing action is influenced by structure while at the same time such action produces, reproduces, and transforms structure over time. This is the basic structuration theory tenet of the *duality of structure* (Giddens, 1984). Figure 14.1 shows how the local context embedded within a national policy environment is the over-arching *context* that influences the knowledge construction process. There are also structural conditions, such as the organizational structure, participant socio-economic status (SES), and participant culture, that influence the process. Figure 14.1 also shows how the *consequences* of the process presented include both system transformations and reproduction of more entrenched structural principles.

Second, SAT reflects CHAT by asserting that elements are connected in activity systems as members of the system orient toward an object. These elements shape, or *mediate*, situated actions and interactions in ongoing activity (Engeström, 1994). System elements include the subject, rules, community members, mediating resources, and division of labor that are involved in accomplishing object-oriented activity over time (Center for Activity Theory and Developmental Work Research, 2004). Figure 14.1 shows these mediating elements as *system conditions* that influence the knowledge construction process.

Third, SAT holds that mediation is related to broader structural features, such that mediated activity draws on social structure as it also repro-

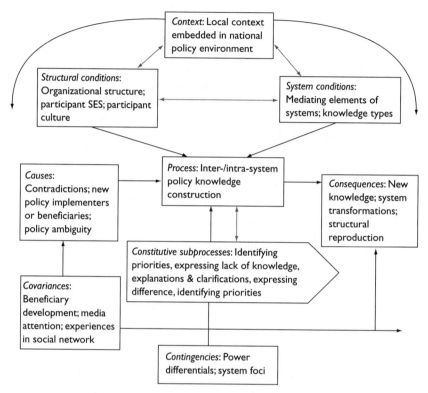

Figure 14.1 Theoretical concepts for constructing knowledge across boundaries.

duces and transforms structure over time through system transformations (Canary, 2010a). This mediated structuration is depicted in Figure 14.1 with the two-way arrow between *structural conditions* and *system conditions*. The *consequences* listed in the diagram include both system and structural outcomes.

Fourth, structural and system oppositional tensions, referred to as contradictions, are viewed as potential mechanisms for transformation within and between activity systems (Canary, 2010a). Figure 14.1 includes contradictions as *causes* for the focal process of constructing policy knowledge. Although not discussed in this chapter, previous research indicates that when contradictions are recognized, participants pursue ways to resolve or manage those contradictions through system transformations, including the construction of new knowledge (Canary, 2010b; Foot, 2001).

Finally, and most relevant to this investigation chapter, SAT asserts that policy knowledge constructed between systems is mediated by elements of intersecting activity systems, and that this process is constrained and

enabled by structural features, while at the same time it produces, reproduces, or transforms social structure (Canary, 2010a). That is, many
organizational processes involve multiple activity systems, and SAT constructs enable analyses to account for intersections of these system elements as well as the confluence of system processes with broader structural
features. Figure 14.1 depicts relationships between the structural context,
structural conditions, system conditions, the focal process, and constitutive
subprocesses. These relationships will be discussed in more detail below in
terms of the specific case presented.

This chapter focuses on one of the six SAT propositions offered by
Canary (2010a), which states, "Elements of systems of ongoing activity
mediate situated action and interaction, such that system elements shape
how and what policy knowledge is constructed within and between activity systems." The project reported below draws on Blackler's (1995)
organizational knowledge typology to explain ways in which elements of
intersecting activity systems shape how and what policy knowledge is constructed through the use of communication processes.

Constructing Policy Knowledge Across Systems

Project Data

This analysis was part of a larger study of the communicative construction
of special education policy knowledge conducted over a five-month period
in a public elementary school district in the southwest United States (Canary,
2007). Participants included 82 educational professionals and 18 parents/
guardians who interacted regarding the United States' Individuals with Disabilities Education Act (IDEA). Educational professionals included regular
and special education teachers, administrators, psychologists, and speech
and language pathologists. There were eight intersecting activity systems representing three types of systems: specialists, schools, and families. Data
included federal, state, and school district policy documents, transcripts of
49 audio-recorded staff and staff–parent meetings, transcripts from 24
audio-recorded semi-structured interviews, 60 district e-mail messages/
threads regarding policy, and field notes of approximately 10 hours of additional observations. Meetings and e-mail messages focused on changes in
policy provisions, implementation practices related to those changes, and
educational decisions for students as part of policy implementation or com-
pliance. Interviews focused on ways professionals and parents learned about
policy and interactions regarding policy changes and implementation.

Data Analysis

Previous reports provided detailed explanations of the data analysis
process involved in the larger project (Canary, 2010a, 2010b; Canary &

McPhee, 2009). To summarize the analysis procedures, the constant comparative method was used to code and categorize the data (Glaser, 1978; Lindlof & Taylor, 2002). The coding process resulted in 108 content codes that were organized into 11 axial codes reflecting elements of activity systems and knowledge construction. These axial codes were activity intersections, community, consensus building, dissensus building, division of labor, giving information, mediating resources, object, rules, seeking information, and subject. This analysis extends previous reports of the study by examining how the policy knowledge construction process reflected the use and development of different knowledge types.

Multi-Dimensional Policy Knowledge

Previous analyses of project data revealed that participants developed policy knowledge that was shaped by mediating elements of intersecting activity systems (Canary & McPhee, 2009). These mediating elements included rules, such as following agendas; aspects of individual system members, such as their existing knowledge; material and language resources, such as technology and metaphors; divisions of labor, such as authority; and community, such as meeting interactions. The discussion below explains how mediating elements were integral to different types of knowledge being used and constructed in the policy process. Additionally, it was previously reported that participants developed policy knowledge with five primary communication processes: identifying priorities, expressing lack of knowledge, offering explanations and clarifications, expressing difference, and posing potential consequences (Canary, 2010b). Distinction of these processes provides a foundation for the following discussion of the role of different knowledge types as participants constructed policy knowledge within and across policy-related systems.

Identifying Priorities

The communicative process of identifying priorities involved the development of primarily *encoded* knowledge, although the construction of encoded knowledge involved the use of different types of knowledge. Encoded knowledge is conveyed by signs and symbols, such as in handouts and policy documents. This is explicit knowledge that can be articulated by members as a resource for constructing policy knowledge within and across activity systems. Identifying policy priorities by distributing informational hand-outs, using policy documents, and defining terms were ways of using and constructing encoded knowledge both within activity systems and between policy-related systems. However, individuals also drew on the *embedded* knowledge of particular activity systems, which is knowledgeability of the routines and relations of a system, represented by system rules and divisions of labor. For example, participants used the rule of following an agenda to identify policy priorities. Accordingly, the knowledge constructed was mediated by the use of agendas, and therefore included participants' embedded knowledge of system rules. Identifying priorities within activity systems was also shaped by shared language and understandings of the community that reflected *encultured* knowledge. Members of related activity systems shared a common understanding of the legitimacy of policy to structure activity, and members of specialist systems shared common understandings of policy terms, using that encultured knowledge to identify policy priorities in their professional systems. For example, a special education administrator stated in an e-mail to a transportation administrator, "Next year we need to make sure we are providing the right amount of instructional time for our students in the self contained programs." Although this e-mail was sent in the fall, administrators of these intersecting activity systems shared a common understanding that procedures such as school and transportation schedules take considerable time to develop, which is embedded knowledge, as well as a common understanding of terms such as "instructional time" and "self contained programs," which is encultured knowledge, to facilitate the development of policy knowledge across systems.

The embedded and encultured knowledge drawn on and reinforced was primarily that of professional activity systems. As would be expected, parents did not identify policy priorities, but they also rarely explicitly drew on embedded and encultured knowledge of their family systems when priorities were identified in decision-making meetings with professionals. Rather, members of specialist or school systems would present policy priorities to parents, and in the process structure parent–professional interactions to comply with those priorities. Thus, although multiple knowledge types were evident in the communication process of identifying priorities, participants clearly privileged knowledge resources of professional systems over family systems and accordingly reinforced the authority of those systems for shaping what – and whose – knowledge counts in the policy process. Figure 14.1 depicts this as one consequence of the knowledge construction process, the reproduction of expert authority and of the power divide between experts (educational professionals) and lay people (parents).

Expressing Lack of Knowledge

Previous analyses indicated that direct and indirect expressions of *lack* of knowledge were important for developing requisite policy knowledge within and across activity systems. For example, direct admissions of lack of knowledge were important for parents to develop knowledge about special education policy. Professionals leading parent–professional decision-making meetings often presented information mechanically according to the organization of policy implementation documents. When parents openly admitted that they did not know or understand a policy feature, there was an opportunity for parents to access the expert system through the encoded document knowledge, the embrained conceptual knowledge of specialists, and the embodied expertise regarding the practice of special education that professionals possessed. Members of school and specialist activity systems also used direct expressions of lack of knowledge, especially in meetings with people perceived to have expert authority, such as the director of special education or school principals. Accordingly, this communication process was important for both within-system and cross-system knowledge development.

Participants also expressed their lack of knowledge indirectly by requesting additional information or clarification about policy features. People in authority (e.g., administrators leading staff meetings, or psychologists leading parent–professional meetings) often used informational hand-outs or policy documents to identify policy priorities. Participants would use these hand-outs as basic encoded information, but express the inadequacy of that information for developing requisite knowledge by requesting clarifications and additional information. Many of these requests stemmed from participants' own embodied knowledge developed in organizational practice. These requests for clarifications and additional information also included questions about specific aspects of the context, demonstrating that understanding of the policy issue involved embedded knowledge of routines of the system and by encultured, shared understandings of the community. For example, participants in several specialist activity systems discussed that there were conflicts between their school-day schedules and school bus schedules. This topic revealed that certain special education students were not getting as many hours of school as other students in the district. One specialist asked at a district meeting, "So I feel like it's not fair for everybody. So, are we wanting the same time to get out? [sic] Or they – because they are VE [students with severe disabilities]?" This request for clarification reflects embodied knowledge that led to a judgment about fairness, the embedded knowledge about how procedures work across related activity systems of the school district, and encultured knowledge about common terms. Accordingly, expressing lack of knowledge was mediated by elements of participants' activity systems as well as elements of related systems as they used embodied, embedded, and encultured knowledge to generate shared encoded policy knowledge across systems.

Offering Explanations and Clarifications

Expressions of lack of knowledge often led to explanations and clarifications that involved different types of knowledge. Explanations and clarifications reflected individuals' existing encoded knowledge of policy, their abstract embrained knowledge, their embedded knowledge of routines, and their shared encultured knowledge. Sometimes participants offered their existing knowledge of policy texts as a resource for constructing common knowledge within and between activity systems, drawing on their encoded knowledge as they interacted with the community. Participants often referenced past practices as a way of explaining current policy changes or policy features, drawing on embedded and encultured knowledge of the community. For example, changes regarding service provisions to private school students involved extended discussions among members of various specialist activity systems that used past policy and procedures as a way to make sense of the new policy. These explanations and clarifications reflected knowledge that was embedded in the rules, routines, and practices of particular activity systems.

Explanations and clarifications were also used to develop policy knowledge across intersecting systems. Professionals often used examples of common classroom or playground practices to explain to parents how policy provisions would work for students. In these cases, explanations and clarifications provided connections between family, school, and specialist activity systems by involving embodied knowledge of what happens in schools, encultured knowledge of normative expectations, and embedded knowledge of common school procedures. Occasionally, parents would explain past procedures for policy implementation regarding their child's education if they had transferred from a different school. In these instances, parents reflected both embrained and encoded knowledge regarding policy that contributed to decision-making for students.

Posing Potential Consequences

Many policy issues and changes were controversial, and involved participants discussing potential consequences of decisions. Posing potential consequences involved various forms of existing knowledge. For instance, participants drew on their own abstract thinking, or embrained knowledge, to introduce potential scenarios about policy changes to the community. Also, participants used their existing encoded knowledge based on their professional position to frame potential consequences of policy features and changes. Potential consequences reflected participants' embedded knowledge of existing system routines based on the division of labor as resources for talking about potential consequences of policies and procedures. For example, a new scholarship program for students with disabilities raised numerous policy concerns among school psychologists. One psychologist noted the potential for legal problems stemming from the new program, "Can you imagine how you can – you've now proven – you've been awarded a scholarship because you're dissatisfied with the [public school special education] program. Now you've opened a whole new course for due process." The knowledge that developed over time regarding connections between IDEA policy provisions and the scholarship program was influenced by comments such as this, which reflected embrained, encoded, encultured, and embedded knowledge. Furthermore, these different types of knowledge used as resources were shaped by mediating elements of participants' activity systems, such as their divisions of labor, community interactions, and policy text resources.

When participants discussed policy across related systems, such as during parent–professional meetings, posing potential consequences also involved several types of knowledge and mediating elements of intersecting systems. Professionals often discussed potential consequences of children entering special education. For example, one psychologist explained to a parent, "Removal for the resource room may result in him losing time with his non-disabled peers. The positive effects would hopefully be a more individualized program where he can have more access to curriculum in ways that he best learns." These consequences were stated based on encoded knowledge of policy as well as embedded knowledge of school systems, but also provided a connection for parents to the school activity system.

Expressing Difference

Participants drew on their existing knowledge, values, and experiences to express differences and shape policy discussions, thereby shaping knowledge about policy. Expressions of difference were mediated by individuals drawing on their existing encoded and embrained knowledge; they used their existing knowledge of mediating resources such as policy language and policy provisions to provide evaluations of policy changes, suggest alternatives, and offer alternative perspectives about issues. This process also was shaped by individuals' perceptions of how to engage in activity, reflecting implicit knowledgeability or embodied knowledge. For example, in one school meeting a special education teacher used embodied knowledge as he noted differences among staff members about how to implement and interpret policy, "[Name] and I disagree strongly on this. I feel it's more important to serve the needs of many rather than one." This comment led to a discussion among system members about how best to interpret policy provisions regarding a specific type of educational service. Expressions of difference also involved shared, or encultured, knowledge of the community as participants used interactions with other members of the system community in meetings to share diverse perspectives that reflected common understandings of their activity. Expressions of difference sometimes were mediated by the division of labor, reflecting embedded knowledge, as participants disagreed with each other or offered diverse opinions based on their hierarchical position or job function, which then influenced policy interpretations for the entire activity community.

Parent–professional interactions rarely involved expressions of disagreement or diverse perspectives. Interviews with parents after decision-making meetings revealed that many parents were hesitant to "cause trouble" for teachers, and so refrained from expressing disagreements regarding policy implementation. The lack of disagreement or diversity in these intersections of professional and family activity systems is consistent with parent reports, noted earlier, that they rely on gaining information from expert professionals. However, it also suggests that the value of knowledge parents possess goes unrecognized in policy implementation, as such interactions reproduce the privileging of expert, encoded knowledge over other ways of knowing in the policy process.

Implications and Conclusions

The above discussion demonstrates that the development of policy knowledge involves much more than memorization of policy texts. Participants in policy-related systems drew on multiple types of knowledge to shape the construction process and consequently shape what new policy knowledge was produced as a resource for future activity. Furthermore, the analysis demonstrated that these knowledge types were expressed in specific communication processes within and across systems involved in the special education process.

This examination of policy knowledge construction provides an expanded conceptualization of policy knowledge. People in policy-related systems clearly use and develop many types of organizational knowledge that all contribute to overall policy knowledge. Knowledge that people draw on to interpret, implement, and use policy is accordingly a combination of encoded, embrained, embedded, embodied, and encultured knowledge. The multi-dimensional policy knowledge that is constructed is then available as a resource to transform systems as they engage in activity. System members develop knowledge about how to use policy, how to assign meaning to policy terms, and how to assimilate policy requirements with other system routines through mediating elements of their own system as well as through mediating elements of intersecting activity systems, such as specialist and administrative systems.

Additionally, analyzing the knowledge construction process through the lens of structurating activity theory illustrates ways in which mediated knowledge construction is both enabled and constrained by broader structural conditions. Participants clearly communicated, either directly or indirectly, that particular experts (i.e., specialists or administrators) were viewed as knowledgeable, while also communicating that parents, as members of policy-related systems, were viewed as less knowledgeable. Interestingly, the focal policy of this investigation, IDEA, includes a requirement that parents be active participants in decision-making for their children's special education programs. However, parents as well as professionals interacted and functioned within an expert-dependent view that professionals' knowledge – whether embrained, encoded, or embedded – counted more for making those decisions than did parents' embodied knowledge of their children and their embedded knowledge of the family systems in which their children are situated. Accordingly, newly constructed policy knowledge also reproduced entrenched views that expert knowledge is more important than lay knowledge when making policy-led decisions. System transformations, whether they be professional or family systems, then use and reproduce this notion of what knowledge counts in policy-led activity.

The expanded conceptualization of policy knowledge and this view of mediated knowledge construction across systems hold implications for other policy contexts as well. Policies, both public and private, pervade contemporary organizational life. Policies are developed to benefit organizations, their members, and non-members alike, but policy knowledge is a critical factor in determining whether a policy will be used effectively. And this chapter clearly demonstrates that simply measuring whether a person has policy text memorized is a poor indicator of that knowledge. Instead, administrators who desire effective policy implementation and use can look to the multiple dimensions of policy knowledge described in this chapter, in combination with assessing mediating elements of relevant activity systems, for determining policy knowledge strengths and weaknesses. Such an assessment would include determining what knowledge types currently are privileged in developing policy knowledge, and the ways in which elements of involved activity systems mediate ongoing construction of policy knowledge.

The five communication processes described in this chapter are a good place to start making such assessments. Efforts are currently underway to develop a quantitative instrument to identify how these five communication processes are evident in policy interactions within organizations. The items under development reflect findings reported in this chapter and elsewhere (Canary & McPhee, 2009; Canary, 2010b) regarding mediating elements, knowledge types, and communication processes. Such an instrument would be a valuable tool for policy administrators to move away from a linear approach to policy communication, and from a uni-dimensional view of policy knowledge to a more interactive, multi-dimensional view of the policy process.

References

Adams, D. (2004). Usable knowledge in public policy. *Australian Journal of Public Administration, 63*, 29–42.

Birkland, T. A. (2005). *An introduction to the policy process: Theories, concepts, and models of public policy making.* Armonk, NY: M. E. Sharpe.

Blackler, F. (1995). Knowledge, knowledge work, and organizations: An overview and interpretation. *Organization Studies, 16*, 1021–1046.

Boer, N. I. (2005). *Knowledge sharing within organizations: A situated and relational perspective.* Rotterdam: Erasmus Research Institute of Management. Retrieved from http://hdl.handle.net/1765/6770.

Canary, H. E. (2007). *The communicative creation of policy knowledge: A structurating-activity approach.* Unpublished dissertation, Arizona State University, Tempe.

Canary, H. E. (2008). Negotiating dis/ability in families: Constructions and contradictions. *Journal of Applied Communication Research, 36,* 437–458.

Canary, H. E. (2010a). Structurating activity theory: An integrative approach to policy knowledge. *Communication Theory, 20,* 21–49.

Canary, H. E. (2010b). Constructing policy knowledge: Contradictions, communication, and knowledge frames. *Communication Monographs, 77,* 181–206.

Canary, H. E., & Cantú, E. (2009, November). *Making decisions about a child's disability: An analysis of culture and translation in meetings.* Paper presented at the annual convention of the National Communication Association, Chicago, Illinois.

Canary, H. E., & McPhee, R. D. (2009). The mediation of policy knowledge: An interpretive analysis of intersecting activity systems. *Management Communication Quarterly, 23,* 147–187.

Center for Activity Theory and Developmental Work Research. (2004). *The activity system.* Retrieved from www.edu.helsinki.fi/activity/pages/chatanddwr/activitysystem.

Clases, C., & Wehner, T. (2002). Steps across the border – cooperation, knowledge production and systems design. *Computer Supported Cooperative Work, 11,* 39–54.

Collins, H. M. (1993). The structure of knowledge. *Social Research, 60,* 95–116.

Cook, S. D. N., & Brown, J. S. (1999). Bridging epistemologies: The generative dance between organizational knowledge and organizational knowing. *Organization Science, 10,* 381–400.

Engeström, Y. (1994). Teachers as collaborative thinkers: Activity-theoretical study of an innovative teacher team. In I. Carlgren, G. Handal, & S. Vaage (Eds.), *Teachers' minds and actions: Research on teachers' thinking and practice* (pp. 43–61). London, UK: Falmer.

Fisher, P., & Owen, J. (2008). Empowering interventions in health and social care: Recognition through "ecologies of practice." *Social Science & Medicine, 67,* 2063–2071.

Foot, K. A. (2001). Cultural–historical activity theory as practice theory: Illuminating the development of a conflict-monitoring network. *Communication Theory, 11,* 56–83.

Gallucci, C. (2003). Communities of practice and the mediation of teachers' responses to standards-based reform. *Education Policy Analysis Archives, 11,* 35. Retrieved from http://epaa.asu.edu/epaa/v11n35.

Giddens, A. (1984). *The constitution of society.* Berkeley, CA: University of California Press.

Glaser, B. G. (1978). *Theoretical sensitivity.* Mill Valley, CA: Sociology Press.

Harry, B., Rueda, R., & Kayanpur, M. (1999). Cultural reciprocity and sociocultural perspective: Adapting the normalization principle for family collaboration. *Exceptional Children, 66,* 123–136.

Jakubik, M. (2007). Exploring the knowledge landscape: Four emerging views of knowledge. *Journal of Knowledge Management, 11*(4), 6–19.

Lam, A. (2000). Tacit knowledge, organizational learning, and societal institutions: An integrated framework. *Organization Studies, 21,* 487–513.

Lindlof, T. R., & Taylor, B. C. (2002). *Qualitative communication research methods.* Thousand Oaks, CA: Sage.

McPhee, R. D., Corman, S. R., & Dooley, K. (1999, May). *Theoretical and methodological axioms for the study of organizational knowledge and communication.* Paper presented at the annual convention of the International Communication Association, San Francisco, California.

Meyer, D. R., Cancian, M., & Nam, K. (2007). Welfare and child support program knowledge gaps reduce program effectiveness. *Journal of Policy Analysis and Management, 26,* 575–597.

Pan, S. L., Newell, S., Huang, J., & Galliers, R. D. (2007). Overcoming knowledge management challenges during ERP implementation: The need to integrate and share different types of knowledge. *Journal of the American Society for Information Science & Technology, 58,* 404–419.

Parsons, W. (2004). Not just steering but weaving: Relevant knowledge and the craft of building policy capacity and coherence. *Australian Journal of Public Administration, 63,* 43–57.

Polanyi, M. (1967). *The tacit dimension.* Garden City, NY: Anchor Books.

Shapiro, J., Monzo, L. D., & Rueda, R. (2004). Alienated advocacy: Perspectives of Latina mothers of young adults with developmental disabilities. *Mental Retardation, 42,* 36–54.

Spender, J.-C. (1996). Making knowledge the basis of a dynamic theory of the firm. *Strategic Management Journal, 17,* 45–62.

Spillane, J. P., Reiser, B. J., & Reimer, T. (2002). Policy implementation and cognition: Reframing and refocusing implementation research. *Review of Educational Research, 72,* 387–431.

Tywoniak, S. A. (2007). Knowledge in four deformation dimensions. *Organization, 14,* 53–76.

Walker, J. S. (2001). Caregivers' views on the cultural appropriateness of services for children with emotional and behavioral disorders. *Journal of Child and Family Studies, 10,* 315–331.

Chapter 15

Coaching to the Craft

Understanding Knowledge in Health Care Organizations

Alexandra G. Murphy and Eric M. Eisenberg

Questions regarding the nature of organizational knowledge draw upon a variety of communication theories and cut across a range of organizational settings and industries. As Kuhn and Jackson (2008) have shown, conceptions of organizational knowledge take two general forms. The first views knowledge as a defined, objective body of information derived through the use of formalized, deductive principles. From this perspective, knowledge "management" comprises the precise documentation, storage, assessment, and retrieval of information, optimizing its timely and accurate distribution and accessibility to relevant members and divisions of the organization.

The second approach challenges the notion of knowledge as a fixed, objective body of information. Instead, this perspective sees knowledge as fluid, dynamic, and continually under revision, perpetually emerging through communication, action, and events (see Kuhn and Jackson, 2008, for a complete review). Put another way, the first perspective sees knowledge management mainly as a matter of creating and retrieving records, while the second emphasizes the importance of continuous, just-in-time access to networks of relationships (Steier & Eisenberg, 1997).

Eisenberg (2008) draws a similar distinction between transmission-based and social construction models of communication in the context of health care teams. Rather than treating the two models as mutually exclusive, he examines the definitions and criteria for effectiveness for each, demonstrating their applicability to particular situations (e.g., sometimes it is useful to think of knowledge in terms of transmission, other times as ongoing social construction). In this chapter, we expand upon this idea to promote a more nuanced understanding of organizational knowledge management as it relates to health care.

In a fashion that echoes Joanne Martin's (1992) description of three perspectives in organizational culture research, our approach begins by identifying three frameworks of analysis for organizational knowledge and communication in health care: routinized, emergent, and political. After elaborating on these three frameworks, we demonstrate the value in considering how all three interact with one another in dimensional pairings and tensions. To do this, we draw from a rather unique data set: the transcripts of a two-day retreat of an interdisciplinary research team. The purpose of the meeting was to make sense of a large amount of observational data on physician transitions and decision-making in emergency rooms. In a sense, we are providing a method of nested reflections as we reflect on their reflections on health care. What we discovered in these reflections was a compelling example of collective sensemaking that may have broad utility as a model for sensemaking in health care organizations.

Three Frames of Knowledge

Knowledge as Routinized

The first framework highlights transmissional approaches to communicating knowledge typically characterized as objective, standardized *routines* (Table 15.1). Most analysis of knowledge management in health care has this focus, highlighting situations where information is not accurately passed from one person to the next (Anderson, 1997; Bose, 2003; Forgionne, Gangopadhyay, Klein, & Eckhardt, 1999; Raghupathi & Tan, 1999). Knowledge management systems in health care seek to establish processes and infrastructures necessary to create, coordinate, and manage patient information among a variety of health services and providers, primarily through electronic and computer-based technologies known as e-health knowledge (Anderson & Aydin, 1997; Forgionne et al., 1999). E-health knowledge allows the immediate and ongoing access to disparate knowledge repositories. One of the top priorities of the new administration in Washington, DC (*c.*2009) is to create a fully integrated, paperless health information system nation-wide.

Recognizing the need to increase the accurate transmission of medical knowledge, health care institutions have integrated a series of recommendations by the Joint Commission (formerly the Joint Commission on Accreditation of Healthcare Organizations, JCAHO) in the form of specialized communication technologies and purposeful patterns of interaction. Commonly employed techniques include medical team callbacks, formalized clinical patient interviews, and structured, asynchronous patient handoffs – all to improve the fidelity of information transfer (Eisenberg, 2008). Once this information is "properly coded, structured, and shared with the right people at the right time, it becomes knowledge" (Bose, 2003, p. 61).

The mindset behind this line of research is a belief in the importance of evidence-based medicine, which depends upon the routinization and dissemination of best treatment practices. The design of the knowledge management-enabled health care system directly supports evidence-based medical practice because the care recommendations made by the system are based on a broadly established knowledge base. To support clinical decision-making, the system is designed to match the characteristics of an individual patient to the clinical knowledge base, and patient-specific assessments or recommendations are then presented to the medical staff or the patient for a decision (Bose, 2003, p. 62).

A framework for the transmission of knowledge as routine follows the assumption that knowledge is an objective outcome based on formalized, clear, and deductive information transfer. The goal is to improve standardized medical care and preclude miscommunication and negative events. And the emphasis on the clarity and fidelity of information transfer helps in the reduction of certain types of medical errors. Sometimes, the wrong medicine is given to a patient because the nurse cannot read a written physician order, or the wrong test may be run because the nurse misheard the verbal order, or a physician misses attending to a critical patient because there were too many distractions occurring and the patient was not prioritized. These kinds of mishaps, however, do not account for all of the medical errors in health care – they are but one level on which knowledge operates.

Knowledge as Emergent

The second framework draws upon theories of social construction (cf. Eisenberg, 2008) to reveal the *emergent* nature of organizational knowledge (Table 15.1). From this perspective, it is the repeated, sometimes ritual interactions of health care actors that best represent what is "known." At the same time, employees of health care organizations engage in joint, collaborative sensemaking over time in response to patients and situations that are never quite identical. The organizational knowledge in question from this perspective emerges through experience, interpersonal relationships, conversations, and collaborative routines employed by these individuals as they struggle to cope with a turbulent organizational environment.

In health research, attention is shifting from considering medical knowledge and expertise as the "God's unassailable truth" to considering the "ongoing negotiation and control of symbolically and socially produced knowledge" (Ellingson, 2008; Kuipers, 1989, p. 100; Murphy, Eisenberg, Wears, & Perry, 2008). This view assumes that knowledge is not predetermined or fixed, but instead emerges as people access their networks of interpersonal relationships to develop interpretations for handling fundamentally ambiguous situations (Blatt, Christianson, Sutcliffe, & Rosenthal, 2006; Schulman, 2004). Seen this way, health professionals interact in order to develop interpretations of equivocal situations which in turn lead to a plan of action.

Sensemaking and resiliency models are the most commonly applied theories in health care from this emergent perspective. Sensemaking is the process that recognizes the emergent, experiential production of knowledge

– meanings "materialize" and are "talked into existence" (Weick, Sutcliffe, & Obstfeld, 2005, p. 409). If meanings materialize as they are talked into existence, it is impossible to predict all the variations in context, experience, and positionality that influence the actions individuals take.

Sensemaking of this kind is less about certainty than it is about resiliency, and what makes this kind of knowledge resilient is its basis in a rich network of relationships. Resiliency, as Blatt and colleagues (2006) describe, is not counter to medical reliability. Rather, it has a different focus than predictive models. Resiliency focuses on how to best recognize and recover from an error and to learn about the vulnerabilities of the system, rather than trying to identify and seek to eliminate the single root cause of the mistake (Vincent, 2003; Wears, 2003). The resiliency approach accepts the inevitability of human errors in the inability to control for idiosyncrasy, unanticipated events, and unexpected outcomes of planned activities (Blatt et al., 2006; Schulman, 2004). Rather than rely on formalized knowledge, the resiliency approach relies heavily on emergent, experiential knowledge, including intuition and tacit understandings, in the hope that the participants can recognize problems as they occur, then improvise and contain them before they escalate into catastrophic outcomes (Schulman, 2004). O'Hair, Kelley, and Williams write about the importance of community-level resiliency and crisis communication in Chapter 13.

Since different individuals have different experiential knowledge and interpret events in different ways, it is important to provide ways to promote communication technologies that allow for collective interaction, thought, and interpretation. We have seen examples of this through the use of a "white board" or a common, visual account of patients and their key symptoms, that on the surface may seem instrumental in transferring information, but in practice offers a common gathering place for physicians and nurses to collect and exchange ideas about patients. There is a movement in the medical literature to call for more synchronous rounds where physicians, and often nurses, are called together to discuss and transfer patient care. In another work, we recommended that medical staff implement a "deliberative pause" that stops the action to allow a (re)interpretation and reflection of events (Murphy et al., 2008).

This perspective maintains that "communication, rather than merely a neutral conduit for transmitting independently existing information, is the primary social process through which our meaningful common world is constructed" (Craig, 2007, p. 127; Eisenberg, 2008). This perspective on knowledge takes into consideration questions of identity, social relationships, context, and the determination of a plausible story. Less emphasized, however, is the political dimension of this story-making process. As Blatt and colleagues (2006) show, resiliency models assume that individuals must not only recognize errors as they happen, but must speak up as well. Their study revealed that often individuals remained silent either because they were not knowledgeable or because they were knowledgeable but did not feel they had voice in the organization. After all, the person with the most persuasive story may not be the most "knowledgeable." Therefore, we next turn our attention to the relationship between power and knowledge as it has been applied in health care research.

Knowledge as Political

The third framework draws on theories of power to show how health care knowledge is *political*, the result of a confluence of interests and variability in power relations (Table 15.1). It reveals how what counts as "fact" is shaped by professional status and accepted hierarchies within health care bureaucracies. Organizational knowledge is always politically driven (Deetz, 1998; Mumby, 1988, 1993; Murphy, 1998, 2003).

A large body of work in health care settings makes the link between knowledge and power in social life by drawing upon the work of Michel Foucault (1980). Foucault's model has been applied in a variety of ways, including a focus on the power of the "gaze" and the objectification and normalization of the patient as body (Henderson, 1994; Sullivan, 1986), the behavior of medical professionals (Allen, 1999; Lynch, 2004), and the expression and suppression of voice in nursing (Huntington & Gilmour, 2001; Heartfield, 1996; Ceci, 2004).

According to Foucault, when someone makes an assertion it becomes an instance of "power" when someone else (the other) takes the statement as "true." There is no de-contextualized, transcendent truth, and to "know" means to be able to give reasons for one's beliefs that are accepted by practical communities as valid (Ceci, 2004, p. 1881; May 1993). If you start with this perspective, it becomes critically important to attend to the social context within which medical decisions are made – to understand how knowledge is determined, by whom, and in what situations. In short, medical communication practices should be recognized as political and studied as such. It is these political relationships that determine who speaks, who listens, who defers, and who is deferred to.

The expression and suppression of knowledge and voice is another common topic in nursing literature. Nurses are "disciplined" to behave in a way and to produce particular professional and gendered activities that limit their participation and reinforce how the role of nursing is perceived by others and by the nurses themselves (Heartfield, 1996; Riley & Manias, 2002). Deetz (1991) found that the most common form of discursive closure – the privileging of certain discourses and the marginalization of others – is the "denial of the right of expression, denying access to speaking forums, the assertion of the need for certain expertise in order to speak, or through rendering the other unable to speak adequately" (p. 187).

We studied the political cues for coordination such as hierarchy, stereotypes, and occupational roles to reveal how socially based power relations

Table 15.1 Three frames of knowledge and communication in health care

View of knowledge	View of communication	Key theoretical approaches	Key practical applications
Knowledge as Routinized	Communication as transmission of information	Knowledge management	E-health knowledge
Knowledge as Emergent	Communication as socially constructed	Sensemaking and Resiliency	White board, Take-5 breaks
Knowledge as Political	Communication as negotiated and rhetorical	Discursive Closure, Dialogue, Voice	Unmoderated listservs, deliberative pauses

permeate the content of knowledge (Murphy et al., 2008). We also identified the different types of authority that nurses, ED physicians, and specialty physicians (or consultants) can claim over the interpretation of patient narratives. Since these health care professionals rarely visit and "hear" the patient story at the same time, they are all getting slightly different versions and frameworks for the narrative, and can draw (sometimes significantly) different interpretations and recommendations for action.

The political perspective is the most ignored in the establishment of communication technologies. It is critical, however, that patterns of interaction include possibilities for dialogue and voice. Some medical staff have found outlets for their voice and a "safe" space to exchange ideas and concerns through unmoderated listservs that provide occupational spaces for dialogue. Another step would be to institute these kinds of patterns within the hospital setting. Also, during the deliberative pauses mentioned to improve resiliency and sensemaking in the social construction of knowledge, it is important to make sure that all parties are represented. Too often, nurses, physicians, and other medical staff remain isolated in occupational exchanges. Purposely mixing these groups can help increase the likelihood of dialogue and voice over time.

Next, we move to an application of the three frames of knowledge in a specific health communication event – physician transitions of care in hospital emergency departments.

Method

This project draws from a unique data set and methodology. We participated in a large, multi-year, multi-site project exploring patient safety and transitions in patient care. Our methodology included extensive participant-observation, interviews, and, most important for this work, data reflection meetings. The focus of this analysis will be on one of these data reflection meetings. We gathered for a two-day, 18-hour retreat with all representative physicians from the participating hospitals to go through the typed and distributed field observation notes and to reflect on what it all meant. The data retreat turned into a collective sensemaking experience as the group discussed examples from the observation notes as well as their own experiences to understand how physicians communicate knowledge about patients during transitions. The entire meeting was tape-recorded and transcribed.

Physician Transitions: Applying the Three Frameworks of Knowledge

Physician transitions are a communication event that can serve as an object of analysis, as noted in the model presented by Glaser (1978) and modified by McPhee (2008). Physician transitions are often described as a risk factor for ongoing patient care (Joint Commission, 2006). Generally speaking, physicians transition patients through some version of physician rounds. These rounds serve multiple purposes, and are rich sites to explore the three frameworks of knowledge in the communication patterns of physicians. First, they are an instrumental, formalized exchange of information about a patient from the outgoing physician to the incoming physician. Also, in many teaching hospitals, rounds are a routinized opportunity for residents to learn from attending physicians and senior residents. They learn clinical, emergent knowledge (gain experience diagnosing patients, clarifying diagnoses, etc.); and, they learn professional and political expectations about how to communicate knowledge – as Myers describes in Chapter 16, they work through an assimilation process as they learn how to "talk and act like a doctor."

After close examination of the transcripts of the data reflection retreat, we found that any one framework ignores or distorts critically important aspects of organizational knowledge and communication. This relates well with Canary's claims in Chapter 14 that participants in policy-related systems draw on multiple types of knowledge to shape the policy construction process. In our work, we identified three clear communication dimensions that emerged along a continuum with two of the three frameworks in a primary dialectical tension and the third frame operating as a condition as defined by Glaser and modified by McPhee (2008). To help picture this, we have diagramed the three frames as points on a knowledge triangle (Figure 15.1). Each side of the triangle corresponds with a communication dimension as revealed by the physician reflections.

The right side of the triangle refers to the "instrumental" dimension of communication when knowledge during physician transitions can be both routine (objective and rote) and emergent (based on judgment and interpretation). The political framework still factors as a condition of the instrumental dimension in that power is bracketed to be neutral or equal.

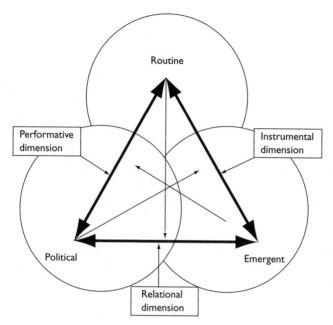

Figure 15.1 The knowledge triangle.

The bottom side of the triangle addresses the "relational" dimension of communication when knowledge is both emergent (socially constructed) and political (based on influence and credibility). In this case, the routine structure and expectations of the rounds function as a condition of the relational dimension. Finally, the left side of the triangle considers the "performative" quality of communication when knowledge is both political (influenced by hierarchy) and routine (ritualized performances). Here, the emergent condition of physician identity plays a part in the performative dimension.

Instrumental Communication Dimension

The instrumental dimension of the knowledge triangle reflects the functional responsibility of physician transitions as a means of transferring knowledge, and focuses both the routine and emergent frames of knowledge. A condition of the instrumental dimension is an assumed neutrality in power that is complicated in the sections that follow. From the physician transcripts, it is clear that transitions have a routine quality. To effectively transfer knowledge about a patient from one physician to another, a baseline set of information must be passed on. There is an expected (and often rote) sequence of information and sound bites provided about each patient: "Patient in Bed two is a 52-year-old, was presented after 8 hours of shortness of breath; patient in bed five is a 49-year-old African American female, hypertensive diabetic." This sequence is so scripted that there is often a side-step and a "let's really talk" that moves the physicians out of the formalized routine of the rounds. While this interruption is often so expected that it is also routine, it does allow a space for the communication of emergent knowledge – or the interpretive data drawn from the physician's experience.

The physicians spoke directly about how what a physician "presents" to another physician during a patient transfer is always influenced by what is happening around them and what they choose to pay attention to (Weick, 1995). In other words, the baseline information is still enacted as individual physicians select and pay attention to certain physical and/or psychological cues among a variety of possible distractions. For example, Sunday evening is notoriously busy because people tend to wait through the weekend to seek care; Friday and Saturday evenings provide more intoxication-related cases. Furthermore, there is considerable folklore surrounding the prevalence of "strange" or unique cases on the night of a full moon. Each of these cues has a way of informing how a physician interprets a patient's conditions and, subsequently, what he or she shares with others.

One physician in the meeting described a particularly difficult situation when four critical patients arrived in the ED at the same time. He explained,

> This girl that I had died two days after childbirth. A perfectly healthy young woman came in the same time with three other critical patients and I am thinking to myself, "here I have four patients and all of them look like they are going to die, but luckily this one is 20 years old and is hemorrhaging, so she'll live." But, she died, and the other two, the one we were putting the pacemaker in and the one who went into septic shock, all lived.

In this case, the physician describes the way he enacted an emergent situation. He first scanned his field, looked for situational cues, and then took action. Since the action taken led to the unanticipated death of the young girl, one read of the situation would be that the physician misinterpreted the cues and passed on erroneous information. However, the physicians in the meeting struggled with what this all meant in the desire for, but the unlikelihood that there could be, predictable outcomes based on routine scenarios in health care. Another physician in the meeting explained,

> Overload is constant and an outcome that is undesirable, which is death of a human being, is always possible whether we know the cause or not. That's different than most of the other [professions] we are trying to draw in here.

The physician was referring to the often used comparison of health care to other high reliability organizations such as air traffic control, airlines, nuclear reactors, or aircraft carriers. In these latter cases, when a death occurs, it is because there was a problem with the system. A scenario could be created where a different choice was made, the right information was acted upon, and a different outcome could be predicted. With health care, however, a death is always a possible outcome even if no mistake was made.

The physicians in the meeting agreed that there is often a contradiction in the desire for routine, predictable outcomes in an environment that calls for emergent, interpretive information. They did not agree, however, on what to do about this situation. They grappled with whether or not it is possible, or even desirable, to strip away subjective qualifiers and interpretations about patients when communicating with one another.

One of the physicians described a situation where a 16-year-old youth came "barreling into the ED and was swearing and cursing at the nurses." He was described as a troubled, modern teenager, that should be "grounded for a week." The youth died in the CT scan about a half-hour later from a head injury. It turned out that he was an honor student and his parents said that he was the best-behaved kid, but the head injury made him act erratically. The physician said, "This judgmental thing went on and [we] completely missed it."

Another physician in the meeting disagreed: "Sometimes the interpreted element helps." If a wife explains that her husband woke up in the middle of the night "pale and sweaty and he looked as if he was going to pass out," a physician must interpret whether or not this sounds like a heart attack. However, the physician continued, "sometimes interpretations are advanced as factual. They are not identified as interpretations. That's where the problem is." A third physician said, "I think interpretations are okay, judgmental behavior is the thing. We know how that works; you say to someone that 'this guy is being a real jerk...'"

Physicians often say things like "bed four is a lovely woman" or "the nice gentleman in bed six" as a way of labeling patients for the incoming physicians as a form of code for their behavior, and to influence how they are treated, or even the order in which they are treated, when the ED is very busy (Eisenberg et al., 2005). One physician in the meeting said, "Let's face it, one of the components is that you are going to direct more of your attention towards someone that you feel positively towards." As another physician said,

It is a dangerous situation when people start putting their spin on things, soon as somebody starts referring to a patient in the vernacular, I think it should be a decoy, saying derogatory things about them, especially psychiatric patients, actually joking about psychiatric patient symptoms is absolutely unprofessional, but happens relatively frequently.

According to the physicians, there is no question that transitions are instrumental in communicating knowledge. They must provide an incoming physician with baseline information about a patient that will be in his or her care. At the same time, they recognize the interpretive process that physicians undertake when constructing emergent knowledge based on their own experiences. At some hospitals, responses to these concerns have focused primarily on clarifying and even sanitizing the routine. These include instituting call-back systems (where the incoming physician repeats back key phrases to demonstrate knowledge), electronic patient tracking and charting, and asynchronous transitioning (with physicians leaving voice recordings with the patient information for the next physician).

Many hospitals have transitioned to computerized charting (Electronic Medical Records or EMRs). This eliminates the need for the physical patient chart that can often get lost or be kept by one person. The computerized chart allows any medical staff to access a patient chart at any time and at the same time. Many times, it includes a patient history of any illnesses or hospital visits during the period of time tracked to help reduce the problem of relying on patients to remember their own medical histories or prescriptions. A computerized chart also reduces the degree of judgmental framing, as physicians are not as likely to reference whether someone is "nice" or not in a written form.

While there are clear benefits to these technologies for communicating routine, factual knowledge, there is a cost to the quality of emergent, socially constructed knowledge. In the hospitals using computerized charting, there is a significant decrease in the amount of informal communication and synchronous conversations. When a chart is lost, medical staff call out, "who has number 13?" When the person with that chart responds, it can start a spontaneous conversation about that patient. Also, an overreliance on the computerized record does not allow as much correction on the part of the patient. Patients often overhear a discussion about their own care and correct facts: "I'm not diabetic" or "I am 35 not 55." Finally, sometimes it is important to know the subjective interpretations of a patient's behavior. As one physician in the meeting explained, "judging is often inappropriate. But, sometimes, it is true [a patient] is acting like an asshole and they are difficult to work with and sometimes it makes a hard case because of that."

Through the instrumental dimension, we can see that while transitions are predictable routine passages of demographic information, there is a clear emergent quality to the information that physicians select and notice about a patient to pass along, especially in unpredictable work environments. Again, an assumption in the instrumental dimension is that power is a condition that is consistent across these episodes and interactions. The next section more directly addresses the emergent and political implications in the physician relationships as they frame and/or accept the framing of another physician during a transition.

Relational Communication Dimension

The relational dimension of physician transitions connects the emergent and the political levels of knowledge. As we saw above, physicians pass along more than objective content about a patient during a transition. They also pass along their interpretive frameworks. During a transition, there is an opportunity for physicians to collaboratively co-construct knowledge as they work together to plan patient care. At the same time, whether or not physicians will accept that subjective framing or work collaboratively with one another will depend on who is speaking – the reputation, perceived experience, and credibility of the physicians participating. In this way, the routine set of norms regarding objectivity, trust, and credibility function as a condition of the relational dimension.

The physicians at the meeting spoke of the following situation at length. It involved a 20-year-old patient who arrived in the ED with a heart rate in the 130s/140s. The resident physician suspected an overdose of the painkiller neurontin. Believing he knew the cause of her condition, he decided not to order any toxicology tests and was just watching her. Her heart rate stayed in the 130s/140s for several hours. Other residents brought it up with him, asking; "Don't you think this could be an overdose?" By the time he ordered the tests, her condition had worsened. It turned out she had also ingested crack cocaine several hours after taking the neurontin.

In this example, the resident physician enacted a diagnosis of an overdose, but in doing so he limited his ability to consider what kind of overdose had occurred. He presented himself as professionally certain. His credibility, however, was damaged as a result of this situation. One of the physicians relating the example said, "As I watched the body language of his fellow residents telling me this story – it was disgust." They continually said things like, "He should have known. He's graduated. HE SHOULD HAVE KNOWN!." He continued to explain that the other residents were very disparaging of the resident physician because of this incident, and expressed angst and anxiety about working with him in the future and what their work-around plans were for dealing with him.

So, there are long-term implications for this mistake. Not only did the patient suffer more severe consequences of her overdose, but also other physicians will no longer trust the credibility of this resident when they are accepting patients he has evaluated. The physician continued,

> And this story will spread through residency of course. Because by the time it gets to us, it's spread through them. They don't come tell us first, they tell each other first. So there are significant *peer issues in this credibility I think weigh more heavily than even we want to accept.*

During the data retreat, this example built on several other examples in the transition transcripts and observation notes. One physician said, "So, we are saying there is situational credibility, professional credibility by the level of experience you have had, then the visual would be another situational factor?" Another responded, "Yeah, I think there are a lot of contextual characteristics that impact the nature of the conversation. From a credibility standpoint ... that's what we have been focusing on." They went on to identify and discuss the difference between relational and situational credibility. One said,

> There is relational credibility, do you have a relationship with this person that has caused you to trust them, have you worked with them at another hospital, you've known them for years or their family, you went to school with them whatever. Right?

One of the physicians continued:

> The credibility probably hinges a lot more on the relationship than on the content of what's being said. Simply because people don't say things like, "this guy just arrived from Mars and is having trouble with the oxygen atmosphere." People say things that normally make sense in context but every now and then you get a story that does not make sense ... and that way it can impact your credibility ... that somebody should have been able to make sense out of, you didn't make sense out of.

At the same time, the physicians were not unified in their views. One held on to the perspective that the "transmission of objective information which makes that picture effectual is the goal rather than if you really want to inherit anybody's impressions or..." Another interrupted, "Well, I think sometimes you do, cause I think some of these things just can't be objectified." A third jumped in,

> But [the first physician] raises a great point too that what we are predicting here is the degree to which the incoming person will believe the frame which is being presented to them, that doesn't mean that that's the best outcome. You can have high credibility, high clarity, whatever, the person accepts it, and really what they should be doing is questioning it, for whatever reason. So, in other words, understanding isn't necessarily the goal here. Then what is it?

Not only can damaged peer credibility and relationships influence the acceptance of an outgoing physician's patient framing, but strong peer relationships can as well. As noted above, when physicians have worked with each other for a long time and have a series of positive interactions, it can create a context for automatic acceptance without a critical evaluative eye in the transition process. For example, the physicians discussed a very well-respected and experienced clinician transferring a patient as "all done" to an incoming physician and simply waiting for transfer to the ICU. As it turned out, the patient was septic [a life-threatening inflammatory infection]. The anesthetist came down as part of a standard evaluation, and detected the sepsis. The physician giving the example explained,

> So, he is signing it over and the anesthetist caught it ... The anesthetist picked it up within five minutes because he didn't have the same relationship with the emergency physician as the guy who accepted the transfer.

The example also demonstrates a professional expectation and a bias toward having "closed up" patients, "wrapped up with a bow." These are considered the "gifts" you give the incoming physicians. They can, however, lead to premature closure of patient care. We will discuss this more in the next section.

Performative Communication Dimension

The performative dimension of the knowledge triangle features the political and routine levels of knowledge. These two levels may seem the most distant, in that one is about objectifying knowledge routines while the other is about how knowledge is subjectively interconnected with power. However, the two come together when considering how resident physicians (low in hierarchy) are socialized to speak and act "like a doctor" in ritualized, cultural performances. A condition, therefore, of the performative dimension is the emergence of physician and, even more specifically, resident identity.

The physicians at the meeting discussed the performative dimension of physician transitions at length. Physicians learn to routinely perform an expected level of "certainty" as they "present" their patient diagnoses. Even the language used to describe this process (i.e., "presenting a patient") indicates the finality expected in the physician knowledge of that patient. Physicians are trained to select cues from a patient's clinical examination to create a plausible "good story" or a diagnosis that is then translated into an easily digestible list of technical facts about that patient. When a patient's case is complicated, or does not provide a "good story," it is presented as a "work in progress."

The physicians at the meeting reflected on a story of a second-year resident who was being asked his diagnosis for one of his patients. He said that he wanted to consult colleagues in the hospital "who deal with this situation more." The attending didn't accept his tentativeness, and said, "Take a deep breath – you can do it." The resident said, "I know I can do it but..." The attending interrupted and reminded him, "You have a license like everyone else."

We give this example in another work that demonstrates how resident physicians are disciplined to respond appropriately during patient rounds and transitions (Eisenberg et al., 2005). Physicians are trained not only in clinical skills, but also in rhetorical ones – they are expected to "talk like a doctor." Talking like a doctor means expressing oneself with certainty and confidence (Eisenberg et al., 2005; Murphy et al., 2008). Medical students learn that "the clinician experiences uncertainty but must project certainty, the certainty craved by not only students, but also patients, and more generally, Western culture's sense of scientific rationality and its tenets of transparency and control" (Lingard, Garwood, Schryer, & Spafford, 2003, p. 611). We call this the "cultural performance of knowledge" (Eisenberg et al., 2005; Murphy et al., 2008). By cultural performance, we refer to the rites and rituals actively displayed by participants for an audience. In this case the audience is the other physicians, and physicians participate in a rite of passage as they transition from resident to physician (Turner, 1988).

The example of the "uncertain" resident was marked as compelling by the physicians at the meeting because he was discussing a case that was not considered complicated by his attending physician. One of the physicians said, "The attending was letting him know that he should know how to proceed." This is not always the case. Physicians must always be certain, but they may not always have the answer. "SSW" is a common acronym in medical schools – swift, sure, and wrong. This is to teach the lesson about how confident, disastrous decisions can be made. The more experienced physicians know when a case is actually complicated enough to warrant them saying with certainty, "this is a work in progress."

During patient transitions, the outgoing physician will also try to manage or frame the situations for the incoming physician based on critical care needs. As noted in the instrumental dimension, physicians will often "mark" patients with common phrases and categories. For example, if a physician describes a patient as a "good story," then there is a clear connection between the patient narrative and the clinical examination, so the incoming physician does not have to be concerned with re-evaluation. A "complicated story" or a "work in progress," on the other hand, indicates a degree of ambiguity in the case. This term is often served as a short-cut for the residents' report and reduces the pressure to offer overly speculative information that might turn out to be misleading or dangerous (Eisenberg et al., 2005). Less experienced residents, however, can confuse the need for certainty with the need to appear to know all things, leading them to "present" a patient case with more finality than it may warrant.

The example of the tentative resident who was reprimanded for not speaking with enough certainty sparked a conversation by the physicians about the issues in politics and professional socialization. Given the work-load in an average ED, there is a political expectation that outgoing physicians will handoff as few "work in progresses" as possible. The ideal, according to one physician, "is that you will hand over all your patients nicely tied up in a box with a bow on top."

Whether or not the incoming physician will or should accept the coding cues from the outgoing physician will have much to do with the relationship and/or reputation of that person, as well as the certainty expressed in the physician cultural performance. One physician at the meeting explained:

> The first year when there is a bunch of people and one of the new people will hear an old transition between two familiar people and then their turn will come and they'll come up with something like "55-year-old man with community acquired pneumonia admitted to medicine." Everyone will say "stop, hold on..." and make them go through the litany of chief complaints, the history, the physical and so forth.

Asking for a more extensive transition reinforces the clinical expertise of the residents by requiring them to demonstrate their diagnostic process. It is also a way of beginning a "credibility assessment" of a new physician. One physician explained,

> So after you work with these people a couple of times then you'll hear kind of the reverse thing, particularly like "okay, we're busy, let's just hit the high spots, anything I need to know if this one goes down? Is there something I need to know?" particularly if the patients are kind of wrapped up ... right up to the point of who is "really sick."

Once professional credibility has been established, doctors will come on shift and say, "Well, who is really sick?" and have the outgoing attending replying, "well, nobody" or just saying "watch nine." Interestingly, this does not mean that shorter transitions are always a sign of trust. If an incoming physician doesn't trust the judgment of the outgoing physician, the incoming physician will simply ask for the basic information required for the transition because he or she knows they are going to re-evaluate all the patients anyway.

Managing Knowledge as Collective Mindfulness

All three frameworks of knowledge – routine, emergent, and political – have implications and applicability for particular situations in health care, and the above examples show that the frameworks of knowledge do not necessarily work independently of each other. As we reflect on the physicians' reflections on transitions, we see three different communication dimensions expressed on each side of the knowledge triangle. At times communication is instrumental, as physicians work through a tension between objective and predictable knowledge routines and subjective, emergent knowledge based on experience. At other times communication is relational, as knowledge emerges through an interpretive, socially constructed and political process. Finally, communication is performative, making knowledge both emergent and routine.

The question remains: What can an organization learn as a result of these events? The key lessons drawn from any of the above examples do not often make their way into the institutional fabric of the hospital or emergency room culture. They tend to stay at the level of the individual or direct participants in the situation, who may or may not be reflective on what they can learn from the event. In this sense, this research allowed us to participate in a rare event where multiple physicians came together to collectively make sense of knowledge and patient transitions. We drew on their conversations for the examples given above. Another important conversation thread takes us through a discussion about how, if at all, any of these issues can be resolved.

One physician described his interaction with trainers of crew resource management (CRM) – a type of systemized training pioneered in air travel. The group came into the ED and said,

> Tell us what your process is and what your system is like. And they couldn't get a coherent answer in their terms because to the people in that world, it is mysterious and undefined and its boundaries are very vague.

Another physician added,

> Well, yeah, it is taught in practice, still as a craft. You apprentice yourself with someone else and you gradually absorb the craft through osmosis. The masters usually do not have much ability to articulate what it is that makes them a master as opposed to not. You can tell the difference. But it's not articulated. But one of the functional goals is to provide feedback to people who are trying to learn the craft. Cause we saw that certainly again, again, and again when someone says you can't say that, don't say that, tell me more. I mean, different ways of coaching residents and students.

The dilemma of the CRM group working with the ED teams as discussed by these physicians gets to the heart of the desire to standardize the transfer of objective information and knowledge, and the acknowledgment of interpretation and need for resiliency in situations. One physician captured the heart of this dilemma:

> What that says though, is it's kind of spooky, because we're saying there is no kind of boundaries as to what it should be but, we need to

coach these people to do this thing. There is no consistent way to deliver the information. But, yet, we are coaching these kids this craft.

Another physician continued:

> Which gets us back to when [another physician] was bringing up that there are these particular objective things like how to get information transferred that needs to be transferred, coded within that are still these relational cues, that lead you to then make sense in different ways, depending on how you're reading that person, so that there is still something happening there that relationally gives you some other information other than chest pain with...

Another physician interrupted,

> So where it becomes a risk in that sense is in what point in a career or in what point in terms of individual do you know its okay to say, "I don't need to stop it. I don't need to pause." Is that something that happens automatically, or is that something that sort of grows in the position? Do some people never get it? Or do all people always get it?

The conversation continued with one physician claiming it comes with "experience, clinical acumen," and another saying it also comes with "the number of near misses" you have. If you trust someone's framing and then it turns out to be wrong, you are not likely to automatically trust again. They talk about how and why the physicians round in the way they do, how and why a physician may believe or not believe what another one says to be a medical fact.

Weick and Sutcliffe (2001) note, "An informed culture learns by means of ongoing debates about constantly shifting discrepancies. The debates promote learning because they identify new sources of hazard and danger and new ways to cope." In this case, the participants debated the dilemma about what constitutes the frameworks of knowledge and what to do with this knowledge institutionally. This is a collective "deliberative pause" that allows learning to take place (Murphy et al., 2008). These collective pauses do not often happen (if at all) in most health care organizations. Rounding could be considered a transitionary pause, but, as noted above, much of these behaviors are more rote than dialogic, more performative than reflective. Hospitals also have M&M (mortality and morbidity) conferences when a problem has occurred, but this is more disciplinary and punitive than learning-based. Weick and Sutcliffe (2001) continue, "If timely, candid information generated by knowledgeable people is available and disseminated, an informed culture becomes a *learning culture*" (p. 136, their emphasis).

After participating with these physicians in a deliberative process, we believe that these reflection skills should be institutionalized in medical settings. Routine and scheduled sensemaking conversations such as the data retreat could be set to allow debriefing and collective learning to take place in an ongoing manner, rather than relying on the random events that may or may not increase physician certainty and credibility. To make this possible, resident physicians should be trained not only in clinical acumen, but also in dialogue and reflection, and a recognition of the relational and political implications of knowledge and communication.

Conclusion

Communication is critical to understanding how knowledge is constituted, framed, and interpreted – not just how information is transferred. How issues are framed and interpreted can have life and death consequences in a health care context. While there is a rich application of knowledge and power in medical settings (and particularly in nursing), when the context is shifted to an organizational focus for recommendations and practice the routine, transmissional level of knowledge is typically the only level of knowledge addressed. We do not believe the routine level should be ignored, or that it is not important. This work simply calls for a shift in health care to also pay attention to the emergent and political construction and negotiation of medical knowledge. The three levels of analysis should be considered collectively, and are not mutually exclusive. There is a need to move beyond the professional emphasis on building better systems for knowledge delivery to consider the relational and political implications of knowledge construction and to institutionalize deliberative pauses for collective mindfulness and long-term organizational learning.

References

Allen, B. (1999). Power/knowledge. In N. K. Racevskis (Ed.), *Critical Essays on Michel Foucault* (pp. 69–82). New York, NY: G. K. Hall & Co.

Anderson, J., & Aydin, C. (1997). Evaluating the impact of health care information systems. *International Journal of Technology Assessment in Health Care, 13(2)*, 380–393.

Blatt, R., Christianson, M. K., Sutcliffe, K. M., & Rosenthal, M. M. (2006). A sensemaking lens on reliability. *Journal of Organizational Behavior, 27*, 897–917.

Bose, R. (2003). Knowledge management-enabled health care management systems: capabilities, infrastructure, and decision-support. *Expert Systems with Applications, 24*, 59–71.

Ceci, C. (2004). Nursing, knowledge, and power: A case analysis. *Social Science and Medicine, 59*, 1879–1889.

Craig, R. (2007). Pragmatism in the field of communication theory. *Communication Theory, 17*, 125–145.

Deetz, S. (1991). *Democracy in an age of corporate colonization*. Albany, NY: SUNY Press.

Deetz, S. (1998). Discursive formations, strategized subordination and self-surveillance. In A. McKinlay & K. Starkey (Eds.), *Foucault, management, and organizational theory* (pp. 151–172). London, UK: Sage.

Eisenberg, E. M. (2008). The social construction of health care teams. In C. Nemeth (Ed.), *Improving healthcare team communication: Building on lessons from aviation and aerospace* (pp. 9–20). Aldershot, UK: Ashgate Publishing.

Eisenberg, E. M., Murphy, A. G., Sutcliffe, K. M., Wears, R., Schenkel, S., Perry, S., & Vanderhoef, M. (2005). Communication in emergency medicine: Implications for patient safety. *Communication Monographs, 72(4),* 390–413.

Ellingson, L. (2008). Changing realities and entrenched norms in dialysis: A case study of power, knowledge, and communication in health-care delivery. In H. M. Zoller & M. J. Dutta (Eds.), *Emerging perspectives in health communication: Meaning culture, and power* (pp. 293–310). New York, NY: Routledge.

Forgionne G. A., Gangopadhyay, J. A., Klein, R., & Eckhardt, R. (1999). A decision technology system for health care electronic commerce. *Topics in Health Information Management, 20(1),* 31–41.

Foucault, M. (1980). *Power/knowledge: Selected interviews and other writings, 1972, 1977* (L. M. C. Gordon, J. Mepham, & K. Soper, Trans.). New York, NY: Pantheon Books.

Glaser, B. (1978). *Theoretical sensitivity.* Mill Valley, CA: Sociology Press.

Heartfield, M. (1996). Nursing documentation and nursing practice: The contribution of Foucault. *Journal of Advanced Nursing, 24,* 98–103.

Henderson, A. (1994). Power and knowledge in nursing practice: The contribution of Foucault. *Journal of Advanced Nursing, 20,* 935–939.

Huntington, A. D., & Gilmour, J. A. (2001). Re-thinking representations, re-writing nursing texts: Possibilities through feminist and Foucauldian thought. *Journal of Advanced Nursing, 35(6),* 902–908.

Joint Commission of Health Care Organizations (2006). National patient safety goals. Washington, DC: Joint Commission.

Kuhn, T., & Jackson, M. (2008). Accomplishing knowledge: A framework for investigating knowing in organizations. *Management Communication Quarterly, 21(4),* 454–485.

Kuipers, J. (1989). Medical discourse in anthropological context: View of language and power. *Medical Anthropology Quarterly, 3(2),* 99–123.

Lingard, L., Garwood, K., Schryer, C., & Spafford, M. (2003). A certain art of uncertainty: Case presentations and the development of professional identity. *Social Science and Medicine, 56,* 603–616.

Lynch, J. (2004). Comment section: Foucault on targets. *Journal of Health Organization & Management, 19(2/3),* 128–135.

Martin, J. (1992). *Cultures in organizations: Three perspectives.* New York, NY: Oxford University Press.

May, T. (1993). *Between genealogy and epistemology: Psychology, politics, and knowledge in the thought of Michel Foucault.* University Park, PA: Pennsylvania State University.

McPhee, R. D. (2008). *Revision of Glaser's 6C model.* Unpublished paper.

Mumby, D. (1988). *Communication and power in organizations. Discourse, ideology, and domination.* Norwood, NJ: Ablex.

Mumby, D. (1993). Critical organizational studies: The next 10 years. *Communication Monographs, 60,* 18–25.

Murphy, A. G. (1998). Hidden transcripts of flight attendant resistance. *Management Communication Quarterly, 11(4)*, 499–535.

Murphy, A. G. (2003). The dialectical gaze: Exploring the subject–object tension in the performances of women who strip. *Journal of Contemporary Ethnography, 32*, 305–335.

Murphy, A. G., Eisenberg, E. M., Wears, R., & Perry, S. J. (2008). Contested streams of action: Power and deference in emergency medicine. In H. M. Zoller & M. J. Dutta (Eds.), *Emerging perspectives in health communication: Meaning culture, and power* (pp. 275–290). New York, NY: Routledge.

Raghupathi, W., & Tan, J. (1999). Strategic uses of information technology in health care: a state-of-the-art survey. *Topics in Health Information Management, 20(1)*, 1–15

Riley, R., & Manias, E. (2002). Foucault could have been an operating nurse. *Journal of Advanced Nursing, 39(4)*, 316–324.

Schulman, P. R. (2004). General attributes of safe organizations. *Quality Safety Health Care, 13*, 39–44.

Steier, F., & Eisenberg, E. M. (1997). From records to relationships: Courting organizational dialogue at NASA. *Cybernetics and Human Knowing, 4*, 51–58.

Sullivan, M. (1986). In what sense is contemporary medicine dualistic? *Culture, Medicine, and Society, 10(4)*, 331–350.

Turner, V. (1988). *The anthropology of performance*. New York, NY: PAJ Publications.

Vincent, C. A. (2003). Understanding and responding to adverse events. *New England Journal of Medicine, 348*, 1051–1056.

Wears, R. L. (2003). A different approach to safety in emergency medicine. *Annals of Emergency Medicine, 42*, 334–336.

Weick, K. E. (1995). *Sensemaking in organizations*. Thousand Oaks, CA: Sage.

Weick, K. E., & Sutcliffe, K. M. (2001). *Managing the unexpected: Assuring high performance in an age of complexity*. San Francisco, CA: Jossey-Bass.

Weick, K. E., Sutcliffe, K. M., & Obstfeld, D. (2005). Organizing and the process of sensemaking. *Organization Science, 16(4)*, 409–421.

Chapter 16

Socializing Organizational Knowledge

Informal Socialization through Workgroup Interaction

Karen K. Myers

Organizational knowledge is context-specific information that enables members to interpret, make decisions, and act (Droege & Hoobler, 2003). In an information-based economy and society, organizational knowledge is a competitive resource essential for organizational success (Huang & Kuo, 2003; King & Zeithaml, 2003; Starbuck, 1992). Knowledge held by organizational members gives the organization capacity to differentiate itself from competitors and to quickly respond to changes in the environment (Erden, von Krogh, & Nonaka, 2008; Leonard-Barton, 1992).

Organizational knowledge is not easily created or distributed, in part, because it is reflected in individuals' perspectives as they acquire meanings through exposure to an organizational context (Nonaka & Takeuchi, 1995; Tagliaventi & Mattarelli, 2006) and develop an understanding of what life is like in connection with the organization. This aspect of organizational knowledge makes it nearly impossible to attain it entirely through secondary sources. In fact, one cannot adequately investigate organizational knowledge without an immersion in the environment, developing an understanding of its context, development, and use (Spender, 1996). Morrison's (2002, p. 1150) definition of organizational knowledge, "knowing about one's larger organizational context," is premised on this notion. This suggests that organizational knowledge includes information and knowledge possessed by an organization that some or all members share (Iverson & McPhee, 2008), and often is found in rules (March, Schulz, & Zhu, 2000), routines (Levitt & March, 1988), and standard operating procedures (Cyert & March, 1963). These properties have important implications for newcomer training and familiarization as new members are socialized.

Organizational socialization is the process by which newcomers are introduced to the task and social elements of an organization (Chao, O'Leary-Kelly, Wolf, Klein, & Gardner, 1994; Van Maanen & Schein, 1979). Organizations socialize members to the "way things are done around here," with the dual purpose of easing coordination of activities between new and existing workers, and shaping newcomers into loyal members (Scott & Myers, 2005; Van Mannen & Schein, 1979). Socialization involves instructing newcomers how to perform necessary job duties (Feldman, 1976), but becoming an organizational insider also involves acquiring organizational knowledge: becoming acquainted with others and learning about individuals associated with the work, the organization, and the local unit (Ashforth, Saks, & Lee, 1988; Gibson & Papa, 2000; Gundry & Rousseau, 1994; Klein, Bigley, & Roberts, 1995; Louis, 1980). A significant objective is to provide organizational knowledge that familiarizes recruits with the traditions of the organization, systems, policies, norms, standard operating procedures, and information such as how work *really gets done* in the social environment.

Socialization is intended to share both task and cultural knowledge with recruits, but when individuals attempt to share knowledge with newcomers, they transmit data with some measure of resonance based on shared understandings, and individuals process information in varying ways due to differences in experience (Boisot, 2001). Thus, acquiring functional organizational knowledge requires familiarity with the context – something newcomers lack. These competing elements make transmitting knowledge to new organizational members fraught with problems. (See Chapter 14 in this volume for other difficulties associated with knowledge distribution.) Until recruits develop minimal contextual understanding, they cannot effectively absorb and internalize much of the information that is shared during formal training, which, ironically, often occurs during the first few days of membership.

This chapter discusses issues related to organizational knowledge from an organizational socialization perspective, especially the types of knowledge that members must acquire to assimilate into roles, and the difficulties in distributing the knowledge through commonly used socialization strategies. Many organizations attempt to socialize newcomers through formal orientation classes. While formal socialization can successfully distribute some types of knowledge, I propose that the most effective means of distributing certain types of knowledge is informal socialization provided in workgroups. Group coordination and interaction gives newcomers an informed perspective, and exposure to experienced members whose behaviors can be observed and mimicked. This may be particularly important in highly interdependent workgroups. Previous research has examined how organizational knowledge is distributed (Choo, 1998; Nonaka & Takeuchi, 1995), but research has not related these findings to the socialization of newcomers.

I begin with a general description of the nature of knowledge relative to organizational socialization, and follow with challenges newcomers face in acquiring organizational knowledge. Next, I discuss the limitations associated with formal socialization for transmitting organizational knowledge when newcomers have little knowledge of the new environment. Informal socialization in the form of workgroup interaction is then offered as the most effective means of sharing crucial contextual and occupational "know-how." In the second section of the chapter, I recount research demonstrating the effectiveness of group socialization for transmitting organizational knowledge. The contexts of those studies are high reliability organizations, specifically municipal fire departments, with firefighting crews the focus. In the last section, I offer implications and questions for future research.

The Nature of Knowledge

Knowledge has explicit and tacit properties depending on its level of abstraction and level of codification. *Explicit* knowledge can be communicated and codified into training manuals, rules, and procedures, thus making it easy to share in training and easy for new members to internalize (Stenmark, 2000/2001). Instructions for filing a report or steps to assemble a machine are examples of knowledge that can be shared explicitly. *Tacit* knowledge, on the other hand, "cannot be easily articulated and thus only exists in people's hands and minds, and manifests itself through their actions" (Stenmark, 2000/2001, p. 10). Tacit knowledge can entail understandings so complex that they are difficult if not impossible to fully describe, such as *how* to sense danger, or *how* to develop trust with co-workers. It also can be embodied knowledge, involving mental and physical properties, such as the coordination required in dance or connecting a hose to a fire hydrant.

Although explicit and tacit knowledge often are dichotomized, the two types of knowledge may be conjoined because many tasks utilize both (Tsoukas, 1996). For example, in learning how to operate a forklift, a new forklift operator might read manuals which offer explicit descriptions of the steps involved in picking up, moving, and repositioning pallets, but only after practicing these techniques does the operator develop a more innate understanding of how to efficiently do the job. Some essential elements of operating the machine may have been learned by reading a set of instructions, but there is much more to know than can be described in a manual. Tacit knowledge acquired through experience helps the operator to improve and develop his or her skill (Gioia, 1986). For many organizational tasks, competency requires both.

Tacit knowledge is important in activities that require physical skill, but it plays a significant role in cognitive skills as well. Tacit knowledge acquired over years of experience enables individuals to make better decisions (Brockmann & Anthony, 2002). This may be due to more experienced members' ability to see similarities in situations and events. Using experience as a guide, individuals are able to make predictions based on similarities they already have encountered. They also are able to make better judgments about what could and might happen due to their developed cognitive schemas suggesting relevant patterns (Ericsson, 1996). This type of knowledge cannot be transferred to newcomers upon their arrival, but is developed incrementally and over time.

Time can also transform knowledge. Knowledge acquisition occurs in two stages that can at times overlap (Anderson, 1976, 1987; Singley & Anderson, 1989): (1) the declarative stage, in which knowledge is general, conscious understanding, and skills can be described explicitly, followed by (2) the procedural stage, during which knowledge becomes deeper and embedded, and is associated with actions and skills related to context (Singley & Anderson, 1989). Although organizational training can be declarative, organizational knowledge is largely procedural, consisting of skills and routines that are organizationally specific (King & Zeithaml, 2003; Nelson & Winter, 1982). For example, new sales representatives can learn about the firm's product line and clients' past purchases, but they cannot as easily be trained on how to deal with new customers' personalities or keying into their particular buying behaviors that influence their willingness to purchase products. In other words, they cannot become competent in sales representative performance without experience.

Baumard (1999) argues that procedural (or tacit) knowledge is learned through observation and practice, and, as a result, becomes highly personalized. Through this lens, members perceive *what ought to be*. Davenport and Prusak (1998, p. 5) report that knowledge is "a fluid mix of framed experience, values, contextual information and expert insight." Although individuals can achieve some competence at certain tasks with relatively little time investment, true expertise, argue Simon and Chase (1973), takes years to develop because it is based on being able to ascertain predictable outcomes. Expertise comes when individuals have made mental models, which involves creating and recreating analogies in their minds (Johnson-Laird, 1983; Miller, Herbig, & Petrovic, 2009). Mere competence may be enough for many organizational tasks, but time and experience are necessary for true expertise.

Learning Challenges for Newcomers

Organizational newcomers are faced with a variety of learning opportunities and challenges. They must learn how to perform their tasks, how to assume their organizational roles, and about "the essence of the firm" (Tsoukas & Vladimirou, 2001, p. 975). Although any two organizations might seem similar to outsiders, newcomers, once inside, are introduced to a multitude of characteristics that make the organizations unique – including norms relating to attitudes, relationships, behaviors, and productivity. Upon entry, many newcomers assume the role of legitimate peripheral participants – recognized members who, because of their newcomer status, are enabled to take limited roles (Lave & Wenger, 1991). As newcomers acculturate and learn their roles, they transition to become fully participating members (Kok, 2006; Taber, Plumb, & Jolemore, 2008). Through their limited involvement, members develop the capability to perform tasks and relate to others in organizationally acceptable ways in the process of carrying out their work. This process is not easy, nor does it happen quickly.

As much as 80 percent of what newcomers must learn is tacit knowledge (Goldblatt, 2000), making it difficult to easily distribute this type of knowledge from more experienced members to new recruits (Fernie, Green, Weller, & Newcombe, 2003). As individuals come and go, members must continually work to disperse and acquire knowledge enabling newcomers to interpret information, often transforming explicit knowledge to tacit knowledge, according to group- and organizationally-constructed norms (Droege & Hoobler, 2003; Nonaka, von Krogh, & Voelpel, 2006). This requires newcomers to make sense of new information and make it usable knowledge, which is crucial for organizational functioning.

Formal Socialization

Many organizations acquaint and socialize newcomers by providing training during their first few hours and days with the organization, often in the form of formal socialization. According to Van Maanen and Schein (1979), formal socialization involves segregating newcomers from other members so that they can participate in orienting and training classes, with the goal being to give recruits a unified representation of the official culture, thus prescribing the *appropriate* member attitude and demeanor associated with that culture. Formal collective socialization also helps to ensure the long-term stability and productivity of the organization. While there are benefits to formal collective socialization, such as stronger identification with the organization and reduced role uncertainty (Jones, 1986), the explicit knowledge that can be transmitted through formal socialization in orientation seminars and documented in employee handbooks is only a small part of what it takes to assimilate. Orientation classes can explicate rules, but those rules are tied to a context and are not very useful until the newcomer becomes familiar with the context (Swap, Leonard, Shields, & Abrams, 2001). Swap and colleagues explain, "Whereas the rules are easily transferred, the pattern recognition that allows for a decision about when [and how] to apply the rule is not so easily taught" (Swap et al., 2001, p. 98).

The nature of knowledge (tacit, procedural, and organizational) means that formalized socialization cannot have full impact until newcomers learn about their context, but, paradoxically, some knowledge is required for newcomers to develop a framework to make sense of the information. Newcomers must relate the new information to what they already understand (Gioia & Ford, 1996). One means of exposing new members to contextualized understandings and normative behaviors is through group interaction. In the next section, the value of workgroup-provided informal socialization is introduced as an effective means of distributing organizational knowledge.

Knowledge Acquisition and Distribution in Groups

Organizations function as a social system within which members coordinate their actions and interactions toward a defined set of goals (Erden et al., 2008; McPhee, Corman, & Dooley, 1999). Much research on organizational knowledge explores how *individual members* acquire and distribute organizational knowledge (e.g., Gundry & Rousseau, 1994; King & Zeithaml, 2003; Spender, 1996; Swap et al., 2001). However, the acts of *individuals* acquiring and distributing knowledge are only one aspect of organizational knowledge. Much of what is accomplished in organizations is not achieved through individuals working in isolation. Teams can be more effective in complex tasks, especially when multiple perspectives aid in sorting through multiple decision outcomes (LaFasto & Larson, 2001; Shaw, 1981). Increasingly, problem-solving, decision-making, innovation, and the completion of physical tasks are the result of group coordination. For the group to effectively complete these tasks, new members must be "brought up to speed" with the rest of the group, at least to some extent, to facilitate group action and coordination. Newcomers are socialized with knowledge that enables them to perform duties, and also knowledge that helps them to establish and maintain functional relationships with co-members. In other words, for them to function as a cohesive group, they must be transformed with knowledge about how to be a part of the group. In these synchronized efforts, members must share and utilize knowledge with other members across levels and between groups and throughout the organization (Tagliaventi & Mattarelli, 2006).

Groups facilitate newcomer learning of knowledge that is tacitly held by other members. For example, many workgroups team members with more experience and tacit knowledge with less experienced members. (This is also useful for members who may not be new to the organization, but new to the group or new to the knowledge.) Less experienced members work interdependently with more experienced members, allowing for frequent and deeper interpersonal interactions in which experiences are shared utilizing both verbal and non-verbal communication (Brockmann & Anthony, 2002). Members learn by observation, but they also gain insight into more experienced members' tacit knowledge through narratives (Orr, 1990; Swap et al., 2001). As members work in groups, stories are shared and extended. Members develop shared meaning through these stories, metaphors, and analogies. As a result, both individual and group knowledge is enhanced (Nonaka, von Krogh, & Voelpel, 2006).

As individuals create or attain knowledge, and communicate it to other group members, it is amplified through the group and becomes shared knowledge. Group-based collective learning occurs as a result of interaction between individuals and groups as various types of knowledge that are both conscious and automatic merge through collective social and work-related processes (Spender, 1996). Indeed, Nonaka and Takeuchi

(1995, p. 62) define socialization as "a process of sharing experiences and thereby creating tacit knowledge such as shared mental models and technical skills." In their view, socialization involves making procedural or tacit knowledge available to others so that they also may acquire it as tacit knowledge. Learning takes place in context, which often makes it more meaningful (Tagliaventi & Mattarelli, 2006). Brockmann and Anthony (2002) argued that socialization in the form of on-the-job training or apprenticeships is particularly effective in sharing tacit knowledge, as it enables groups to learn and behave in a coordinated fashion.

Knowing can be both an input and output of collective sensemaking, knowledge creation, and decision-making. Choo (1998) examined knowledge distribution across various levels and applications in the organization. Knowledge is transformed in substantial ways as it moves from being a local resource which may be utilized by one or a few individuals, to being utilized as a system-wide resource allowing its use individually, collectively, and organizationally. This process is described as *social learning*, "a body of knowledge presumed by members of a collective to be generally applicable and accessible, and which simultaneously shapes both individual and collective behavior" (Kuhn, 2000, p. 6). Social learning theory as developed by Bandura (1986) proposes that observational learning (learning by watching others) is governed by four processes, including the amount of attention given to the performance, and the observer's ability to retain the knowledge, ability to produce the performance, and motivation. Kuhn (2000) argues that social knowledge is both normative and generative because it enables members to make sense of situations and events. Organizational knowledge sharing between group members or between individuals in other groups or across the organization plays a role in the development of collaboration and trust (Farrell, 1976; McPhee et al., 1999).

Social and technical knowledge may be distributed in an organization along functional and social ties. Although it is more evident how technical knowledge impacts work participation, social status and perceived expertise also have a powerful impact on workgroup participation. When group members with fewer social connections share knowledge with others, their contributions typically are stifled or received with less favor than if the knowledge had been shared by a socially connected member (Thomas-Hunt, Ogden, & Neale, 2003). Fernie and colleagues' (2003) investigation into knowledge sharing attempted to dispel apparent managerial misconceptions that knowledge is freely shared between individuals and groups in organizations. They argued that current managerial practices do not account for the fact that knowledge is embedded in social contexts, thus making distribution uneven and problematic, even among willing individuals. (See Chapter 15 in this volume for a more extensive discussion on social and political dimensions of knowledge.)

Team composition and, especially, social relationships between organizational members affect knowledge distribution among group members.

In workgroups with members who share positive feelings for one another, newcomers benefit from the increased communication. When relationships, loyalty, and trust exist, members are more likely to interact, sharing hard-earned tacit knowledge. Nevertheless, these teams can also experience negative outcomes, such as groupthink and unnecessary obedience to authority, which limit critical thinking and knowledge generation (Seibold, Kang, Gailliard, & Jahn, 2010). In other situations where productive relationships do not exist, members are not motivated to share hard-earned lessons (Wittenbaum, Hollingshead, & Botero, 2004). At the far end of the spectrum are dysfunctional groups. Here, group members are negatively valenced toward each other and much less likely to be supportive, share stories, or make an effort to educate newer members (Brockmann & Anthony, 2002; Swap et al., 2001). In situations with negative or minimal relationships, observational learning may be effective, but overall, knowledge is limited by the lack of sharing that would otherwise contribute to the individual- and group-level knowledge.

Carried a step further, socializing interaction can lead to conflict that may be functional or dysfunctional. Dysfunctional conflict can involve personal attacks against other team members undermining group effectiveness (Amason, 1996). In groups experiencing dysfunctional conflict, knowledge distribution and amplification are undermined by personal feelings that restrict communication and the desire to mimic others. On the other hand, functional conflict can foster new ideas and a healthy group climate. Functional conflict can result from newer members questioning normative behaviors and underlying assumptions (Amason), potentially causing all members to reassess their understandings and practices. In this way, conflict can serve to expand knowledge of the entire group.

Socialization through Group Interaction

Knowledge is embedded in structure, technology, and process (Grover & Davenport, 2001), but merely possessing information or data is not useful unless that information can be made meaningful and useful in achieving individual, group, or organizational objectives (Iverson & McPhee, 2008). In groups that coordinate physical activities, shared knowledge is most evident in their interdependent action (Stacey, 2001). As team members interact with one another, they begin to make assumptions about one another's behaviors and become more interdependent. They learn to perform in ways that support one another's competencies and possible lack thereof. Their practices become integrated so that they no longer must rely on explicit coordination as their actions become a relatively seamless stream of activity (Hutchins, 1996; Weick & Roberts, 1993). Newcomers become more socialized by imitating and adapting their behaviors to fit into the already cohesive group (Hutchins, 1996). Not only is physical coordination enhanced through shared mental maps, but so too is problem-solving and decision-making. Through distributed cognition, teams can more quickly sort through alternatives and solve problems than can individual members (Erden et al., 2008; Hutchins, 1990).

Communicating organizational objectives helps to increase organizational knowledge by ensuring that individual members understand their role in achieving those objectives. As the organization's paradigm is communicated, it provides members with a "master routine" (Wilkins & Ouchi, 1983, p. 475). Working together can provide other advantages, especially in high-stress or dangerous situations. As described by Weick and Roberts (1993, p. 358), "Agents working alone have less grasp of the entire system than they do when working together." Under these conditions group members are most likely to develop collective mental processes which may translate into "connections between behaviors" (p. 359); in this way, "intelligence is to be found in patterns of behavior rather than in individual knowledge" (pp. 359–360). Although collective group efforts can result in more intelligent work and improved efficiencies, practicing interactivity in order to improve group routines also serves to informally socialize members while instilling organizational knowledge.

Socialization through group interaction is especially evident in dangerous, team-based organizations. In the next section, I illustrate how informal workgroup interaction is key in distributing organizational knowledge to newcomers. The socialization offered through this type of interaction is

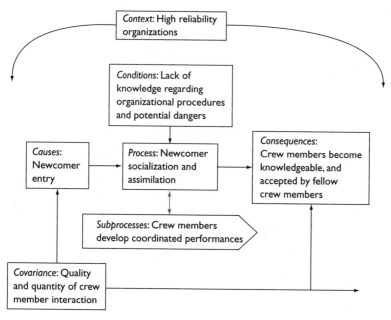

Figure 16.1 Model of knowledge flows based upon McPhee's (2008) amended diagram of Glaser's (1978) six coding families.

foundational in assuming functional roles. In this discussion, I borrow McPhee's (2008) 7C model. Although originally intended for use in grounded theory as a tool to organize data codes (Glaser, 1978), it is a useful means to demonstrate elements involved in the sharing of organizational knowledge in high danger workgroups (see Figure 16.1).

Knowledge Distribution in High Reliability Organizations

High reliability organizations (HROs) are a distinctive *context*. They operate in conditions of high danger, but through careful planning and coordination HROs are able to avoid accidents (Babb & Ammons, 1996). HROs function under a different set of presumptions than other organizations because they do not focus primarily on efficiency and profitability as measures of success. Instead, HROs emphasize member reliability (Weick, 1987; Weick & Roberts, 1993; Weick, Sutcliffe, & Obstfeld, 1999). Productivity and reward systems focus on uniformity and reliability to keep members and publics safe (Grabowski & Roberts, 1997; Myers, 2005a; Scott & Myers, 2005). In HROs such as combat-ready military units, police departments, hospital emergency rooms, and fire departments, members' ability to perform predictably well in unison with other team members constitutes crucial knowledge and a vital intangible resource.

In HROs technology can be a source of failure and accidents, but most concern is related to the human inability to perceive the wide range of potential problems related to complex systems (Bierly & Spender, 1995; Weick, 1987). Hannan and Freeman (1984, p. 153) defined reliability as the "unusual capacity to produce collective outcomes of a certain minimum quality repeatedly." Although this may be thought to imply highly standardized routines that are adhered to without variation (Hannan & Freeman, 1984), the notion of high reliability implies consistent awareness to system anomalies. In the face of potentially unstable situations, reliability comes from "stable cognitive processes" used to detect system variations (Weick et al., 1999). Reliability is, therefore, an input which helps to produce reliability as an output (Schulman, 1993). What is noteworthy is that HRO members seldom see the object of their preoccupation. In other words, failures – the targets of the work – are rare occurrences in HROs. Their *condition* is a lack of contextualized understanding of both the organization, but also the types of situations they may encounter and how they will respond. This creates a challenge in training newcomers, specifically, distributing knowledge about how to respond to accidents.

The strong HRO culture and its associated rules are designed to enhance performance reliability in emergency situations. Through group interaction, featured in Figure 16.1 as *subprocesses*, new members quickly learn about norms and also about the importance of following the norms of the culture (Bierly & Spender, 1995; Pascale, 1985; Scott & Myers, 2005).

When workers are faced with events and situations that put themselves and others in danger, rules and norms can serve to protect members from harm. Protective norms include behaviors such as demonstrating team commitment, a dedication to work hard, an ability to cope with difficult emotional situations in the line of duty (Scott & Myers, 2005), and decision-making that serves the collective. Those who do not learn to follow rules of the organization–group culture experience sanctions such as non-acceptance (Haas, 1977; Myers, 2005a, 2005b), but deep levels of trust – trust in their knowledge, and also trust in their character – develop between members of the workgroup for those who do. In most HROs, being accepted as a member indicates the recruit is part of the metaphorical family, trusted to watch out for him- or herself and for each other. This type of cohesiveness helps keep members connected to fellow group members, thus helping to ensure safety for the entire team (Weick, 1993). High-level cohesiveness enables members to effectively draw upon each other's knowledge and to coordinate their performances. One particularly cohesive group is a firefighting crew, in which members must coordinate their efforts for their own safety and also the safety of community members.

Organizational Knowledge and Socialization in Firefighting Crews

Myers and colleagues conducted several studies focused on the socialization and assimilation (*event/process*) of municipal firefighters (Myers, 2005a, 2005b; Myers & McPhee, 2006; Scott & Myers, 2005). They examined organizational knowledge socialization, such as how new firefighters learn organizational- and workgroup-based norms, and how they learn to coordinate with fellow crew members for maximum predictability and reliability. Their findings confirm the crucial role of crew-based interaction in distributing knowledge to probationary firefighters.

Many probationary firefighters (firefighters with less than a year's tenure) reported that their formal socialization – three months in the training academy – was valuable, but they did not really understand how the training applied to their firefighting roles. In fact, they did not really begin to understand firefighting until they were placed in their first station and began working in a firefighting crew (Myers, 2005a). At the station, each of the three more senior members of their four-person crew played a substantial role in socializing the newcomer about various aspects of organization-based knowledge (*constitutive subprocesses*). For example, captains (crew leaders) often guide crew meal-time discussions about past incidents intended to teach less experienced firefighters about the crew's experience and capabilities, and how the members of their crew work together. One captain remarked that he teaches them what they need to know to survive (Myers, 2005b). Other crew members carefully observe the new firefighter's behaviors, both on calls and back at the station, to guide the newbie about organizational and crew expectations. And as a collective, crew members were instrumental in guiding probationary firefighters about which rules were closely followed and which were mostly ignored.

Probationary firefighters reported that they learned the most thorough interaction with others in the trenches (Myers, 2005a). They learned how to take charge, control themselves and the environment, and be more efficient by watching more experienced firefighters and the emergency medical technicians in their crews perform their work. Observing and working side-by-side with seasoned veterans provided them valuable knowledge – how to perform like a firefighting professional. In situ, they watched and listened to their co-workers as they described how they were assessing an incident, how they were making a decision, and how they were responding to potential danger in the fire or medical situation.

Although not always welcome, another socializing influence found in Myers' (2005b) research was crew-based critical evaluation. New members must prove themselves trustworthy and reliable. This requirement compels new firefighters to quickly learn about and adopt culturally prescribed attitudes and behaviors in order to impress fellow crew members. Members must demonstrate that they are able to fit in and capable of performing reliably within their crew (*consequence*). Because their performance is primarily based on their ability to coordinate actions with crewmates, developing reliable relationships with co-workers is particularly important.

To the neophytes, listening to stories and narratives shared by others in the crew was invaluable for learning and crucial because of the difficulty, even inability, to train for the multitude of potential situations they may encounter. By sharing their organizational knowledge, experienced members help to extend the technical and social knowledge of the entire crew. However, sharing stories was not the norm in all crews (*covariance*). In some crews, conflicts between crew members stifled communication and distribution of knowledge. In other situations, members felt less unity and connection with one another. These crew members seemed less inclined to offer constructive suggestions and to swap stories educating the less experienced. Unfortunately, those newcomers were given less opportunity to learn from others in the crew, and overall knowledge within the crew was minimized.

Theoretical and Practical Contributions Toward Understanding Organizational Knowledge and Socialization

Organizational socialization has received considerable attention in the past several decades. Van Maanen and Schein (1979) identified *formal* versus *informal* socialization as strategic choices made by management and used in organizational socialization. The effectiveness of formal versus informal socialization tactics relative to the desired content of that socialization largely has been overlooked. Given the importance of providing newcomers with organizational knowledge that will enable them to successfully function in the organizational environment, it is surprising how little research has focused on how organizational knowledge is best provided in socialization. Although explicit knowledge, such as organizational goals, rules, and policies, can successfully be provided to members in formal socialization, as I have argued, practices that often are the foundation of organizational functioning appear to be best shared through informal means at the workgroup level.

The extensive literature on organizational knowledge and the intricacies surrounding its distribution offer several theoretical and practical insights into the difficulties of newcomer socialization. First, due to the need to understand the relevant context, it is apparent that new members require exposure to the role, work, and culture of the organization before they are capable of making sense of and utilizing organizational knowledge. This is further evidence for the presumption that newcomers become more assimilated with time. Nevertheless, experience in the organization does not necessarily cause members to feel more assimilated into the organization's culture (Jablin, 2001). Many factors, such as perceived supervisor supportiveness (Jokisaari & Nurmi, 2009), co-worker friendships (Myers, 2009), and social networks, mediate the relationship between time and assimilation, in part because of the effect these relationships have on an individual's organizational knowledge.

Second, this line of research extends socialization theory by identifying the conditions for selecting formal or information socialization (Van Maanen & Schein, 1979). The need for experience in the organization makes questionable the effectiveness of formal orientation seminars upon newcomers' arrival. A significant amount of organizational knowledge is procedural, making it impossible to provide in orientation classes. Particularly in emergency response situations, each situation is different, requiring an ability to assess the situation and quickly make crucial, often life-or-death, decisions. Even though these decisions are made quickly, they are not random, and often are based on knowledge acquired in the field. Although organizations can socialize newcomers to some aspects of their new organization and role, individuals cannot fully appreciate or internalize much that they will need to know until after they are immersed in the environment. One option would be to allow newcomers to shadow experienced members for a period prior to formal socialization, thereby enabling them to better contextualize the training.

Third, informal socialization provided by workgroups, especially in supportive workgroups with strong communication norms, is foundational for organizational knowledge distribution. Interdependency among group members likely contributes to this method of socialization, because members are motivated to develop the newcomers' competencies for the entire group's success.

Future research should continue to explore the role of organizational knowledge in newcomer assimilation. Many questions should be pursued, such as how and where members attain the most and most crucial organizational knowledge. How do newcomers distinguish good organizational knowledge from bad, for example, or favored practices from less than favorable practices? Drawing on Orlikowski's (2002) work, how do they put that knowledge into practice? Beyer and Hannah's (2002) study found that newcomers with previous experience in a wide array of organizations had an easier time of transitioning into new professional identities. Does that principle apply to newcomers' attainment and internalization of organizational knowledge? Specifically, do newcomers with related previous organizational experience find it easier to understand and apply knowledge in their new contexts? Are there situations in which previous experience is a hindrance?

If the primary source of organizational knowledge is informal group socialization, what is the medium – stories, memorable messages, or observation, or is it embodied through activity? Can group members be encouraged and trained to better provide this type of socialization? If groups can be trained and encouraged to actively participate in sharing organizational knowledge with newcomers, are the groups strengthened by that participation? At an organizational level, it may be helpful to explore how other structures and processes that have been shown to affect socialization (e.g., job characteristics, recruitment practices, and organizational culture; Bauer, Morrison, & Callister, 1998) influence acceptance and use of organizational knowledge.

Conclusion

Drucker (1973) and others have suggested that in our post-capitalist society knowledge is the only meaningful economic resource. However, with workers changing jobs at ever increasing rates (US Bureau of Labor, 2008), distributing and enhancing organizational knowledge to maintain and increase competitiveness, becomes an even bigger managerial challenge. This chapter highlights difficulties associated with socializing newcomers to organizational knowledge, primarily in HROs. Organizational newcomers, and especially HRO workers, require sufficient exposure to the culture before they can make sense of and utilize training information as knowledge. This necessitates socialization beyond formal collective socialization. Over time interaction provided in workgroups may be the best source of the knowledge contributing to successful functioning in the organizational environment, not just for newcomers, but more experienced members too. Co-creating and distributing organizational knowledge among group members not only increases effectiveness of the individual member, but the cohesiveness and value of the entire workgroup.

References

Amason, A. C. (1996). Distinguishing the effect of functional and dysfunctional conflict on strategic decision making: Resolving a paradox for top management teams. *Academy of Management Journal, 39*, 123–148.

Anderson, J. R. (1976). *Memory, language, and thought.* Hillsdale, NJ: Erlbaum.

Anderson, J. R. (1987). Skill acquisition: Compilation of weak-method problem solutions. *Psychological Review, 94*, 192–210.

Ashforth, B., Saks, A. M., & Lee, R. T. (1998). Socialization and newcomer adjustment: The role of organizational context. *Human Relations, 51*, 897–926.

Babb, J., & Ammons, R. (1996). BOP (Bureau of Prisons) inmate transport: A high reliability organization. *Corrections Today, 58*, 108–110.

Bandura, A. (1986). *Social foundation of thought and action: A social cognitive theory.* Englewood Cliffs, NJ: Prentice-Hall.

Bauer, T., Morrison, E. W., & Callister, R. R. (1998). Organizational socialization: A review and direction for future research. In G. R. Ferris & K. M. Rowland (Eds.), *Research in personnel and human resource management,* Vol. 16 (pp. 149–214). Greenwich, CT: JAI Press.

Baumard, P. (1999). *Tacit knowledge in organizations.* Thousand Oaks, CA: Sage.

Beyer, J., & Hannah, D. (2002). Building on the past: Enacting established personal identities in a new work setting. *Organization Science, 13*, 636–652.

Bierly, P. E., & Spender, J. C. (1995). Culture and high reliability organizations: The case of the nuclear submarine. *Journal of Management, 21*, 639–656.

Boisot, M. (2001). The creation and sharing of knowledge. In C. W. Choo & N. Bontis (Eds.), *The strategic management of intellectual capital and organizational knowledge* (pp. 65–77). New York, NY: Oxford University Press.

Brockmann, E. N., & Anthony, W. P. (2002). Tacit knowledge and strategic decision making. *Group & Organization Management, 27*, 436–455.

Chao, G., O'Leary-Kelly, A., Wolf, S., Klein, H., & Gardner, P. (1994). Organizational socialization: Its content and consequences. *Journal of Applied Psychology, 79*, 730–743.

Choo, C. W. (1998). *The knowing organization: How organizations use information to create meaning, create knowledge, and make decisions.* New York, NY: Oxford University Press.

Cyert, R., & March, J. (1963). *A behavioral theory of the firm.* Englewood Cliffs, NJ: Prentice-Hall.

Davenport, T. H., & Prusak, L. (1998). *Working knowledge: How organizations manage what they know.* Boston, MA: Harvard Business School Press.

Droege, S. B., & Hoobler, J. M. (2003). Employee turnover and tacit knowledge diffusion: A network perspective. *Journal of Managerial Issues, 15*, 50–64.

Drucker, P. (1973). *Management: Tasks, responsibilities, practices.* New York, NY: Harper & Row.

Erden, Z., von Krogh, G., & Nonaka, I. (2008). The quality of group tactic knowledge. *Journal of Strategic Information Systems, 17*, 4–18.

Ericsson, K. A. (1996). The acquisition of expert performance: an introduction to some of the issues. In K. A. Ericsson (Ed.), *The road to excellence* (pp. 1–50). Mahwah, NJ: Lawrence Erlbaum.

Farrell, T. (1976). Knowledge, consensus, and rhetorical theory. *Quarterly Journal of Speech, 62*, 1–14.

Feldman, D. (1976). A contingency theory of socialization. *Administrative Science Quarterly, 21,* 433–452.

Fernie, S., Green, S., Weller, S., & Newcombe, R. (2003). Knowledge sharing: Context, confusion, and controversy. *International Journal of Project Management, 21,* 177–187.

Gibson, M., & Papa, M. (2000). The mud, the blood, and the beer guys: Organizational osmosis in blue-collar work groups. *Journal of Applied Communication Research, 28,* 68–88.

Gioia, D. A. (1986). Symbols, scripts, and sensemaking: Creating meaning in the organizational experience. In J. H. P. Sims & D. A. Gioia (Eds.), *The thinking organization* (pp. 49–74). San Francisco, CA: Jossey-Bass.

Gioia, D. A., & Ford, C. M. (1996). Tacit knowledge, self-communications, and sensemaking in organizations. In L. Thayer (Ed.), *Organization communication: Emerging perspectives* (pp. 83–102). Norwood, NJ: Ablex.

Glaser, B. (1978). *Theoretical sensitivity.* Mill Valley, CA: Sociology Press.

Goldblatt, D. (2000). Introduction. In D. Goldblatt (Ed.), *Knowledge and the social sciences: Theory, method and practice.* London, UK: Routledge.

Grabowski, M., & Roberts, K. (1997). Risk mitigation in large-scale systems: Lessons from high reliability organizations. *California Management Review, 39,* 152–162.

Grover, V., & Davenport, T. H. (2001). General perspectives on knowledge management: Fostering a research agenda. *Journal of Management Information Systems, 18,* 5–21.

Gundry, L., & Rousseau, D. M. (1994). Critical incidents in communicating culture to newcomers: The meaning is the message. *Human Relations, 47,* 1063–1088.

Haas, J. (1977). Learning real feelings: A study of high steel ironworkers' reactions to fear and danger. *Sociology of Work and Occupations, 4(2),* 147–170.

Hannan, M. T., & Freeman, J. (1984). Structural inertia and organizational change. *American Sociological Review, 49,* 149–164.

Huang, C. C., & Kuo, C. M. (2003). The transformation and search of semi-structured knowledge in organizations. *Journal of Knowledge Management, 7,* 106–123.

Hutchins, E. (1990). The technology of team navigation. In J. Galegher, R. E. Kraut, & C. Egido (Eds.), *Intellectual teamwork: Social and technical bases of collaborative work* (pp. 191–220). Hillsdale, NJ: Erlbaum.

Hutchins, E. (1996). Organizing work by adaptation. In M. Cohen & L. Sproull (Eds.), *Organizational learning* (pp. 20–57). London, UK: Sage.

Iverson, J. O., & McPhee, R. D. (2008). Communicating knowing through communities of practice: Exploring internal communicative processes and differences among CoPs. *Journal of Applied Communication Research, 36,* 176–199.

Jablin, F. (2001). Organizational entry, assimilation, and exit. In F. Jablin & L. Putnam (Eds.), *The new handbook of organizational communication* (pp. 732–818). Thousand Oaks, CA: Sage.

Johnson-Laird, P. N. (1983). *Mental models.* Cambridge, UK: Cambridge University Press.

Jokisaari, M., & Nurmi, J. (2009). Change in newcomers' supervisor support and socialization outcomes after organizational entry. *Academy of Management Journal, 52,* 527–544.

Jones, G. (1986). Socialization tactics, self-efficacy, and newcomers' adjustments to organizations. *Academy of Management Journal, 29,* 262–279.

King, A. W., & Zeithaml, C. P. (2003). Measuring organizational knowledge: A conceptual and methodological framework. *Strategic Management Journal, 24,* 763–772.

Klein, R., Bigley, G., & Roberts, K. (1995). Organizational culture in high reliability organizations: An extension. *Human Relations, 48,* 771–793.

Kok, A. J. (2006). Enhancing information literacy in an interdisciplinary collaboration. *Journal of Technology in Human Services, 24,* 83–103.

Kuhn, T. (2000). *Examining the evolution of individual and collective knowledge: Communication networks and the dynamic process of organizational change.* Paper presented at the National Communication Association, Seattle, WA, November.

LaFasto, F., & Larson, C. (2001). *When teams work best.* Thousand Oaks, CA: Sage.

Lave, J., & Wenger, E. (1991). *Situated learning: Legitimate peripheral participation.* Cambridge, UK: Cambridge University Press.

Leonard-Barton, D. (1992). Core capabilities and core rigidities: A paradox in managing new product development. *Strategic Management Journal, 3,* 111–125.

Levitt, B., & March, J. (1988). Organizational learning. In W. Scott (Ed.), *Annual review of sociology,* Vol. 14 (pp. 319–340). Greenwich, CT: JAI Press.

Louis, M. (1980). Surprise and sensemaking: What newcomers experience when entering unfamiliar organizational settings. *Administrative Science Quarterly, 23,* 225–251.

March, J., Schulz, M., & Zhou, X. (2000). *The dynamics of rules: Studies of change in written organizational codes.* Stanford, CA: Stanford University Press.

McPhee, R. D. (2008). *Revision of Glaser's 6C model.* Unpublished paper.

McPhee, R. D., Corman, S., & Dooley, K. (1999, May). *Theoretical and methodological axioms for the study of organizational knowledge and communication.* Presented at the annual meeting of the International Communication Association, San Francisco, CA.

Miller, A., Herbig, B., & Petrovic, K. (2009). The explication of implicit team knowledge and its supporting effect on team processes and technical innovations: An action regulation perspective on team reflexivity. *Small Group Research, 40,* 28–51.

Morrison, E. (2002). Newcomers' relationships: The role of social network ties during socialization. *Academy of Management Journal, 45(6),* 1149–1160.

Myers, K. K. (2005a). A burning desire: Assimilation into a fire department. *Management Communication Quarterly, 18(3),* 344–384.

Myers, K. K. (2005b). *Organizational knowledge and assimilation in a high reliability organization.* Unpublished dissertation. Arizona State University, Tempe, AZ.

Myers, K. K. (2009). Workplace relationships. In S. Smith & S. R. Wilson (Eds.), *New directions in interpersonal communication* (pp. 135–156). Thousand Oaks, CA: Sage.

Myers, K. K., & McPhee, R. D. (2006). Influences on member assimilation in workgroups in high reliability organizations: A multilevel analysis. *Human Communication Research, 32,* 440–468.

Nelson, R. R., & Winter, S. G. (1982). *The evolutionary theory of economic change*. Cambridge, MA: Belknap Press of Harvard University Press.

Nonaka, I., & Takeuchi, H. (1995). *The knowledge-creating company: How Japanese companies create the dynamics of innovation*. New York, NY: Oxford University Press.

Nonaka, I., von Krogh, G., & Voelpel, S. (2006). Organizational knowledge creation theory: Evolutionary paths and future advances. *Organization Studies, 27*, 1179–1208.

Orlikowski, W. J. (2002). Knowing in practice: Enacting a collective capability in distributed organizing. *Organization Science, 13*, 249–273.

Orr, J. E. (1990). Sharing knowledge, celebrating identity: Community memory in a service culture. In D. Middleton & D. Edwards (Eds.), *Collective remembering* (pp. 169–189). London, UK: Sage.

Pascale, R. (1985). The paradox of "corporate culture": Reconciling ourselves to socialization. *California Management Review, 27*, 26–42.

Schulman, P. R. (1993). The analysis of high reliability organizations: A comparative framework. In K. Roberts (Ed.), *New challenges to understanding organizations* (pp. 33–54). New York, NY: Macmillan.

Scott, C., & Myers, K. K. (2005). The socialization of emotion: Learning emotion management at the fire station. *Journal of Applied Communication Research, 33*(1), 67–92.

Seibold, D. R., Kang, P., Gailliard, B. M., & Jahn, J. L. S. (2010). Communication that damages teamwork: The dark side of teams. In P. Lutgen-Sandvik & B. Davenport-Sypher (Eds.), *The destructive side of organizational communication: Processes, consequences and constructive ways of organizing*. New York, NY: Taylor Francis/Routledge, in press.

Shaw, M. E. (1981). *Group dynamics: The psychology of small group behavior*, 3rd Edn. New York, NY: McGraw-Hill.

Simon, H. A., & Chase, W. G. (1973). Skill in chess. *American Scientist, 61*, 394–403.

Singley, M. K., & Anderson, J. R. (1989). *The transfer of cognitive skill*. Cambridge, MA: Harvard University Press.

Spender, J. C. (1996). Organizational knowledge, learning and memory: Three concepts in search of a theory. *Journal of Organizational Change Management, 9*, 63–78.

Stacey, R. D. (2001). *Complex responsive processes in organizations: Learning and knowledge creation*. London, UK: Routledge.

Starbuck, W. H. (1992). Learning by knowledge-intensive firms. *Journal of Management Studies, 29*, 713–740.

Stenmark, D. (2000/2001). Leveraging tacit organization knowledge. *Journal of Management Information Systems, 17*, 9–25.

Swap, W., Leonard, D., Shields, M., & Abrams, L. (2001). Using mentoring and storytelling to transfer knowledge in the workplace. *Journal of Management Information Systems, 18*, 95–114.

Taber, N., Plumb, D., & Jolemore, S. (2008). "Grey" areas and "organized chaos" in emergency response. *Journal of Workplace Learning, 20*, 272–285.

Tagliaventi, M. R., & Mattarelli, E. (2006). The role of networks of practice, value sharing, and operational proximity in knowledge flows between professional groups. *Human Relations, 59*, 291–319.

Thomas-Hunt, M. C., Ogden, T. Y., & Neale, M. A. (2003). Who's really sharing? Effects of social and expert status on knowledge exchange within groups. *Management Science*, *49*, 464–477.

Tsoukas, H. (1996). The firm as a distributed knowledge system: A constructionist approach. *Strategic Management Journal*, *17*, 11–25.

Tsoukas, H., & Vladimirou, R. (2001). What is organizational knowledge? *Journal of Management Studies*, *38*, 973–993.

US Bureau of Labor Statistics (2008). "Employee Tenure in 2008." Available at: www.bls.gov/news.release/pdf/tenure.pdf.

Van Maanen, J., & Schein, E. (1979). Toward a theory of organizational socialization. *Research in Organizational Behavior*, *1*, 209–264.

Weick, K. (1987). Organizational culture as a source of high reliability. *California Management Review*, *29*, 112–127.

Weick, K. (1993). The collapse of sensemaking in organizations: The Mann Gulch disaster. *Administrative Science Quarterly*, *38*, 628–652.

Weick, K., & Roberts, K. (1993). Collective mind in organizations: Heedful interrelating on flight decks. *Administrative Science Quarterly*, *38*, 357–381.

Weick, K., Sutcliffe, K., & Obstfeld, D. (1999). Organizing for high reliability: Processes of collective mindfulness. In B. M. Staw & R. Sutton (Eds.), *Research in organizational behavior*, Vol. 23 (pp. 81–123). Greenwich, CT: JAI Press.

Wilkins, A. L., & Ouchi, W. G. (1983). Efficient cultures: Exploring the relationship between culture and organizational performance. *Administrative Science Quarterly*, *28*, 468–481.

Wittenbaum, G. M., Hollingshead, A. B., & Botero, I. C. (2004). From cooperative to motivated information sharing in groups: Moving beyond the hidden profile paradigm. *Communication Monographs*, *71*, 286–310.

Conclusion
Moving Forward with Communicative Perspectives on Organizational Knowledge

Robert D. McPhee, Heather E. Canary, and Joel O. Iverson

This volume displays many ways that communication ideas and paths of inquiry are relevant to the concept and phenomenon of organizational knowledge. The term *organizational knowledge* itself is contested in many ways that we have not discussed. For example, Lyon and Chesebro (Chapter 5) note the relevance of Foucault's ideas about power/knowledge, but that theme is not an evident concern of other chapters. Also, the organization-level ideas of absorptive capacity and cross-organization knowledge sharing have been researched extensively as higher-level corollaries to our ideas about learning and transmission. Additionally, the issue of the research discovery and epistemic status of knowledge is frequently raised in the general organizational theory literature, but is outside our domain here.

Our main aim, instead, is to contribute to the growth of understanding that communication scholars have contributed, and continue to contribute, to an increasingly important understanding of organizational knowledge. Some organizational theorists have advanced conceptions of firms *as being* knowledge; for others knowing is among the fundaments of organization. Similarly, authors have depicted firms *as being* communication (Kuhn, 2008; Putnam & Nicotera, 2009; Taylor & Van Every, 2000; Weick, 1979); and for nearly all others, communication is a vital idea. But many analyses of organizational knowledge have given communication a peripheral, simplified, or reified role in theories (Tsoukas, 2005). Our authors make communication both a conceptual and explanatory construct in organizational knowledge studies (and, via that theoretic route, in organizational studies generally).

Explicit and Tacit Knowledge

One over-arching theme explored in several chapters of this book is that organizational knowledge consists of both tacit and explicit dimensions. Indeed, several contributors (Corman & Dooley in Chapter 9, Deng & Poole in Chapter 12, Flanagin & Bator in Chapter 10, Kuhn & Porter in Chapter 2; Myers in Chapter 16; and Shumate in Chapter 11), if not all, have noted how the entire notion of knowledge management (KM) is revolutionized by Polanyi's (1967, p. 4) assertion that "we can know more than we can tell." Efforts to harness and manage knowledge have often focused on tapping tacit knowledge and converting it to explicit knowledge. These efforts reflect the knowledge-based view of the firm that emerged in organizational studies in the 1990s and emphasized that competitive advantage was tied to use of knowledge as an asset (see Chapter 4, by Jackson & Williamson, in this volume; see also Nonaka & von Grogh, 2009, for overview). However, many contributors to this volume have also criticized this focus of KM by disputing both the notion that these dimensions are separate (or opposite ends of a continuum) and the notion that "conversion" is a desirable goal (see, for example, Kuhn & Porter in Chapter 2; Myers in Chapter 16).

It is understandable how Polanyi's concept of tacit knowledge gained traction in organizational circles. Especially made attractive in Nonaka and Takeuchi's (1995) treatise on creating knowledge in Japanese companies, and on the subsequent development of what Nonaka and colleagues label "organization knowledge creation theory" (Nonaka & von Grogh, 2009), sustained academic attention to tacit knowledge moved conceptualizations of organizational knowledge to a new level. However, by conceiving of tacit and explicit knowledge as opposite ends of a continuum, this view abandoned Polanyi's definition of the tacit dimension, and, as a result, impoverished understandings of how explicit and tacit dimensions of knowledge function in organizations.

A view that aligns with Polanyi's original conceptualization of the tacit dimensions requires a reorientation away from the continuum and from the idea of conversion across that continuum. Tacit knowledge cannot be "converted" to explicit knowledge any more than the image on one side of a coin can be converted to the image on the other side. Both sides of a coin are necessary for it to maintain its integrity and identification as a token of exchange. At the same time, knowing is both tacit and explicit (Tsoukas, 2005, p. 143); indeed, interpreting explicit statements is always a partly tacit process, while reflection inherently leads to verbal expression of previously tacit content.

What we should be concerned about as organizational communication scholars, on the other hand, is the importance of communication for teasing out connections between explicit and tacit knowledge. As Tsoukas (2005, p. 158) argued, "we need not so much to operationalize tacit knowledge ... as to find new ways of taking, fresh forms of interacting, and novel ways of distinguishing and connecting." Chapters in this book have made a valuable contribution toward this end.

One important move made possible by authors of this book is to identify the role of communication in knowledge development and sharing. This focus moves away from the explicit/tacit philosophical debate to address the practical question of *how* organizational knowledge develops, spreads, and changes across organizations. Some chapters have specifically addressed the explicit/tacit dimensions, such as Chapter 9 by Steve Corman and Kevin Dooley, and Chapter 11 by Michelle Shumate. Both of these chapters set the debate aside and focus specifically on the many challenges that lie in knowledge sharing of even the most codifiable knowledge, or what some would call "explicit" knowledge. Other authors, such as Tim Kuhn and Amanda Porter in Chapter 2 and Karen Myers in Chapter 16, clearly reject the notion of conversion or a divide, and argue for an integrated view of knowledge that transcends a strictly cognitive view of what resides "within" a person.

Another contribution to moving beyond the tacit/explicit divide is made by authors who do not explicitly discuss the dimensions but rather offer alternative conceptualizations of knowledge processes. For example, in Chapter 6, Paul Leonardi examines differences across workgroups (and across the globe) in conceptualizations of where knowledge lies. Although he does not make specific reference to Polanyi's concept of tacit and explicit dimensions, readers can easily infer from his conclusions that a full understanding of organizational knowledge must account for the unarticulated, culturally-bound, and assumption-laden tacit knowledge as well as the theoretical, concept-based, codified explicit knowledge.

Another alternative to the explicit–tacit divide is provided in Chapter 14, as Heather Canary presents ways in which five types of knowledge were used in a case of developing cross-system policy knowledge. She adopts Blackler's (1995) typology of embrained, encultured, embodied, encoded, and embedded knowledge to demonstrate that knowledge development is social, situated, and involves the influence of a number of elements of both specific systems and broader social contexts. Her conclusions comport with Duguid's (2005) assertion that, "...if we want to understand individuals' capacities and motives for sharing knowledge, we need to look not just at the knowledge, but at the communities in which their knowing *how* was shaped." This suggestion is also evident in Chapter 5, as Alexander Lyon and Joseph Chesebro examine the politics of knowledge. Both chapters are especially useful for recognizing that much more occurs in organizational knowledge processes than in individual cognitive progressions. As Duguid noted, communities and elements of social systems shape knowledge processes, and this volume presents ways in which communication is pivotal in that shaping.

Chapter 15, by Alexandra Murphy and Eric Eisenberg, also offers an alternative to the explicit–tacit divide with a communication-centered approach to knowledge frames and corresponding dimensions of knowledge. Applying their framework to the health care context, Murphy and Eisenberg demonstrate how organizational knowledge is routinized, emergent, and political, and that these frames of knowledge reflect performative, relational, and instrumental dimensions of knowledge. From this perspective, the explicit–tacit distinction is an over-simplification.

Whether expanding upon and/or challenging the tacit–explicit dimensions of organizational knowledge, these chapters imply a deep interrelation of the two. Furthermore, they point to the processual nature of both knowledge and organizational communication. One resulting pivotal issue, now focal in organizational communication studies, concerns the communicative constitution of organization.

Organizational Knowledge and Organizational Constitution

As mentioned in the introductory chapter, we asked our authors to, whenever possible, rephrase their results using the "6C" model presented by Glaser (1978) and modified by McPhee (2008) to the "7C" model. Some authors found this model to be compatible with at least parts of their arguments. For instance, Canary found all the model's "Cs" in her account of school special education policy knowledge construction, partly because of her exploration of the structuration of normative knowledge "given" by a national institution, as it is enacted by successive local subsystems. O'Hair, Kelley, and Williams, in Chapter 13, also concentrate on dispersion of knowledge processes, and distinguish causes, contexts awakened by them, knowledge concentration and dispersion processes per se, and consequences of such processes. Shumate (Chapter 11) provides a multivariate and non-linear account of knowledge flow that is a nice fit to the variety of relations articulated by the model.

Others found it more difficult, or even impossible, to characterize their arguments in these terms. Usually, this is due to the fact that their chapters actually focused, in a general way, on the communicative nature of organizational knowledge rather than its processual context. Very often, the debates and reconceptions of the tacit-versus-explicit distinction were more or less at the core of these chapters, as discussed extensively above. But there were varied conceptual concerns for other chapters. For instance, in Chapter 5 Lyon and Chesebro discuss the politically charged nature of knowledge legitimacy and constructed relevance to the organization, a conceptual repositioning rather than an explanatory structure that could be fit into the 7C model. Similarly, in Flanagin and Bator's (Chapter 10) discussion of communication technologies, the goal is a conceptual transition from "managing knowledge" to "managing (or even co-organizing) knowledge processes" (p. 22), and, again, not an explanatory account. We conclude that the 7C model is a revealing but loose fit for communicative studies of organizational knowledge. The nature of communication itself, and of knowledge as a resource/outcome of communication, is essentially contested. In the theories of knowledge communication, multiple conceptions of the explicit/tacit distinction and the corresponding stated/implicated distinction in communication lead to multiple loci for central descriptive and thus explanatory concepts. Just so, in practice knowledge managers can fund, institute, control, or distribute power to social sites of knowledge, not essentially production or profit centers. Choices about these matters are clearly political and perspective-dependent. Thus, we can broaden our conceptions of knowledge practices, but we cannot as scholars direct or anticipate the knowledge constitution practices or resources of tomorrow's organizations.

A newly grounded set of distinctions is the McPhee–Zaug–Iverson notion of "four flows" of communicative constitution of organizations. A number of authors have advanced the argument that communication has constitutive force in specific application to organizations, as noted above. McPhee and Iverson (2009) describe a developing framework for understanding constitutive force as resulting from a system of differentiated and self-regulating practices. They hold that no one kind of practice, or model of communication, is sufficient to explain the constitution of organizations. They suggest, instead, four fundamentally different processes or ongoing flows of organizational communication: (1) membership negotiation; (2) reflexive self-structuring; (3) activity coordination; and (4) institutional positioning. Not only do these involve different paths to social constitution; they also produce and reproduce social knowledge in varied ways. Moreover, since the four flows model is based on structuration theory, it can take advantage of Giddens' (1984) serendipitous recasting of the 7C model. In his primarily interpretive analysis, "Causes" is represented more precisely as concepts of embedded praxis, processual constraints (and dually enablements), power to react (and thus enact), and conditions of social process itself. The idea of context is similarly elaborated, as a fundamental condition and structural resource for action. And Giddens regularly notes that a prime unrecognized consequence of agentive interaction is the reproduction/transformation, and thereby constitution, of a social system.

Membership negotiation. The first flow of organizational constitution, membership negotiation, maintains and transforms the relation between the individual agent and the enacted entity "the organization." As we become and represent ourselves as members of organizations, or move into varied positions, and simultaneously constitute the organization as a membership focus, we use and have to learn and thereby legitimize certain knowledge stocks that hence are produced/reproduced as the foundation of organizing. This flow is surprisingly rarely explored in organizational knowledge studies, but research streams note knowledge sharing both to new members and among experienced members as part of membership negotiation on an ongoing basis (Bechky, 2003; Michel, 2007; Nonaka & Takeuchi, 1995).

Among our chapter authors, Myers (Chapter 16) is the one that most focally discusses membership and its position practices. She notes how membership results initially from socialization, which in turn is a process of knowledge sharing and the legitimation of its sharing via trust development. She portrays a peculiar trajectory of knowledge complementarity beginning with sharing of basic codified knowledge, which is then enacted as members, in initial relations of humility and listening, are initiated into practices and develop tacit knowledge that in turn empowers both their skillful use of explicit learning and the development of trust that legitimates even more demanding participation in high-risk settings.

In other chapters, parts of this cycle are shown to recur as the membership relation matures. As Kuhn and Porter (Chapter 2), Corman and Dooley (Chapter 9) and Leonardi (Chapter 6) demonstrate in varied ways, knowledge sharing takes on the negotiated form of sharing in a context of problematic heterogeneity. Ultimately, Palazzolo (Chapter 7), Hollingshead, Brandon, Yoon, and Gupta (Chapter 8), and Shumate (Chapter 11) show that the fundamental level of knowledge co-membership consonant with organizational membership is the recognition of the other's knowledge command, sufficient to ground search and coordination processes. This level of membership recognition seems to parallel the relation of belonging (Iverson, Chapter 3) on the social level. Knowledge thus depends on a sufficient mix of skill knowledge and social relatedness, sufficient to allow membership relations to ground cooperative practices.

Reflexive self-structuring. Membership is one facet, but not the most distinctive, in organizational constitution. Organizations are distinctive, among social forms, in the distribution, development, and planning of their self-guidance, self-shaping, and self-knowing processes and products. A well-researched example is organizational formal structure. As Canary (Chapter 14) shows, formal structure mediates and channelizes knowledgeable interaction that, in its appropriation in activity system contexts, allows members to act and interact effectively. Moreover, the *raison d'être* of national-level disability education policy is its application at the local level, which inexorably *is* its knowledgeable reproduction and rearticulation in local systems. A good deal of research has emphasized the knowledge-limiting effects of formal structure (for an intriguing example, see Jacobides, 2008), but Canary demonstrates the mediating and constituting effects of a wider array of formal mechanisms (also evinced in Kowtha, 2008).

A similar dynamic is apparent in the self-structuring that occurs when organizations and organizational systems search for, implement, and use information and communication technology. As O'Hair and colleagues (Chapter 13), Deng and Poole (Chapter 12), Jackson and Williamson (Chapter 4), and Leonardi (Chapter 6) show from varied perspectives, technology is no longer seen, even in contemporary knowledge management, as an objective resource allowing the accumulation of a shared, objective knowledge stock that can be a supply for organizational work; such a view elides the adaptive structuration of a reflexively chosen structural resource. Its employment rests on interpretive insights about its features (Deng & Poole), while those same features can constrain, but in correlative ways enable, knowledgeable activity.

Activity coordination. There is a constant temptation, in the current literature outside communication, to regard knowledge as a shared resource stockpiled as a basis for production, or as simply shaped via various structural or formalized mechanisms. But a plethora of work (see, for example, Bechky, 2003) analyzes specific processes of knowledge sharing and transformation in activity coordination processes.

Our studies emphasize the constitutive force of knowledge as intertwined with communicative praxis, in two main ways. First, knowledge collections or instruments can themselves depend on practices of varying kinds for their impact. For instance, Shumate notes the new processes involved in technologically based knowledge management systems, and argues that more powerful practices are enabled and constrained in new ways, with partly unintended consequences of blurring boundaries and motivating politically charged alliance-building. Leonardi and Canary each highlight the different practices, in different nation and school subsystems, for interpreting/implementing documents in ongoing cooperative work, and how problems can highlight their differences as system contradictions. Corman and Dooley show how a knowledge collection and analysis practice can provide impetus and guidance for new cooperative systems of experts in organizations.

Second, is a more situationally adaptive emphasis on knowledge enactment as intertwined with social interaction and relation systems. An example of this stance is the analysis McPhee and Iverson (2009, p. 8) give of the activity coordination flow. Knowledge is recognized to abide in social interaction and relation systems. They argue that coordination especially follows from three processes.

> One is the development of, and reliance on, a joint medium of task representation.... This may be a computer monitor or other display device, a simplified vocabulary, or any way of indicating what the task is and where the group is at in dealing with it. A second process is specific role negotiation, as standard roles are adjusted or forsaken when current contingencies require it. Finally, a process with varied but recognizable communicative dimensions is "support," means of indicating that help is willing and waiting.

Another important example is the contribution the Montreal School of communication theory has made to the study of coordination processes. McPhee and Iverson (2009) detail how coorientation, narrative, and dialectical communication phenomena have unique coordinative force within a more general structuration model of coordination.

We should note how this knowledge flow is equally taken up in the communication and organizational research traditions outside this volume. For instance, important types of knowledge collections or instruments are public information goods analyzed by Monge, Fulk, Flanagin, and their colleagues. Here, more or less generalized knowledge record stocks are contributed to and used in ways that vary across individuals in connection with political as well as economic considerations.

Institutional positioning. Institutional positioning is the flow that theorizes the organization at the macro level. "Institutional positioning in large measure rests on individuals representing the organization, especially spanning boundaries as representatives communicating with the outside constituencies" (McPhee & Iverson, 2009, p. 83). Institutional position can tie to current literatures such as adaptive capacity literature that examines building connections to other organizations as a system survival strategy as an alternative to cost cutting (Staber & Sydow, 2002).

Our chapters, with the exceptions of those by Canary and by O'Hair and colleagues, focus less on institutional positioning, and present a view of knowledge from within the organization. However, much KM literature extols the need for effective KM for an organization to remain competitive in the knowledge economy, and theories of OK seem readily applicable to organized complexes of corporate units. McPhee and Iverson (2009, p. 83) indicate that "Institutional positioning is also vital to secure resources, support income, and legitimacy for the organization." O'Hair and colleagues' chapter focuses on several elements of institutional positioning, including collaboration, boundary spanning, and environmental scanning. O'Hair et al. also recognize the importance of developing relationships among stakeholders that are enacted in multi-organizational KM. Canary focuses most clearly on institutional positioning through policies that shape the environment of the organization. She illuminates the structurational process of creating and enacting larger and, in some cases, macro levels of structures. This fits well within the purview that McPhee and Zaug (2000) articulate with institutional positioning.

Although most chapters are internal to organizations, several have implicit (though not tacit) institutional positioning implications. Corman and Dooley's chapter analyzes data to consider the merits of rethinking traditional structures based on KM for competitiveness and effectiveness to better position the LAS college. Leonardi's analysis of global knowledge sharing offers useful insights for institutional positioning in a global environment.

Due to the importance of institutional positioning for an organization to be successful, we encourage more communication theorizing of knowledge at this level (type) of organizational work. Considering the knowledge enacted in organizational activities that represent the organizations, such as negotiation, decision-making, and boundary-spanning (Kuhn, 2002), exploration of institutional positioning as knowledge work would be very productive. Additionally, we contend that theorizing institutional positioning from a practice perspective, for example, would assist in theorizing the transition from micro- to macro-level issues. Also, understanding how institutional positioning phenomena distinctively encompass both "macro" and "micro" levels of analysis would be quite useful.

Conclusion

Overall, we feel that our chapters make important and complementary advances in the study of communication and organizational knowledge. Communication theory is clearly a basic resource for understanding and improving on the explicit/tacit dichotomy. And the constitutive force of organizational knowledge for organizations rests on the broader force of knowledgeable communication practices using communication resources.

Future theoretical and research endeavors concerning organizational knowledge are undoubtedly called for throughout this volume. As communication scholars collaborate with scholars across disciplines, there will be opportunities to bring communicative phenomena to the fore of OK research. Studies of organizational knowledge processes are an excellent place to further the theoretical discussion of the interplay of materiality and ideality. Such studies will necessarily involve longitudinal studies that address both "scaling-up" and "scaling-down" processes in efforts to further explain practical connections among micro-, meso-, and macro-organizational processes.

Our chapters also provide implications for practice. One suggestion that follows from most chapters is the need for organizational practitioners to be more reflective of both knowledge *practices* and knowledge *resources*. We organized this book around broad topics of practices, connections, technologies, and contexts. These broad topics are actually issues of concern for practitioners. Taking a reflective posture toward knowledge processes will foster consideration of both intended and unintended consequences of OK practices and resources in place as a strategy for fostering effective and productive processes. Finally, several contributors note the importance of embracing the complex nature of knowledge and instead of trying to simplify (and therefore impoverish) knowledge processes, practitioners can use a richer conceptualization of organizational knowledge to generate practices and resources that take full advantage of the many dimensions of knowledge.

References

Bechky, B. A. (2003). Sharing meaning across occupational communities: The transformation of understanding on a production floor. *Organization Science, 14*, 312–330.

Blackler, F. (1995). Knowledge, knowledge work, and organizations: An overview and interpretation. *Organization Studies, 16*, 1021–1046.

Duguid, P. (2005). "The art of knowing": Social and tacit dimensions of knowledge and the limits of the community of practice. *The Information Society, 21*, 109–118.

Glaser, B. (1978). *Theoretical sensitivity*. Mill Valley, CA: Sociology Press.

Jacobides, M. G. (2007). The inherent limits of organizational structure and the unfulfilled role of hierarchy: Lessons from a near-war. *Organization Science, 18*, 455–477.

Kowtha, N. R. (2008). Engineering the engineers: Socialization tactics and new engineer adjustment in organizations. *IEEE Transactions on Engineering Management*, *55*, 67–81.

Kuhn, T. (2002). Negotiating boundaries between scholars and practitioners: Knowledge, networks, and communities of practice. *Management Communication Quarterly*, *16*, 106–112.

Kuhn T. (2008). A communicative theory of the firm: Developing an alternative perspective on intra-organizational power and stakeholder relationships. *Organization Studies*, *29*, 1227–1254.

McPhee, R. D. (2008). *Revision of Glaser's 6C model*. Unpublished paper.

McPhee, R. D., & Iverson, J. (2009). Agents of constitution in the *Communidad*: Constitutive processes of communication in organizations. In L. L. Putnam & A. Nicotera (Eds.), *Building theories of organization: The constitutive role of communication* (pp. 49–87). New York, NY: Routledge.

McPhee, R. D., & Zaug, P. (2000). The communicative constitution of organizations: A framework for explanation. *Electronic Journal of Communication*, 10 (1–2), www.cios.org/getfile/McPhee_V10n1200.

Michel, A. A. (2007). A distributed cognition perspective on newcomers' change processes: The management of cognitive uncertainty in two investment banks. *Administrative Science Quarterly*, *52*, 507–557.

Nonaka, I., & Takeuchi, H. (1995). *The knowledge-creating company: How Japanese companies create the dynamics of innovation*. New York, NY: Oxford University Press.

Nonaka, I., & von Grogh, G. (2009). Tacit knowledge and knowledge conversion: Controversy and advancement in organizational knowledge creation theory. *Organization Science*, *20*, 635–652.

Polanyi, M. (1967). *The tacit dimension*. Garden City, NY: Anchor.

Putnam, L. L., & Nicotera, A. (Eds.) (2009). *Building theories of organization: The constitutive role of communication* (pp. 1–19). New York, NY: Routledge.

Staber, U., & Sydow, J. (2002). Organizational adaptive capacity: A structurational perspective. *Journal of Management Inquiry*, *11*, 408–424.

Taylor, J. R., & van Every, E. J. (2000). *The emergent organization: Communication as its site and surface*. Mahwah, NJ: Erlbaum.

Tsoukas, H. (2005). *Complex knowledge: Studies in organizational epistemology*. Oxford, UK: Oxford University Press.

Weick, K. E. (1979). *The social psychology of organizing*. New York, NY: Random House.

Index

information: and communication
technologies (ICTs) xvi, xix, 11,
89–90, 93, 108–9, 173–9, 181–2,
184–7, 209; information-processing
approach 191; information system
(IS) 6, 54, 57, 191, 212, 215, 230,
265; processing 145–6, 173–5,
177–8, 182, 184–5, 191, 212–13,
215
inimitable xviii, 57–8, 61–2, 64–6
innovation 4, 80, 82, 182–3, 186, 211,
214, 217, 232, 290
institutional positioning 308, 311

knowing xv, xviii, xix, 8, 10, 18–31,
36, 39, 41–4, 46–9, 58, 66, 72, 98,
101, 103, 106–7, 118, 136, 168–9,
176–7, 185, 202, 210, 245–6, 260,
285, 291, 304–6, 309
knowledge: assets 53, 54–5, 58, 61,
63–6, 121, 180, 228; construction 5,
245, 248, 250, 252–3, 255–6,
260–1, 282, 307; cultural xv, xvii–
xviii, 3, 175, 286; directory 129;
embedded xvi, 248, 250–1, 255–9,
261, 306; embodied 248–51, 257–9,
287; embrained 248, 257–9;
emergent xvii, 60, 62, 153, 270,
272, 274, 280; encoded 248–9, 251,
255, 257–60; encultured 248–9,
251, 256–60; explicit xvii, 55, 66,
151–3, 156, 158, 166–9, 175–6,
192, 200, 211–12, 215–16, 218,
246–8, 255, 287, 289, 297, 305–6;
exploitation 211, 217; exploration
211, 217; flow 11, 191–6, 198–204,
224, 236, 293, 307, 310; implicit 63,
246, 259; improvisational xvi, xvii;
management (KM) i, xix, 4, 8, 11,
27–8, 31, 36–7, 53–9, 62–6, 70, 72,
74, 80–1, 83, 91, 114, 118, 120,
130, 143, 151–3, 158, 166, 168–9,
173–4, 176–87, 191–200, 202–4,
210, 212, 218, 223–5, 230, 232,
237, 264–5, 269, 305, 309–11;
network 12, 120, 125–7, 129, 167,
198–9, 226–7, 230–1, 234–5;
personal 24, 83, 249; practices 9–11,
36, 41, 49, 55, 58, 61, 63, 84, 308,

312; production 157, 181, 185;
routine 12, 265, 269; shared 10, 20,
79, 89, 113, 133, 177, 194, 196, 230,
290–2; sharing 36, 39, 79, 81, 144–6,
237, 306; structure 118, 122, 129,
152, 229; synoptic xiv–xvii; tacit 12,
151–2, 167, 175–6, 192, 196, 200,
211–12, 216–17, 246–7, 287–92,
304–6, 309; types 200–1, 246–9,
251, 253, 255–6, 260–1; typologies
5, 246–7, 249
knowledge-accomplishing activities
xviii, 19, 22, 28–9, 177
knowledge-intensive 73–4, 79, 89,
157, 193, 218
knowledgeability 21, 245, 248, 255,
259

laboratory studies 114–15
leader 2, 74–5, 81–4, 127, 130, 144,
146, 162, 237, 295
learning i, xix, 3, 35–6, 38–9, 41, 44,
46–7, 56, 66, 70, 75–6, 79, 92–3,
115, 117, 119–20, 129, 144–5, 167,
174, 204, 210, 216, 218, 230,
281–2, 286–8, 290–2, 296, 304,
309
legitimacy xvii, 21–6, 28–30, 64, 73,
201, 203, 229, 256, 307, 311

membership 38, 45, 49, 115, 121, 138,
140–2, 144, 146, 162, 191, 195,
203–4, 230, 286, 308–9; negotiation
45, 308
mental models 3, 136–7, 139–40, 288,
291
metacommunication 24, 28, 30–1

negotiation 21, 37–43, 45, 50, 73, 137,
217, 266, 282, 308, 310–11
network model 11, 115, 155, 191,
193–5, 201, 203–4, 212
network structure 115, 199, 213–18

outcome xvi–xvii, 7, 21, 23, 25, 30,
42, 72, 130, 133, 135, 137, 139,
143–4, 151, 199, 218–19, 224, 228,
237, 249, 253, 266–7, 272–3, 276,
288, 290, 292, 294, 307